Guide to

SQL

Guide to
SQL

Database Management
for IBM PCs
and Compatibles

Richard H. Baker

Scott, Foresman and Company
Glenview, Illinois   London

1-2-3 is a registered trademark of Lotus Development Corporation.
dBASE and dBASE III Plus and Ashton-Tate are registered trademarks of Ashton-Tate.
IBM is a registered trademark of International Business Machines Corporation.
Microsoft is a trademark of Microsoft Corporation.

ORACLE and SQL*Calc are registered trademarks of the Oracle Corporation.
SQL*Plus, SQL*Forms, SQL*Report, and Pro*C are trademarks of Oracle Corporation.
QuickC is a registered trademark of Microsoft Corporation.
XyWrite is a trademark of XYQUEST, Inc.

NOTE: The fanciful names used in the examples in this book are fictitious. The purpose of them is to make reading and writing a little more enjoyable. It is not the author's intention to use them as commentary on any person or institution.

Library of Congress Cataloging-in-Publication Data

Baker, Richard H.
   Guide to SQL : database management for IBM PCs and compatibles / Richard H. Baker.
     p.   cm.
   Includes index.
   ISBN 0-673-38356-3
   1. SQL (Computer program language) 2. IBM Personal Computer-
-Programming. 3. Data base management. I. Title.
QA76.73.S67B35 1989
005. 13′3--dc 19   88-26332
                                             CIP

ISBN 0-673-38356-3

1   2   3   4   5   6   KPF   93   92   91   90   89   88

Cover photo: Courtesy of International Business Machines Corporation.

Notice of Liability
The information in this book is distributed on as "As Is" basis, without warranty. Neither the author nor Scott, Foresman and Company shall have any liability to customer or any other person or entity with respect to any liability, loss, or damage caused or alleged to be caused directly or indirectly by the programs contained herein. This includes, but is not limited to, interruption of service, loss of data, loss of business or anticipatory profits, or consequential damages from the use of the programs.

Scott, Foresman professional books are available for bulk sales at quantity discounts. For information, please contact Marketing Manager, Professional Books Group, Scott, Foresman and Company, 1900 East Lake Avenue, Glenview, IL 60025.

CONTENTS

v

INTRODUCTION

SQL isn't exactly named right. It's an acronym for Structured Query Language. SQL cannot stand independently as a programming language. Strictly speaking, it does not query databases, although it participates in that exercise. To some minds, it's not very well structured.

SQL is not a complete programming language. Depending on how you count them, it has only about two dozen basic commands. Most of the time you'll use only one of those, although with many variations. For this reason, SQL is not destined to fully replace any of the languages now in use. More appropriately, it will find its way inside them. For example, there are now database management applications in which the traditional syntax of dBASE III Plus suddenly yields to a series of SQL statements. SQL probably will not replace the database management systems now in use on personal computers. It will extend them into new dimensions of possibility.

SQL is like a trained specialist: It does one thing very well. That singular task is to manage a database. As the comments about its name suggest, this involves more than just processing queries. Still, SQL is tailored to the very specific job of database management. Like any well-tailored product, it is a very good fit.

SQL's supposed lack of structure is a matter of opinion. With a limited number of available commands, it does not need a great deal of structure. The opposite of structure is flexibility.

Thus, SQL is a flexible, highly specialized means to extend and improve the management of your database. The complaints are not very important because SQL itself is important. SQL is almost certainly destined to be the heart of personal computer database management systems to come.

FAMILAR FACE—TO SOME

SQL is not particularly new. It is an import from the mainframe and minicomputer world. IBM developed it several years ago as a standard way to address its large-computer databases. As personal computers have approached minicomputers in power and capacity, their database management duties have been expanded to match. The extension of SQL to personal computers helps give PC users the same kinds of tools as their mainframe brethren have.

IBM, naturally enough, was the first major user of SQL, which now drives two of the company's large-computer database products. A third has been developed for the Extended Edition of Operating System/2 (OS/2) for personal computers. To place a database manager within an operating system is itself a reflection of IBM mainframe practice.

SQL is not particularly hard to understand. Its commands are ordinary words that mean about what you expect them to mean. Its syntax requirements are minimal; the words string together into ordinary expressions, and most are complete sentences.

The most difficult part of using SQL is that it requires a kind of attitude that is different from that required by dBASE or the programming languages you may have used before. Most familiar languages are primarily *procedural*. They tell the computer what to do, step by detailed step. dBASE commands the computer to DO this or that; BASIC shows itself to the world by ordering PRINT; Pascal offers the formally polite DO BEGIN. All these commands, in various ways, tell the computer to take some kind of direct action.

SQL issues only the most minimal orders. In its vocabulary, SELECT is pretty strong language. Any procedural commands SQL does issue are secondary to its main purpose. SQL's workings are mainly *descriptive*. Through SQL, you describe the data you want to add, edit, or display. In a way, SQL extends the principles of good management to database operations. You tell the computer what you want to accomplish. You don't necessarily provide step-by-step instructions for the task.

To SQL, procedural commands are only necessary embellishments. Their purpose is to order the computer to do something with the data SQL receives. This will sometimes require that you incorporate SQL commands into another language that has the necessary procedural powers, or that you add embellishments as most vendors of SQL products have done. Still, you might be surprised at what you and SQL can do just by describing things.

People who have experience with Lisp, Prolog, or other forms of artificial intelligence may find this idea easier to grasp than those who come from other programming environments. For this reason, SQL lends itself to interactive use, responding to individual commands as you type them, as you would respond to the infamous dot prompt of dBASE.

Most implementations of SQL also provide for dBASE-like command files that execute prewritten lists of SQL commands automatically. When used in a full-scale application program, SQL is more likely to appear within some other language that handles the application's procedural necessities. The SQL product provides an expanded list of commands that goes beyond those of standard SQL.

INTRODUCING THE ORACLE

The first complete SQL system for personal computers is not from IBM. The Oracle Corporation of Menlo Park, CA, claims that honor with Professional ORACLE, its SQL-driven database system for higher-powered members of the IBM-PC compatible family. Like SQL itself, ORACLE appeared first on mainframes; a PC version was released early in 1987. This book is based on Professional ORACLE (which, for simplicity, will just be called ORACLE from here on). However, SQL is already such a universal standard that the commands and procedures you learn from this book should serve you equally well on future SQL products as well.

Meanwhile, don't sell ORACLE short. It's tempting to think of ORACLE as the Steve DeBerg of database managers. For the many who don't know, Mr. DeBerg is a professional quarterback whose ability and experience are exceeded only by his obscurity. His main distinction in a long career with several teams is that he has repeatedly been the quarterback who was displaced by a rising young star. He's lost jobs to some of the best players in the game.

By virtue of its early release, ORACLE may be seen as filling a similar role, filling in while database fans waited for SQL to appear in the newest dBASE or in the extended OS/2. Like Steve DeBerg, ORACLE deserves more attention. ORACLE is a full-featured database that makes full use of extended memory—requires it, in fact. As ORACLE's advertisements have pointed out, it was available before the better-known products.

For some users, ORACLE may have two significant drawbacks.

The first is a hefty list price of $1,295, although at least one sales promotion sharply cut that figure. The second is found in ORACLE's equally chunky system requirements: An AT- or 386-class computer with at least 1536K of RAM and 7.5K of free space on the hard disk.

DUAL/DUAL PURPOSES

This book will serve a dual purpose. It will teach SQL by way of ORACLE. You can use the knowledge in any way you wish, with ORACLE or with a later arrival.

It will serve another purpose as well. Because many readers will no doubt be familiar with the widely-used syntax of dBASE, the book is written so they can use their current knowledge as a frame of reference. Whenever possible, an ORACLE/SQL procedure will be illustrated with an equivalent in dBASE. A main object of this book is to serve as a bridge from the world of dBASE to the world of SQL. You may notice, though, that as this book proceeds, it uses fewer dBASE comparisons and pays more attention to advanced SQL features, including those specific to ORACLE's implementation.

At the same time, those who don't know dBASE need not feel left out. You'll find SQL explained thoroughly in its own right. If you're new to database management, this book will start from the beginning. One reason is that, to some extent, even database veterans will have to do the same. SQL offers just enough new ideas to require some adjustment even at the basic levels.

In short, this book is written for everyone who wants to explore the database frontier of SQL. The future of database management on personal computers is in the pages to come.

These pages also will demonstrate standard ORACLE/SQL techniques in a setting of useful applications. When you are finished, not only will you understand SQL better, but you'll have a collection of useful routines to start putting that knowledge to work.

WHAT SQL REALLY IS

You can't just go down to your local computer store and ask for SQL. Well, you can ask, but you won't find it. Because it is so highly specialized, SQL does not appear as a single, self-contained, all-purpose product. Instead, it will usually appear in one of these two forms:

- SQL will be integrated into a full-featured database management product, as in dBASE IV.
- A *SQL server* will serve as a central database manager, responding to SQL commands, but will require one or more *front-end* products to actually issue those commands.

ORACLE falls into the second category. In fact, ORACLE is the blanket name for an entire package of database products. The ORACLE Relational Database Management System, or ORACLE RDBMS, is the SQL-driven core program. As you will see in the startup instructions in Chapter 2, you load this database server separately from the front-end products, or *tools* as they are called in ORACLE.

The most basic of these tools is called SQL*Plus. This is the front-end facility through which you can issue SQL commands from the keyboard to the database. You also can issue an extended set of nonstandard commands that are peculiar to ORACLE. These commands are the "plus" in SQL*Plus.

Early chapters of this book will concentrate primarily on the basic SQL commands, although some commands from SQL*Plus will necessarily be included. Later chapters will give you more of the extended SQL*Plus commands, plus a taste of the more sophisticated front-end products that also are included in the ORACLE package. These include SQL*Forms, with which you can create and use custom screen displays; SQL*Calc, a SQL-based spreadsheet; and Pro*C, with which you can incorporate SQL commands into the C programming language.

TERMINOLOGY AND CONVENTIONS

To keep things as simple as possible, this book will normally use *ORACLE* to refer to the overall program and *SQL* to refer to the command language. When you find a reference to an extension feature such as those in a program such as *SQL*Plus*, that reference will usually be specific to the ORACLE implementation of SQL. For example, it often is necessary to distinguish between standard SQL commands and their SQL*Plus extensions, because there are some differences in entering and editing the two types of commands. Also, many readers may want to distinguish between standard SQL commands and those that are specific to ORACLE. (Tables accompanying Chapter 2 provide full listings of commands in the two groups.)

This book also deals with commands entered in three different contexts: DOS, ORACLE, and dBASE. Since all are entered from distinctive on-screen prompts, you'll find these prompts included in the commands. For example, a DOS command will look like this:

C> ORACLE

You need not type the C>, which is the standard DOS prompt seen by hard disk users. You simply enter ORACLE. (This book will also follow the convention in which ENTER means to type an entry, then hit the <Enter> or <Return> key. TYPE means simply to type the entry.)

A dBASE command will include the dot prompt normally seen on a dBASE screen. An example:

. DISPLAY ALL

SQL commands are a little more complicated. They can be entered on one line or many, as you prefer. It is easier to understand a long command if you break it up into individual clauses; this will be the practice in this book. Also, SQL*Plus provides a distinctive system of prompts: SQL> for the first line of a command and numbers for succeeding lines. Thus, a SQL command will usually appear in this form:

```
SQL> SELECT *
   2   FROM EMP
   3   WHERE DEPTNO = 30;
```

As with the DOS and dBASE commands, the prompt and line numbers will be supplied automatically; you need not type them yourself.

PART

1 GETTING STARTED

Getting Acquainted with SQL

DON'T BE INTIMIDATED

SOME BASIC SQL OPERATIONS

BASIC SQL PRINCIPLES

Thousands of people have learned how to create databases with the dBASE line of database managers. The current dBASE, its predecessors, and its imitators and likely successors have earned the designation "standard" in the personal computer world. Thousands of other people probably have determined that they will never try to learn how to create databases with dBASE or anything like it.

Although SQL has something to offer both groups, it gives both another thing to worry about. Hard-core dBASE users have worked hard to learn one database system. The advent of SQL appears to mean that they must discard much of their hard-earned knowledge and learn something new. Those who have avoided dBASE thus far—whether by accident or by design—now must contend with yet another kind of database management system.

It doesn't help to know that SQL has come to personal computers from the larger processors that many users have come to regard as "impersonal computers." In fact, the main reason for the recent interest in SQL is that it provides a common data management language for computers of all sizes.

DON'T BE INTIMIDATED

SQL is primarily a language you use to *describe* the data you want to store in, add to, or retrieve from a database. Both SQL and dBASE have commands and functions that describe data; the difference is that dBASE works primarily with *procedural* commands—commands that tell the computer to take some kind of action. To retrieve a particular set of data, you USE the database, SET a filter or a relation with another file, then LIST or DISPLAY the results. Significantly, all these procedural commands begin with verbs.

Nearly every SQL command also starts with a verb. By far the most frequently used is SELECT. From that point on, however, SQL commands function more as adjectives. SELECT introduces a description of the data you want to retrieve; a FROM clause identifies the source of that data, and an optional WHERE clause sets any further conditions you might wish to establish.

Another difference between SQL and dBASE is that dBASE commands usually operate on one record at a time, although that certainly isn't always the case. SQL typically operates on *sets* of records, extracting one set from another.

In addition to its data description commands, dBASE has a host of procedural commands that add up to a nearly full-featured programming language. In dBASE, you can format screens, use CASE commands for menu selections, and repeat an operation a stated number of times. SQL does none of these things. It does an excellent job of describing data, but it does little else. That's why it needs extensions, such as those in SQL*Plus, other add-on products, or a conventional programming language such as C.

A dBASE DATABASE

Coming chapters will demonstrate SQL commands in detail. For now, here is a taste of some basic SQL operations, compared with their equivalents in dBASE III Plus. For this demonstration, consider the law firm McKnife, Tawdry, Diver, and Brown. A dBASE database file of its personnel roster might have this structure:

```
Structure for database : D:LA__FLAW.dbf
Number of data records:         11
Date of last update    : 11/06/87
Field  Field Name  Type        Width  Dec
    1  LAST        Character     15
    2  FIRST       Character     15
    3  BRANCH      Numeric        1
    4  ASSIGN      Character     15
    5  HIRED       Date           8
    6  SALARY      Numeric        9     2
**  Total  **                    64
```

You might have noticed that dBASE always claims one space for itself; here, for example, the field widths add up to only 63 spaces, but the program actually uses 64 spaces.

The firm has 11 employees in two branches; to see who and where they are, issue these commands:

```
. USE LA__FLAW
. LIST ALL
```

dBASE will scroll out the roster shown in Figure 1-1. This is typical of the kind of personnel database you often encounter in

FIGURE 1-1   A Typical dBASE Employee Roster

```
Record#  LAST          FIRST       BRANCH ASSIGN           HIRED     SALARY
      1  MCKNIFE       DARREN          1  SR. PARTNER     01/09/49   5000.00
      2  TAWDRY        ALLEN           2  JR. PARTNER     09/12/65   4000.00
      3  COSSACK       MICHAEL         1  CRIMINAL        07/17/82   4500.00
      4  BUNSEN        BURNER          2  FAMILY          10/09/78   2975.00
      5  TUCKER        FRIAR           1  TAX             08/14/77   2850.00
      6  BOYSENBERRY   ANN             1  CIVIL           12/31/85   2450.00
      7  ROX           GOLDIE          2  SECRETARY       01/23/82   1300.00
      8  MASON         PERCY           2  CRIMINAL        06/09/29   3850.00
      9  BAILEY        F. BILL         1  CRIMINAL        12/17/80   4800.00
     10  BORQUE        BOBBY           1  PARALEGAL       12/03/81    950.00
     11  HARTLESS      JAMES           2  PERSONAL INJURY 08/08/83   7500.00
```

training exercises in which the author has been watching a little too much television.

THE SQL EQUIVALENT

You can do almost exactly the same thing in SQL. ORACLE presents the same information in a structure like this:

```
Name                                        Null? Type
-------------------------------------------  ------ ------
LAST                                         CHAR(15)
FIRST                                        CHAR(15)
BRANCH                                       NUMBER(1)
ASSIGN                                       CHAR(15)
HIRED                                        DATE
SALARY                                       NUMBER(9,2)
```

This is a SQL *table,* the counterpart of a dBASE file. To retrieve the contents of this table, the SQL command is:

```
SQL> SELECT * FROM LA_FLAW
```

The SQL> is the standard prompt you'll see when using SQL*Plus with ORACLE. It's much like the familiar DOS C> or the dBASE dot prompt. It means the program is waiting for a command.

SELECT is the basic SQL command. It tells the program to retrieve the data you are about to specify. Nearly every data retrieval command in SQL begins with SELECT.

The asterisk is a wild card that is used in much the same way as it is in a DOS file specification. In SQL, it literally means "select everything." More specifically, it means "select every column" in the SQL table that you will describe in the next part of the command.

Now, the FROM clause identifies that table. In this case, it is the SQL table also called LA__FLAW. You should get the result shown in Figure 1-2.

There's not much difference, is there? The main distinction is the way that SQL displays dates. Whereas dBASE uses the form:

12/17/80

SQL uses this form

17–DEC–80

You also probably noticed that ORACLE's description of the roster includes a mysteriously vacant column headed *Null?* This column reports whether a column will accept a null entry. In this case, there are no notations to the contrary, so every column will accept a null entry. As you might suspect, there are some cases for which you will want a different result.

A *null* value is something dBASE doesn't recognize. Users who are unfamiliar with this concept can find it hard to understand. A null is an entry that's blank. This is not the same thing as an entry that has a value of zero, a fine but important distinction in SQL. Don't worry if you don't fully understand it right

FIGURE 1-2   Selections from the Oracle Version

```
LAST              FIRST            BRANCH ASSIGN            HIRED       SALARY
----------------  ---------------- ------ ---------------- ----------  -------
MCKNIFE           DARREN                1 SR. PARTNER      09-JAN-49     5000
TAWDRY            ALLEN                 2 JR. PARTNER      12-SEP-65     4000
COSSACK           MICHAEL               1 CRIMINAL         17-JUL-82     4500
BUNSEN            BURNER                2 FAMILY           09-OCT-78     2975
TUCKER            FRIAR                 1 TAX              14-AUG-77     2850
BOYSENBERRY       ANN                   1 CIVIL            31-DEC-85     2450
ROX               GOLDIE                2 SECRETARY        23-JAN-82     1300
MASON             PERCY                 2 CRIMINAL         09-JUN-29     3850
BAILEY            F. BILL               1 CRIMINAL         17-DEC-80     4800
BORQUE            BOBBY                 1 PARALEGAL        03-DEC-81      950
HARTLESS          JAMES                 2 PERSONAL INJURY  08-AUG-83     7500

11 records selected.
```

now. As the book progresses, it will present more details on the "care and feeding" of nulls. It will even tell you how to use them creatively.

There also are some differences between dBASE and SQL in the SALARY entries. The dBASE file structure specifies the usual two decimal places for monetary figures:

6 SALARY   Numeric   9   2

In its current form, the SQL table does not. A later exercise will involve modifying the way the program displays this item by using a command from SQL*Plus, one of ORACLE's extensions to basic SQL.

SOME BASIC SQL OPERATIONS

The soul of a database operation is the ability to select from a large collection of data only the information you want. For example, dBASE lets you distill the roster of all employees into a list of those assigned to Branch 2. From here on, assume that dBASE users have already issued the command

. USE LA__FLAW.

You can then enter:

. LIST ALL FOR BRANCH = 2

The resulting display is shown in Figure 1-3.
The command in SQL that does the same thing is:

```
SQL> SELECT *
   2   FROM LA__FLAW
   3   WHERE BRANCH = 2;
```

FIGURE 1-3   The dBASE Display from Branch 2

Record#	LAST	FIRST	BRANCH	ASSIGN	HIRED	SALARY
2	TAWDRY	ALLEN	2	JR. PARTNER	09/12/65	4000.00
4	BUNSEN	BURNER	2	FAMILY	10/09/78	2975.00
7	ROX	GOLDIE	2	SECRETARY	01/23/82	1300.00
8	MASON	PERCY	2	CRIMINAL	06/09/29	3850.00
11	HARTLESS	JAMES	2	PERSONAL INJURY	08/08/83	7500.00

SQL is like a good newspaper editor in that it requires you to name your source (in this case, LA_FLAW). You must do this every time; SQL has no equivalent to the dBASE command USE, which remains in effect until canceled or superseded.

You don't have to put all of a SQL statement on one line, although you can if you like. Following the example of other SQL manuals, this book will break the SQL statements into separate lines to make them easier to follow. The semicolon indicates the end of the command. ORACLE supplies the SQL> prompt and the succeeding line numbers. You need not type these yourself.

Meanwhile, the dBASE commands are meant to be written in one continuous line, even though they might not appear that way in print. There's an irony here. SQL lets you spread your commands over as many lines and spaces as you like; enter a semicolon at the end of the command to indicate that you've completed it. dBASE also lets you use multiple lines, but it uses the semicolon to signal just the opposite; it indicates that the command is continued on the next line. Sometimes that 180-degree difference will be important.

If you keep the semicolons straight, the previous SQL query will result in what is shown in Figure 1-4. The outcome is much the same as it is with dBASE.

MULTIPLE SEARCHES

There are many ways to describe the data you want. The next search procedure eliminates several unwanted data items, concentrating on three that presumably are important to the searcher. It seeks the names, job assignments, and salaries of

FIGURE 1-4   Department 30 via Oracle

LAST	FIRST	BRANCH	ASSIGN	HIRED	SALARY
TAWDRY	ALLEN	2	JR. PARTNER	12-SEP-65	4000
BUNSEN	BURNER	2	FAMILY	09-OCT-78	2975
ROX	GOLDIE	2	SECRETARY	23-JAN-82	1300
MASON	PERCY	2	CRIMINAL	09-JUN-29	3850
HARTLESS	JAMES	2	PERSONAL INJURY	08-AUG-83	7500

6 records selected.

managers who earn more than $2,800 per month. The dBASE version is:

```
. LIST LAST, ASSIGN, SALARY FOR BRANCH = 2 .AND.
SALARY > 2800
```

It produces this result:

Record#	LAST	ASSIGN	SALARY
2	TAWDRY	JR. PARTNER	4000.00
4	BUNSEN	FAMILY	2975.00
8	MASON	CRIMINAL	3850.00
11	HARTLESS	PERSONAL INJURY	7500.00

The SQL version is:

```
SQL> SELECT LAST, ASSIGN, SALARY
  2   FROM LA__FLAW
  3   WHERE  BRANCH  =  2
  4   AND SALARY > 2800;
```

Its outcome is

LAST	ASSIGN	SALARY
TAWDRY	JR. PARTNER	4000
BUNSEN	FAMILY	2975
MASON	CRIMINAL	3850
HARTLESS	PERSONAL INJURY	7500

THE OR OPTION

The above search called up records that meet all of several conditions. You can also call for records that meet any but not all of those conditions. The technique is to use OR instead of AND. With the unique punctuation required by dBASE, such a command might be:

```
. LIST LAST, ASSIGN, SALARY FOR BRANCH = 2 .OR.
SALARY > 2800
```

Only one word has been changed, but the results are much different:

Record#	LAST	ASSIGN	SALARY
1	MCKNIFE	SR. PARTNER	5000.00
2	TAWDRY	JR. PARTNER	4000.00
3	COSSACK	CRIMINAL	4500.00
4	BUNSEN	FAMILY	2975.00
5	TUCKER	TAX	2850.00
7	ROX	SECRETARY	1300.00
8	MASON	CRIMINAL	3850.00
9	BAILEY	CRIMINAL	4800.00
11	HARTLESS	PERSONAL INJURY	7500.00

The SQL command gets the same change:

```
SQL> SELECT LAST, ASSIGN, SALARY
   2  FROM LA__FLAW
   3  WHERE BRANCH = 2
   4  OR SALARY > 2800;
```

and the same major difference occurs in the results:

LAST	ASSIGN	SALARY
MCKNIFE	SR. PARTNER	5000
TAWDRY	JR. PARTNER	4000
COSSACK	CRIMINAL	4500
BUNSEN	FAMILY	2975
TUCKER	TAX	2850
ROX	SECRETARY	1300
MASON	CRIMINAL	3850
BAILEY	CRIMINAL	4800
HARTLESS	PERSONAL INJURY	7500

9 records selected.

Some of these people are paid less than $2,800, and some are from Branch 1. They meet one or the other of the command's conditions, but they don't meet both.

SEARCHING FOR EXCEPTIONS

A third alternative is to search for records that do not meet a particular criterion. It's not quite certain why you would want to execute this next command except for learning purposes, but that's a good enough reason for it to be included here. This search looks for every employee who is not in Branch 2 and who was hired before January 1, 1980. In dBASE, the command is written:

- LIST LAST, ASSIGN, BRANCH FOR BRANCH <> 2 .AND. HIRED < CTOD('01/01/80')

Only a couple of veterans fit that particular mold:

Record#	LAST	ASSIGN	BRANCH
1	MCKNIFE	SR. PARTNER	1
5	TUCKER	TAX	1

The same is true of the SQL version:

```
SQL> SELECT LAST, ASSIGN, BRANCH
  2   FROM LA__FLAW
  3   WHERE BRANCH <> 2
  4   AND HIRED < '01–JAN–80';
```

The results are the same, but now they appear in the SQL format.

Both dBASE and SQL use the operator <> to mean "not equal." Each also has an alternative that means the same thing. In dBASE, BRANCH # 2 means the same thing as BRANCH <> 2 does. In SQL, the equivalent is BRANCH != 2. Use the version that makes the most sense to you.

Another distinction is that dBASE requires you to use the function CTOD( ), which converts the date field from a string to a date before it conducts that part of the search; SQL doesn't make that requirement. It does have some date conversion functions to match those in dBASE, but in SQL these are used mainly for formatting and date arithmetic.

CHANGING THE FORMAT

One difference between the dBASE and SQL LA__FLAW files is that they display the salary and commission figures in different formats. As promised, here's the way to fix that.

In dBASE, use the command MODIFY STRUCTURE. This displays the existing structure and gives you a chance to change things such as the number of decimal places in a numeric field. In

ORACLE, you must go beyond basic SQL and use a SQL*Plus command called COLUMN:

SQL> COLUMN SALARY FORMAT $99,999.99 HEADING "BASE PAY";

The FORMAT command is similar to the PICTURE command, which is available to dBASE programmers. It specifies a leading dollar sign, a comma for the thousands, and two decimal places. This particular COLUMN command also alters the heading of the SALARY column. This command:

SQL> SELECT FIRST, LAST, SALARY
    2   FROM LA__FLAW;

will produce this result:

FIRST	LAST	BASE PAY
DARREN	MCKNIFE	$5,000.00
ALLEN	TAWDRY	$4,000.00
MICHAEL	COSSACK	$4,500.00
BURNER	BUNSEN	$2,975.00
FRIAR	TUCKER	$2,850.00
ANN	BOYSENBERRY	$2,450.00
GOLDIE	ROX	$1,300.00
PERCY	MASON	$3,850.00
F. BILL	BAILEY	$4,800.00
BOBBY	BORQUE	$950.00
JAMES	HARTLESS	$7,500.00

11 records selected.

STAY TUNED

This has been just a brief introduction to SQL. The purpose has been to demonstrate its basic structure and approach. Although there are differences from the more familiar dBASE, there are many similarities as well. The SQL SELECT means roughly the same thing as dBASE's LIST or DISPLAY does.

To some minds, SQL may seem more natural than dBASE. To others, it may not. Basically, SQL and dBASE both describe similar data in similar ways.

BASIC SQL PRINCIPLES

The sports pages recently told the story of two minor league baseball players. One spoke no English; the other spoke no Spanish. They spent long bus rides teaching each other their native languages. The resulting friendship endured even when the two found themselves on opposing sides in the National League playoffs.

SQL and dBASE have a similar relationship. They do the same thing, but they speak different languages while doing it. Users of either can learn to speak the other's language. They now find themselves both in close contact and in high-level competition with each other.

LEARNING THE NEW LANGUAGE

The differences between dBASE and SQL start with the concept of a database. In dBASE, it's not unusual to think of a database as a single file—a list of data with a .Dbf at the end of its file name. In fact, when you display the structure of a dBASE file, dBASE itself refers to the file as a database. A dBASE database can also be a series of linked files. The mechanism of linking them has been improved through a succession of dBASE products, but it still falls short of the automatic linkages in an SQL database.

In SQL, it is best to think of a database as a system of tables. A SQL table is comparable to a dBASE data file. Together, these tables can be treated as an organized collection of information. In some cases, this system may consist of only one table. In most advanced systems, there will be a group of linked tables. There is no limit on the number of tables that can be included in a database. It is easiest to understand SQL if you understand its perception of what a database is.

Related dBASE files can be linked together to form a database, as can related SQL tables. Such databases are known as *relational* systems. The meaning of the term relational is a subject of endless debate among computer professionals and members of the academic community. E. F. Codd, who originated the relational concept, has set forth an extensive set of rules for determining whether a database is relational. Hardly any product known to Codd meets all of them. In any event, they are the rules of a mathematician who works at the top level of database theory.

Most users need not know all, or even most, of the rules. C. J. Date, a Codd associate and the author of several books on database management, offers two standards that can serve as general guidelines:

1. The user sees the data in the form of tables.
2. The commands and operators available to the user are used to create new tables.

SEEING TABLES

Take another look at the outputs displayed earlier in this chapter. When dBASE was asked to LIST the contents of the file, it produced a familiar row-and-column structure. Each row is a *record*. Each record contains information about a particular employee. Each column is a *field,* a particular piece of information about an employee. The employee's name is one such item. The branch office assignment is another.

dBASE doesn't always present its data in tabular form. When you want to ADD a new record or EDIT an existing one, dBASE presents a screen that displays only the single record with which you want to work. A dBASE program that produces a custom-formatted screen display usually also works one record at a time. The major exception to this record-by-record presentation is the BROWSE command, which does offer the data in tabular form for additions and alterations.

SQL produces a very similar-looking table. In fact, that's why SQL users call it a table. Furthermore, they have some highly technical names for the rows and columns—they're called rows and columns. Accordingly, when the earlier exercise changed the format of the salary figures, it used the command COLUMN rather than FIELD. In a SQL table, as in a dBASE data file, each column lists a category of information, and each row describes an individual case.

There is yet another system of nomenclature used at the high-theory level. A table is called a *relation,* a column is called an *attribute,* and a row is called a *tuple.* These terms reflect the mathematical origins of relational database theory. They mean something to mathematicians. For the rest of us, the knowledge might be useful should we encounter this terminology some day.

SETTING THE TABLES

The second of Date's principles is that the user can use the command language to form new tables. That's what was done earlier in this chapter in some of the exercises that selected certain columns and rows (or fields and records). For example, in several exercises, SQL produced what appeared to be a new table listing only those employees who work in Branch 2. Other commands revealed only selected rows. By the end of that demonstration you were seeing commands that displayed only selected rows and columns.

These selective displays are called *virtual tables*. The original LA__FLAW table is still intact. You see what appears to be a different table, composed of parts of the original.

It is also possible to create a virtual table from two or more original tables. Such a table selects information from the various original tables and presents it on-screen as though it were a single table in its own right. If you give a virtual table a name, it is called a *view*. dBASE III Plus also offers a view facility, but it seems to have attracted little attention. As you'll see in coming chapters, the view is an integral part of SQL.

Once you have created a table (or a view), you can use SQL to take various actions to manipulate the data in that table. The *query* is one such action. As you've seen already, it SELECTS certain items from the table to create and display a new virtual table. You can do this with a relatively short list of variations on the basic SELECT command. The ORACLE reference guide lists a modest twenty-five commands for SQL itself. Most of these are used primarily for database administration and security rather than for day-to-day queries and updates.

ARE YOU MY TYPE?

Whether in dBASE or SQL, each field or column contains one type of value. dBASE presented the structure of its version of LA__FLAW like this:

```
Structure for database  : D:LA__FLAW.dbf
Number of data records:        11
Date of last update     : 11/06/87
Field    Field Name    Type         Width    Dec
  1      LAST          Character      15
  2      FIRST         Character      15
  3      BRANCH        Numeric         1
  4      ASSIGN        Character      15
  5      HIRED         Date            8
  6      SALARY        Numeric         9       2

** TOTAL **                          64
```

The fields LAST and FIRST contain names. Names are composed of letters and, occasionally, punctuation marks. Accordingly, dBASE accepts these data as being of the *Character* type. As mentioned earlier, the employee and branch office numbers are also treated as character data, since there is no reason to perform any mathematical operations on them. The salary figures, however, are contained in *numeric* fields. These fields contain numbers that you might want to add or subtract. For example, you might want to determine the total payroll or the sum of salaries paid in a particular branch office.

A third major data type is the *date* field. It contains—no surprise—dates. The computer stores these in a format you can use to calculate the number of days between two dates.

dBASE has two other data types. A *logical* field contains only one of two possible entries: yes or no. A *memo* field accepts large amounts of textual information, such as notes or comments on the other data in the record. Its capacity is almost unlimited, but you cannot search or manipulate a file on the basis of the contents of this field.

SQL Fields Forever

SQL uses either seven or fifteen data types, depending on how you count them. All but the most advanced users usually can content themelves with four of these. All four are counterparts to dBASE types:

- The *char* type is like the dBASE character type, but it has an abbreviated name. In ORACLE, a char column can contain up to 240 letters, numbers, spaces, and punctuation marks.
- The *number* type corresponds to the numeric field in dBASE. It consists of digits, signs, and decimal points. You can perform mathematical operations with the contents of this type of column.
- Except for the way it displays its output, the SQL *date* type is nearly the same as its dBASE counterpart. You can add and subtract dates to find the differences between them. The functional difference is that in addition to calculating dates, SQL can also work with hours, minutes, and seconds.
- SQL has a *long* data type that is similar to the dBASE memo field. A long column can have up to 65,535 characters. As in dBASE, there are strict limits on how you can use this data type in database manipulations.

There is no SQL counterpart to the dBASE logical field. As will be demonstrated shortly, though, there's a way you can use null values to the same effect.

GETTING TABLES TOGETHER

Because SQL is the language of a relational database, the information in one table can be related to the information in another. For example, the BRANCH column in LA__FLAW contains identification numbers for two offices. A separate table called DEPT can contain further information about each branch office. In dBASE, that file could have this structure:

```
Structure for database  : D:DEPT.dbf
Number of data records:        4
Date of last update     : 10/19/87
Field    Field Name    Type        Width    Dec
   1     BRANCH        Numeric        1
   2     MANAGER       Character     25
   3     CITY          Character     15
** Total **                          41
```

Since there are only two offices at present, a listing of this file would have only two rows, one for each branch office.

```
BRANCH        MANAGER   CITY
-----------   --------------   --------------------
         1    MCKNIFE   LOS ANGELES
         2    TAWDRY    DENVER
```

LA__FLAW and DEPT have one field or column in common: BRANCH. You can use that common data element to form a link between the two tables. If you retrieve information about an employee from LA__FLAW, you can also retrieve information from DEPT about where and for whom this employee works. A later chapter will explain exactly how to do it. The basic process is to create a view, or a virtual table, with some selected information from LA__FLAW and some from DEPT.

REVIEW QUESTIONS

1. Write the SQL equivalent of these dBASE commands:

   ```
   USE EMP
   LIST ALL
   ```

2. Write an SQL*Plus command to format the COMM column of the EMP table with a leading dollar sign, a comma to indicate thousands, and two decimal places.
3. How many tables make up a SQL database?
4. Which part of a SQL table represents a field?
5. What are the four most common data types in SQL?

ANSWERS

1. SELECT * FROM EMP
2. SQL> COLUMN SAL FORMAT $99,999.99 HEADING SALARY
3. Within practical limits, you can use any number.
4. A column.
5. Char, Number, Date, and Long.

Getting Acquainted with ORACLE

LOADING AND STARTING ORACLE

ENTERING AND EDITING SQL COMMANDS

CONVERTING dBASE FILES TO SQL

Your first look at the ORACLE package of SQL products may not be confidence-building. The driver who delivers the software package may stoop a little under its weight. You'll need nearly a foot of shelf space in which to store the three volumes of instruction manuals. The program itself comes in two boxes, each capable of holding ten disks. For what little it's worth, the disk boxes aren't completely full; together, they hold nineteen disks.

You can ignore most of the books and disks until some time in the future when you feel better prepared to deal with them. You can ignore some of them forever, if you'd like to. ORACLE is actually a package of several programs, all driven by SQL, including SQL*Forms, a facility to draw on-screen data entry forms; SQL*Report, which, as its name suggests, produces reports; and SQL*Calc, a SQL-driven spreadsheet with the facade and texture of Lotus 1-2-3. (An optional accessory lets you run the SQL database from 1-2-3 itself.) Standard equipment also includes Pro*C, which lets you put SQL commands in a C language program.

Two remaining programs form ORACLE's core. They will also be at the heart of this book. One is the ORACLE Relational Database Management System (ORACLE RDBMS). As you might expect, it manages the ORACLE database. It uses standard SQL, the relatively short list of commands that is common to nearly every SQL product. The other key program is SQL*Plus, which offers a range of commands that is more extended than that offered by standard SQL, particularly in the area of formatting the results of a query. Because SQL is a highly specialized language in its basic form, it needs this kind of help.

ORACLE is derived from a large-computer product. It makes only the barest concessions to the DOS (disk operating system) that is standard in the PC-compatible world. This will become apparent the moment you unpack those nineteen disks and find the manual entitled *Installation and User's Guide*. Look up the section entitled *Hardware Requirements*.

You'll find some of the expected requirements: a floppy disk drive from which to load the program, a hard disk onto which to load it, and a monitor. In addition, there are some requirements that aren't quite as conventional:

- A computer that uses the 80286 or 80386 memory chip and is 100% compatible with the industry standards for these models. Your PC, XT or clone won't run ORACLE.
- A total of at least 1536K of random access memory (RAM)— more if you expect to run large applications. ORACLE's programmers have tapped into the so-called "protected mode" of advanced memory chips. This lets the SQL server use more memory than the maximum of 640K that the original versions of DOS acknowledge.
- At least 7.5 megabytes of free space on your hard disk.

In short, this is a high-powered program, and it requires a high-powered computer. ORACLE makes good use of the power it draws. First, it steps past the normal memory-handling limits of DOS to tap extended memory. This is the otherwise "useless" form of RAM that you can install on the motherboard of a 286- or 386-class computer. ORACLE will also use the memory that is available on add-in boards, but you must set it up as extended memory rather than as the similarly named expanded memory that most of these boards provide.

LOADING AND STARTING ORACLE

When you load ORACLE into its memory cave, nearly all of it moves into the extended memory. Only about 80K lodges itself in the lower 640K of RAM. That leaves the bulk of your conventional memory to run SQL*Plus, other ORACLE accessories, or conventional DOS programs, which you can reach through a HOST command in SQL*Plus.

With those nineteen disks, the process of installing ORACLE is time-consuming but not difficult. The *Installation Guide* and on-screen prompts will walk you through the process. The manual describes different procedures for network and single-use versions and for different types of computers and monitors. Just don't expect the process to be quick. You'll install SQL*Plus and the database server in individual steps. Then, at your option, you can install the forms, spreadsheet, or programming-language accessories. By the way, the *Installation Guide* is the only book in ORACLE's vast documentation that is specific to the PC. Others are written for users of all types of computers, from mainframes to PCs.

The first step, of course, is to run to the computer store and buy enough blank disks to back up the entire original set of nineteen. Copy each of the program disks using the DISKCOPY command or the alternative method of your choice. Keep in mind that ORACLE has used the DOS BACKUP command to create some of its distribution disks, so use a copy method that will leave the backed-up files intact. The use of BACKUP also means you will have to have a copy of RESTORE in the root directory of your hard disk when you install ORACLE.

ORACLE ORGANIZATION

During the installation process, ORACLE will create its own directory, called ORACLE5, and several subdirectories. Once it has fitted itself into this structure, ORACLE will all but ignore the DOS file and directory arrangement. It will use its own file and memory management system, which includes subdivisions such as partitions and clusters. For example, you create the LA__FLAW table, then search your hard disk in vain for a DOS file by that name. The table exists, but not as a separate DOS file as it would in dBASE. Instead, the table is inside a database file that holds multiple SQL tables. One of these tables is a list of your own currently active tables. To get a look, enter:

SQL> SELECT * FROM TAB

You should see a list of any tables you have created, plus several ORACLE has created for you.

It is possible for an advanced user to alter and expand the file management structure. Beginners should stick to the default blueprint, which is adequate for most uses.

HITTING THE STARTER

The first step in firing up ORACLE is not unexpected—simply type:

C> ORACLE

and then hit <Enter>.

What happens next may not be what you expect. The command activates a batch file that begins to stuff the SQL database management system into your computer's RAM. Along the way your screen will display some messages, many of them cryptic. If all goes well, the final message will read:

ORACLE WARM STARTED

That's nice. It means that the database is ensconced in memory and is ready to be used by one of the front-end programs such as SQL*Plus. That's why you now find yourself back at the DOS prompt. Next, you must issue the command to load SQL*Plus. Enter the logical:

C> SQLPLUS

Again, a batch file will superintend a loading process. At this point you will discover that ORACLE is protected by a password system. Fortunately, the *Installation Guide* provides a means to get into the system for the first time. When ORACLE asks for your user name, enter:

SYSTEM

Then, when asked for the password, enter:

MANAGER

The *Installation Guide* suggests that you immediately alter this stock system by supplying a different password. The command that does this is:

SQL> GRANT CONNECT TO SYSTEM IDENTIFIED BY <your new password>

The meaning of this command will be explored in more detail in the chapter on database security. For now, it's important to know that the user name SYSTEM has a special meaning to ORACLE. When you log in under that name, ORACLE gives you certain privileges necessary to manage the security system. The password should be something of your own choice that others cannot immediately guess, thereby giving you sole entry to the system until you grant access privileges to someone else. You can also grant privileges to yourself, under a new user name.

Once you have passed the password checkpoint, you will find youself at the SQL> prompt, ready to issue a SQL command.

GO CONFIGURE

As you gain a little experience, you will probably take an interest in two configuration files that the program executes as it fires up. One is LOGIN.SQL; the other is CONFIG.ORA.

The LOGIN file is simply a listing of SQL commands to be executed as the program is loaded. Mine looks like this:

```
set numwidth 7
set pagesize 25
set linesize 79
define __editor 'c:\xy\editor'
set pause on
```

The first three commands were provided by ORACLE. They set up a standard-size screen display. I added the last two myself. The first defines the text editor I use to edit commands; within the quotes are the drive, directory, and starting command for a word processor.

When a SQL command produces more than a screenful of output, the PAUSE command lets you examine it one screen at a time; press <Enter> to move to the next screen. This is valuable when you SELECT many items from a large database. It's even handier when you are using HELP. Most of the help files consume more than one screen. With PAUSE, you can get a look at their valuable information before they go whizzing off into the limbo above your monitor.

You can also SET PAUSE ON or SET PAUSE OFF at any time you have the SQL> prompt available.

My CONFIG.ORA has these brief contents:

```
oracle__tio=VIDEO
oracle__home=C:\ORACLE5
oracle__spooler=D:SPOOL.LST
```

The first command identifies the proper video driver for your computer; the *Installation Guide* has more details on this select-ing the right driver. The second defines the "home" disk directory for ORACLE. This is one of many things you can change; it's wise not to do so, however, until you've had some experience.

The third command is my own addition. The SPOOL command in SQL*Plus logs the results of an ORACLE session. You can send this output to a disk file or to the printer. The command here designates the file that will receive it.

The commands in both configuration files set defaults for your personal use. You can overcome nearly any of them with SQL*Plus commands.

FINDING GOOD HELP THESE DAYS

Approximately one-nineteenth of the ORACLE disk set is devoted to help files. During the installation process, there will be a point at which you can decide whether to install the on-screen help system by loading these files. The instructions are not clear, though, on a second step that must be taken to make the help system available; without it, you will still find yourself help-less.

In the subdirectory \ORACLE5\DBS is a batch file named HELPINS.BAT. Go to the DOS prompt and run that file. Thereafter when you call for help you will get some. The procedure for getting help is, while in SQL*Plus, enter HELP plus the subject on which you need assistance. For example:

HELP SELECT

will retrieve information on the ever-popular SELECT command.

GOING HOME

The command to leave SQL*Plus is:

SQL> EXIT

This will return you to the DOS prompt—but with the database manager still loaded in RAM. Just as it took two steps to install ORACLE and SQL*Plus, it takes two steps, plus an optional third, to get out of them.

The recommended command to leave ORACLE is:

C> IOR S

This activates a utility that is intended for network use. It will check for other users on the system and will not remove the database server from memory until everyone is finished. If you're sure that you're alone on the system, you can skip that command and go to the next step:

C> REMORA ALL

Alternatively, you can shut down the computer; everything in RAM will disappear. Another alternative is simply to forget the database manager server is present. Unless SQL*Plus or one of the accessory tools is active, the database takes only about 80K of your 640K of conventional RAM. You can run many programs in the remaining 560K.

ENTERING AND EDITING SQL COMMANDS

Much has been said over the years about the dBASE dot command. Little of what has been said is repeatable here. In its original form, dBASE presented its user with a single period on an otherwise cavernous screen. That period was the program's prompt to enter a command. Later versions of dBASE have embellished the screen display and have provided an optional menu-driven system. The dot is still there, however. If it does nothing else, it prompts you to enter ASSIST, the command that activates the menus.

SQL*Plus has no menus. Instead of a dot, it presents you with a prompt that reads SQL>. Unlike later versions of dBASE, there has been no further attempt to adorn the screen. The prompt indicates the position of what is called the *command line,* although you might be hard-pressed to distinguish this line from the acres of blank screen that often surrounds it.

In addition to the standard SQL commands, a total of forty-two commands are unique to SQL*Plus. Most of these deal with file management or with editing and writing commands. They also provide some limited formatting capacity. At the peak of its formatting power, SQL*Plus can emulate the dBASE report generator. Other ORACLE add-ons let you design on-screen forms, emulate a spreadsheet, or use SQL commands within a conventional programming language.

Since ORACLE's SQL*Plus is an enhancement to standard SQL, there are two kinds of commands you can enter:

- SQL commands, which work with the information in the database. These commands are the universal language of SQL.
- SQL*Plus commands, which are ORACLE's own additions to the basic SQL command set. SQL*Plus commands format the results, set options, and edit and store SQL commands.

If you will be using some other version of SQL, it will be more than helpful to know which commands are common to all SQL systems and which are peculiar to ORACLE. If you're using ORACLE, there's another reason to remember the distinction: It affects the way you enter and edit a command.

Table 2-1 lists the standard SQL commands, their definitions, and some approximate dBASE equivalents. Table 2-2 is a similar list of SQL*Plus commands.

SQL COMMAND SYNTAX

You can enter a command on one line or on several lines. While entering a SQL command, any time that you hit <Enter> to begin a new line, the program will prompt you with a new line number. Once you've completed the full command, enter a semicolon to signal that you're finished. The program will then process the command in the database. In this book, most SQL commands are broken up, with a clause on each line. This makes the commands easier to follow and to understand. In your own use, you may break or not break as you prefer.

If you're like most new SQL users, you will have trouble remembering the command-ending semicolon. You probably have developed the habit of typing a command then hitting <Enter>. If you do this in SQL*Plus, all you'll get is the next line number. No problem. Simply enter the semicolon on the new line. Hit <Enter> again, and SQL*Plus will ignore your mistake. However, not all errors are so easily overcome, as you'll see in a moment.

Some users would say that even this correction isn't easy. One knowledgeable expert—an "oracle" on the subject of ORACLE— maintains that you can't use a semicolon alone on a line. I've done it hundreds of times, though, usually after I've forgotten to properly punctuate the previous line. You can try it yourself and see who's right.

You can use as many tabs or spaces as you need between

TABLE 2-1. SQL commands

This table lists standard SQL commands with explanations and equivalents in dBASE III Plus. In some cases, the dBASE equivalents are direct; in others they are only approximate. There are no dBASE equivalents for many of the SQL space management and security commands. The SQL commands are generic to SQL database management. SQL*Plus commands are specific to Oracle. See the text for details.

SQL	dBASE	DESCRIPTION
/* . . . */ or REM	* or &&	Comment indicators in programs or command files. SQL uses */ to begin a comment and */ to end it. Comments in dBASE extend from the indicator to the end of the line.
ALTER PARTITION		Add a file to a database partition.
ALTER SPACE		Alters the space definition in SQL.
ALTER TABLE	MODIFY STRUCTURE	Add or redefine a SQL column or a dBASE field.
AUDIT		Audit the use of a table, view, or other Oracle facility.
COMMENT		Insert a comment about a table or column into the data dictionary.
CREATE CLUSTER		Create a cluster, which may contain two or more tables.
CREATE DATABASE LINK		Create a link to a user name in a remote database.
CREATE INDEX	INDEX ON \<field> TO \<index file>	Create an index for a table.
CREATE PARTITION		Create a new partition in the database.
CREATE SPACE		Define the space allocation of a table.
CREATE SYNONYM	SELECT \<.Dbf file> ALIAS \<alias name>	Create an alternative name for a table or view.
CREATE TABLE	CREATE	Create a table and define its columns.
DROP		Delete a cluster, database link, etc. from the database.
GRANT	See the PROTECT utility of the network version.	Establish user privileges.
INSERT	INSERT	Add new rows to a table or view.
LOCK TABLE		Provide read-only access to a table.
NOAUDIT		Cancel a previous AUDIT command.
RENAME	RENAME	Change the name of a table, view, or synonym.
REVOKE		Revoke database privileges previously established with GRANT.
SELECT	DISPLAY or LIST	Select specified rows and columns from one or more tables.
UPDATE	UPDATE	Change the value of information in a table.
VALIDATE INDEX		Check the integrity of an index.

TABLE 2-2. SQL*Plus Commands

This table lists SQL*Plus commands with explanations and equivalents in dBASE III Plus. As with standard SQL commands, in some cases the dBASE equivalents are direct; in others they are only approximate. SQL*Plus commands are unique to Oracle.

SQL*Plus	dBASE	DESCRIPTION
@ or START	DO	Execute a command file.
#		End a comment begun with a DOCUMENT command.
$	RUN or !	Go to DOS. Same as HOST.
/	See the HISTORY feature.	Run the command in the SQL buffer.
ACCEPT	ACCEPT	Accept user input.
APPEND		Add text to the current line in the command buffer.
BREAK		Specify which events will cause a break, and what action is taken at that time.
CHANGE	See the HISTORY feature.	Change the current line in the command buffer.
CLEAR		Clear the command buffer.
COLUMN	MODIFY STRUCTURE or PICTURE	Specify the format of a column display and heading.
COMMIT	Executed with QUIT	Save all changes in the database.
COMPUTE	? <formula>	Perform computations on groups of selected rows.
CONNECT		Log on under a new user name.
COPY	COPY	Copy data from one database to another. Used only in networks on Oracle.
DEFINE	STORE	Assign a value to a variable.
DEL	<Esc>	Delete the current line of the command buffer.
DESCRIBE	LIST STRUCTURE	Display a brief description of the table.
DISCONNECT	QUIT	Save file modifications and log off Oracle.
DOCUMENT		Begin an extended comment.
HOST	RUN or !	Return temporarily to the operating system.
INPUT	See HISTORY function	Add a new line to the command buffer.
LIST	See HISTORY function	List contents of command buffer.
PAUSE	WAIT	Display a message and wait for a user response.
QUIT	QUIT	Leave SQL*Plus and return to the operating system. Same as EXIT.
REMARK	* or &&	Begin a remark in a command file.
ROLLBACK		Discard unsaved changes.
RUN	See HISTORY function	Run the command in the current buffer.

SQL*Plus	dBASE	DESCRIPTION
SAVE		Save the contents of the command buffer to disk.
SET	SET	Set a SQL parameter to a specified value.
SHOW	DISPLAY STATUS	Display the current status of SQL parameters.
TIMING		Analyze SQL performance.
TTITLE	See REPORT facility	Display a title at the top of a report.
UNDEFINE	RELEASE	Delete the definition of a user variable.

individual words of the command. You're free to use this formatting flexibility in any way that makes sense to you. With only a few exceptions, which will be explained as they occur throughout the book, you have your choice of uppercase letters, lowercase letters, or any combination of the two.

If you spot a mistake on the command line you are currently writing, correcting it is a simple matter of backspacing to the error and entering the change. If you have already completed the erroneous line and have pressed <Enter>, you must rewrite the command or use the editing commands described later in this chapter to make the correction.

The Difference with SQL*Plus

A SQL*Plus command usually is entered on a single line. Because the end of the line is assumed to be the end of the command, putting a semicolon at the end of the command is unnecessary. You can include it, but its use is optional.

There is a way to break a long SQL*Plus command into more readable segments if you must do so. Here's an example:

```
SQL> COLUMN BRANCH-
        HEADING OFFICE
```

The hyphen tells SQL*Plus that the line is continued. If you don't use the hyphen, the program assumes that the end of the line is the end of the command. This command will place the heading OFFICE on the column ORACLE knows as BRANCH.

EDITING SQL COMMANDS

SQL*Plus has a *command buffer,* which stores the last SQL command you entered. This does not refer to the last SQL*Plus command; the buffer stores only the last command that comes from standard SQL. If you want to repeat a SQL command that is still in the buffer, you can issue the simple command:

SQL> RUN

SQL*Plus will run again whatever command is stored in the buffer.

The buffer is also the key to editing a SQL command when you want to make a change or correct an error. First, use the LIST command to redisplay the command:

SQL> LIST

You then should see:

```
1   SELECT *
2   FROM LA__FLAW
3*  WHERE DEPT = 2;
```

This command would have been in the buffer. The *current line,* usually the last one you entered, will be marked with an asterisk. Now, look at what happens when you enter:

SQL> RUN

Perhaps you didn't notice that there is a mistake in this command. ORACLE did. It will respond with this message:

```
WHERE DEPT = 2
        *
ERROR at line 3: ORA-0704:     invalid column name
```

The asterisk is now below the likely point of error. Indeed, LA__FLAW has no column called DEPT. How do you correct it? Correct it by typing:

SQL> CHANGE /DEPT/BRANCH/

To use the CHANGE command, put the text you want to correct between the first pair of slashes, then enter the text with which you want to replace it. The CHANGE command works almost exactly as does the search-and-replace function of a word processor. SQL*Plus will then display the altered line:

```
3* WHERE BRANCH = 2
```

To check the altered command in full, use the LIST command:

```
SQL> LIST
    1  SELECT *
    2  FROM LA__FLAW
    3* WHERE BRANCH = 2
```

If this is what you want to see, then the next command you should use is RUN. SQL*Plus again will display the revised command and then execute it.

This particular command displayed every column in the table. Perhaps, however, that isn't what you needed, and you want to change the first line of the command. But the active line—the one indicated with the asterisk and the one you now can edit—is still the third. To solve this problem, enter:

```
SQL> LIST 1
```

SQL*Plus will respond with:

```
    1* SELECT *
```

SQL*Plus now displays Line 1, and Line 1 becomes the current line. You now can issue a change command to specify which columns you want to see:

```
SQL> CHANGE /*/LAST, ASSIGN/
```

The amended line now reads:

```
    1 * SELECT LAST, ASSIGN
```

In full, your command is now:

```
    1  SELECT LAST, ASSIGN
    2  FROM LA__FLAW
    3* WHERE BRANCH = 2
```

Maybe this still isn't right; perhaps you would like the salaries included, too. Use LIST 1 again. This time, the next command is

```
SQL> APPEND , SALARY
```

Be careful here. APPEND adds text to the end of the current line. With this command, you are adding a comma, a space, and the word *SALARY*. If the text you want to enter begins with a space, begin the text entry with two spaces. SQL*Plus will recognize the first space as part of the command and the second as part of the text. Your edited command is now:

```
1   SELECT LAST, JOB, SALARY
2   FROM LA__FLAW
3*  WHERE BRANCH = 2
```

Wait, though—it could be even better—you want to have the names in alphabetical order. This requires that you add a line to the command:

SQL> INPUT

This will add a new line just below the currently active one, which at this point is Line 3. You will receive a prompt with the new line number, and you may enter the new line:

4 ORDER BY LAST

Why confine this report to members of Branch 2? Delete the line that contains this specification by entering:

SQL> LIST 3

Then enter:

SQL> DEL

Line 3 will now be the dear-departed Line 3.

Since only SQL commands are stored in the buffer, this technique does not work with SQL*Plus commands. Table 2-3 lists the full range of available editing commands.

If you need more sophisticated editing power, an EDIT command will automatically activate any word processor you specified in the configuration file. The contents of the buffer will be transferred to a file that the word processor will be prepared to edit.

After you are finished editing the command, save the file. SQL*Plus will transfer the revised command back into the buffer and return you to the SQL> prompt. You can then execute the revised command with RUN.

TABLE 2-3.   SQL*Plus Editing Commands

COMMAND	PURPOSE
APPEND <text>	Add the string <text> to the end of a line.
CHANGE /<old>/<new>/	Change <old> to <new>
CHANGE /<text>/	Delete <text>
CLEAR BUFFER	Delete all material from buffer.
DEL	Delete one line.
INPUT	Add a new line below the current line.
INPUT <text>	Add a new line containing <text>.
LIST	List all lines in the buffer.
LIST *n*	List Line *n*.
LIST *n1 n2*	List Lines *n1* through *n2*.
RUN	Run the current command.

A GOOD HOST

Most major programs these days have a command that lets you temporarily drop back to DOS. In SQL*Plus, that command is:

SQL> HOST

You'll see the DOS prompt, representing an opportunity to execute a DOS function or to call some other function. When you type EXIT at the DOS command, you'll find yourself back in SQL*Plus, facing the SQL> prompt.

You can issue a DOS command on the same line on which you enter HOST. For example, to reach dBASE III Plus for the examples in this chapter, I typed:

SQL> HOST DBASE

You can even enter multiple commands such as:

SQL> HOST EDITOR D:CHAP2

This procedure was also used to prepare this book. EDITOR is the command that starts my word processor using XyWrite III Plus. The rest of the command tells XyWrite to load the file that contains the text for this chapter.

CONVERTING dBASE FILES TO SQL

The dBASE command file CONVERT.PRG, Listing 2-1, is the first of two steps by which you can convert a dBASE file to SQL.

```
*   LISTING 2-1
*   FILE NAME: CONVERT.PRG
*   BY: Richard H. Baker
*   DATE: November 6, 1987
*   DESC: Converts dBASE database to SQL Command File
*
*
*
SET TALK OFF
SET ECHO OFF
CLEAR
CLOSE DATABASES
TEXT
dBASE III Plus to SQL Conversion

This program will generate an SQL command file from a
dBASE III Plus database. Running the SQL command file will
then convert the dBASE data into an SQL table.

ENDTEXT
ACCEPT 'dBASE file to convert: ' TO dbfile
dbfile = UPPER(dbfile)
ACCEPT 'Name of SQL file to generate: 'TO sqlfile
sqlfile = UPPER(SQLFILE)
SELECT 1
USE &DBFILE
COPY STRU EXTENDED TO TEMPFILE
SELECT 2
USE TEMPFILE
GOTO TOP
SET ALTERNATE TO CONVERT.SQL
SET ALTERNATE ON

* Assemble command to create table.

CMD = 'CREATE TABLE '+SQLFILE+'('
? CMD
DO WHILE .NOT. EOF()
   DO CASE
   CASE FIELD_TYPE = 'C'
      CMD = FIELD_NAME + ' CHAR(';
      + LTRIM(STR(FIELD_LEN)) + ')'
   CASE FIELD_TYPE = 'N'
      CMD = FIELD_NAME + ' NUMBER(';
      + LTRIM(STR(FIELD_LEN)) + ',';
      + LTRIM(STR(FIELD_DEC)) + ')'
   CASE FIELD_TYPE = 'L'
      CMD = FIELD_NAME + ' NUMBER(1)'
   CASE FIELD_TYPE = 'D'
      CMD = FIELD_NAME + ' DATE'
   ENDCASE
   IF RECNO() < RECCOUNT()
      CMD = CMD + ','
   ELSE
      CMD = CMD + ');'
   ENDIF
   ? CMD
   SKIP
ENDDO EOF
*
```

```
*
*      Build command string from field variables
*
FIELD_COUNT = RECCOUNT()
SELECT 1
GOTO TOP
DO WHILE .NOT. EOF()
    BUILD_COUNT = 1
    CMD = 'INSERT INTO ' + SQLFILE + ' VALUES('
    DO WHILE BUILD_COUNT <= FIELD_COUNT
        FIELD_NAME = FIELD(BUILD_COUNT)
        DO CASE
        CASE TYPE(FIELD_NAME) = 'C'
            CMD = CMD + "'" + TRIM(&FIELD_NAME) + "'"
        CASE TYPE(FIELD_NAME) = 'N'
            CMD = CMD + LTRIM(STR(&FIELD_NAME))
        CASE TYPE(FIELD_NAME) = 'D'
            CMD = CMD + "TO_DATE('"+ DTOC(&FIELD_NAME) + "','MM/DD/YY')"
        CASE TYPE(FIELD_NAME) = 'L' .AND. &FIELD_NAME
            CMD = CMD + '1'
        CASE TYPE(FIELD_NAME) = 'L' .AND. .NOT. &FIELD_NAME
            CMD = CMD + 'NULL'
        ENDCASE
        IF BUILD_COUNT < FIELD_COUNT
            CMD = CMD + ', '
        ELSE
            CMD = CMD + ');'
        ENDIF &&BUILD_COUNT < FIELD_COUNT
        BUILD_COUNT = BUILD_COUNT + 1
    ENDDO && BUILD_COUNT <= FIELD+COUNT
    ? CMD
    SKIP
ENDDO NOT EOF
CLOSE ALTERNATE
CLOSE DATABASES
ERASE TEMPFILE.DBF
CLEAR
@ 10,0 SAY 'Conversion Completed'
@ 11,0 SAY 'SQL command file CONVERT.SQL now on current ;
    drive/directory'
@ 12,0 SAY 'Run it under SQL to generate new SQL table '+SQLFILE
WAIT "Press any Key to Return to dBASE"
CLEAR
RETURN
```

You will be prompted first for the name of the dBASE file to be converted, then for the name you want to give the new SQL table. You can use the same name for both. You also can enter the names with or without extensions.

CONVERT then uses COPY STRUCTURE EXTENDED to create a temporary file. This file is a database, the contents of which describe the structure of the dBASE file you want to convert.

The program then steps through this file, reading each field in the temporary file and building the SQL command to create that same field in the SQL database. Once the command has been assembled, CMD writes that command in an alternative file that will become the SQL command file.

The program goes through a similar process twice. The first time it uses the temporary file to assemble a CREATE TABLE command. This command usually will be long, because it must include the specifications for each field in the dBASE file.

The second pass uses the dBASE file itself. This time it assembles an individual command to INSERT each record in the dBASE file into the SQL counterpart. dBASE then saves the assembled commands under the name CONVERT.SQL.

THE SQL COMMAND FILE

The dBASE CONVERT program does not actually convert the file. It creates a SQL command file with the appropriate columns and data entries in it. The SQL command file then creates the new table.

A SQL command file is much like a dBASE command file with one difference. Since SQL without extensions has only a few commands, it usually is simpler. In either case, the basic idea is the same: Assemble a list of commands, then activate them automatically.

Listing 2-2 is the CONVERT.SQL command file that dBASE created from the LA_FLAW database. The first command CREATE creates the table; each of the remaining INSERT commands inserts a new row of data.

```
REM     Listing 2-2
REM     CONVERT.SQL
REM     Example of SQL command file
REM     created by CONVERT.PRG


CREATE TABLE LA_FLAW(
LAST        CHAR(15),
FIRST       CHAR(15),
BRANCH      NUMBER(1,0),
ASSIGN      CHAR(15),
HIRED       DATE,
SALARY      NUMBER(9,2));
INSERT INTO LA_FLAW VALUES('McKnife', 'Darren', 1, 'Sr. Partner',
    TO_DATE('01/09/49','MM/DD/YY'), 5000);
```

```
INSERT INTO LA_FLAW VALUES('Tawdry', 'Allen', 2, 'Jr. Partner',
    TO_DATE('09/12/65','MM/DD/YY'), 4000);
INSERT INTO LA_FLAW VALUES('Cossack', 'Michael', 1, 'Criminal',
    TO_DATE('07/17/82','MM/DD/YY'), 4500);
INSERT INTO LA_FLAW VALUES('Bunsen', 'Burner', 2, 'Family',
    TO_DATE('10/09/78','MM/DD/YY'), 2975);
INSERT INTO LA_FLAW VALUES('Tucker', 'Friar', 1, 'Tax',
    TO_DATE('08/14/77','MM/DD/YY'), 2850);
INSERT INTO LA_FLAW VALUES('Boysenberry', 'Ann', 1, 'Civil',
    TO_DATE('12/31/85','MM/DD/YY'), 2450);
INSERT INTO LA_FLAW VALUES('Rox', 'Goldie', 2, 'Secretary',
    TO_DATE('01/23/82','MM/DD/YY'), 1300);
INSERT INTO LA_FLAW VALUES('Mason', 'Percy', 2, 'Criminal',
    TO_DATE('06/09/29','MM/DD/YY'), 3850);
INSERT INTO LA_FLAW VALUES('Bailey', 'F. Bill', 1, 'Criminal',
    TO_DATE('12/17/80','MM/DD/YY'), 4800);
INSERT INTO LA_FLAW VALUES('Borque', 'Bobby', 1, 'Paralegal',
    TO_DATE('12/03/81','MM/DD/YY'), 950);
INSERT INTO LA_FLAW VALUES('Hartless', 'James', 2, 'Personal Injury',
    TO_DATE('08/08/83','MM/DD/YY'), 7500);
```

To run it, fire up SQL*Plus and issue this command:

SQL> START CONVERT

Include any necessary drive and directory indicators, but you need not add the .SQL suffix. For example, this version would be correct:

SQL> START D:\SQL\CONVERT

ORACLE will run the series of SQL commands as a program, creating and filling the new table.

CONVERTING DATES

In a couple of cases, the two CONVERT files must do some fancy stepping over differences between dBASE and SQL syntax. Date fields are particularly tricky. Like dBASE, SQL has a series of functions to translate dates between character and date types. The SQL function to transform a character version to date status is:

TO_DATE('<text>','<format>')

The text is the character rendition of the date in question; the format entry tells SQL how to read the text. When the dBASE CONVERT program finds a date field, it uses this sequence to assemble the SQL command:

"TO_DATE('"+ DTOC(&FIELD_NAME) + "','MM/DD/YY')"

This translates the contents of the current dBASE field into character form, then includes them in the command. The program then adds a statement to the effect that the dates are in the format MM/DD/YY, which is the standard dBASE format.

A typical SQL clause created by this sequence is:

TO__DATE('01/09/49','MM/DD/YY')

LOGICAL NULLS

CONVERT also uses SQL's null values to compensate for its lack of a logical field type. In setting up the structure of the new SQL table, CONVERT.PRG turns dBASE logical fields into SQL number columns.

When reading the individual data from the database, CONVERT provides two options for handling a logical field:

```
CASE TYPE(FIELD__NAME) = 'L' .AND. &FIELD__NAME
CMD = CMD + '1'
CASE TYPE(FIELD__NAME) = 'L' .AND. .NOT. &FIELD__NAME
CMD = CMD + 'NULL'
```

In translation, if the field is logical and its value is the logical .T., the value 1 will appear in the corresponding SQL row and column. If the value is a logical .F., that block will have a null value. You can simulate the search for a logical field by searching for fields that are NULL or NOT NULL.

For example, if PAID was a logical field in the dBASE file, you would use this command to search for records in which PAID was logically true:

```
SQL> SELECT <fields>
  2    FROM <table name>
  3    WHERE PAID IS NOT NULL;
```

To select records that were logically false in the dBASE file, the command would be:

```
SQL> SELECT <fields>
  2    FROM <table name>
  3    WHERE PAID IS NULL;
```

The basis of this technique is the singular character of a null value. A null is an empty space. It has no value, not even a value of zero. In a manner of speaking, it is a logical nothing, the opposite of a logical something. Simply take the dBASE true and false and substitute the SQL alternatives of something and nothing.

REVIEW QUESTIONS

1. What DOS accessory does ORACLE use during installation?
2. How can you obtain a directory of your SQL tables?
3. What user name and password can you use to log onto ORACLE until you have established your own?
4. What does the PAUSE command do in SQL*Plus?
5. What is the difference between a SQL command and a SQL*Plus command?
6. Why are the SQL commands in this book usually written in several short lines?
7. You need to edit Line 2 of a three-line command. How would you get there?
8. What is the command to return temporarily from SQL*Plus to DOS?

ANSWERS

1. RESTORE. Many ORACLE files have been placed on the distribution disk using the DOS BACKUP. RESTORE retrieves these files.
2. Query the table called TAB. You cannot obtain this directory through DOS.
3. The user name is SYSTEM, identified by the password MANAGER.
4. It halts scrolling of the screen display.
5. A SQL command is part of standard SQL. A SQL*Plus command is an extension added by ORACLE.
6. For convenience and readability. You can enter a SQL command on as many lines as you wish, as long as you end the command with a semicolon.
7. Use LIST 2 to make the second line the current line.
8. HOST.

PART

2 LEARNING SQL

3

Creating and Managing a Table

CREATING A TABLE

INSERTING AND UPDATING

"Yo, Addie. You wanted to see me?"

"Yes, I did, Dennis. I want to talk about our MBO situation. You do know what an MBO is, don't you?"

"Oh, yeah, Major Brownie-Point Operation."

"That's Management by Objectives. And it's very important. Oh, I know. Some people use it as a glorified quota system. I assure you, though, that the new management . . ."

"Ah, yes. The Marine Bank of the Great Plains. Having saved little old Underwood Federal from the clutches of the federal government, they are now the new management."

"I'm very familiar with all that. Anyway, I agree with management. I think it's very important that we set realistic objectives for this office and for every employee. For example, I'd like to start setting some goals for cross-selling."

"Whoa, there."

"You know what I mean. When a customer signs up for one kind of account, we want to sell that customer our other services as well; it's called dual relationships."

"We're supposed to have relationships with our customers now? Hey, I might get to like the new owners after all."

"That's not it, and you know it."

"Yeah, I know. I sure miss the good old days with UnderFed. You'd sign up a customer for a checking account, a savings account, or your basic certificate of deposit. Then you'd march him over to the display with the glorious prizes spread out, and he could say, 'I'll take the toaster for $25, the electric fry pan for $30, and the rest in a gift certificate.'"

"You know that kind of marketing is obsolete. That's one reason UnderFed got into such deep financial trouble. That's why the federal regulators stepped in and found a new owner. I realize that, because Marinecorp brought me in to manage this branch, many of you probably think of me as. . . well, an outsider, but I'd like to think I'm part of the team here."

"I'd like you to start developing a computer system to keep track of employees and their MBO performance."

"What's wrong with that computer behind you?"

"Oh, that's just a prop. I don't actually know how to use it. I want you to set up a system that the employees can use on their own PCs—when they're actually working, that is."

"I don't know. That's a really big job."

"I realize that. I also know it will take some time and effort. You can use Misty Presto and Hubert Tuba, if you'd like to. You'll have to set up a comprehensive database system—one that will keep track of the employees and their selling performance. It should also produce the reports we need for management information."

"What kind of information does management need?"

"Anything it wants. You know, I like Marinecorp, and they've treated me very well, but it seems as though some of the people in top management got their causes mixed up a few years ago. They got the idea that government reporting requirements should be turned over to private industry."

"There's a lot of that going around."

"I agree. What I really hope to do is to set up a system that will make it easier to prepare those reports every month. It will save both of us a lot of time."

"I sure can think of ways to put that time to good use."

"Just get busy. And Dennis . . ."

"Yeah, Addie."

"Don't slam the door on your way out."

Later, Dennis Madison announced to a pair of his subordinates, "I've figured out a good, old-fashioned way to design this system. We're going to have a little competition. You, Mr. Tuba, will start working in dBASE III Plus."

"Thank you, sir. I'm sure I'll justify the faith you've placed in me."

"And you, Miss Presto, will do the same thing using ORACLE and SQL."

"I can hardly wait to get started."

"So, get to it. Start with a personnel roster. Before we can figure out how our people are doing, we have to figure out who our people are, so let's get busy and design some databases. Let me see how you do; may the best person win. One more thing. . . . "

"What's that?"

"Think of this as a challenge. You are about to enter the hallowed halls of higher management. You are about to learn the most valued thing any manager can learn. You are about to become research assistants."

CREATING A TABLE

The command to create a SQL table is CREATE TABLE. Once more, the command to create a SQL table is CREATE TABLE. Why the repetition? The answer is simple: You tend to gloss over things as obvious as this is when you read them. They require so little effort that you end up exerting too little effort.

A CREATE TABLE command must include the specifications of the table you want to create. These are:

- The name of the table
- The name of each column in the table
- The width of each column
- The type of data in each column

There is also some optional information that you might want to include.

PUTTING YOUR SPECIFICATION IN A COMMAND

When the two employees returned with their newly created databases, Madison looked first at Tuba's dBASE design. It looked like this:

```
Structure for database: D:ROSTER.dbf
Number of data records:     10
Date of last update:    10/23/87
```

Field	Field Name	Type	Width	Dec
1	EMPNO	Numeric	4	
2	LAST	Character	10	
3	FIRST	Character	10	
4	INITIAL	Character	1	
5	DEPT__NO	Numeric	2	
6	POSITION	Character	10	
7	SALARY	Numeric	9	2
** Total **			47	

"Very good, my man. Now, let's see what Miss Presto has been able to do with SQL." (Remember dBASE always claims one space for itself.)

"Glad to show you, Mr. Madison," she replied, entering the command:

SQL> describe roster

ORACLE quickly produced these results:

Name	Null?	Type
EMPNO	NOT NULL	NUMBER(4)
LAST		CHAR(10)
FIRST		CHAR(10)
MI		CHAR(1)
DEPT__NO		NUMBER(2)
POSITION		CHAR(10)
SALARY		NUMBER(9,2)

"There is one difference," Miss Presto pointed out. "Hubert's version uses a field called INITIAL. My computer told me I couldn't do that. I guess ORACLE uses that word for something else. Because the program uses the word, I can't use it."

"That's what's called a reserved word, I say with reservations. Let's see the name you gave it. My, my, you called it MI. Now, being wise in the ways of dBASE, I know how Mr. Tuba created his database. How did *you* do it?"

"I wrote out a SQL command," Presto replied.

Like any good CREATE command, hers had two major parts:

- The clause CREATE TABLE plus the name of the table.
- A list of the columns, including their names, types, and lengths. The entire list is within a pair of parentheses.

The full command is:

```
SQL>   CREATE TABLE ROSTER
    2    (EMP__NO    NUMBER(4) NOT NULL
    3    LAST       CHAR(10),
    4    FIRST      CHAR(10),
    5    MI         CHAR(1),
    6    DEPT__NO   NUMBER(2,0),
    7    POSITION   CHAR(10),
    8    SALARY     NUMBER(8,2));
```

NAMING A TABLE

Like any database file, a SQL table must have a name. As with nearly any kind of computer operation, the user has to observe certain rules when creating names. Because ORACLE doesn't maintain its databases as DOS does its files, you aren't bound by the familiar file-naming rules. Instead, ORACLE imposes its own requirements. The name of an ORACLE table must:

- *Begin with a letter:* The letter can be either uppercase or lowercase. You can't start with a number or a punctuation mark.
- *Be no more than thirty characters long.* That's a big jump in flexibility over the eight letters that DOS allows. After the first letter, you can use letters, numerals, or an underscore. A few other punctuation marks also are allowed, but they will usually prove to be more confusing than useful.
- *Be different from any other name now in use.* This includes the names of views as well as the names of tables.
- *Not duplicate an ORACLE reserved word.* At last count, ORACLE had a full 140 of these and this total is subject to change. As the characters in the database drama found out, INITIAL is one of these. You probably won't learn every one, but ORACLE knows them all. When you use a reserved word, an error message will let you know.

ORACLE will usually ignore the difference between uppercase and lowercase letters, but there is an exception. ORACLE will become case-sensitive if you put the name in quotation marks as follows:

```
CREATE TABLE "ROSTER"
CREATE TABLE "Roster"
CREATE TABLE "roster"
```

Thus the creation of three different tables. The quotation marks also let you get away with what ordinarily would be improper practice. "Cheat Sheet" or "87 Taxes" would be acceptable; without the quotation marks, these would be highly illegal—even plea bargaining would be out of the question.

NAMING COLUMNS

Creating a table and naming a column can be done on one line. Creating individual columns can be done that way, too. If your table is at all complicated, though, you'll want to break the clauses into individual lines. There will be one clause per column. For each clause, you must specify in the following order:

- The column's name
- The data type
- The length (a description which will vary somewhat with the data type)
- Whether null values are allowed

For example, in the ROSTER table, EMP_CODE CHAR(3) creates a column called EMP_CODE. DEPT_NO NUMBER(2,0) specifies a column of number values up to two digits in length, with no decimal places allowed. For example, a specification such as AMOUNT NUMBER(6,2) would create a column called AMOUNT that would have a total of six digits, two of which could be to the right of the decimal point.

The column name always comes first, and it cannot duplicate any column name that is already in the table. The rules for naming columns are otherwise the same as the rules for naming tables.

The column type follows. As explained in Chapter 1, SQL users typically use only three of the many available data types: *Char, Number,* and *Date.* The final entry is the description, which can be the length of a Char value—the length and decimal places of a Number column. A date column needs no description. Table 3-1 lists and describes all the SQL data types.

Unlike dBASE users, SQL users don't have to worry much about creating columns that are too wide; dBASE claims enough memory to hold the maximum width you specify, no matter what the column actually contains. ORACLE, however, allocates enough memory to accommodate the contents themselves, without regard to the maximum width.

ALLOW NULL VALUES?

A null value indicates that one or more values in the column are empty. The ability to use a null value often can be useful when

TABLE 3-1.   SQL Data Types and Specifications

CHAR(8)	Char values consist of upper and lower case letters and punctuation marks. The width is the maximum length in characters. In this case the column may have up to eight characters. SQL allows up to 240.
NUMBER	Number values consist of the digits 0 through 9 with an optional + or − sign and a decimal point. When used without a length specification, this column can contain as many as forty digits, not counting a decimal point or sign.
NUMBER(4)	Specifies a Number value up to as many characters as indicated, in this case, four. When used with a length specification, a number column may be as many as 105 digits wide. However, for mathematical purposes, Oracle will recognize only 40 significant digits of a longer column.
NUMBER(8,2)	This column may contain up to eight digits, with two to the right of the decimal point. If you omit a specification for the number of decimal places, the effect will be that of floating decimals with any number of places, up to the maximum width of the column itself.
DATE	This column will hold the value of any date and time from 4712 BC through 4712 AD. It will display times of day as well as dates.
LONG	This column is similar to Char but may be up to 65,535 characters long. No more than one Long column may be in any table. You cannot query or order a table on the basis of data in a Long field.

there are missing values in your data. At other times, you may not want to allow null values, in effect requiring that the column contain some tangible value.

In the ROSTER table, you may not want to allow null values for the social security number. Every employee must have one, and you will be required to use it often. Accordingly, the command to create that column might read:

    SS_NO   CHAR(11) NOT NULL

This would require that every employee's record include a Social Security number. If anyone tries to add a record without the Social Security number, ORACLE will point out the error.

INSERTING AND UPDATING

After checking out the very similar database structures, Madison asked his two underlings to display the contents of their employee rosters. Tuba entered the dBASE command:

    . LIST ALL

Misty Presto, only a few keystrokes behind, rapped out:

SQL> SELECT * FROM ROSTER

Madison put the two together as they appear in Figure 3-1. "All very good," he said. "I see all are present and accounted for. However, I have one little surprise for you. We just hired a new employee."

"That means we'll each have to add this person's record to our databases," Presto said.

"Couldn't have said it better myself," said Madison.

ADDING A NEW ROW

This time, Tuba had the advantage. He ordered dBASE to APPEND a new record. He was presented with a full-screen display calling for the new entries field by field.

FIGURE 3-1   Two Versions of the Same Roster

```
DBASE:

Record#   EMPNO LAST        FIRST      INITIAL DEPT_NO POSITION       SALARY
      1       1 DAVIDSON    ADDIE      H             1 MANAGER     24000.00
      2       2 MADISON     DENNIS     W             1 ASST MGR    21000.00
      3       3 PRESTO      MISTY      D             1 RECEPTION   42500.00
      4       4 TUBA        HUBERT     G             2 NEW ACCT    11000.00
      5       5 SUTTON      WILMA      W             3 TELLER      12500.00
      6       6 MAHONEY     SUZANNE    S             3 TELLER      12400.00
      7       7 BUCHINSKY   CHARLES    B             4 SECURITY    15000.00
      8       8 PALMER      VERA       M             3 TELLER      13450.00
      9       9 COLLINS     KATHLEEN   D             2 NEW ACCT    13300.00
     10      10 ZIMMERMAN   ROBERT     D             2 NEW ACCT    18000.00

SQL

  EMPNO LAST        FIRST      M DEPT_NO POSITION     SALARY
------- ----------  ---------- - ------- ----------   -------
      1 DAVIDSON    ADDIE      H       1 MANAGER       24000
      2 MADISON     DENNIS     W       1 ASST MGR      21000
      3 PRESTO      MISTY      D       1 RECEPTION     42500
      4 TUBA        HUBERT     G       2 NEW ACCT      11000
      5 SUTTON      WILMA      W       3 TELLER        12500
      6 MAHONEY     SUZANNE    S       3 TELLER        12400
      7 BUCHINSKY   CHARLES    B       4 SECURITY      15000
      8 PALMER      VERA       M       3 TELLER        13450
      9 COLLINS     KATHLEEN   D       2 NEW ACCT      13300
     10 ZIMMERMAN   ROBERT     D       2 NEW ACCT      18000
```

Misty realized, though, that SQL would require that she construct a command to INSERT a new record. It was more complicated than the dBASE method—and more complicated than she had expected. She entered this command:

```
SQL> INSERT INTO ROSTER
   2    VALUES(11,'ROWE-HATTON',
   3    'PHYLLIS','F',2,'NEW_ACCT',11250);
```

It should have worked. In fact, this is a thoroughly correct and "legal" command. INSERT requires a list of VALUES to be inserted. List them in the order of the table's columns. Put Char entries between single quotes. Misty Presto did all that. Even so, ORACLE responded with an error message:

```
INSERT INTO ROSTER
*
ERROR at line 1: ORA-1401: inserted value too large for column
```

This message stumped the entire group for a while. It turned out that the error was not in line 1 at all. However, there was one item that was too large for its column. The table called for a last name of up to ten letters. The new employee had a hyphenated, eleven-letter name.

"I ran into the same thing," Tuba reported. "dBASE just lopped off the last letter when it appended the new record. I solved that by using MODIFY STRUCTURE and lengthening the LAST field to fifteen characters."

MODIFYING COLUMN SPECIFICATIONS

"Can you do that?" Madison asked the other contestant.

"I think so," After checking the ORACLE manual, she wrote out this command:

```
SQL> ALTER TABLE ROSTER
   2    MODIFY (LAST CHAR(15));
```

What the book told Misty is that ALTER TABLE is the command that modifies the structure of an existing column. Name the table, then add the word MODIFY. After that, type in the new specifications just as you would for a CREATE TABLE command. Be careful to have as many opening parentheses as you do closing ones. In this case, the command extended the LAST column to fifteen characters. When Misty repeated the INSERT command it worked perfectly. ORACLE verified this with:

1 record created.

To check that all was in order, she entered:

```
SQL> SELECT LAST, POSITION, SALARY
  2   FROM ROSTER
  3   WHERE EMP_NO = 11;
```

ORACLE responded with:

LAST	POSITION	SALARY
ROWE-HATTON	NEW_ACCT	11250

INSERTING SELECTED COLUMNS

"Now, I'm afraid I have another little problem to throw at you," Madison announced. "It seems we've hired yet another new employee—I don't know what we're going to do. All we have to put in the record is his name. We'll have to leave everything else blank for now."

"No problem," said Tuba from the dBASE side. "I'll just APPEND another new record. When I don't have the information, I'll just leave the fields blank."

"And how are things in SQL-land?" Madison asked. "So far, I notice that data entry hasn't exactly been your strong point. How would you handle this situation—data entry-wise, I mean?"

"Oh, I know that already. I just use a variation of the INSERT command, naming the columns for which I do have information. The rest will have null values until we change them."

"I like a good null as well as anyone does. Let's see it." The command is:

```
SQL> INSERT INTO ROSTER (LAST, FIRST)
  2   VALUES ('BANKERSON','HARVEY');
```

"Very good. Now, let's display the entire table." If all has gone well—and who's to say it hasn't—the results shown in Figure 3-2 should appear.

FIGURE 3-2   The Roster Table with Two New Additions

```
EMP_NO LAST              FIRST        M DEPT_NO POSITION     SALARY
------- ----------       ----------   - ------- ----------   -------
      1 DAVIDSON          ADDIE        H       1 MANAGER       24000
      2 MADISON           DENNIS       W       1 ASST MGR      21000
      3 PRESTO            MISTY        D       1 RECEPTION     42500
      4 TUBA              HUBERT       G       2 NEW ACCT      11000
      5 SUTTON            WILMA        W       3 TELLER        12500
      6 MAHONEY           SUZANNE      S       3 TELLER        12400
      7 BUCHINSKY         CHARLES      B       4 SECURITY      15000
      8 PALMER            VERA         M       3 TELLER        13450
      9 COLLINS           KATHLEEN     D       2 NEW ACCT      13300
     10 ZIMMERMAN         ROBERT       D       2 NEW ACCT      13300
     11 ROWE-HATTON       PHYLLIS      F       2 NEW_ACCT      11250
        BANKERSON         HARVEY
```

UPDATING A RECORD

Meanwhile, at the law firm of McKnife, Tawdry a personnel crisis was taking place.

"Percy Mason is getting along in years," Tawdry pointed out. "I think we should give him a healthy pension and send him packing."

"I know he's expressed an interest in joining his brother's business."

"What's that?"

"Mason's brother, Paul, operates this sort of regional distillery in the Southeast. Perhaps you've heard their slogan: 'We'll sell no 'shine before it's time.'"

"Oh, yes. That one."

"What Percy would really want to do is go into semiretirement. I figure we could set him up with a branch office in Atlanta."

"Then who would we get to take his place? He is a skilled defense attorney. Very few have perfected, as he has, the use of a forced confession as a defense tactic."

"There is one other who has. He's only been around for a few years, but I hear his ratings are good."

"You mean . . ."

"Yes, Ben Mukluk."

The job of updating the database fell to secretary Goldie Rox. She usually works in Denver but was flown in for this assignment. First, she recorded Mason's assignment to the new branch office, giving it the number of 3:

```
SQL> UPDATE LA__FLAW
   2   SET BRANCH = 3
   2   WHERE LAST = 'MASON';
```

The UPDATE command again requires the table name. It then uses a SET command to change the branch number to 3. WHERE then specifies the row or rows in which this change is to be made.

INSERTING DATE VALUES

Rox faced an extra challenge when she set up the command to add the new attorney to the staff. The table included the hiring date, and adding a date requires a particular kind of command. The full command went this way:

```
SQL> INSERT INTO LA__FLAW
   2   VALUES('MUKLUK','BENJAMIN',2,'CRIMINAL',
   3   TO__DATE('11/09/87','MM/DD/YY',4700);
```

As usual, the INSERT command names the table. Line 2 inserts several Char values and a number; another number appears at the end of Line 3. Most of Line 3 is devoted, however, to the date entry.

The TO__DATE function converts Char entries to Dates. The first of the two entries within the brackets identifies the date to be entered. Since it is a Char value at this point, it is set off with single quotes. The next entry, also in single quotes, describes the format of the preceding entry. It tells SQL how to interpret the preceding entry.

Had the date Nov. 9, 1987 been specified as '09-11-87,' a format clause of "DD-MM-YY' would have caused ORACLE to interpret it correctly. Checking out the revised table, Rox got the results shown in Figure 3-3.

It wasn't necessary in this case, but it would have been possible to record the exact moment Mukluk was hired. The date function would have read:

```
TO__DATE(11/09/87 11:06','MM/DD/YY HH:MM')
```

FIGURE 3-3 The Revised Law Firm Table

```
LAST              FIRST            BRANCH ASSIGN           HIRED      SALARY
----------------  ---------------- ------ ---------------- ---------- -------
MCKNIFE           DARREN                1 SR. PARTNER      09-JAN-49   5000
TAWDRY            ALLEN                 2 JR. PARTNER      12-SEP-65   4000
COSSACK           MICHAEL               1 CRIMINAL         17-JUL-82   4500
BUNSEN            BURNER                2 FAMILY           09-OCT-78   2975
TUCKER            FRIAR                 1 TAX              14-AUG-77   2850
BOYSENBERRY       ANN                   1 CIVIL            31-DEC-85   2450
ROX               GOLDIE                2 SECRETARY        23-JAN-82   1300
MASON             PERCY                 3 CRIMINAL         09-JUN-29   3850
BAILEY            F. BILL               1 CRIMINAL         17-DEC-80   4800
BORQUE            BOBBY                 1 PARALEGAL        03-DEC-81    950
HARTLESS          JAMES                 2 PERSONAL INJURY 08-AUG-83   7500
MUKLUK            BENJAMIN              2 CRIMINAL         09-NOV-87   4700
```

The result would have looked like this:

9-NOV-87 11:06

UPDATING ONE TABLE FROM ANOTHER

"Well, it's sort of good," said branch manager Addie Davidson when she saw the Roster program. I mean, it's useful and all that, but don't you think we ought to have a separate file just for the new-accounts people, because they do most of the selling? You can't expect people in other kinds of jobs to do as well."

"I think," said Madison, "that our smiling security guard could do a lot of selling if we allowed him to take the right approach." I take it, though, that you'd like a separate database table that just lists the new-accounts employees."

"That's right."

"Your command is my wish."

There was no need now to involve the two associates. Madison had picked up SQL and was on a roll. First he entered this command to create the new table:

```
SQL> CREATE TABLE REPS
   2  (REP_CODE        CHAR(4),
   3  LAST             CHAR(15),
   4  FIRST            CHAR(15),
   5  BRANCH_NO        NUMBER(3),
   6  DEPT_NO NUMBER(2));
```

He then began to cleverly apply his recently gained knowledge of SQL:

```
SQL> INSERT INTO REPS (LAST, FIRST, DEPT__NO)
   2   SELECT LAST, FIRST, DEPT__NO
   3   FROM ROSTER
   4   WHERE DEPT__NO = 2;
```

"Pretty slick," he congratulated himself, knowing he had just emulated the UPDATE command of dBASE. The SQL version consists of the INSERT command and a list of values to be inserted. The second line begins a process of SELECTING certain records and columns from ROSTER. In other words, Madison used a query to select data for the new table. The records and columns to be inserted in REPS are those that satisfy the query. In this case, INSERT copied data from the three columns that both tables had in common for employees assigned to Department 2. The new file would look like this:

REP__	LAST	FIRST	BRANCH__NO	DEPT__NO
	TUBA	HUBERT		2
	COLLINS	KATHLEEN		2
	ZIMMERMAN	ROBERT		2
	ROWE-HATTON	PHYLLIS		2

It was still necessary to fill in the two new columns. The first part was easy:

```
SQL> UPDATE REPS
   2   SET BRANCH__NO = 79;
```

Because everyone in this branch works for Branch 79, this command simply updates every row. The dBASE equivalent would be:

.REPLACE ALL BRANCH__NO WITH 79

It's reasonable to ask, then, why the table should have that column at all. The reasonable answer is that it's useful for the training exercise you have just completed. Otherwise, you're right. It is useless.

Filling in the other column was a little more difficult. Not only does ORACLE truncate its name in the display, but each entry is to be different. Madison also decided that employees' initials probably would be useful as identification codes. To be sure, there are other codes available, such as the employee and social security numbers. Many who had to work with this data, though, would recognize the employees' initials but would not know the numbers.

To update the first row, Madison entered:

```
SQL> UPDATE REPS
   2   SET REP__CODE = 'HT'
   3   WHERE LAST = 'TUBA';
```

For the next, he entered

```
SQL> UPDATE REPS
   2   SET REP__CODE = 'KC'
   3   WHERE LAST = 'COLLINS';
```

and so on, through the rest of the table. When he was finished, the new table looked like this:

REP__	LAST	FIRST	BRANCH__NO	DEPT__NO
HT	TUBA	HUBERT	79	2
KC	COLLINS	KATHLEEN	79	2
RZ	ZIMMERMAN	ROBERT	79	2
PR	ROWE-HATTON	PHYLLIS	79	2

ADDING A COLUMN

"You know what would really be helpful?" asked Addie Davidson after she reviewed this latest effort.

"Always willing to be of help," Madison replied.

"Perhaps we could add something to the ROSTER table. The way the phone system works around here, I'm always having trouble getting my own employees on their assigned extensions."

"You want a data table that will make the phones work right? That's a tall order. You're asking me to retrieve a lost art from the oral tradition of electronic communication."

"It would be nice if you could do that, but all I'm asking is that you provide a column for the employees' extension numbers."

"Nothing to it," Madison said, and he was nearly right. To add a column to a database, use ALTER TABLE and then ADD, then enter a description of the column to be added. This description must be in parentheses, and it takes the same form as the description in CREATE. The command to add a new column to the ROSTER table went something like this:

```
SQL> ALTER TABLE ROSTER
   2  ADD (PHONE      NUMBER(4);
```

"Well, it does go something like that," Madison muttered. Instead of adding the column, ORACLE responded with an error message:

```
ADD (PHONE      NUMBER(4)
                          *
ERROR at line 2: ORA-0907: missing right parenthesis
```

"Always gotta watch those brackets," Madison realized. "Your tax brackets, your wall brackets, your SQL brackets. Leave one out, and look what happens. I guess I'll just have to get this command into a different bracket." Making use of the ORACLE error-correction system, Madison entered:

```
SQL> LIST 2
```

ORACLE responded by presenting the offending line:

```
2* ADD (PHONE      NUMBER(4)
```

The correction, then, was simple:

```
SQL> APPEND )
```

ORACLE then displayed the corrected line:

```
2* ADD (PHONE      NUMBER(4))
```

"That's the way it should have looked in the first place," Madison said to himself. Because this was the case, he commanded:

```
SQL> RUN
```

ORACLE displayed, then executed, the full revised command:

```
1   ALTER TABLE ROSTER
2*  ADD (PHONE      NUMBER(4))
```

The program then confirmed that all had gone as expected, or at least as Madison had commanded:

Table altered.

To be sure, Madison then used the DESCRIBE command to check the new version. It looked like this:

Name	Null?	Type
EMP__NO		NUMBER(4)
LAST		CHAR(15)
FIRST		CHAR(10)
MI		CHAR(1)
DEPT__NO		NUMBER(2)
POSITION		CHAR(10)
SALARY		NUMBER(8,2)
PHONE		NUMBER(4)

Initially, all the fields in a newly created column are null. Madison expressed his recognition of that fact in these terms: "Now I supposed she's going to want me to enter all the phone numbers into the file," Madison muttered. He was right.

REVIEW QUESTIONS

1. A CREATE TABLE command must contain four elements. What are they?
2. What would a SQL table called __6thGrade be likely to contain?
3. What does the specification NOT NULL indicate?
4. What is the wild card character used to select every column in a table?
5. With what command would you modify a table named DETRITUS to change the length of a Char column called JUNK to 12 spaces?
6. Whoops. Percy Mason has decided not to retire after all and will appear in a few selected cases. How do you reassign him back to Branch 2?
7. Dennis Madison created a new table called REPS by transferring information from another table. How would you use

the same technique to create yet another table called NON__REPS?

ANSWERS

1. Table name, column names, column widths, and data types.
2. Nothing. A name that begins with either a punctuation mark or a number is considered "illegal." You won't find it in your state penal code, but ORACLE will punish you just the same.
3. It means that null values are not accepted; the entry must not be blank.
4. An asterisk.
5. SQL> ALTER TABLE DETRITUS
    2   MODIFY (JUNK CHAR(12));
6. SQL> UPDATE LA__FLAW
    2   SET BRANCH = 2
    3   WHERE LAST = 'MASON';
7. SQL> INSERT INTO REPS (LAST, FIRST, DEPT__NO)
    2   SELECT LAST, FIRST, DEPT__NO
    3   FROM ROSTER
    4   WHERE DEPT__NO != 2

Basic Query
Techniques

The daily staff meeting at McKnife, Tawdry, Diver, and Brown has been called to order. The first order of business: "What's the status of *Kateley* v. *Eliason*?"

"That's a divorce case. The complicating factor is that the two aren't married. However, I expect we'll have a settlement very soon."

"Fine. Now what's this about *Michigan* v. *Northwestern*. That sounds like a football game."

"It is, in a manner of speaking. As I'm sure you know, recruiting of college athletes has changed greatly in the last few years. The players don't want cars and money any more. They insist on getting degrees. Not only that, but the best players won't settle for basket-weaving programs. They want degrees in business administration or prelaw."

"So what has this to do with our case?"

"Since things changed, Northwestern has had some really great recruiting years. They've dominated the Big 10. In fact, right now they're ranked third in the country, behind Columbia and Duke. Now, some of the old football powers in the conference have filed suit. They claim that, because Northwestern offers so many meaningful degree programs to its athletes, the school is engaging in unfair competition."

"How's it look?"

"Our clients from Northwestern are in a pretty tough position. We had to show them the records of a linebacker who's majoring in English lit. We might be able to settle, however, if we can get him to transfer to one of the social sciences."

SIMPLE SELECTIONS

SELECT is the basic command in a SQL query. It's so fundamental the first few chapters would have been incomplete without some mention of SELECT, even though this book had not yet presented it to you officially. Now it's time to take an in-depth look at this vital command.

Figure 4-1 shows the structure and contents of four tables you'll be using in this chapter. Two of them, LA_FLAW and ROSTER, have appeared previously. Two others, BRANCHES and CASES, are making their debuts in this chapter. All four

FIGURE 4-1 The Four Tables for Chapter 4

```
SQL> SELECT * FROM LA_FLAW;

LAST              FIRST           BRANCH ASSIGN           HIRED      SALARY
----------------  --------------- ------ ---------------- ---------- -------
MCKNIFE           DARREN               1 PARTNER          09-JAN-49    5000
TAWDRY            ALLEN                2 PARTNER          12-SEP-65    4000
COSSACK           MICHAEL              1 CRIMINAL         17-JUL-82    4500
BUNSEN            BURNER               2 FAMILY           09-OCT-78    2975
TUCKER            FRIAR                1 TAX              14-AUG-77    2850
BOYSENBERRY       ANN                  1 CIVIL            31-DEC-85    2450
ROX               GOLDIE               2 SECRETARY        23-JAN-82    1300
MASON             PERCY                3 CRIMINAL         09-JUN-29    3850
BAILEY            F. BILL              1 CRIMINAL         17-DEC-80    4800
BORQUE            BOBBY                1 PARALEGAL        03-DEC-81     950
HARTLESS          JAMES                2 PERSONAL INJURY  08-AUG-83    7500
MUKLUK            BENJAMIN             2 CRIMINAL         09-NOV-87    4700


SQL> SELECT * FROM BRANCHES;

 BRANCH LOCATION         SUPER
 ------ ---------------- ----------------
      1 Los Angeles      McKnife
      2 Denver           Tawdry
      3 Atlanta          Mason


SQL> SELECT * FROM CASES;

CASE                            CLIENT                          COUNSEL
------------------------------- ------------------------------- ----------------
MICHIGAN V. NORTHWESTERN        J. ROCKY MULLER                 COSSACK
PEASE V. QUIETTE                RENE QUIETTE                    BOYSENBERRY
KATELEY V. ALLISON              HARLEY ALLISON                  BUNSEN
PEOPLE V. CLOVERHOUSE           PUGH CLOVERHOUSE                MUKLUK
GREENHEAD V. CLOVERHOUSE        PUGH CLOVERHOUSE                COSSACK


SQL> SELECT * FROM ROSTER;

EMP_NO LAST             FIRST       M DEPT_NO POSITION   SALARY
------ ---------------- ----------- - ------- ---------- -------
     1 DAVIDSON         ADDIE       H       1 MANAGER     24000
     2 MADISON          DENNIS      W       1 ASST MGR    21000
     3 PRESTO           MISTY       D       1 RECEPTION   42500
     4 TUBA             HUBERT      G       2 NEW ACCT    11000
     5 SUTTON           WILMA       W       3 TELLER      12500
     6 MAHONEY          SUZANNE     S       3 TELLER      12400
     7 BUCHINSKY        CHARLES     B       4 SECURITY    15000
     8 PALMER           VERA        M       3 TELLER      13450
     9 COLLINS          KATHLEEN    D       2 NEW ACCT    13300
    10 ZIMMERMAN        ROBERT      D       2 NEW ACCT    13300
    11 ROWE-HATTON      PHYLLIS     F       2 NEW ACCT    11250
       BANKERSON        HARVEY

12 records selected.
```

displays are the results of SELECT commands that follow this basic format:

```
SQL> SELECT *
    2   FROM <table>
```

The use of an asterisk can be a time-saver when you are entering direct queries from the keyboard. However, SQL experts warn against it. Once you reach the level of a command file or application program, the asterisk could cause unexpected effects. The star is a wild card, and if a program changes the active table, it could be wilder than you expect.

You can SELECT specific columns from the specified table. For example, in dBASE you can:

```
. USE CASES
. LIST COUNSEL
```

dBASE will display only the names listed in the Counsel field.

```
Record#   COUNSEL
      1   COSSACK
      2   BOYSENBERRY
      3   BUNSEN
      4   MUKLUK
      5   COSSACK
```

The SQL equivalent is:

```
SQL> SELECT COUNSEL
    2   FROM CASES;
```

The result is much the same as the dBASE result:

```
COUNSEL
------------------------
COSSACK
BOYSENBERRY
BUNSEN
MUKLUK
COSSACK
```

A DISTINCT ADVANTAGE

Very quickly, though, SQL's way of querying is going to gain an edge over dBASE's. Cossack is assigned to two of the cases in this list. If your object were simply to list those staff members who have active cases, the last report is a bit of an overkill. It would be even more killing were you doing this with a larger staff. The solution is:

```
SQL> SELECT DISTINCT COUNSEL
  2   FROM CASES;
```

The word DISTINCT distinguishes this command from the previous version. It has a profound effect on the output. Not only is Cossack listed only once, but ORACLE neatly puts the list in alphabetical order. The alphabetization is not automatic, by the way, but it happened in this case.

```
COUNSEL
-----------------------
BOYSENBERRY
BUNSEN
COSSACK
MUKLUK
```

Will dBASE do this? Yes, but it takes more than one word. First, you must:

```
. INDEX ON COUNSEL TO COUNSEL UNIQUE
```

Then you can:

```
. LIST COUNSEL
```

. . . and see results like these:

```
Record#   COUNSEL
      2   BOYSENBERRY
      3   BUNSEN
      1   COSSACK
      4   MUKLUK
```

In dBASE, UNIQUE serves the same function as SQL's DISTINCT does. To make use of UNIQUE, though, you must include it in an indexing operation. SQL just quietly responds to your query.

RETRIEVING COMPUTED VALUES

The next exercise is the sort of thing you won't find prominently featured in the dBASE manual, although, as you'll see, dBASE can do it. It is a central feature of SQL. You can retrieve a column that doesn't exist.

The salary column is supposed to contain monthly figures. Suppose, instead, you'd like to see annual salaries. In SQL, it's simple. Just SELECT an imaginary column that is twelve times the monthly pay:

```
SQL> SELECT LAST, SALARY * 12
   2   FROM LA__FLAW;
```

Because ORACLE easily can create your pseudocolumn, it will do just that:

LAST	SALARY*12
MCKNIFE	60000
TAWDRY	48000
COSSACK	54000
BUNSEN	35700
TUCKER	34200
BOYSENBERRY	29400
ROX	15600
MASON	46200
BAILEY	57600
BORQUE	11400
HARTLESS	90000
MUKLUK	56400

12 records selected.

For the record, dBASE will do this too:

```
. USE LA__FLAW
. LIST LAST, SALARY*12
```

Record#	LAST	SALARY*12
1	MCKNIFE	60000.00
2	TAWDRY	48000.00
3	COSSACK	54000.00
4	BUNSEN	35700.00
5	TUCKER	34200.00
6	BOYSENBERRY	29400.00
7	ROX	15600.00
8	MASON	46200.00

9	BAILEY	57600.00
10	BORQUE	11400.00
11	HARTLESS	90000.00
12	MUKLUK	56400.00

There is one improvement you can make with SQL. The ALIAS feature will let you set your own column heading, replacing the cryptic headings you otherwise might get. Simply enter an alias after the column to which it refers:

```
SQL> SELECT LAST, SALALRY * 12 ANNUAL
    2   FROM LA__FLAW;
```

LAST	ANNUAL
MCKNIFE	60000
TAWDRY	48000
COSSACK	54000
BUNSEN	35700
TUCKER	34200
BOYSENBERRY	29400
ROX	15600
MASON	46200
BAILEY	57600
BORQUE	11400
HARTLESS	90000
MUKLUK	56400

12 records selected.

You also can ask SQL to invent a new column, including its contents:

```
SQL> SELECT LAST, 'Annual Salary ',
    2   SALARY * 12
    3   FROM LA__FLAW;
```

LAST	'ANNUALSALARY'	SALARY*12
MCKNIFE	ANNUAL SALARY	60000
TAWDRY	ANNUAL SALARY	48000
COSSACK	ANNUAL SALARY	54000
BUNSEN	ANNUAL SALARY	35700
TUCKER	ANNUAL SALARY	34200

BOYSENBERRY	ANNUAL SALARY	29400
ROX	ANNUAL SALARY	15600
MASON	ANNUAL SALARY	46200
BAILEY	ANNUAL SALARY	57600
BORQUE	ANNUAL SALARY	11400
HARTLESS	ANNUAL SALARY	90000
MUKLUK	ANNUAL SALARY	56400

12 records selected.

You can do this in dBASE, too. The next question is: Why would you want to? The ALIAS column head seems a much better choice.

SELECTIVE RETRIEVAL

You can use SELECT to designate which columns you want to retrieve. With the addition of WHERE, you can also specify the rows you wish to see. Take, for example, this query. It asks for the last names (first column displayed) and assignments (second column displayed) of everyone assigned to Branch 2:

```
SQL> SELECT LAST, ASSIGN
   2   FROM LA__FLAW
   3   WHERE BRANCH = 2;
```

LAST	ASSIGN
TAWDRY	PARTNER
BUNSEN	FAMILY
ROX	SECRETARY
HARTLESS	PERSONAL INJURY
MUKLUK	CRIMINAL

SQL uses SELECT and WHERE in the same way that dBASE uses LIST and FOR. In dBASE, LIST or DISPLAY lets you specify the columns of fields; FOR indicates the records to be retrieved. To get the Branch 2 report from dBASE, you would command:

```
. LIST LAST, ASSIGN FOR BRANCH = 2
```

MORE FLEXIBLE QUERIES

Strictly speaking, a SQL table needs to be in no particular order. As far as ORACLE is concerned, the columns can be in whatever order they happen to fall. The order of rows is equally random. You add rows to the bottom of the table as you create new records.

You don't always want to see your data in such a random order. That's where a new class of more flexible commands can help. You can determine the order of the display when you issue the retrieval command.

RETRIEVING IN ORDER

For example, LA__FLAW lists its personnel in the kind of random order just described. Perhaps, instead, you'd like to see this list displayed in order of salary, from highest to lowest.

dBASE makes this tough. You must start by SORTING the file, using a /D flag to create a new file in descending order:

. SORT ON SALARY/D TO TEMP

Then you must:

. USE TEMP
. LIST LAST, SALARY

The results will then be displayed the way you intended them to be:

Record#	LAST	SALARY
1	HARTLESS	7500.00
2	MCKNIFE	5000.00
3	BAILEY	4800.00
4	MUKLUK	4700.00
5	COSSACK	4500.00
6	TAWDRY	4000.00
7	MASON	3850.00
8	BUNSEN	2975.00
9	TUCKER	2850.00
10	BOYSENBERRY	2450.00
11	ROX	1300.00
12	BORQUE	950.00

ORACLE takes a much easier route to the same destination:

```
SQL> SELECT LAST, SALARY
   2   FROM LA__FLAW
   3   ORDER BY SALARY DESC;
```

Here, the last line is the important one. ORDER BY is a command that lists records in the order that you specify, in this case, by salary. You then add DESC to designate that the salaries should appear in descending order. The SQL display will thus be much like the sorted dBASE version.

In either dBASE or SQL, you can use SELECT to specify the order in which the columns as well as the rows will appear. If, for instance, you want the first name first, you can just say so. If you want the salaries in increasing order, you can just say that, too:

```
SQL> SELECT FIRST, LAST, SALARY
   2   FROM LA__FLAW
   3   ORDER BY SALARY;
```

Because you asked, you shall receive:

FIRST	LAST	SALARY
BOBBY	BORQUE	950
GOLDIE	ROX	1300
ANN	BOYSENBERRY	2450
FRIAR	TUCKER	2850
BURNER	BUNSEN	2975
PERCY	MASON	3850
ALLEN	TAWDRY	4000
MICHAEL	COSSACK	4500
BENJAMIN	MUKLUK	4700
F. BILL	BAILEY	4800
DARREN	MCKNIFE	5000
JAMES	HARTLESS	7500

12 records selected.

You could do much the same thing in dBASE, but, again, it's a multi-step process:

```
. INDEX ON SALARY TO SALARY
. LIST FIRST, LAST, SALARY
```

The dBASE record numbers give you a clue that the file is not stored in the same order in which it appears:

Record#	FIRST	LAST	SALARY
10	BOBBY	BORQUE	950.00
7	GOLDIE	ROX	1300.00
6	ANN	BOYSENBERRY	2450.00
5	FRIAR	TUCKER	2850.00
4	BURNER	BUNSEN	2975.00
8	PERCY	MASON	3850.00
2	ALLEN	TAWDRY	4000.00
3	MICHAEL	COSSACK	4500.00
12	BENJAMIN	MUKLUK	4700.00
9	F. BILL	BAILEY	4800.00
1	DARREN	MCKNIFE	5000.00
11	JAMES	HARTLESS	7500.00

IN, BETWEEN, AND LIKE

The SQL BETWEEN command gives you a way to search for records that fall within a certain range. Say, for example, that you want to know who falls within a particular salary bracket. The command would be this:

```
SQL> SELECT LAST, SALARY
  2  FROM LA__FLAW
  3  WHERE SALARY BETWEEN 3000 AND 5000;
```

The result is:

LAST	SALARY
MCKNIFE	5000
TAWDRY	4000
COSSACK	4500
MASON	3850
BAILEY	4800
MUKLUK	4700

6 records selected.

BETWEEN is really a shortcut. In dBASE, which has no comparable command, you'd have to take the long way around and use the .AND. operator:

. LIST LAST, SALARY FOR SALARY >=3000 .AND. SALARY <=5000

By the same token:

```
SQL> SELECT LAST, SALARY
    2   FROM LA__FLAW
    3   WHERE SALARY NOT BETWEEN 3000 AND 5000;
```

will list everyone whose salaries fall outside the specified range:

LAST	SALARY
BUNSEN	2975
TUCKER	2850
BOYSENBERRY	2450
ROX	1300
BORQUE	950
HARTLESS	7500

Again, SQL offers a quick way around this dBASE command:

. LIST LAST, SALARY FOR SALARY < 3000 .OR. SALARY > 5000

IN can be an even shorter cut. It spells out a list of values and calls for records that match values in the list:

```
SQL> SELECT LAST
    2   SQL> SELECT LAST, ASSIGN
    2   FROM LA__FLAW
    3   WHERE ASSIGN IN ('Civil', 'Criminal');
```

This will produce a list of people whose assignments are one or the other specified in the list:

LAST	ASSIGN
COSSACK	CRIMINAL
BOYSENBERRY	CIVIL
MASON	CRIMINAL
BAILEY	CRIMINAL
MUKLUK	CRIMINAL

Again, the dBASE equivalent is more complex:

. LIST LAST, ASSIGN FOR ASSIGN = 'Criminal' .OR. ASSIGN = 'Civil'

You need an .OR. statement for every alternative—a considerable chore, should the list be much longer than the two values in this example.

LIKE gives you the means to make wild card searches. In the SQL deck, two cards are wild:

- The __ (underscore) stands for any single character.
- The % (percent) stands for any number of characters, including none at all.

Several members of the law firm have last names that begin with M. To find them, try this search:

```
SQL> SELECT LAST
   2   FROM LA__FLAW
   3   WHERE LAST LIKE 'M%';
```

You should get:

```
LAST

------------------------
MCKNIFE
MASON
MUKLUK
```

The CASES table has two entries that involve the same client. You can find him with:

```
SQL> SELECT CASE
   2   FROM CASES
   3   WHERE CASE LIKE '%Cloverhouse';
```

Such a command would cause two items to be displayed:

```
CASE

------------------------------------------------
PEOPLE V. CLOVERHOUSE
GREENHEAD V. CLOVERHOUSE
```

Again, there's a dBASE equivalent that tends to be on the lightly documented side. It searches Character fields for a particular string:

. LIST CASE FOR 'CLOVERHOUSE' $CASE

MUCH ADO ABOUT NULLS

When we last saw the Roster database at the UnderFed branch of Marinecorp, it contained several null values for one awkwardly situated employee. It still does. A null value, remember, is a missing value. In SQL, this employee's salary is a null. So, if you were to mount this search:

SQL> SELECT LAST
   2   FROM ROSTER
   3   WHERE SALARY IS NULL;

it would give this result:

LAST

BANKERSON

If you try to do anything like this in dBASE, you'll get nothing but an error message. To retrieve this same record would require this command:

. LIST LAST FOR SALARY = 0

This would produce the same result. The difference is this. Say, for instance, you want to compute the average of all salaries in this table (a subject that is discussed in the chapter on numerical operations). dBASE would average all thirteen salaries, including Bankerson's zero, giving a result of $3,451.92. SQL would average only the twelve records that have actual entries, ignoring the null in Bankerson's row. Figured that way, the average salary is $3,739.58.

SEARCHING MULTIPLE TABLES

You don't need ORACLE to manage a single table. You don't need dBASE, for that matter. Get an inexpensive, flat-file manager, buy a basic clone computer on which to run it, and you've saved a lot of money. Advanced programs such as ORACLE and dBASE are useful because of their ability to *relate* one file to another.

Take, for instance, the two files LA__FLAW and BRANCHES. The former lists employees' names and other data, including a branch number; the latter lists branch numbers and their corresponding locations and supervisors. If you relate the two tables, you can take one or more names from the first and use the second to find out where they are, to whom they report, or both.

A SIMPLE JOIN

A query that retrieves data from more than one table is called a *join*. An example of a simple join is:

```
SQL> SELECT *
  2   FROM LA__FLAW, BRANCHES
  3   WHERE LA__FLAW.BRANCH = BRANCHES.BRANCH;
```

This simple command produces output that is excessive. Because of the asterisk, this command retrieves everything from both tables. The result is shown in Figure 4-2.

Notice in particular that the branch number appears twice. It is the field that the two tables have in common. The command retrieved it once from LA__FLAW, then picked up the matching information from BRANCHES.

FIGURE 4-2 Two Joined Tables—in Their Entirety

LAST	FIRST	BRANCH	ASSIGN	HIRED	SALARY	BRANCH	LOCATION	SUPER
MCKNIFE	DARREN	1	PARTNER	09-JAN-49	5000	1	LOS ANGELES	MCKNIFE
COSSACK	MICHAEL	1	CRIMINAL	17-JUL-82	4500	1	LOS ANGELES	MCKNIFE
TUCKER	FRIAR	1	TAX	14-AUG-77	2850	1	LOS ANGELES	MCKNIFE
BOYSENBERRY	ANN	1	CIVIL	31-DEC-85	2450	1	LOS ANGELES	MCKNIFE
BAILEY	F. BILL	1	CRIMINAL	17-DEC-80	4800	1	LOS ANGELES	MCKNIFE
BORQUE	BOBBY	1	PARALEGAL	03-DEC-81	950	1	LOS ANGELES	MCKNIFE
TAWDRY	ALLEN	2	PARTNER	12-SEP-65	4000	2	DENVER	TAWDRY
ROX	GOLDIE	2	SECRETARY	23-JAN-82	1300	2	DENVER	TAWDRY
HARTLESS	JAMES	2	PERSONAL	08-AUG-83	7500	2	DENVER	TAWDRY
MUKLUK	BENJAMIN	2	CRIMINAL	09-NOV-87	4700	2	DENVER	TAWDRY
BUNSEN	BURNER	2	FAMILY	09-OCT-78	2975	2	DENVER	TAWDRY
MASON	PERCY	3	CRIMINAL	09-JUN-29	3850	3	ATLANTA	MASON

12 records selected.

Line 3 is the key to the join. It expresses what is known as the *join condition*. In this case, the condition is the relatively simple one that the branch number in one file match the branch number in the other. In SQL, this condition is expressed as:

LA_FLAW.BRANCH = BRANCHES.BRANCH

Strictly speaking, the two columns in a join condition need not have the same name, as you'll see in an example later in this chapter. They need not even be of the same data type. It makes sense, however, to keep both names and types the same, otherwise, you're asking for trouble.

To distinguish the matching columns in each of the two files, each is preceded by the table name and a period. Thus, BRANCHES.BRANCH identifies the BRANCH column in the BRANCHES table.

DOING IT IN dBASE

It is possible to do the same thing with dBASE, but it's not nearly as quick or easy as it is with ORACLE. First, you must prepare a rather elaborate set of instructions to describe the relationship between the two files:

```
. SELECT 1
. USE LA_FLAW
. INDEX ON BRANCH TO LA_BRAN
. SELECT 2
. USE BRANCHES
. INDEX ON BRANCH TO BR_BRAN
. SELECT 1
. SET RELATION TO BRANCH INTO BRANCHES
```

Here, one of the toughest things to do is to avoid setting the relationship backward. This is also one of the most important things to do. If you start with BRANCHES and set the relationship into LA_FLAW, dBASE will zip through each of the three records in BRANCHES, find a matching record in the other file, and then quit. You will have retrieved three records. Deciding which file is to be related to which, and in what direction, can cause long periods of frustration that are punctuated by the exhilaration of error messages and wrong results.

There's no sense in using dBASE to retrieve the massive display shown in Figure 4-2. Why not try for something a little more specific? After setting up the program as above, issue the command:

. LIST LAST, BRANCHES−>BRANCH, BRANCHES−>SUPER

This produces a simple list of employees and their supervisors:

Record#	LAST	BRANCHES−>BRANCH	BRANCHES−>SUPER
1	MCKNIFE	1	MCKNIFE
3	COSSACK	1	MCKNIFE
5	TUCKER	1	MCKNIFE
6	BOYSENBERRY	1	MCKNIFE
9	BAILEY	1	MCKNIFE
10	BORQUE	1	MCKNIFE
2	TAWDRY	2	TAWDRY
4	BUNSEN	2	TAWDRY
7	ROX	2	TAWDRY
11	HARTLESS	2	TAWDRY
12	MUKLUK	2	TAWDRY
8	MASON	3	MASON

Notice that in multiple-file dBASE queries the file name is included in the field identification. The main difference is in the punctuation; a simulated arrow is used instead of a period. The SQL version of a similar command is:

```
SQL> SELECT FIRST, LAST, ASSIGN, LOCATION
   2   FROM LA__FLAW, BRANCHES
   3   WHERE LA__FLAW.BRANCH = BRANCHES.BRANCH;
```

Here, you ask for the first and last names, the assignments, and the branch locations. Here are the results:

FIRST	LAST	ASSIGN	LOCATION
DARREN	MCKNIFE	PARTNER	LOS ANGELES
MICHAEL	COSSACK	CRIMINAL	LOS ANGELES
FRIAR	TUCKER	TAX	LOS ANGELES
ANN	BOYSENBERRY	CIVIL	LOS ANGELES
F. BILL	BAILEY	CRIMINAL	LOS ANGELES
BOBBY	BORQUE	PARALEGAL	LOS ANGELES

ALLEN	TAWDRY	PARTNER	DENVER
GOLDIE	ROX	SECRETARY	DENVER
JAMES	HARTLESS	PERSONAL INJURY	DENVER
BENJAMIN	MUKLUK	CRIMINAL	DENVER
BURNER	BUNSEN	FAMILY	DENVER
PERCY	MASON	CRIMINAL	ATLANTA

12 records selected.

The branch numbers are nowhere to be seen, yet, just as in the earlier instance, ORACLE used them to make the connection between the files.

USING AN ALIAS

When using a join, it's a good idea to identify all columns by using their table names. When in doubt, it hardly ever hurts to be as specific as you can. However, typing names such as LA_FLAW.LAST or BRANCHES.SUPER can become a pain after a while. The dBASE equivalents, LA_FLAW−>LAST and BRANCHES−>SUPER almost ensure that you'll try to write minimum-length queries.

Both programs let you use an alias for the table name, in much the same way that SQL lets you create an alias for a column heading. If you create a table-name alias that is shorter than the original name, you can avoid some difficult typing. You can also create an alias that is longer than the original name, but there's little point in doing this. dBASE even lets you create an alias that's the same as the table name—something like saying "Ray Luca alias Ray Luca." A more sensible approach is to pick an alias of one or two letters. Here's how you would set it up in dBASE:

```
. SELECT 1
. USE LA_FLAW ALIAS L INDEX LA_BRAN
. SELECT 2
. USE BRANCHES ALIAS B INDEX BR_BRAN
. SELECT 1
. SET RELATION TO BRANCH INTO B
```

Then you could write a command such as:

```
. LIST L−>LAST, L−>ASSIGN, B−>LOCATION
```

Assigning an alias in SQL is part of the SELECT command itself:

```
SQL> SELECT L.LAST, L.ASSIGN, B.LOCATION
   2    FROM LA_FLAW L, BRANCHES B
   3    WHERE L.BRANCH = B.BRANCH;
```

Line 2 is the key to this command. When specifying the tables, you also assign them their one-letter aliases. This lets you use those aliases even in a line that comes before the alias assignments. The results of this query are:

LAST	ASSIGN	LOCATION
MCKNIFE	PARTNER	LOS ANGELES
COSSACK	CRIMINAL	LOS ANGELES
TUCKER	TAX	LOS ANGELES
BOYSENBERRY	CIVIL	LOS ANGELES
BAILEY	CRIMINAL	LOS ANGELES
BORQUE	PARALEGAL	LOS ANGELES
TAWDRY	PARTNER	DENVER
ROX	SECRETARY	DENVER
HARTLESS	PERSONAL INJURY	DENVER
MUKLUK	CRIMINAL	DENVER
BUNSEN	FAMILY	DENVER
MASON	CRIMINAL	ATLANTA

12 records selected

NOT ALL JOINS ARE CREATED EQUAL

In the examples used so far, the relationship between the two tables has been simple and direct. The department number in one has been the same as the department number in another. In SQL parlance, the relationship is stated this way:

```
WHERE LA_FLAW.BRANCH = BRANCHES.BRANCH;
```

This kind of relationship is called an *equi-join*. It can be signified by an equals sign (=) in the WHERE clause. It is the kind of relationship you usually establish when you use the SET RELATION command in dBASE.

Other kinds of relationships are also possible. The logical people who created SQL have a name for relationships that are not equi-joins. They are called *non-equi-joins*. The tipoff is the use of the symbols > (greater than) or < > (not equal) or some other operator, instead of the equals sign. That includes SQL's IN and BETWEEN.

It's come to the attention of junior partner Allen Tawdry that several people in the organization are being paid more than he is. He decides to find out who they are. In any event, Tawdry reasons, the firm should establish a standard schedule of pay grades. He decides to do this, and he creates this SQL table:

GRADE	LOW	HIGH
1	1	2000
2	2001	3000
3	3001	4000
4	4001	5000
5	5000	9999

There's a mistake in this table, but if you didn't catch it, don't worry, neither did he—at least not for a while. Tawdry then constructed a query that would:

- Report each employee's salary.
- Report the pay grade into which each employee's salary falls.
- Display the output in order of pay grade and in order of salary within each grade.

Whatever else you might say about the underpaid Mr. Tawdry, he was about to leave dBASE in the dust. This type of query is not impossible in dBASE; we are now in an area, though, where constructing a dBASE query becomes difficult and awkward—more trouble than it's worth. In SQL, the query is more complex than most of those you've seen so far in this book. Still, it is reasonably simple:

```
SQL> SELECT GRADE, LAST, SALARY
   2   FROM LA__FLAW, PAYGRADES
   3   WHERE SALARY BETWEEN LOW AND HIGH
   4   ORDER BY GRADE, SALARY;
```

A CLOSER LOOK AT A POWERFUL QUERY

The first line, as usual, is a SELECT statement. It calls for three columns: GRADE from the PAYGRADES file and LAST and SALARY from the LA__FLAW file. The second line identifies the two tables to be joined. Thus far, there's nothing unusual about this procedure.

Line 3 is the join condition. It uses the BETWEEN operator, a clue that this is not an equi-join. It specifies the salaries that fall between the low and high figures for each grade.

Line 4 is also unexceptional. It specifies that the output be in order of grade and by salary within each grade—just what the partner ordered. Thus, four fairly ordinary SQL commands add up to a query that could put the dBASE report writer to shame. Tawdry issues this query and gets this result:

GRADE	LAST	SALARY
1	BORQUE	950
1	ROX	1300
2	BOYSENBERRY	2450
2	TUCKER	2850
2	BUNSEN	2975
3	MASON	3850
3	TAWDRY	4000
4	COSSACK	4500
4	MUKLUK	4700
4	BAILEY	4800
4	MCKNIFE	5000
5	MCKNIFE	5000
5	HARTLESS	7500

13 records selected.

Poor Allen Tawdry. Not only do several people exceed his earnings, but partner McKnife appears to do so twice. Now the error in the PAYGRADES table begins to become apparent. Another clue is the fact that thirteen records were selected; the firm has only twelve employees. A close examination reveals that McKnife appears in two different salary grades, in each case with the same $5,000 salary.

Watch Your Ranges

There's an important lesson here for anyone who works with ranges. You have to be careful when you specify ranges. Tawdry made a common mistake. Look at PAYGRADES again:

GRADE	LOW	HIGH
1	1	2000
2	2001	3000
3	3001	4000
4	4001	5000
5	5000	9999

The break point between grades 4 and 5 is $5,000. As this table is written, the $5,000 salary falls in both grades 4 and 5. Since McKnife's salary happens to be an even $5,000, he appears in both pay grades. The other break points are done correctly. To bring the last row up to standard, enter:

```
SQL> UPDATE PAYGRADES
  2   SET LOW = 5001
  3   WHERE GRADE = 5;
```

The corrected PAYGRADES now should read:

GRADE	LOW	HIGH
1	1	2000
2	2001	3000
3	3001	4000
4	4001	5000
5	5001	9999

This, in turn, should produce the following output from Tawdry's command:

GRADE	LAST	SALARY
1	BORQUE	950
1	ROX	1300
2	BOYSENBERRY	2450
2	TUCKER	2850
2	BUNSEN	2975
3	MASON	3850

```
3   TAWDRY              4000
4   COSSACK             4500
4   MUKLUK              4700
4   BAILEY              4800
4   MCKNIFE             5000
5   HARTLESS            7500
```

12 records selected.

Five of Tawdry's coworkers earn more than he does. For whatever consolation it might bring, all are in higher pay grades.

JOINING A TABLE TO ITSELF

There is another way to approach Tawdry's problem (that is, querying the file, not increasing his pay). He could join a table to itself.

dBASE people don't even want to think about this. In SQL, it is a valid and useful way to construct a query. Tawdry could find out the names of those whose pay exceeds his with this query:

```
SQL> SELECT X.LAST, X.SALARY, Y.LAST, Y.SALARY
   2   FROM LA__FLAW X, LA__FLAW Y
   3   WHERE Y.LAST = 'TAWDRY'
   4   AND X.SALARY > Y.SALARY;
```

The key to this technique is in Line 2. It gives two different aliases, X and Y, to the same file. Then, it sets up a two-pronged WHERE condition.

The first of these conditions appears in Line 3. In the version of LA__FLAW that carries the alias Y, this command will look only for the row that carries Tawdry's last name.

The second condition, in Line 4, looks into the X version and selects those records for which the SALARY column exceeds that in the single record selected from the Y version. The resulting output is a bit overdone, but it shows what you can do when you join a file to itself:

```
LAST            SALARY  LAST          SALARY
--------------  ------- ------------  ---------
MCKNIFE           5000  TAWDRY           4000
COSSACK           4500  TAWDRY           4000
BAILEY            4800  TAWDRY           4000
```

| HARTLESS | 7500 | TAWDRY | 4000 |
| MUKLUK | 4700 | TAWDRY | 4000 |

TIPS FOR EFFECTIVE SEARCHING

Even a complex SQL search is really only a combination of simple statements. If you can keep this in mind, you can easily combine these simple statements to form a query that provides the answer you seek.

Put yourself in Tawdry's position. Better, imagine yourself in Tawdry's position. Because you really are looking for the answer to a question, the best way to begin a query is to state the question. For example, "Who has an active case and a salary that is higher than mine?" Perhaps more to the point, "Who is making more money than I am but isn't working on a case?"

The next step is to isolate the things you want to know. In the case of either question, these would be the salary and the case identification. This sets you up for the final step: constructing a query that plucks these two pieces of information from your SQL database.

REVIEW QUESTIONS

1. An asterisk can be very useful in a SQL command, but in some circumstances it can be extremely hazardous. Why is that?
2. Write a SQL query that would have the same effect as these dBASE commands have:

   . USE ROSTER
   . LIST FIRST, LAST

3. What is the distinction of the command SELECT DISTINCT?
4. Write a SQL command that retrieves the last names and annual salaries of members of the law firm who make more than $40,000 per year.
5. Rewrite the previous query to display the output in order of salary.
6. Write a join condition that would link the tables ROSTER and REPS.
7. Write the SQL clause that would specify a join condition between the tables LA_FLAW and CASES.

8. What's the difference between an equi-join and a non-equi-join?

9. Darren McKnife sees Tawdry messing around with the salary figures and decides to find out who's earning more than *he* is. Help him construct a query.

ANSWERS

1. The asterisk is a wild card that retrieves every column in the table. In a programmed environment, it is better always to specify the columns you want, in order to guard against surprises.

2. SQL> SELECT FIRST, LAST FROM ROSTER;

3. It will select only one example of a duplicated value.

4. SQL> SELECT LAST, SALARY * 12
         FROM LA__FLAW
         WHERE SALARY * 12 > 40000;

5. SQL> SELECT LAST, SALARY
         FROM LA__FLAW
         WHERE SALARY * 12 > 40000
         ORDER BY SALARY;

6. ROSTER.LAST = REPS.LAST

7.   LA__FLAW.LAST = CASES.COUNSEL

8. In an equi-join, there is a direct one-to-one relationship between the records in each file. In a non-equi-join, this need not be the case.

9. SQL> SELECT X.LAST, X.SALARY, Y.LAST, Y.SALARY
     2   FROM LA__FLAW X, LA__FLAW Y
     3   WHERE Y.LAST = 'MCKNIFE'
     4   AND X.SALARY > Y.SALARY;

5

Advanced Query Techniques

COMBINING SEARCH TECHNIQUES

PRINCIPLES OF SUBQUERY ARCHITECTURE

SUBQUERIES FOR MULTIPLE VALUES

MULTIPLE QUERIES FROM MULTIPLE TABLES

It's time to venture into the world of advanced query techniques in SQL. You may find the experience something like a computerized adventure game. The message on your screen might be something like this:

In front of you is a dense forest. Sages have told you that beyond this thicket lies a promised land in which your every query will be answered. Before you can reach that land, however, you must traverse the forest of unmapped darkness. You decide to:

1. Turn your back and retreat to the familiar domain of Ashton and Tate.
2. Proceed into the forest, armed with SQL, this book, and the knowledge that the rewards will be well worth the effort.

Congratulations. You chose B. (You did choose B, didn't you?) You should heed these two further warnings:

- *Be careful what you ask for. You just might get it.* This is a basic rule of nature. The more complex something is, the more opportunities there are for something to go wrong. This is as true of SQL queries as it is of anything else. If you make a mistake in constructing a SQL query, you may get some unexpected results. There's no great danger, unless you also make the mistake of relying on these results.
- *It's easy to write a complex query when a simple one will do.* Don't get carried away with the ability to write the multi-headed queries you're about to encounter. There are times—many times—when SQL can produce even highly sophisticated results with a fairly simple query. C. J. Date points out that the ability to construct complex queries was the original reason for the inclusion of the word "structured" in "Structured Query Language." In modern use, this ability has lost importance as SQL users have discovered easier ways to accomplish the same things.

None of the foregoing is intended to frighten you; it is intended to help you put advanced SQL queries in perspective. As you enter this discussion, there are two important things to remember.

First, this is not prime dBASE territory. A clever dBASE user can make that program do nearly anything—the key word here is *make*. What you're about to see would require considerable effort in dBASE. You would be forcing the program to accomplish something it does not easily do. However, as Date's comment suggests, this kind of activity is integral to SQL.

Second, these advanced capabilities are not as important as you might think. dBASE meets most database management needs without being forced; likewise, SQL meets most people's needs with relatively simple search commands. The advanced SQL commands are good to have when you need them. You probably won't need them often.

With that in mind, it's time to look in again on Allen Tawdry, who's becoming obsessed with the salary question.

COMBINING SEARCH TECHNIQUES

There are many ways Tawdry could search for higher-paid employees. For example, he might place some importance on members of the firm who are earning their higher salaries by actually handling cases. He might join the LA__FLAW and CASES tables in this way:

```
SQL> SELECT L.LAST, L.SALARY, C.CASE, C.CLIENT
  2   FROM LA__FLAW L, CASES C
  3   WHERE C.COUNSEL = L.LAST;
```

A LINK BY ANY OTHER NAME

The object of this command is to produce the names and salaries of firm members whose names appear in the CASES table. These two tables have no field that shares a common name—an unalterable prerequisite for a dBASE RELATIONship. The same names do appear, however, in columns that have different names: COUNSEL in the CASES table and LAST in LA__FLAW.

Line 3 of this command sets up a simple equi-join of these two columns. The fact that they have different names makes no difference, as long as you specify the names properly. The use of table aliases makes that fairly easy. The search should lead to the results shown in Figure 5-1.

A SQL join doesn't actually use a command called JOIN. The

FIGURE 5-1   Cases and Salaries Joined

```
LAST              SALARY CASE                           CLIENT
----------------  ------- ------------------------------ ----------------
BOYSENBERRY        2450 PEASE V. QUIETTE               QUIETTE
BUNSEN             2975 KATELEY V. ALLISON             ALLISON
COSSACK            4500 MICHIGAN V. NORTHWESTERN       MULLER
COSSACK            4500 GREENHEAD V. CLOVERHOUSE       CLOVERHOUSE
MUKLUK             4700 PEOPLE V. CLOVERHOUSE          CLOVERHOUSE
```

dBASE equivalent does, though. A set of dBASE commands that does much the same thing is:

```
. SELECT 1
. USE LA__FLAW ALIAS L
. SELECT 2
. USE CASES ALIAS CA
. JOIN WITH L TO E:TEMP FOR CA–>COUNSEL = L–>LAST
FIELDS L–>LAST, L–>SALARY, CA–>CASE, CA–>CLIENT
```

A MORE COMPLEX JOIN

One thing still is missing. This search fails to isolate those staff members who meet both requirements: they have active cases, and they have salaries higher than Tawdry's. You can state these two conditions with a join command that includes a combination of query techniques:

```
SQL> SELECT L.LAST, L.SALARY, C.CASE, C.CLIENT
   2    FROM LA__FLAW L, CASES C
   3    WHERE C.COUNSEL = L.LAST
   4    AND L.SALARY >=
   5        (SELECT SALARY
   6        FROM LA__FLAW
   7        WHERE LA__FLAW.LAST = 'TAWDRY');
```

The first three lines are the same as before: an equi-join between the COUNSEL and SALARY columns. The new lines impose an added condition. This condition is stated in the form of an entirely separate query that is known as a *subquery*.

The subquery is a self-contained SQL command in its own

FIGURE 5-2   Further Filtration Based on Salary

```
LAST                 SALARY CASE                            CLIENT
---------------      ------- ------------------------------ --------------
COSSACK                 4500 MICHIGAN V. NORTHWESTERN       MULLER
COSSACK                 4500 GREENHEAD V. CLOVERHOUSE       CLOVERHOUSE
MUKLUK                  4700 PEOPLE V. CLOVERHOUSE          CLOVERHOUSE
```

right. Were you to run Lines 5 through 7 by themselves, you would select one item: Tawdry's salary from LA_FLAW.

Line 4 specifies as a search condition that the salaries selected by the main query be equal to or higher than the results of the subquery, in other words, higher than Tawdry's. This is in addition to the requirement in Line 3 that the selected staff members have active cases.

In this case, the subquery imposes an added condition for the primary search. The narrowed-down results are shown in Figure 5-2.

PRINCIPLES OF SUBQUERY ARCHITECTURE

Meanwhile, over at the UnderFed branch of Marinecorp S&L, Dennis Madison was arriving at subqueries by a route of his own. As you might recall from a previous episode, one of his assignments was to build a new table consisting only of new-accounts representatives, who have a distinctive sales responsibility. After creating the table, he used this command to transfer data from the main ROSTER:

```
SQL> INSERT INTO REPS (LAST, FIRST, DEPT_NO)
   2    SELECT LAST, FIRST, DEPT_NO
   3    FROM ROSTER
   4    WHERE DEPT_NO = 2;
```

Lines 2, 3 and 4 comprise a query in their own right—a subquery. SQL actually started at the end, running the subquery first. Then, it INSERTed the results of that query into the new table. (A subquery normally appears in parentheses; this particular query is an exception to that rule.) "Amazing," said Madison to himself. "You start from the end, and SQL takes you right to the beginning. It seems appropriate, somehow."

FROM SUBQUERY TO QUERY

Actually, the end-to-beginning approach is the way that SQL processes *nested queries,* the official name for queries that contain subqueries. As you will see in the next chapter, and as you may know already, a program like SQL processes any mathematical expressions that appear within parentheses before processing any other expressions. SQL does the same with any bracketed command, including a subquery. It processes the subquery first, then feeds the results to the higher-level query, also known as the *outer query.* If you recognize this pattern and follow it yourself, you can easily construct even the most complex command when you need it.

dBASE users can look at a subquery in terms of the conditions it sets for the main query. The WHERE clause of a subquery is similar to a SET FILTER command in dBASE. Once a filter has been set in dBASE, the program will behave as if the only records that exist are those that meet the filter condition. In SQL, the program behaves as if the only records that exist are those that meet the conditions set forth in the subquery.

Here's how Madison might have gone about this, even with very limited knowledge of the organization. Assume that he knew little else except that Zimmerman was one of the people who should be included in the REPS table. The others should be people in Zimmerman's occupational specialty. Madison could first try to identify that specialty:

```
SQL> SELECT POSITION
  2    FROM ROSTER
  3    WHERE LAST = 'ZIMMERMAN';
```

SQL would quickly present the singular response:

```
POSITION
----------------
NEW ACCT
```

Using this information, Madison could then find a list of other employees in the same position:

```
SQL> SELECT LAST, POSITION
  2    FROM ROSTER
  3    WHERE POSITION = 'NEW ACCT';
```

This produces:

```
LAST                POSITION
----------------    ------------------
TUBA                NEW ACCT
COLLINS             NEW ACCT
ZIMMERMAN           NEW ACCT
ROWE-HATTON         NEW ACCT
```

COMBINE TWO STEPS IN ONE

The real value of a subquery is that it can combine two or more SQL commands into one. Madison's first command, to identify Zimmerman's position, and the second, to find others in the same position, could be combined like this:

```
SQL> SELECT LAST, POSITION
  2    FROM ROSTER
  3    WHERE POSITION =
  4        (SELECT POSITION
  5        FROM ROSTER
  6        WHERE LAST = 'ZIMMERMAN');
```

Lines 4, 5, and 6 are Madison's original query for Zimmerman's position. The first three lines are the outer query. The results of the inner query become the conditions of the WHERE clause in the outer query. In short, this query does exactly the same thing as the original two did.

COMBINE THREE STEPS IN ONE

Madison still hasn't finished the job. The original objective was to insert selected data into a new table. At this point, he has only identified the names of the people whose data should be inserted. He still could plug the results of his two-level query into an INSERT command that would have three levels: the command, a query, and a subquery. It might look something like this:

```
SQL> INSERT INTO REPS (LAST, FIRST, DEPT_NO)
  2    SELECT LAST, FIRST, DEPT_NO
  3    FROM ROSTER
  4    WHERE POSITION =
  5        (SELECT POSITION
```

```
6          FROM ROSTER
7          WHERE LAST = 'ZIMMERMAN');
```

Working again from the bottom up, the query that SELECT's Zimmerman's position is now at the third level down. It occupies Lines 5 through 7. Again, the results become the criteria for the WHERE statement at the next level up. This query, in Lines 2, 3, and 4, is a modified version of the employee selection command used earlier. It has been changed to provide the data required by the new main command. This command INSERTs the selected data into the new table.

Broken into its three main components, this command shouldn't be particularly hard to understand. You can issue multiple queries, one at a time, feeding the results of each into the next, or you can write one command and let SQL do the rest for you.

The sharp-eyed may have noticed that the original INSERT command makes use of department numbers, whereas the subsequent queries look for descriptions of the employees' positions. If everyone in the department always has the same title, that's a sign of wasteful database design. Two different columns identify essentially the same information. There will be more on this subject in the chapter on database design.

SUBQUERIES FOR MULTIPLE VALUES

The subquery that asked for Zimmerman's position is one of the simplest found in SQL. It returns only a single value and transmits it to the next higher level. The higher-level query produced several values. It retrieved several records and reported the contents of multiple columns in those records.

SQL has four commands that specifically work with multiple values in subqueries: ANY, ALL, IN, and (what were you expecting?) NOT IN. Each works with the multiple results of a subquery, but they all do so in subtly different ways.

ANY OR ALL

Allen Tawdry's exhaustive and exhausting research has now taken him far afield of his original purpose. He finds himself poking into all manner of research that he chooses to call "compensation administration." Once, he issued this command:

```
SQL>  SELECT LAST, SALARY
    2     FROM LA__FLAW
    3     WHERE SALARY > ANY
    4            (SELECT SALARY
    5             FROM LA__FLAW
    6             WHERE BRANCH = 2);
```

The subquery calls for the salaries of everyone in Branch 2. Then, the outer query looks for those salary values which exceed *any* figure in the values retrieved by the subquery—in other words, the lowest salary in Branch 2. It finds:

LAST	SALARY
MCKNIFE	5000
TAWDRY	4000
COSSACK	4500
BUNSEN	2975
TUCKER	2850
BOYSENBERRY	2450
MASON	3850
BAILEY	4800
HARTLESS	7500
MUKLUK	4700

Edit this command to change one key word. Instead of ANY, use ALL to look for those salaries that exceed *every* salary in Branch 2. After editing, SQL*Plus displays this revised version (the display of an edited command is a little different from the display of the original entry):

```
    1   SELECT LAST, SALARY
    2     FROM LA__FLAW
    3     WHERE SALARY > ALL
    4            (SELECT SALARY
    5             FROM LA__FLAW
    6*            WHERE BRANCH = 2)
```

The output is:

no records selected

This means that there is no one in the firm whose salary exceeds the highest one in Branch 2. To demonstrate, try the same command using Branch 1 as the base:

```
1    SELECT LAST, SALARY
2    FROM LA__FLAW
3    WHERE SALARY > ALL
4          (SELECT SALARY
5          FROM LA__FLAW
6*        WHERE BRANCH = 1)
```

Now you're looking for anyone whose salary exceeds every salary paid for Branch 1. There is someone:

LAST	SALARY
HARTLESS	7500

To complete the cycle, modify the search again. Use ANY with Branch 1, and you should turn up everybody in the firm whose pay exceeds that of the lowest-paid employee in the branch. Because paralegal Bobby Borque also happens to be the lowest-paid employee in the firm, this search should turn up everyone else:

```
SQL> RUN
1    SELECT LAST, SALARY
2    FROM LA__FLAW
3    WHERE SALARY > ANY
4          (SELECT SALARY
5          FROM LA__FLAW
6          WHERE BRANCH = 1)
```

The result is:

LAST	SALARY
MCKNIFE	5000
TAWDRY	4000
COSSACK	4500
BUNSEN	2975
TUCKER	2850
BOYSENBERRY	2450
ROX	1300

MASON   3850
BAILEY   4800
HARTLESS   7500
MUKLUK   4700

11 records selected.

IN OR NOT IN

IN and NOT IN are actually abbreviations for forms of ANY and ALL. The phrase:

SALARY = ANY

means the same thing as this phrase does:

SALARY IN

By the same token:

SALARY < > ALL

and:

SALARY NOT IN

produce identical results.

Take this query of Underfed's ROSTER:

```
SQL> SELECT LAST, SALARY, POSITION
   2    FROM ROSTER
   3    WHERE POSITION IN
   4         (SELECT POSITION
   5          FROM ROSTER
   6          WHERE LAST = 'ZIMMERMAN');
```

Because Zimmerman is a new-accounts representative, the subquery will again filter out the employees in that position:

LAST	SALARY	POSITION
TUBA	11000	NEW ACCT
ZIMMERMAN	13300	NEW ACCT
COLLINS	13300	NEW ACCT
ROWE-HATTON	11250	NEW ACCT

Change the key word to NOT IN:

```
1    SELECT LAST, SALARY, POSITION
2    FROM ROSTER
3    WHERE POSITION NOT IN
4          (SELECT POSITION
5          FROM ROSTER
6*         WHERE LAST = 'ZIMMERMAN')
```

and you get instead the records of everyone else:

LAST	SALARY	POSITION
DAVIDSON	24000	MANAGER
MADISON	21000	ASST MGR
PRESTO	42500	RECEPTION
MAHONEY	12400	TELLER
BUCHINSKY	15000	SECURITY
PALMER	13450	TELLER

TO EXIST OR NOT TO EXIST

EXISTS and its companion NOT EXISTS can serve as substitutes for many of the commands just discussed. C. J. Date believes that, in most cases, they are superior substitutes. The less sophisticated may not agree. The proper use of EXISTS requires that you understand the truly existential logic behind it. Basically, EXISTS is true if the subquery to which it refers returns at least one record. Consider this command:

```
SQL> SELECT LAST
2    FROM LA_FLAW
3    WHERE EXISTS
4          (SELECT *
5          FROM CASES
6          WHERE CASES.COUNSEL = LA_FLAW.LAST);
```

In response to this command, the program spools through each last name, item by item. At each name the program questions whether using that last name would cause the subquery to return at least one value. If so, EXISTS is true, and the subquery condition is true. The results become:

```
LAST
------------------------
COSSACK
BUNSEN
BOYSENBERRY
MUKLUK
```

These are, in fact, the staff members who have active cases in the CASES file (to my great relief, because it took me many attempts to construct an EXISTS command that works).

The warning about becoming unnecessarily complex does apply here. In Chapter 4, a much simpler query got the same results. It was necessary to tailor that earlier query, though, to accommodate the one lawyer who has two cases pending. Here, that did not present a problem.

NOT EXISTS, as you might suspect, does just the opposite of EXISTS:

```
SQL> SELECT LAST
   2    FROM LA__FLAW
   3    WHERE NOT EXISTS
   4        (SELECT *
   5         FROM CASES
   6         WHERE CASES.COUNSEL = LA__FLAW.LAST)
```

The results now are:

```
LAST
--------------------
MCKNIFE
TAWDRY
TUCKER
ROX
MASON
BAILEY
BORQUE
HARTLESS
```

EXISTS in dBASE

dBASE users might find it easier to understand EXISTS if it is expressed in their own language. You can start with the principle stated earlier in this chapter: A subquery in SQL is much like a

SET FILTER condition in dBASE. This means that you can use a filter condition to emulate an EXISTS condition.

To establish the just-discussed relationship between LA__FLAW and CASES you would first have to index the files on their common fields:

```
SELECT 1
USE LA__FLAW ALIAS LA INDEX NAME
SELECT 2
USE CASES ALIAS CA INDEX COUNSEL
```

It is not necessary to SET a RELATION between the two; in fact, it would be more than difficult, because the two indexed fields have different names (although their contents are similar). You then can set this filter condition:

```
SET FILTER TO LA->LAST = CA->COUNSEL
```

Then, if you are very patient, you can skip record by record through CASES. Because the file has been indexed, the records will appear in alphabetical order, as they do in the COUNSEL field, and not the order in which they physically appear in the data file.

At each new CASES record, you can return to LA__FLAW and ask to see the last name and any other pertinent data from that file. You will get a single record, matching the currently selected record in CASES. SKIP to the next record in CASES, move back to LA__FLAW, and ask again for the current record. This time the last name in that record should match the COUNSEL entry in the second record in CASES. You can proceed to the end of the CASES file or until you get tired, whichever comes first.

This kind of repeated skipping and searching is best done through a dBASE command file. The brief program EXISTS.PRG, shown in Listing 5-1, automates the steps just described. Its output is essentially the same as the earlier example that used the SQL EXISTS command.

```
* LISTING 5-1
* EXISTS.PRG
* Emulates EXISTS command in SQL
*
SET TALK OFF
SET ECHO OFF
CLEAR
SELECT 1
```

```
USE LA_FLAW ALIAS LA INDEX NAME
SELECT 2
USE CASES ALIAS CA INDEX COUNSEL
SELECT 1
GOTO TOP
SET FILTER TO LA->LAST = CA->COUNSEL
SELECT 2
GOTO TOP
DO WHILE .NOT. EOF()
    SELECT 1
    GOTO TOP
    ? LAST
    SELECT 2
    SKIP
ENDDO
RETURN
```

MULTIPLE QUERIES FROM MULTIPLE TABLES

You also can use multiple queries in ways that simulate the dBASE .AND. and .OR. operators. For example, Tawdry might want a list of staff members whose salaries exceed either his or that of his partner, Darren McKnife. He might do it this way:

```
SQL> SELECT LAST, SALARY
  2    FROM LA_FLAW
  3    WHERE SALARY >
  4        (SELECT SALARY
  5        FROM LA_FLAW
  6        WHERE LAST = 'TAWDRY')
  7    OR SALARY >
  8        (SELECT SALARY
  9        FROM LA_FLAW
 10        WHERE LAST = 'MCKNIFE');
```

He would get:

LAST	SALARY
MCKNIFE	5000
COSSACK	4500
BAILEY	4800
HARTLESS	7500
MUKLUK	4700

MULTIPLE SUBQUERIES

This search uses two subqueries that are separated by an OR. It will retrieve those records that satisfy either or both of the subqueries. Perhaps Tawdry really wants to see only those employees whose salaries exceed those of both partners. He could edit the command, starting with:

SQL> list 7

Then, he could enter this correction:

SQL> CHANGE/OR/AND

The revised line now reads:

7* AND SALARY >

One word has made a significant change. When Tawdry issues the order RUN, SQL*Plus first displays the full command in its new form:

```
 1    SELECT LAST, SALARY
 2    FROM LA_FLAW
 3    WHERE SALARY >
 4         (SELECT SALARY
 5         FROM LA_FLAW
 6         WHERE LAST = 'TAWDRY')
 7    AND SALARY >
 8         (SELECT SALARY
 9         FROM LA_FLAW
10*        WHERE LAST = 'MCKNIFE')
```

Then it produces these singular results:

LAST	SALARY
HARTLESS	7500

Several people receive salaries exceeding that of one partner or the other. Only one employee's pay exceeds both.

UNIONS AND INTERSECTIONS

SQL has three commands that are specifically designed for queries that compare two subqueries. They more or less duplicate the use of AND and OR, with some small but critical differences.

- UNION is equivalent to OR. It will find every record that matches *either* of the subqueries to which it applies.
- INTERSECT is a counterpart to AND. It will retrieve every row that matches *both* queries.
- MINUS is nearest to the dBASE .NOT. operator. It will get you every row that meets the condition of the *first* query, but not of the *second*. MINUS is not standard SQL, by the way, but an extension provided by ORACLE. The IBM implementation of SQL has a similar function called DIFFERENCE.

A simple use of the UNION command would be:

```
SQL> SELECT SALARY
   2   FROM LA__FLAW
   3   WHERE SALARY >
   4         (SELECT SALARY
   5          FROM LA__FLAW
   6          WHERE LAST = 'TAWDRY')
   7   UNION
   8         (SELECT SALARY
   9          FROM LA__FLAW
  10          WHERE LAST = 'MCKNIFE')
```

It produces:

```
SALARY
----------
    4500
    4700
    4800
    5000
    7500
```

All in all, it would have been easier to use the more productive OR command. What's more, UNION, INTERSECT, and MINUS are unusually tricky. They can produce error messages by the ream. All three require an exact and exacting match between the number of columns in the main and the subordinate queries. The corresponding columns must also be of the same type, although not necessarily of the same length.

You may find it unusually hard to construct a query that meets all these requirements. There are easier alternatives, so why should you bother? In many cases, you should not. There are a couple of situations, though, in which UNION, MINUS, or INTERSECT is the only possibility.

UNION and Multiple Files

You must use UNION or one of its brethren whenever the two connected subqueries involve more than one table. Here's an example:

```
SQL> SELECT LAST
  2   FROM ROSTER
  3   WHERE LAST IN
  4          (SELECT LAST
  5          FROM REPS)
  6   UNION
  7          (SELECT LAST
  8          FROM ROSTER
  9          WHERE POSITION = 'TELLER')
```

Here, you are looking for Marinecorp employees who satisfy either of two conditions:

- Their names appear in the REPS table.
- They are identified as tellers in the ROSTER table.

In this case, UNION effectively unites the two tables and reports the information they have in common in the form specified by the outer query:

```
LAST
--------------------
COLLINS
MAHONEY
PALMER
ROWE-HATTON
TUBA
ZIMMERMAN
```

MINUS in Place of a Subquery

You also can use UNION and its friends to avoid a subquery. MINUS is particularly useful here. Say, for example, that you want a list of all the Marinecorp employees who are not also listed in the separate REPS table. The conventional way to do this would be:

```
SQL> SELECT LAST, DEPT__NO
   2   FROM ROSTER
   3   WHERE DEPT__NO NOT IN
   4         (SELECT DEPT__NO
   5          FROM REPS);
```

With MINUS you can do the same thing a little more easily:

```
SQL> SELECT LAST, DEPT__NO
   2   FROM ROSTER
   3   MINUS
   4   SELECT LAST, DEPT__NO
   5   FROM REPS;
```

The second query in this command has much the same effect as the subquery in the first version has. It may be a little easier to type and understand, though. As you had hoped (because that's what I just told you to hope), this command will produce a list of everyone who is not listed in the REPS file. In this case, that means everyone who is not in Department 2:

LAST	DEPT__NO
BUCHINSKY	4
DAVIDSON	1
MADISON	1
MAHONEY	3
PALMER	3
PRESTO	1

8 records selected.

INTERSECT Gets the Opposite Result

If you substitute INTERSECT for MINUS in this command, you get a list of records that meet both conditions. Because one condition is that the records be in REPS, you'll get only those:

```
SQL> SELECT LAST, DEPT__NO
   2   FROM ROSTER
   3   INTERSECT
```

```
4    SELECT LAST, DEPT_NO
5    FROM REPS;
```

The result as predicted:

```
LAST                DEPT_NO
-----------------   -------------
COLLINS                  2
ROWE-HATTON              2
TUBA                     2
ZIMMERMAN                2
```

UNION in the Same Situation

UNION is the third possibility. It combines the two tables to display any record that appears in either. Thus:

```
SQL>  SELECT LAST, DEPT_NO
  2    FROM ROSTER
  3    UNION
  4    SELECT LAST, DEPT_NO
  5    FROM REPS;
```

Produces a list of the entire staff:

```
LAST                DEPT_NO
-----------------   -----------
BUCHINSKY               4
COLLINS                 2
DAVIDSON                1
MADISON                 1
MAHONEY                 3
PALMER                  3
PRESTO                  1
ROWE-HATTON             2
TUBA                    2
ZIMMERMAN               2
```

12 records selected.

Another Way to Use Multiple Tables

If you are querying two tables, you don't necessarily have to use two subqueries. The previous chapter demonstrated how to reach two tables with a single main query. You can do the same thing in a subquery. This query asks for the assignments of McKnife, Tawdry employees stationed in Denver. Then it reports the names of employees throughout the firm who share those assignments:

```
SQL> SELECT LAST, ASSIGN
   2   FROM LA__FLAW
   3   WHERE ASSIGN IN
   4        (SELECT ASSIGN
   5        FROM LA__FLAW, BRANCHES
   6        WHERE LOCATION = 'Denver'
   7        AND LA__FLAW.BRANCH = BRANCHES.BRANCH);
```

The key to this query is Line 5. It selects the two tables for processing within the subquery. The subquery then proceeds just as though it were a multi-table main query, then it feeds its results into the outer query:

```
LAST            ASSIGN
-----------------------------------
COSSACK         CRIMINAL
BAILEY          CRIMINAL
MUKLUK          CRIMINAL
MASON           CRIMINAL
BUNSEN          FAMILY
MCKNIFE         PARTNER
TAWDRY          PARTNER
HARTLESS        PERSONAL INJURY
ROX             SECRETARY
```

This has been a case of saving the best for last. The use of a multi-file subquery such as this solves many of the difficulties you might encounter with other advanced forms of searching.

SQL offers multiple ways to search multiple tables. Many of these methods come very close to duplicating each other. Some come even closer and actually do duplicate each other. All these methods have their uses. Otherwise, they wouldn't be present. It pays to remember, though, that the simpler the query, the more reliable the results. Use advanced queries when it's necessary. Always ask, though, whether you can accomplish the same thing more simply. Quite often, you can.

REVIEW QUESTIONS

1. Write a query that will retrieve the last names, salaries, cases, and clients for all law firm members who are working on active cases and whose salaries are less than those of either of the two partners. Hint: this will require a subquery.
2. In what order does SQL process nested queries?
3. Dennis Madison may suspect there are other people in the organization with his title. How would he search for them?
4. Write a query to retrieve the last names and salaries of law firm employees whose salaries are less than that of the highest-paid employee in Branch 3.
5. What SQL query phrase would have the same meaning as LAST NOT IN?
6. Under what conditions is an EXIST query true?
7. UNION is the equivalent of what comparison operator?
8. If you connect two SELECT statements with INTERSECT, which records do you receive?

ANSWERS

1.
```
SQL> SELECT L.LAST, L.SALARY, C.CASE, C.CLIENT
   2    FROM LA_FLAW L, CASES C
   3    WHERE C.COUNSEL = L.LAST
   4    AND L.SALARY >=
   5         (SELECT SALARY
   6         FROM LA_FLAW
   7         WHERE LA_FLAW.LAST = 'TAWDRY'
   8         OR LA_FLAW.LAST = 'MCKNIFE');
```

2. From the innermost parentheses, working outward.

3.
```
SQL> INSERT INTO REPS (LAST, FIRST, DEPT_NO)
   2    SELECT LAST, FIRST, DEPT_NO
   3    FROM ROSTER
   4    WHERE POSITION =
   5         (SELECT POSITION
   6         FROM ROSTER
   7         WHERE LAST = 'MADISON');
```

4.
```
SQL> SELECT LAST, SALARY
   2    FROM LA_FLAW
   3    WHERE SALARY < ANY
```

```
          4              (SELECT SALARY
          5              FROM LA__FLAW
          6              WHERE BRANCH = 3);
```

5. LAST <> ALL.

6. When the subquery to which it refers returns at least one record.

7. .OR.

8. Those records that satisfy both conditions.

6

Working with Numbers

Things were relatively quiet at the UnderFed branch of Marine-corp. With help from Hubert Tuba and Misty Presto, Dennis Madison had refined the Roster table. Wilma Sutton's resignation was now official. Harvey Bankerson, the human null value, had been promoted to assistant regional manager. Madison had modified the Roster table to reflect these two changes. He had even entered all the office phone numbers.

Madison also had made constructive use of the overkill he had discovered earlier, in which the department numbers simply duplicated the job assignments. He changed Zimmerman's title to supervisor and relaxed, figuring that he could do the rest some other time.

There was also a lull at McKnife, Tawdry. It came mainly in the form of great sighs of relief from staff members. It appeared that Allen Tawdry at last had exhausted every possible SQL query he could use on their salary records. In fact, Tawdry even was thinking of handling a case once in a while. He had accomplished one constructive act. Much as Madison did, he discovered that the original table's job assignment entries were ill-suited to the firm's needs. He devised a new system of primary assignments, with a separate column for those who had specialties within the larger groups.

The updated versions of the two main tables appear in Figure 6-1.

MAINTAINING APPEARANCES

Actually, it was Madison's turn to start antagonizing his coworkers by playing around with salary figures. First, however, he gained an amazing insight. As he told Addie Davidson, "Contrary to public opinion, SQL is not deficient in its formatting capabilities."

"It's not? What, pray tell, brought you to that conclusion?"

"I've found out that it has no formatting capabilities. How can you be deficient in formatting capabilities if you have no formatting capabilities to be deficient in?"

"I beg to differ."

"Nothing unusual about that."

"SQL does format numbers," Addie pointed out. "It just may not format them the way you're accustomed to seeing them."

FIGURE 6-1 The Revised Tables

```
SQL> SELECT * FROM ROSTER;

EMP LAST          FIRST         I   DEPT_NO POSITION   SS_NO        DATE_HIRE   SALARY EXTE
--- ------------- ------------- -   ------- ---------- -----------  ---------   ------ ------
AD  DAVIDSON      ADDIE         H         1 MANAGER    123-45-6789  09-SEP-79    24000 101
DM  MADISON       DENNIS        W         1 ASST MGR   234-56-7890  07-JUL-81    21000 102
MP  PRESTO        MISTY         D         1 RECEPTION  456-78-9012  19-JUN-78    42500 100
HT  TUBA          HUBERT        G         2 NEW ACCT   567-89-0123  17-MAY-87    11000 109
SM  MAHONEY       SUZANNE       S         3 TELLER     789-01-2345  18-JAN-79    12400 107
CB  BUCHINSKY     CHARLES       B         4 SECURITY   890-12-3456  18-DEC-86    15000 108
VP  PALMER        VERA          M         3 TELLER     901-23-4567  23-SEP-85    13450 106
KC  COLLINS       KATHLEEN      D         2 NEW ACCT   987-65-4321  15-OCT-85    13300 105
RZ  ZIMMERMAN     ROBERT        D         2 SUPERVISOR 876-54-3210  14-OCT-85    13400 1041
PR  ROWE-HATTON   PHYLLIS       F         2 NEW ACCT   765-43-2109  07-NOV-87    11250 103

10 records selected.



SQL> SELECT * FROM LA_FLAW;

LAST              FIRST             BRANCH ASSIGN     SPECIALTY        HIRED       SALARY
----------------  ----------------  ------ ---------- ---------------- ---------   ------
MCKNIFE           DARREN                 1 PARTNER                     09-JAN-49     5000
TAWDRY            ALLEN                  2 PARTNER                     12-SEP-65     4000
COSSACK           MICHAEL                1 CRIMINAL                    17-JUL-82     4500
BUNSEN            BURNER                 2 CIVIL      FAMILY           09-OCT-78     2975
TUCKER            FRIAR                  1 CIVIL      TAX              14-AUG-77     2850
BOYSENBERRY       ANN                    1 CIVIL      LITIGTION        31-DEC-85     2450
ROX               GOLDIE                 2 SECRETARY                   23-JAN-82     1300
MASON             PERCY                  3 CRIMINAL                    09-JUN-29     3850
BAILEY            F. BILL                1 CRIMINAL                    17-DEC-80     4800
BORQUE            BOBBY                  1 PARALEGAL                   03-DEC-81      950
HARTLESS          JAMES                  2 CIVIL      PERSONAL INJURY  08-AUG-83     7500
MUKLUK            BENJAMIN               2 CRIMINAL                    09-NOV-87     4700

12 records selected.
```

"How's that?"

"Usually, SQL will display as many digits as it needs for accuracy. In ORACLE, the usual standard display width is ten digits. Now, I'll agree that isn't much of a format, but it is a format."

"Sounds more like a floor mat."

"If you like."

"Say, I thought you were supposed to be the computer dummy around here. How'd you get so smart?"

"Would you have taken on this job if you thought I was able to do it myself?"

"Well . . . ."

"Well, well. As I thought. But since I'm supposed to be so

helpless with a keyboard—not to mention a mouse—I'll leave it to you to improve on the standard format."

THE COLUMN COMMAND

Actually, bare-bones SQL does not have any way to escape from its spartan standard format. This means that the makers of SQL products must furnish something. ORACLE provides a command called COLUMN within its SQL*Plus bundle of extensions. Other implementations of SQL provide their own kinds of formatting.

Madison began to experiment. First, he asked for this ungarnished presentation:

```
SQL> SELECT LAST, SALARY
   2    FROM ROSTER;
```

He obtained this result:

```
LAST                 SALARY
---------------   -----------
DAVIDSON             24000
MADISON              21000
PRESTO               42500
TUBA                 11000
MAHONEY              12400
BUCHINSKY            15000
PALMER               13450
COLLINS              13300
ZIMMERMAN            13400
ROWE-HATTON          11250
```

He then made use of the SQL*Plus COLUMN command to add a little pizzazz to the display:

```
SQL> COLUMN SALARY FORMAT $99,999
```

The previous SELECT command was still in the buffer. Because the succeeding COLUMN command comes from SQL*Plus, not from generic SQL, it did not displace the SQL command that was still in storage. Accordingly, all Madison had to do was type RUN, hit <Enter>, and repeat the previous SQL command. Although it was the same command, the results looked different:

LAST	SALARY
DAVIDSON	$24,000
MADISON	$21,000
PRESTO	$42,500
TUBA	$11,000
MAHONEY	$12,400
BUCHINSKY	$15,000
PALMER	$13,450
COLLINS	$13,300
ZIMMERMAN	$13,400
ROWE-HATTON	$11,250

10 records selected.

The COLUMN command identifies the column you wish to format. "Wish I'd thought of that," Madison mused. FORMAT then provides a model for the output, much like the dBASE PICTURE command does. Table 6-1 shows examples of the available formats and their resulting displays.

SOME BASIC ARITHMETIC

SQL and dBASE both will do the usual arithmetic you expect from a computer. They can add and subtract, and they know the multiplication table better than many humans know it. The salary figures in the Roster table are computed on an annual

TABLE 6-1   Available COLUMN Formats for Numbers

VALUE	FORMAT	RESULT	COMMENT
1234.5678	9999.99	1234.57	The value is rounded to two decimal places.
	9,999	1,235	Comma denotes thousands, unless there are fewer than three digits ahead of the decimal.
	$9,999.99	$1,234.57	Dollar sign added to previous formats. Formats can be combined.
000123	None	123	Leading zeroes usually are dropped.
	09999	000123	Add leading zeroes.
−123456	None	−123456	A minus sign usually precedes a negative number.
123	B99		If there are no zeroes, the B has no effect.
123.456	99.99	##.##	Format is too small for number.
12000	9.99EEEE	1.2E + 04	Exponential notation.

basis. Say, however, that you want to find out their monthly equivalents. In dBASE you would:

. LIST SALARY, SALARY/12

That would get you:

Record#	SALARY	SALARY/12
1	24000.00	2000.00
2	21000.00	1750.00
3	42500.00	3541.67
4	11000.00	916.67
5	12400.00	1033.33
6	15000.00	1250.00
7	13450.00	1120.83
8	13300.00	1108.33
9	13400.00	1116.67
10	11250.00	937.50

If you need a more precise output, you could issue this
command:

. SET DECIMALS TO 4

The output would then look like this:

Record#	SALARY	SALARY/12
1	24000.00	2000.0000
2	21000.00	1750.0000
3	42500.00	3541.6667
4	11000.00	916.6667
5	12400.00	1033.3333
6	15000.00	1250.0000
7	13450.00	1120.8333
8	13300.00	1108.3333
9	13400.00	1116.6667
10	11250.00	937.5000

Like dBASE, SQL*Plus has an extended list of SET commands. These are not part of standard SQL.

dBASE programmers enjoy entire lists of formatting commands and functions that largely duplicate ORACLE's COLUMN.
dBASE also has one lesser-known and little-used way to format
the output from direct, dot-prompt commands. A TRANSFORM( )

function lets you use the same templates and PICTURE clauses that are available to the programmers. In this case, you might do this:

```
. LIST TRANSFORM(SALARY,'$99999.99'),
TRANSFORM(SALARY/12, '$9999.99')
```

The output now looks like this:

Record#	TRANSFORM (SALARY,'$99999.99')	TRANSFORM (SALARY/12)
1	$24000.00	$2000.00
2	$21000.00	$1750.00
3	$42500.00	$3541.67
4	$11000.00	$$916.67
5	$12400.00	$1033.33
6	$15000.00	$1250.00
7	$13450.00	$1120.83
8	$13300.00	$1108.33
9	$13400.00	$1116.67
10	$11250.00	$$937.50

The awkward column headings and doubled-up dollar signs before the short numbers still make this less than perfect.

SOMEBODY DOES IT BETTER

If you use the COLUMN command of SQL*Plus, you gain much more flexibility. Take these two commands, for example:

```
SQL> COLUMN ANNUAL FORMAT $99,999
SQL> COLUMN MONTHLY FORMAT $99,999.99
```

The formats are similar to those you encountered a little while ago. What, though, are these column names? Neither appears in ROSTER or in any of its related tables. The answer is that you can use SQL to apply the titles of your choice to the columns in its display. You can give a column an alias, even if the column doesn't actually exist yet. The COLUMN commands here set the formats in which these columns will appear when they are created in response to a future query. This query comes next:

```
SQL> SELECT LAST,
   2    SALARY ANNUAL,
```

```
3   SALARY/12 MONTHLY
4   FROM ROSTER;
```

This command selects three columns from ROSTER. The first is LAST; there is nothing unusual about this part of the command. The second column is SALARY, but the command in Line 2 dictates that in the display it will be called ANNUAL.

Line 3 goes a step further. It creates a *computed column* that is composed of calculated values—each salary divided by twelve. As far as the user can see, such a column actually exists. You, of course, know that the table has no such column; you have created it.

This pseudocolumn will bear the heading MONTHLY. It so happens that ANNUAL and MONTHLY are the two headings for which you just created formats. With this in mind, take a look at the results:

```
LAST                 ANNUAL   MONTHLY
-----------------    --------  --------
DAVIDSON             $24,000   $2,000.00
MADISON              $21,000   $1,750.00
PRESTO               $42,500   $3,541.67
TUBA                 $11,000     $916.67
MAHONEY              $12,400   $1,033.33
BUCHINSKY            $15,000   $1,250.00
PALMER               $13,450   $1,120.83
COLLINS              $13,300   $1,108.33
ZIMMERMAN            $13,400   $1,116.67
ROWE-HATTON          $11,250     $937.50
```

10 records selected.

PRINCIPLES OF COLUMN LABELING

This ability to label columns, both real and contrived, is a major SQL advantage. dBASE does create a computed column, and it shows some limited formatting ability; nevertheless, SQL is clearly the leader here. It allows for a wider range of formats and your choice of column headings.

Usually, a column alias is a single word and will be displayed in capital letters. Creating a variation on this theme can be

TABLE 6-2 Sample Column Heading Formats

COMMAND	RESULTS
SQL> COLUMN SALARY "BY YEAR"	BY YEAR
SQL> COLUMN COMP "SALARY + COMMISSION"	SALARY + COMMISSION
SQL> COLUMN "Salary"	Salary

accomplished easily; enclose your chosen heading in quotation marks. By doing this, you can create such variations as:

- A heading that consists of more than one word or includes a space.
- A title that contains mathematical symbols or other characters that the computer might otherwise misinterpret.
- A heading that includes lowercase letters.

Table 6-2 shows examples of these techniques.

USING MATH EXPRESSIONS

SQL has an unexceptional assortment of mathematical operators. Just as in dBASE, you can perform a calculation based on numbers in the database. Simply include a math expression in a SQL command. This expression can contain:

- One of the four standard mathematical symbols +, −, *, or /.
- The name of any column whose type is number.
- Any number value

The command that converted the annual salaries into monthly figures used the expression SALARY * 12. In doing so, it combined all three elements: a column name, a math operator, and a number.

CALCULATIONS IN dBASE

"I have a memo from the regional manager," Addie Davidson announced one morning.

"What's on dear Allison's mind?" asked Madison.

"It would be better if you called her Miss Wunderland. What's on her mind is that she wants to give everyone a bonus for working so hard last year."

"Hey, for that, I'll call her anything she'd like. How big is the bonus?"

"Two percent of the annual salary. Now, I know this office is full of computer freaks, so I'm sure you'll all soon be figuring out how much you'll get."

"That's okay. I'll do it for everybody," said Hubert Tuba, the dBASE expert. "No, you won't. I'll do it with SQL," said Misty Presto.

Hubert's efforts did produce the desired figures. His command sequence was:

. LIST LAST, SALARY, (SALARY*.02), SALARY + (SALARY*.02)

"Well, that does do the job," mused Madison as he perused the output (shown in Figure 6-2). "This output, though, doesn't do the job very well. Oh, the numbers are there, all right. But glom onto those column headings. I know you can't tell me the meaning of life, but maybe you can tell me what those headings mean."

"Well," Tuba explained. "The one headed SALARY, I'm sure you can figure out."

"Sure."

"Then (SALARY * .02) is the bonus."

"Uh-huh."

"And the third column is the total amount everyone's going to get: the salary plus the bonus."

"I hate to say this, Hubert old man, but I think dBASE has let you down a little on this one. Let's see what Misty Presto has managed to do."

FIGURE 6-2   The Bonus Figures via dBASE

```
Record#   LAST          SALARY (SALARY*.02) SALARY + (SALARY*.02)
      1   DAVIDSON     24000.00       480.00              24480.00
      2   MADISON      21000.00       420.00              21420.00
      3   PRESTO       42500.00       850.00              43350.00
      4   TUBA         11000.00       220.00              11220.00
      5   MAHONEY      12400.00       248.00              12648.00
      6   BUCHINSKY    15000.00       300.00              15300.00
      7   PALMER       13450.00       269.00              13719.00
      8   COLLINS      13300.00       266.00              13566.00
      9   ZIMMERMAN    13400.00       268.00              13668.00
     10   ROWE-HATTON  11250.00       225.00              11475.00
```

CALCULATIONS IN SQL COMMANDS

To get the SQL version of the same display, Presto had used:

```
SQL> COLUMN BONUS FORMAT $99,999.99
SQL> COLUMN TOTAL FORMAT $99,999.99
SQL> SELECT LAST, SALARY,
  2    SALARY * .02 BONUS,
  3    SALARY + (SALARY * .02) TOTAL
  4    FROM ROSTER
```

The first two commands set formats for the computed columns to be completed in the SELECT command. The SELECT command itself specified headings for the two calculated items. The output was much more presentable, as Madison saw (Figure 6-3).

"Way to go," said Madison. "Not only do we have the figures here, but even I can tell what they are."

You can turn off an existing COLUMN specification with the command:

```
COLUMN SALARY CLEAR
```

Of course, you would specify the column or computed column whose definition you want to remove. If you want to check on your currently active column definitions, the command COLUMN with nothing else will produce a report like this:

```
column    MONTHLY ON
format    $99,999
```

FIGURE 6-3   SQL Computes a More Attractive Bonus Offer

```
    LAST          SALARY        BONUS         TOTAL
    ------------  --------  ------------  -----------
    DAVIDSON      $24,000      $480.00    $24,480.00
    MADISON       $21,000      $420.00    $21,420.00
    PRESTO        $42,500      $850.00    $43,350.00
    TUBA          $11,000      $220.00    $11,220.00
    MAHONEY       $12,400      $248.00    $12,648.00
    BUCHINSKY     $15,000      $300.00    $15,300.00
    PALMER        $13,450      $269.00    $13,719.00
    COLLINS       $13,300      $266.00    $13,566.00
    ZIMMERMAN     $13,400      $268.00    $13,668.00
    ROWE-HATTON   $11,250      $225.00    $11,475.00

    10 records selected.
```

```
column   SALARY ON
format   $99,999
```

OBSERVING PRECEDENCE

As in dBASE and virtually every other computer program, SQL observes a certain precedence, a specific order in which it evaluates mathematical operators. Usually, ORACLE will look first for multiplication and division operators and calculate those expressions. Then, it will take on any addition or subtraction expressions. If there is more than one operator of equal precedence, the program will work from left to right. If ORACLE encountered this expression:

SALARY − EXPENSES + .02 * SALARY

it would first do the multiplication. Then, it would subtract EXPENSES from salary. From the result of that operation it would subtract the result of the multiplication. This result would be a net bonus calculated by subtracting the expenses from salary.

You can control the calculation order by using parentheses. Take, for instance, this version:

SALARY − (EXPENSES + .02 * SALARY)

The program will first go inside the parentheses and calculate whatever it found there. If it finds another set of parentheses, it will calculate whatever is inside those. Within the parentheses, the program will observe its usual priorities. It will do the multiplication, then subtract the result from EXPENSES. The result of this entire operation would then be subtracted from SALARY. The effect here would be to compute the bonus, add the expenses, and subtract the whole thing from the poor worker's salary.

USING MATH FUNCTIONS

In addition to its plus-and-minus operators, SQL has an assortment of mathematical functions. There is less variety than you would find in a spreadsheet, but the selection is greater than that available in dBASE. The SQL numerical functions are listed in

Table 6-3 along with their dBASE counterparts and examples of their output.

ROUNDING A NUMBER

As an example of how one of these functions works, the ROUND function rounds a number to a specified number of decimal places.

TABLE 6-3   SQL Mathematical Functions

SQL	DBASE	OUTPUT	COMMENT
ABS(−43)	ABS(−43)	43	Absolute value of a number or expression.
AVG(2,4,6)	AVERAGE	4	Produces the average (arithmetic mean) of the indicated values. In dBASE, AVERAGE is a command that averages the figures in a selected field.
CEIL(43.6)	INT(43.6+1)	44	Rounds upward. dBASE has no direct counterpart, but the formula shown will produce the same result.
FLOOR(43.6)	INT(43)	43	Rounds downward.
GREATEST(2,4)	MAX(2,4)	4	Returns the larger of two values.
LEAST(2,4)	MIN(2,4)	2	Returns the smaller of two values.
MOD(9,4)	MOD(9,4)	1	Returns the modulus, or remainder of the first number divided by the second.
POWER(4,2)		16	Raises the first number to the power indicated by the second. dBASE has no directly comparable function.
ROUND(4.123,2)	ROUND(4.123,2)	4.12	Rounds the first value to the number of decimal places indicated by the second value.
ROUND(4.123)	ROUND(4.123)	4	When no decimal places are specified, returns the nearest whole number.
SIGN(−5)		−1	Returns −1 if the number is negative, 0 if the number is zero, and 1 if the number is positive. There is no dBASE equivalent.
SQRT(16)	SQRT(16)	4	Returns the square root of the indicated number. Will return a null value if the number is zero.
TRUNC(12.34,1)		12.3	Truncates the number to the indicated number of decimal places. Does not round the number.

If you issued this command:

```
SQL> SELECT SALARY/12 MONTHLY
   2   FROM ROSTER:
```

you would get:

```
MONTHLY
-----------
 $2,000.00
 $1,750.00
 $3,541.67
   $916.67
 $1,033.33
 $1,250.00
 $1,120.83
 $1,108.33
 $1,116.67
   $937.50
```

10 records selected.

If you altered the command to round off these figures, the results would be different. Since no decimal places are specified, the program assumes that you want none. This command:

```
SQL> SELECT ROUND(SALARY/12) ROUNDED
   2   FROM ROSTER;
```

produces:

```
ROUNDED
-----------
      2000
      1750
      3542
       917
      1033
      1250
      1121
      1108
      1117
       938
```

10 records selected.

TRUNCATING INSTEAD OF ROUNDING

The TRUNC function is similar to ROUND, but it merely lops off any decimal places beyond those you specify. If there is no specification, TRUNC cuts off all the decimals. It does not attempt to round the figure that remains. This means that this command:

```
SQL>  SELECT TRUNC(SALARY/12) LOPPED
   2    FROM ROSTER;
```

produces results that are slightly, but significantly, different from those in the previous exercise:

```
LOPPED
--------
    2000
    1750
    3541
     916
    1033
    1250
    1120
    1108
    1116
     937
```

10 records selected.

WORKING WITH GROUPS OF NUMBERS

The functions discussed so far work on individual number values. For example, when SQL was commanded to round or truncate the values in the SALARY column, it did so to every figure it found. There is another set of functions that operate on groups of numbers. Usually, the group will be a designated column in a selected group of records.

These group functions will usually ignore null values. In contrast, dBASE will treat an empty numerical field as a zero and include it in the calculation.

ABOUT AVERAGE

For example, the AVG function computes the mean value of the selected column and rows. An example:

```
SQL> SELECT AVG(SALARY)
  2   FROM ROSTER;
```

This computes the average salary of all employees whose records appear in ROSTER. It returns a single figure:

```
AVG(SALARY)
---------------
      17730
```

You can include other mathematical operators with the group functions. Say, for instance, that you want to compare the average salary at McKnife, Tawdry with that at UnderFed. One table reports the employees' annual salaries; the other uses monthly figures. To make a meaningful comparison, this command converts the law firm's monthly salaries into their annual equivalents, then averages the results:

```
SQL> SELECT AVG(SALARY * 12)
  2   FROM LA__FLAW;
```

The result is:

```
AVG(SALARY*12)
------------------
       44875
```

COUNTING SELECTED VALUES

You will nearly always use group functions in SELECT commands. This gives you access to all the options that SELECT has to offer. For example, you could use a WHERE statement to average or count the records that meet a particular specification. This command counts those employees whose salaries are higher than $12,000:

```
SQL> SELECT COUNT(SALARY)
  2   FROM ROSTER
  3   WHERE SALARY > 12000;
```

The result is:

```
COUNT(SALARY)
-----------------
              8
```

OTHER OPERATORS ILLUSTRATED

A complete list of group functions is shown in Table 6-4. Table 6-4 shows some examples of how to put them to practical use:

To find the maximum salary in UnderFed's ROSTER table:

```
SQL> SELECT MAX(SALARY)
  2    FROM ROSTER;
```

The result is:

```
MAX(SALARY)
---------------
        42500
```

This command computes annual salaries from the monthly figures in LA__FLAW:

```
SQL> SELECT MAX(SALARY * 12)
  2    FROM LA__FLAW;
```

TABLE 6-4   SQL Group Functions

SQL	dBASE	COMMENT
AVG(SALARY)	AVERAGE SALARY	Averages values in selected columns and rows. The dBASE version is used as a command rather than as a function.
COUNT(SALARY)	COUNT SALARY	Counts the number of records that meet the supplied specification.
MAX(SALARY)		Finds the maximum value in the indicated columns and rows. There is no direct dBASE equivalent.
MIN(SALARY)		Finds the minimum value in the indicated columns and rows. Again, there is no direct dBASE counterpart.
VARIANCE(SALARY)		Computes the variance of the indicated values.

It also reports the top yearly pay for comparison with the output from ROSTER:

```
MAX(SALARY*12)
------------------
          90000
```

At the other extreme, here's a command to calculate the lowest monthly salary in ROSTER:

```
SQL> SELECT MIN(SALARY/12)
  2    FROM ROSTER;
```

It produces this unformatted result:

```
MIN(SALARY/12)
------------------
      916.666667
```

On the other hand, the minimum salary in LA__FLAW:

```
SQL> SELECT MIN(SALARY)
  2    FROM LA__FLAW;
```

is:

```
MIN(SALARY)
--------------
         950
```

How about the sums of the annual salaries?

```
SQL> SELECT SUM(SALARY)
  2    FROM ROSTER;
```

Here's the total from ROSTER:

```
SUM(SALARY)
--------------
       177300
```

And the comparable calculation for LA__FLAW:

```
SQL> SELECT SUM(SALARY * 12)
  2    FROM LA__FLAW;
```

It produces this result:

```
SUM(SALARY*12)
------------------
          538500
```

MORE SELECTIVE USE OF OPERATORS

You can use WHERE statements to apply averages, sums, and other operators to selected groups of records. This command computes the average salary for the criminal specialists at McKnife, Tawdry:

```
SQL> SELECT AVG(SALARY)
  2    FROM LA__FLAW
  3    WHERE ASSIGN = 'CRIMINAL';
```

The result is:

```
AVG(SALARY)
---------------
         4462.5
```

In contrast, this formula:

```
SQL> SELECT AVG(SALARY)
  2    FROM LA__FLAW
  3    WHERE ASSIGN = 'CIVIL';
```

determines that the lawyers who handle civil cases average slightly less in salary:

```
AVG(SALARY)
---------------
        3943.75
```

At UnderFed, you can use the department number and the SUM function to calculate the total new accounts payroll:

```
SQL> SELECT SUM(SALARY)
  2    FROM ROSTER
  3    WHERE DEPT__NO = 2;
```

The result is:

```
SUM(SALARY)
---------------
        48950
```

This command counts the number of people in administrative positions at UnderFed. Because administration is listed as Department 1, you can do it this way:

```
SQL> SELECT COUNT(LAST)
  2    FROM ROSTER
  3    WHERE DEPT__NO = 1;
```

This command counts the last names, but you could count the records in any column:

```
COUNT(LAST)
---------------
          3
```

One thing to remember, though: This function does not count null values.

A MORE COMPLEX EXAMPLE

You can work with more than one column, real or computed, when using group functions. This command finds the maximum and minimum salaries in ROSTER. Then, it computes and displays these figures along with the difference between them:

```
SQL> SELECT MAX(SALARY) MAXIMUM,
  2    MIN(SALARY) MINIMUM,
  3    MAX(SALARY) − MIN(SALARY) DIFFERENCE
  4    FROM ROSTER
```

The result is:

```
MAXIMUM  MINIMUM  DIFFERENCE
---------- ----------- ---------------
     42500     11000        31500
```

Computations such as this are often useful in salary administration.

OPTIONS IN USING FUNCTIONS

All group functions have two options that you can use. This command:

SELECT COUNT(DISTINCT SALARY)

will count only those salary figures that are unique, omitting any duplicate values. This command:

SELECT COUNT(ALL SALARY)

will override SQL's normal tendency to ignore null values. With ALL in the picture, SQL will treat nulls as zeros, just as dBASE does.

REVIEW QUESTIONS

1. Write a COLUMN command to format the SALARY column with two decimal places, a comma for thousands, and no dollar sign.
2. What is a computed or calculated column?
3. What would the following be likely to produce?

    COLUMN QTR1 + QTR2 "6-Mo Plan Performance"

4. The functions ROUND( ) and TRUNC( ) are much alike, but they have one key difference. What is it?
5. Of 1,200 people who respond to a survey, fifty decline to report their household incomes. Were you to use the AVG( ) function to calculate a mean income, how many of the responses would be included in the average?
6. Write a query to determine the average salary for UnderFed employees in Department 7.

ANSWERS

1. COLUMN SALARY FORMAT 99,999.99.
2. A column which does not exist in a table but which can be displayed using calculated values.
3. The sum of the QTR1 and QTR2 under the heading "6-Mo Plan Performance." A column heading placed in double quotes will usually be reproduced exactly, regardless of SQL's normal preferences.

4. ROUND( ) converts the value to the nearest whole number. TRUNC( ) simply removes the digits to the right of the decimal point.

5. You would get the mean of 1,150 income figures. The unreported incomes would appear as null values and would not be included in the average.

6. SQL> SELECT AVG(SALARY)
   FROM ROSTER
   WHERE DEPT_NO = 1;

Words and Characters

"That's very nice," said Addie Davidson, when she saw what Dennis Madison had done with numerical operations. "Now, let's see what you can do with characters."

"Heh heh."

"Why did you chuckle?"

"'Cause I could see it coming from a mile away."

"What did you see coming?"

"You asked me if I could work with characters. Now you're just sitting there waiting for me to open my mouth and make some stupid, demeaning comment about the fine people who are employed here. Well, I'm too sharp for you today. You're not going to get me to say a thing."

"Well, I don't want you to say anything about our employees. I just want to see what SQL can do with character values. Char, I think they're quaintly called."

"Some of these characters don't seem to have very much value."

"I thought you said you weren't going to make a smart remark like that."

"I lied."

"Get to work."

DISPLAYING CHAR VALUES

Names, addresses, titles, and other text items are Char values, counterparts to the CHARACTER type in dBASE. Put a group of Char values together, as in a word or a sentence, and you have a *string*. Char values usually are displayed exactly as they are stored in a SQL table. However, you can use the COLUMN command to modify their display just as you can with numerical values. Here's the BRANCHES table that accompanies LA__FLAW:

```
SQL> SELECT * FROM BRANCHES;

BRANCH LOCATION           SUPER
--------- ------------------- ------------
        1 LOS ANGELES        MCKNIFE
        2 DENVER             TAWDRY
        3 ATLANTA            MASON
```

CHANGING THE COLUMN WIDTH

Suppose you want to include data from the LOCATION column in a SELECT command, but you are afraid that the full output from your command would be too wide for practical display or printing. You decide to see if you could shorten LOCATION to help solve the space problem. To test this possibility, enter:

SQL> COLUMN LOCATION FORMAT A8

This tells SQL*Plus to format an alphanumeric column (designated by the *A*) in a display eight columns wide. Here are the results:

```
BRANCH LOCATION        SUPER
---------- ------------    ------------
       1 LOS ANGE        MCKNIFE
         LES
       2 DENVER          TAWDRY
       3 ATLANTA         MASON
```

This probably isn't exactly what you had in mind. SQL divided the name but did not worry about doing so at a natural word break. You'll need some other solution. Cancel the COLUMN command with:

SQL> COLUMN LOCATION CLEAR

dBASE DOES IT WORSE

For what it's worth, dBASE would not be up to this particular task, either (with the exception of formatting commands available in the REPORT function or through a command file). To shorten the display from the dot command, you must first MODIFY STRUCTURE to cut the target column down to size. That leaves you with this structure:

```
Structure for database  : BRANCHES.DBF
Number of data records:        3
Date of last update     : 12/07/87
Field Field Name  Type      Width  Dec
     1 BRANCH      Numeric         1
```

2 LOCATION	Character	8
3 SUPER	Character	15
** Total **		25

A LIST command of this structure produces:

Record#	BRANCH	LOCATION	SUPER
1	1	LOS ANGE	MCKNIFE
2	2	DENVER	TAWDRY
3	3	ATLANTA	MASON

Los Angeles is in even worse shape than it was the last time we saw it. It's been truncated, a term Dennis Madison would no doubt enjoy, were he working with this database. Instead of being split off to the next line, the last three letters have simply disappeared.

In fact, they really have disappeared for good. When you return the LOCATION field to its original 15 characters, you get:

Record#	BRANCH	LOCATION	SUPER
1	1	LOS ANGE	MCKNIFE
2	2	DENVER	TAWDRY
3	3	ATLANTA	MASON

It's exactly the same as it was before. The missing letters did not return. Fortunately, this is a small database and you can easily edit the one damaged record. In a larger file this could have been a disaster.

USING CHAR EXPRESSIONS

Just as you can use expressions and functions with numerical values, you can use similar expressions and functions with characters.

STRINGING THINGS TOGETHER

Take concatenation, for example. When he first encountered the concatenation operator in SQL, Dennis Madison found himself crooning to the tune of an old song: "Concatenation . . . is funny . . . ." He couldn't think of an appropriate rhyme, though, and dropped the idea.

Concatenation is the process of attaching two strings end to end, like knotting two lengths of string or plugging an appliance into an extension cord. In dBASE, the concatenation operator is +. You might use it to generate a single-column list of office locations and their supervisors:

. LIST LOCATION + ',   '+SUPER

The results might be something like you expected, but not exactly:

```
Record#   LOCATION+",   "+SUPER
--------  ----------------   ----------
     1    Los Angeles      , McKnife
     2    Denver           , Tawdry
     3    Atlanta          , Mason
```

To get what you really want, trim off the leading blanks like this:

. LIST TRIM(LOCATION)+', '+SUPER

You still have an awkward-looking column heading, though:

```
Record#   TRIM(LOCATION)+",   "+SUPER
--------  ----------------------   ----------
     1    Los Angeles, McKnife
     2    Denver, Tawdry
     3    Atlanta, Mason
```

Concatenation in SQL

The SQL symbol for concatenation is two vertical bars: ||. (The bar is the shifted backslash key on most PC keyboards). A SQL statement to list the branches and supervisors would go something like this:

```
SQL> SELECT LOCATION || ',' || SUPER
   2    FROM BRANCHES;
```

This command concatenates, in order and for each row, the contents of the LOCATION column, a comma, and the contents of the SUPER column. It all comes out like this:

```
LOCATION||','||SUPER
--------------------------------
LOS ANGELES,MCKNIFE
DENVER,TAWDRY
ATLANTA,MASON
```

Not Good Enough

This could stand some improvement. First, SQL gives you the option of using alias names for column headings. This looks like a very good place to take advantage of this feature. You can do it by editing the previous command. Unless you've done something in the meantime, it should still be in the program's buffer area. The editing sequence was described in Chapter 2. In this example, the SQL> prompt indicates commands that you enter; the numbered lines are the computer's response:

```
SQL> LIST 1
   1*   SELECT LOCATION ||','|| SUPER
SQL> APPEND SUPERVISORS
   1*   SELECT LOCATION ||','|| SUPER SUPERVISORS
SQL> RUN
   1    SELECT LOCATION ||','|| SUPER SUPERVISORS
   2*   FROM BRANCHES
```

The concatenation operation has produced a pseudocolumn. Here, you have given this column the heading SUPERVISORS. The results now look like this:

```
SUPERVISORS
--------------------------------
LOS ANGELES,MCKNIFE
DENVER,TAWDRY
ATLANTA,MASON
```

Stupid Computer

The above example demonstrated how bullheaded a computer can be. It did exactly what you told it to do: reported the locations and the supervisors, separated by commas. It had no idea that you wanted to put spaces after the commas.

Even a stupid computer can learn, though. Here, the lesson plan calls for some additional editing of the command:

```
SQL>  LIST 1
   1*   SELECT LOCATION || ',' || SUPER SUPERVISORS
SQL>  CHANGE/','/',   '/
   1*   SELECT LOCATION || ',   ' || SUPER SUPERVISORS
SQL>  RUN
   1    SELECT LOCATION || ',   ' || SUPER SUPERVISORS
   2*   FROM BRANCHES
```

Now the results should be more to your liking:

```
SUPERVISORS
-----------------------------------
LOS ANGELES, MCKNIFE
DENVER, TAWDRY
ATLANTA, MASON
```

'YOU'RE NOT MY TYPE'

What would happen if you were to try to concatenate a character with a numerical value? In dBASE, such a command might be this:

```
. USE ROSTER
. LIST LAST + SALARY
```

All this would get you is the error message:

Data type mismatch.

APPLES + ORANGES

You can't connect strings and numbers in dBASE. First, you must change the number to a character string using a conversion function:

```
. LIST LAST + STR(SALARY)
```

When both elements are of the character type, they fit together neatly:

```
Record#   LAST + STR(SALARY)
--------  -----------------------------------
       1  DAVIDSON          24000
       2  MADISON           21000
```

3	PRESTO	42500
4	TUBA	11000
5	MAHONEY	12400
6	BUCHINSKY	15000
7	PALMER	13450
8	COLLINS	13300
9	ZIMMERMAN	13400
10	ROWE-HATTON	11250

QUESTIONABLE ADVANTAGE

In SQL, such a conversion isn't absolutely necessary. If you try to link two mismatched data types, SQL tries to convert the values into types that will work in the operation you are trying to perform. Thus, if you were to try to concatenate the last name and salary, ORACLE would convert the salary type to Char for the sake of this operation. In the same way, if you were to store a numerical value such as a department number in a Char column, then for some reason try to add it to a Number value, SQL would make the switch from characters to numbers.

You'll get an error message only if ORACLE tries to make a conversion and for some reason isn't able to complete it. This might happen, for example, if you tried to calculate a department number like A11.

There's reason to wonder, though, whether automatic conversion is really a good idea. It certainly is wrong to rely on it. Because the conversion is an automatic process, it also is beyond your control. It might not always produce the results you expect. SQL may interpret your intentions incorrectly. Because the conversion process is hidden, you may not be able to figure out readily what went wrong. Should anyone else try to decipher your work, it may not be obvious that you relied on automatic type conversion.

The best course is not to rely on it. Automatic conversion can occasionally compensate for a mistake on your part. It is much better, though, to tell the computer exactly what you mean, including correct use of the correct data types. Use the data conversion functions shown in Table 7-1; this way, you leave nothing to chance.

TABLE 7-1   Major Type Conversion Functions

INITIAL DATA TYPE	FUNCTION	RESULTING DATA TYPE	COMMENT
Number	TO__CHAR(*number*)	Char	Converts a Number type to Char.
Date	TO__CHAR(*date*)	Char	Converts a Date type to Char (see Chapter 8).
Char	TO__DATE(*string*)	Date	Converts a character string to a date (see Chapter 8).
Number	TO__DATE(*number*)	Date	Converts a numerical entry to a date.
Char	TO__NUMBER(*string*)	Number	Converts a Number value to an equivalent string.

AVOIDING THE APOSTROPHE CATASTROPHE

A Char value in a SQL command must be enclosed in single apostrophes. Say, for instance, that you want to retrieve the records of your transactions with Joe's Barber Shop or your charitable contributions to St. Vincent's Rescue Mission. You might be inclined to refer to them this way:

'Joe's Barber Shop'
'St. Vincent's Rescue Mission'

If you use these forms, SQL will recognize these institutions only as *Joe* and *St. Vincent*. To the program, the remaining characters in the names would be gibberish that probably would produce error messages. Worse, there would be no error messages because the computer would interpret the leftover letters as a command, and somehow would succeed in executing that command.

There's a simple way to avoid this problem. When you need to put an apostrophe within a Char expression, simply use a double apostrophe. Thus, the right forms would be:

'Joe''s Barber Shop'
'St. Vincent''s Rescue Mission'

USING CHAR FUNCTIONS

SQL has an assortment of functions that operate on Char values, just as it has functions that operate on Number values. A full list of Char functions is shown in Table 7-2.

TABLE 7-2   Functions That Work on Char Values

SQL	dBASE	OUTPUT	COMMENT
ASCII('NEVER')	ASC('NEVER')	78	Returns the ASCII code for the first letter of the indicated string, in this case 78 for the capital N.
CHR(78)	CHR(78)	N	Translates an ASCII code into its character equivalent.
DECODE()			See p. 141 for a full explanation.
INITCAP('NOW OR NEVER')		Now Or Never	Capitalizes the first letter of each word in the string. Translates all other letters to lowercase. There is no dBASE equivalent.
INSTR('NOW OR NEVER')	AT(' ','NOW OR NEVER')	4	Finds the location of the first space within the indicated string.
LOWER('NOW OR NEVER')	LOWER('NOW OR NEVER')	now or never	Converts the entire string into lowercase letters.
LPAD('NOW', 5, '*')		**NOW	Adds leading characters to increase the string in the first entry to the length of the second. The third entry is optional; if no character is specified, the function will add blanks.
LTRIM('**NOW', '*')		NOW	Trims the string indicated in the first entry, removing any characters indicated in the second. The dBASE LTRIM() function removes only leading blanks.
RPAD('NOW', 5, '*'		NOW**	Same as LPAD() but adds characters to the right.
RTRIM('NOW**', '*')		NOW	Same as LTRIM() but works from the right.
SOUNDEX('NOU')		NOW	Retrieves values that sound like the indicated letters.
SUBSTR('NOW OR NEVER', 4, 2)	SUBSTR('NOW OR NEVER', 4, 2)	OR	Extracts a portion of a string, starting at the position indicated by the first number, continuing for the number of characters indicated by the second.
UPPER('Now or Never')	UPPER('Now or Never')	NOW OR NEVER	Makes all letters uppercase.

DECODE -ING VALUES

The function that's hardest to explain in a table is DECODE( ). You can use it to translate the values in one column into other, corresponding values. For example, you could use DECODE( ) to assign job classification codes to the various positions at Under-Fed. Such a classification might be useful in setting basic pay scales. The command:

```
SQL> SELECT LAST, POSITION,
   2    DECODE(POSITION, 'MANAGER',89, 'ASST MGR',85,
   3        'SUPERVISOR',82, 'NEW ACCT',80,
   4        'TELLER', 80, 'SECURITY',77, 0) "JOB CLASS"
   5    FROM ROSTER
```

Within the brackets are two major elements:

- The name of the column whose values you want to translate
- A list of values from that column and their translated equivalents

Here, you are assigning the manager's job to Class 89, the assistant manager to Class 85, and so on. You can assign more than one job to the same class. For example, tellers and new accounts representatives are both in Class 80. The arguments within the brackets of this command simply list one job and then its translated value, continuing through every job. The zero at the end is a default value to be assigned to any job that isn't mentioned in the command. After the command comes an alias to be used as a heading for the resulting pseudocolumn. This command produces:

LAST	POSITION	JOB CLASS
DAVIDSON	MANAGER	89
MADISON	ASST MGR	85
PRESTO	RECEPTION	0
TUBA	NEW ACCT	80
MAHONEY	TELLER	80
BUCHINSKY	SECURITY	77
PALMER	TELLER	80
COLLINS	NEW ACCT	80

| ZIMMERMAN | SUPERVISOR | 82 |
| ROWE-HATTON | NEW ACCT | 80 |

10 records selected.

Among other things, this display makes it clear that you forgot to include the receptionist. She may never forgive you for this.

You could perform this operation in dBASE, but it involves some manipulation. You would have to create a new field for the job class then issue a list of substitution commands. The first might be:

REPLACE JOB__CODE WITH 89 FOR POSITION = 'MANAGER'

You will then have to proceed through the remainder of the job list with similar replacements.

DECODE( ) is not limited to use with Char values. In SQL it is a universal function, available for use with any data type that needs translation.

JUST IN INITCAP(CASE)

Like dBASE, SQL has an UPPER( ) function that translates a string into uppercase letters and a LOWER( ) function that translates a string into lowercase letters. Unlike dBASE, SQL also has an INITCAP( ) function that capitalizes the first letter of every word in the string. For example:

```
SQL> SELECT INITCAP(FIRST), INITCAP(LAST)
  2    FROM ROSTER;
```

It changes the all-capitals contents of the ROSTER table into the more readable:

```
INITCAP(FIRS INITCAP(LAST
------------- -------------
Addie         Davidson
Dennis        Madison
Misty         Presto
Hubert        Tuba
Suzanne       Mahoney
```

Charles   Buchinsky
Vera   Palmer
Kathleen   Collins
Robert   Zimmerman
Phyllis   Rowe-Hatton

If you give each column an alias, you can do even better:

```
SQL> SELECT INITCAP(FIRST) "FIRST NAME",
  2    INITCAP(LAST) "LAST NAME"
  3    FROM ROSTER;
```

FIRST NAME   LAST NAME
--------------- ---------------------

Addie   Davidson
Dennis   Madison
Misty   Presto
Hubert   Tuba
Suzanne   Mahoney
Charles   Buchinsky
Vera   Palmer
Kathleen   Collins
Robert   Zimmerman
Phyllis   Rowe-Hatton

10 records selected.

SOUNDING IT OUT

If you aren't sure of the spelling of a name, give it a shot. Then let the SOUNDEX( ) function try to find the right version. SOUNDEX( ) will accept a phonetic spelling and try to match it with something in the database that sounds the same. For example:

```
SQL> SELECT FIRST, LAST
  2    FROM ROSTER
  3    WHERE SOUNDEX(LAST) = SOUNDEX('ROHATON');
```

This command retrieved:

FIRST   LAST
--------------- ---------------

PHYLLIS   ROWE-HATTON

You must come very close to an accurate phonetic spelling. Don't create a routine in which you expect this function to work correctly every time. Here, for example, are a couple of commands that won't work:

```
SQL> SELECT FIRST, LAST
  2    FROM ROSTER
  3    WHERE SOUNDEX(LAST) − SOUNDEX('PESTO');
```

no records selected

```
SQL> SELECT FIRST, LAST
  2    FROM ROSTER
  3    WHERE SOUNDEX(LAST) = SOUNDEX('SIMMERMAN');
```

no records selected

And here is one that will work:

```
SQL> SELECT LAST
  2    FROM ROSTER
  3    WHERE SOUNDEX(LAST) = SOUNDEX('DAVEDZEN');
```

```
LAST
--------------------
DAVIDSON
```

USING CHAR CONSTANTS

You can display a constant Char value as if it were a column of its own. Here, the COLUMN command, normally used to create a column heading, is used to get rid of what otherwise would be an awkward heading:

```
SQL> COLUMN Y HEADING '  ';
SQL> COLUMN Z HEADING '  ';
```

Columns Y and Z don't exist yet, but the next command will take care of that:

```
SQL> SELECT 'Employee:' Y,
  2    L.LAST,
  3    'Supervisor:' Z,
  4    B.SUPER SUPERVISOR
```

```
    5    FROM LA__FLAW L, BRANCHES B
    6    WHERE L.BRANCH = B.BRANCH;
```

HEADLESS HORSEMEN

Since it appears in single quotation marks, the term Employee: will be treated as the contents of its column instead of the head. As Line 1 commands, this column will be known as Y. As a previous COLUMN command has dictated, Y shall be headless. The same is true of Column Z, whose contents are uniformly Supervisor:. Remaining command lines identify this as a join using aliases for the two source tables. Now for a look at the results of all this:

	LAST		SUPERVISOR
Employee:	MCKNIFE	Supervisor:	MCKNIFE
Employee:	COSSACK	Supervisor:	MCKNIFE
Employee:	TUCKER	Supervisor:	MCKNIFE
Employee:	BOYSENBERRY	Supervisor:	MCKNIFE
Employee:	BAILEY	Supervisor:	MCKNIFE
Employee:	BORQUE	Supervisor:	MCKNIFE
Employee:	TAWDRY	Supervisor:	TAWDRY
Employee:	ROX	Supervisor:	TAWDRY
Employee:	HARTLESS	Supervisor:	TAWDRY
Employee:	MUKLUK	Supervisor:	TAWDRY
Employee:	BUNSEN	Supervisor:	TAWDRY
Employee:	MASON	Supervisor:	MASON

12 records selected.

BE MORE REFINED

It's possible to make a few additional refinements. This table shows the three office managers as supervising themselves. That probably is not what you wanted. Perhaps a version that eliminates self-supervisors would be in order:

```
SQL> RUN
    1    SELECT 'Employee:' Y,
    2    L.LAST,
```

```
3    'Supervisor:' Z,
4    B.SUPER SUPERVISOR
5    FROM LA__FLAW L, BRANCHES B
6    WHERE L.BRANCH = B.BRANCH
7    AND L.LAST <> B.SUPER
```

The added line eliminates those records in which the last name and the supervisor's name are the same. It produces:

	LAST		SUPERVISOR
-----------	------------------	------------	--------------
Employee:	COSSACK	Supervisor:	MCKNIFE
Employee:	TUCKER	Supervisor:	MCKNIFE
Employee:	BOYSENBERRY	Supervisor:	MCKNIFE
Employee:	BAILEY	Supervisor:	MCKNIFE
Employee:	BORQUE	Supervisor:	MCKNIFE
Employee:	ROX	Supervisor:	TAWDRY
Employee:	HARTLESS	Supervisor:	TAWDRY
Employee:	MUKLUK	Supervisor:	TAWDRY
Employee:	BUNSEN	Supervisor:	TAWDRY

9 records selected.

REVIEW QUESTIONS

1. What happens when you put a group of Chars together?
2. What does the format command A12 produce?
3. What's wrong with this concatenation command:
   PLACE ||','|| PRODUCT?
4. What happens when you try to mix data types in SQL?
5. How would SQL reproduce the text entry 'Goodey's Ladies Book'?
6. Assume that you're a teacher with a list of the usual letter grades for a group of students. Create a DECODE statement that would report the grades and their associated numerical ranges.

ANSWERS

1. They become a string.
2. An alphanumeric column that is twelve characters wide.
3. There will be no space after the comma. To correct it, place a comma and a space between the single quotes.

4. The program will try to convert the types to some workable combination.

5. You would see only *Goodey*. SQL would assume that the apostrophe was the end of the string. The correct form would be 'Goodey''s Ladies Book'.

6. The scores in each grade are your choice, of course, but the statement might go like this:

DECODE('A','92–100','B','85–91','C','78–84','D','70–78','F', 'BELOW 70')

Working with Dates

SQL's date-management facilities are expansive enough to satisfy antiquarians and futurists alike. ORACLE will work with any date between 4712 BC and 4712 AD.

Pick any date within this range, and SQL knows its day of the week. The program also knows all twelve months, both spelled out and abbreviated. The date function doesn't stop with days, but breaks down each day into its component hours, minutes, and seconds. There's also a broad range of formatting capability. If you want SQL to say, "This eleventh day of December in the year of our Lord Nineteen-Hundred-and-Eighty-Seven," you can get SQL to say that.

GET A GOOD-LOOKING DATE

Computers don't work easily with dates. It's only been in the last few years, for example, that programmers have found satisfactory ways to handle the impending turn of the century. The usual date-handling technique is to assign each date a serial number, which the program uses internally. What you see on the screen is a representation of that number, translated from a form the computer can understand to a form you can understand.

When ORACLE makes that transition, it uses the standard format DD-MON-YY. Thus, if you simply command:

```
SQL> SELECT FIRST, LAST, DATE_HIRED
    2    FROM ROSTER;
```

you would get:

FIRST	LAST	DATE_HIRE
ADDIE	DAVIDSON	09-SEP-79
DENNIS	MADISON	07-JUL-81
MISTY	PRESTO	19-JUN-78
HUBERT	TUBA	17-MAY-87
SUZANNE	MAHONEY	18-JAN-79
CHARLES	BUCHINSKY	18-DEC-86
VERA	PALMER	23-SEP-85
KATHLEEN	COLLINS	15-OCT-85
ROBERT	ZIMMERMAN	14-OCT-85
PHYLLIS	ROWE-HATTON	07-NOV-87

10 records selected.

There's nothing terribly wrong with this display. The one visible problem is SQL's normal tendency to truncate a column heading to the width of the column itself. Many times, though, you'll want more flexibility.

HOW dBASE DOES IT

The standard-equipment dBASE command and display are:

```
. LIST FIRST, LAST, DATE__HIRED

Record#  FIRST        LAST                  DATE__HIRED
-------- -----------  -------------------   ---------------
       1 ADDIE        DAVIDSON              09/09/79
       2 DENNIS       MADISON               07/07/81
       3 MISTY        PRESTO                06/19/78
       4 HUBERT       TUBA                  05/17/87
       5 SUZANNE      MAHONEY               01/18/79
       6 CHARLES      BUCHINSKY             12/18/86
       7 VERA         PALMER                09/23/85
       8 KATHLEEN     COLLINS               10/15/85
       9 ROBERT       ZIMMERMAN             10/14/85
      10 PHYLLIS      ROWE-HATTON           11/07/87
```

dBASE normally reports the full column headings and supplies record numbers. More important right now, it uses a standard date format that is different from the one that SQL uses. dBASE also has some available date formatting functions, but not the variety of them that ORACLE has available.

CHANGING THE STANDARD DISPLAY

If you'd like, you can ask ORACLE to display its dates in the dBASE format. This sequence of two commands will do it:

```
SQL> COLUMN "DATE HIRED" FORMAT A20
SQL> SELECT FIRST, LAST,
   2    TO__CHAR (DATE__HIRED, 'MM/DD/YY') "DATE HIRED"
   3    FROM ROSTER;
```

It bears repeating that the COLUMN command is a SQL*Plus enhancement, not a standard SQL command. It's useful enough, though, that most other implementations of SQL will probably include some way to do the same things. In this case, the command issues instructions to display the column DATE HIRED in a format that is twenty characters in width. This makes things a little neater for display in this book. The command eliminates the cryptic effects of finding the full TO_CHAR( ) command used as a column heading. It also overcomes a play-it-safe tendency of SQL*Plus; when not instructed otherwise, the program will set up the largest column width it conceivably could need. The program thinks big while doing this, so the resulting claim usually covers acres of on-screen real estate.

Give Me an Argument

DATE HIRED is actually created as a pseudocolumn in Line 2 of the main command. The preceding TO_CHAR( ) function sets up the new column's contents. Within the function's brackets are two elements. In SQL as in most of computerdom, these are known as *arguments*. Each argument contains a *parameter,* which helps define exactly what the function will do.

Here, the first argument takes the date values from the actual column DATE_HIRED and transforms them to a character representation. The character-to-date, or CTOD( ) function in dBASE does the same thing. The second argument sets up a format for the character conversion. In this case, it calls for the standard dBASE display. To no one's surprise, then, the resulting output looks something like a dBASE display:

FIRST	LAST	DATE HIRED
ADDIE	DAVIDSON	09/09/79
DENNIS	MADISON	07/07/81
MISTY	PRESTO	06/19/78
HUBERT	TUBA	05/17/87
SUZANNE	MAHONEY	01/18/79
CHARLES	BUCHINSKY	12/18/86
VERA	PALMER	09/23/85
KATHLEEN	COLLINS	10/15/85
ROBERT	ZIMMERMAN	10/14/85
PHYLLIS	ROWE-HATTON	11/07/87

10 records selected.

Comparing Format Options

Both SQL*Plus and dBASE offer some formatting flexibility in displaying date fields or parts of them. Here's a dBASE command that makes use of several available options:

. LIST OFF DOW(DATE_HIRED), CMONTH(DATE_HIRED), DAY(DATE_HIRED), YEAR(DATE_HIRED)

These call for, in order:

- The day of the week, which appears in numerical form.
- The month, in character form. A related function, MONTH( ), returns a numerical version.
- The day of the month.
- The year.

LIST OFF is a version of the LIST command that omits column headings. In this case, the heading would be an awkward repetition of the full command. In SQL, you can replace such a display with a column alias. In dBASE, you can tell it to LIST OFF. Here are the results, preceded as usual by the record numbers:

```
 1   1 September    9   1979
 2   3 July         7   1981
 3   2 June        19   1978
 4   1 May         17   1987
 5   5 January     18   1979
 6   5 December    18   1986
 7   2 September   23   1985
 8   3 October     15   1985
 9   2 October     14   1985
10   7 November     7   1987
```

The days of the week appear in numerical form in Column 2. This indicates that either these examples have been made up or that the Personnel Department operates seven days a week.

MORE FLEXIBILITY IN SQL

A SQL command that produces approximately the same thing would be this:

```
SQL> SELECT TO_CHAR(DATE_HIRED, 'DAY, MONTH DD,
     YYYY')
  2  FROM ROSTER;
```

Instead of the dBASE functions, this command establishes a template for the display. As before, it calls for the day of the week, which SQL will spell out; a comma, the month, the day, and the year follow the day.

```
TO_CHAR(DATE_HIRED,'DAY,MONTHDD,YYYY')
-----------------------------------------------------------
SUNDAY     , SEPTEMBER 09, 1979
TUESDAY    , JULY      07, 1981
MONDAY     , JUNE      19, 1978
SUNDAY     , MAY       17, 1987
THURSDAY   , JANUARY   18, 1979
THURSDAY   , DECEMBER  18, 1986
MONDAY     , SEPTEMBER 23, 1985
TUESDAY    , OCTOBER   15, 1985
MONDAY     , OCTOBER   14, 1985
SATURDAY   , NOVEMBER  07, 1987
```

10 records selected.

Capitals Count

Not only will SQL respond to a template; it will also try to honor your choice in capital letters. For example, DAY will retrieve *MONDAY;* Day will produce *Monday.* This version of the previous command will show how it works:

```
SQL> SELECT TO_CHAR(DATE_HIRED, 'Day, Month DD,
     YYYY')
  2  FROM ROSTER;
```

The capitalization of the template has been changed; here are the results:

```
TO_CHAR(DATE_HIRED,'DAY,MONTHDD,YYYY')
-----------------------------------------------------------
Sunday     , September 09, 1979
Tuesday    , July      07, 1981
Monday     , June      19, 1978
```

```
Sunday      , May          17, 1987
Thursday    , January      18, 1979
Thursday    , December     18, 1986
Monday      , September    23, 1985
Tuesday     , October      15, 1985
Monday      , October      14, 1985
Saturday    , November     07, 1987
```

10 records selected.

To add a finishing touch, use a COLUMN command:

SQL> COLUMN "DATE HIRED" FORMAT A30

Now use the column name in the command:

```
SQL> SELECT TO__CHAR(DATE__HIRED,
  2    'Day, Month DD, YYYY') "DATE HIRED"
  3    FROM ROSTER;
```

Now you should see the following:

```
DATE HIRED
------------------------------------------------
Sunday    , September 09, 1979
Tuesday   , July       07, 1981
Monday    , June       19, 1978
Sunday    , May        17, 1987
Thursday  , January    18, 1979
Thursday  , December   18, 1986
Monday    , September  23, 1985
Tuesday   , October    15, 1985
Monday    , October    14, 1985
Saturday  , November   07, 1987
```

10 records selected.

Abbreviated Variations

Long and short forms of the template entries also produce full or spelled-out results. Here are some edited versions of the previous command, along with the resulting output:

```
SQL> LIST 1
  1*  SELECT TO__CHAR(DATE__HIRED, 'Day, Month DD,
      YYYY') "DATE HIRED"
```

```
SQL> CHANGE /Month/Mm/
   1*  SELECT  TO__CHAR(DATE__HIRED,  'Day,  Mm  DD,
       YYYY') "DATE HIRED"
SQL> run
   1   SELECT  TO__CHAR(DATE__HIRED,  'Day,  Mm  DD,
       YYYY') "DATE HIRED"
   2*  FROM ROSTER
```

DATE HIRED

```
Sunday    , 09 09, 1979
Tuesday   , 07 07, 1981
Monday    , 06 19, 1978
Sunday    , 05 17, 1987
Thursday  , 01 18, 1979
Thursday  , 12 18, 1986
Monday    , 09 23, 1985
Tueday    , 10 15, 1985
Monday    , 10 14, 1985
Saturday  , 11 07, 1987
```

10 records selected.

```
SQL> list 1
   1*  SELECT  TO__CHAR(DATE__HIRED,  'Day,  Mm  DD,
       YYYY') "DATE HIRED"
SQL> CHANGE /Mm/Mon/
   1*  SELECT  TO__CHAR(DATE__HIRED,  'Day,  Mon  DD,
       YYYY') "DATE HIRED"
SQL> RUN
   1   SELECT  TO__CHAR(DATE__HIRED,  'Day,  Mon  DD,
       YYYY') "DATE HIRED"
   2*  FROM ROSTER
```

DATE HIRED

```
Sunday    , Sep 09 , 1979
Tuesday   , Jul 07 , 1981
Monday    , Jun 19 , 1978
Sunday    , May 17, 1987
Thursday  , Jan 18 , 1979
Thursday  , Dec 18, 1986
```

Monday   , Sep 23, 1985
Tuesday , Oct 15, 1985
Monday   , Oct 14, 1985
Saturday , Nov 07, 1987

10 records selected.

Table 8-1 lists the major date-formatting commands.

There are enough variations to produce the legalistic "year of our Lord" presentation at the beginning of this chapter. For the record, the command that produced this was:

```
SQL> SELECT TO_CHAR(SYSDATE,
  2   '"This "DDTH "day of "Month" in the year of our Lord "Year')"
  3   FROM DUMMY;
```

TABLE 8-1 Date Formatting Elements

ELEMENT	MEANING
YYYY	Year.
SYYYY	Applies a minus sign (−) to any BC date.
YY	Displays last two digits of year. A single Y displays one digit; YYY displays three.
YEAR	Spells out year in capital letters.
Year	Spells out year in capital and lowercase letters.
SYEAR	Applies minus sign (−) to spelled-out B.C. years.
Q	Displays quarter.
MM	Displays month in figures.
MON	Abbreviates name of month in capital letters.
Mon	Puts the abbreviation in capital and lowercase letters.
DDD	Day of year in numbers.
DD	Day of month in numbers.
D	Day of week in numbers.
DAY	Name of day in capital letters.
Day	Name of day in capital and lowercase letters.
DY	Abbreviated name of day in capital letters.
Dy	Abbreviated name of day in capital and lowercase letters.
AM or PM	Displays the appropriate meridian indicator.
A.M. or P.M.	Displays the meridian indicator with periods.
HH or HH12	Displays the hour in a 12-hour format.
TH	Added to any code, produces an ordinal. For example, DDTH would produce "14TH."
SP	Spells out the numerical value to which it is attached. DDSP would produce "FOURTEEN."
SPTH OR THSP	Spells out number and makes it an ordinal. DDSPTH produces "FOURTEENTH."

Single quotes enclose the whole template. Within these single quotes, double quotes enclose the text that appears in the final presentation. Be careful to include all necessary spaces. Outside the double quotes (look carefully) are SQL commands for the date, followed by *TH;* the month spelled out; and the year. Another set of double quotes appears outside the single quotes that mark the boundaries of the template. This is the part of the command in which you specify the column heading. In this case, the heading will be blank.

You can also include periods, commas, and other punctuation marks in a template. You need not enclose these within double quotation marks as you must enclose other characters, but the entire template must always be bracketed by single quotes.

Not Bad for a Dummy

The structure of the last command suggests that there is a table called DUMMY. In fact, there is. It comes with your ORACLE package and is the most simple table in all SQL. The table DUMMY has one column, also called DUMMY, and one row, whose value is zero.

For such a simple entity, DUMMY is quite useful. It does much the same thing that a dBASE question mark does: it returns a single value. Had we asked SQL to produce the "year of our Lord" sequence from the hiring dates in the Roster table, the phrase would have been repeated ten times, once for each row in ROSTER. Applying it to the single, simple row in DUMMY, the phrase is produced only once, which is enough.

DISPLAYING THE TIME OF DAY

You can format a SQL time command to display the time as well as the date:

```
SQL> SELECT TO_CHAR(
   2    DATE_HIRED, 'MM/DD/YY MM:HH AM') "DATE HIRED"
   3    FROM ROSTER;
```

This produces the following:

```
DATE HIRED
------------------------------------------------
09/09/79 09:12 AM
07/07/81 07:12 AM
```

```
06/19/78  06:12 AM
05/17/87  05:12 AM
01/18/79  01:12 AM
12/18/86  12:12 AM
09/23/85  09:12 AM
10/15/85  10:12 AM
10/14/85  10:12 AM
11/07/87  11:12 AM
```

10 records selected.

The template of this command has an AM at the end, and all the times reported appear to be in the morning. Is this really the case? Actually, this table was created by importing it from dBASE using the conversion program in Chapter 2. No times were ever added to the date values, but ORACLE appears to have created some anyway. Their origin is uncertain, but the correspondence between hour and month is probably no coincidence.

What would happen, though, if you were to amend the template to specify PM instead of AM? After editing, the command would read:

```
1   SELECT TO__CHAR(
2   DATE__HIRED, 'MM/DD/YY MM:HH PM') "DATE HIRED"
3*  FROM ROSTER
```

There's no need to print the results here. They are exactly the same as those produced by the previous command.

DATE ARITHMETIC

When you're "up to your neck" in date formats and other fun formulas, it's hard to remember that your original objective was to evaluate the employees. David Madison did eventually remember this. Because he was experimenting with SQL dates at the time, he asked himself the logical question, "Which employees are due for our appraisal, and when are they due?"

dBASE DATE ARITHMETIC

Employees are normally appraised at one-year intervals; Hubert Tuba, using dBASE, contrived a simple command:

. LIST DATE__HIRED, DATE__HIRED + 365

It produced results that were more or less expected:

Record#	DATE__HIRED	DATE__HIRED + 365
1	09/09/79	09/08/80
2	07/07/81	07/07/82
3	06/19/78	06/19/79
4	05/17/87	05/16/88
5	01/18/79	01/18/80
6	12/18/86	12/18/87
7	09/23/85	09/23/86
8	10/15/85	10/15/86
9	10/14/85	10/14/86
10	11/07/87	11/06/88

The problem, of course, is that dBASE added only 365 days to each date. It recorded everyone's first anniversary on the job, but this is more or less useless information—dBase also ignored leap years.

SQL PRESENTS ANOTHER PROBLEM

Misty Presto had gone through a similar exercise in SQL:

```
SQL> COLUMN "REVIEW DATE" FORMAT A20
SQL> SELECT LAST, DATE__HIRED,
  2     DATE__HIRED + 365 "REVIEW DATE"
  3     FROM ROSTER;
```

"You did a little better than Hubie did," Madison observed. "You formatted the column, and you included the people's names. You still, however, have nothing more than anniversary dates. In fact, you have less than anniversary dates. Mr. Tuba, see if you can find what's wrong with this output?"

LAST	DATE__HIRE	REVIEW__DATE
DAVIDSON	09-SEP-79	08-SEP-80
MADISON	07-JUL-81	07-JUL-82
PRESTO	19-JUN-78	19-JUN-79
TUBA	17-MAY-87	16-MAY-88

MAHONEY	18-JAN-79	18-JAN-80
BUCHINSKY	18-DEC-86	18-DEC-87
PALMER	23-SEP-85	23-SEP-86
COLLINS	15-OCT-85	15-OCT-86
ZIMMERMAN	14-OCT-85	14-OCT-86
ROWE-HATTON	07-NOV-87	06-NOV-88

10 records selected.

"It seems that my anniversary falls a day short," Tuba observed, "as do Mrs. Rowe-Hatton's and Miss Davidson's. What could have caused that?"

"Leap year," said Madison. "When you add 365 days, and there's a 366th in there somewhere, you're in trouble. I'd say SQL outsmarted itself this time."

USING A DATE FUNCTION

Actually, SQL is even smarter than Madison realized. It has a function, ADD_MONTHS, that adds months instead of days to a date. Here, it is applied to the previous query:

```
SQL> SELECT LAST, DATE_HIRED "DATE HIRED",
  2    ADD_MONTHS(DATE_HIRED, 12) "REVIEW DATE"
  3    FROM ROSTER;
```

The command produces these results:

LAST	DATE HIRED	REVIEW DATE
DAVIDSON	09-SEP-79	09-SEP-80
MADISON	07-JUL-81	07-JUL-82
PRESTO	19-JUN-78	19-JUN-79
TUBA	17-MAY-87	17-MAY-88
MAHONEY	18-JAN-79	18-JAN-80
BUCHINSKY	18-DEC-86	18-DEC-87
PALMER	23-SEP-85	23-SEP-86
COLLINS	15-OCT-85	15-OCT-86
ZIMMERMAN	14-OCT-85	14-OCT-86
ROWE-HATTON	07-NOV-87	07-NOV-88

10 records selected.

USING THE SYSTEM DATE

"I see another problem," said Madison. "It's normal for a new employee's first appraisal to come after 90 days."

"I have a solution to that," Presto exclaimed. "First, let's use the SYSDATE( ) function. That refers to the system date—the little calendar they keep inside the computer. If you want to find it, all you have to do is type this":

```
SQL> SELECT SYSDATE
   2   FROM DUMMY;
```

And the answer was:

```
SYSDATE
------------------
11-DEC-87
```

COUNTING THE DAYS

"That's very nice," said Madison, "but what can we do with it?"

"Well, we can figure out how many days there are until Christmas."

The query was:

```
SQL> COLUMN TODAY FORMAT A20
SQL> SELECT
   2   TO__CHAR(SYSDATE, 'MM/DD/YY HH:MM  PM')
       TODAY,
   3   TO__DATE('25-DEC-87') − SYSDATE LEFT
   4   FROM DUMMY;
```

The answer arrived in more detail than anyone had expected:

```
TODAY               LEFT
------------------- ----------
12/11/87 08:12 AM    13.6269
```

"I guess we'd better hurry before it gets down to 13.6268 days," said Madison. "Really, I do think ORACLE is cutting it much too fine."

"I can do something about that," said Presto. She entered the following:

```
SQL> SELECT
   2   TO__CHAR(SYSDATE, 'MM/DD/YY  HH:MM  PM')
       TODAY,
   3   TO__DATE('25-DEC-87') − ROUND(SYSDATE) LEFT
   4   FROM DUMMY;
```

This version added a ROUND( ) function. When applied to a number, such a function usually will round off decimal places. When applied to an ORACLE date, it rounds to the nearest day:

```
TODAY                 LEFT
--------------------  ------
12/11/87  08:12  AM     14
```

"I suppose that if we waited until after noon to do this, it would say we had only 13 days left," said Madison. He was right.

APPLYING DATE ARITHMETIC

This still did not solve the problem of calculating appraisal dates. However, Misty Presto had just begun her demonstration of how to use the system date. "I was going to find out the names of the people who have been here for fewer than 90 days. Of course, we already know who that person is." Even so, she ran this query:

```
SQL> SELECT LAST, DATE__HIRED "DATE HIRED"
   2   FROM ROSTER
   3   WHERE DATE__HIRED > SYSDATE−90;
```

This query asks for the names of all the employees who were hired fewer than 90 days prior to the current date. As expected, the results are:

```
LAST              DATE HIRED
----------------  -----------------
ROWE-HATTON       07-NOV-87
```

"I even know how to find out when her review date really is," said Presto, and she entered:

```
SQL> SELECT LAST, DATE__HIRED + 90 "REVIEW DATE"
   2   FROM ROSTER
   3   WHERE DATE__HIRED > SYSDATE − 90;
```

The first line adds 90 days to the hiring date and assigns this figure to the REVIEW DATE column. The WHERE clause, as before, limits the search to those who have been employees for 90 or fewer days:

```
LAST             REVIEW DATE
---------------  -----------------
ROWE-HATTON      05-FEB-88
```

THE FINAL APPRAISAL SCHEDULE

"Okay," said Madison. "You've screened out all the fewer-than-90-days' wonders. Now, what about all those other people?"

"Well, you see, once I figured out how to add and subtract dates and use these functions, I figured out that I could do this in a WHERE clause, too." She entered:

```
SQL> SELECT LAST,
  2    TO_CHAR(DATE_HIRED, 'Month') "REVIEW DATE"
  3    FROM ROSTER
  4    WHERE DATE_HIRED < ADD_MONTHS(SYSDATE,-3)
```

"I see," said Madison. "Down there in Line 4, you added months, but you really subtracted them. Very clever. Now, I suppose we're going to see the results of all this." He was right again:

```
LAST           REVIEW DATE
-------------  -----------------
DAVIDSON       September
MADISON        July
PRESTO         June
TUBA           May
MAHONEY        January
BUCHINSKY      December
PALMER         September
COLLINS        October
ZIMMERMAN      October
```

9 records selected.

"Even more clever than I thought," said Madison. "You used a formatting template to isolate the month in which the review is

TABLE 8-2 SQL Date Functions

FUNCTION	EXAMPLE	COMMENT
ADD__MONTHS()	ADD__MONTHS(SYSDATE,3)	Accepts date, adds indicated number of months.
GREATEST()	GREATEST(DATE1, DATE2)	Returns the later of two dates.
LEAST()	LEAST(DATE1, DATE2)	Returns the earlier of two dates.
LAST__DAY()	LAST__DAY(DATE__HIRED)	Returns the last day of the month in which the indicated date occurs.
MONTHS__BETWEEN	MONTHS__BETWEEN (DATE__HIRED, SYSDATE)	Calculates the number of months between two dates.
TO__CHAR	TO__CHAR(DATE__HIRED, 'MM/DD/YY')	Converts a date value to a character display, using the indicated template. Similar to the dBASE DTOC() function.
TO__DATE	TO__DATE(DATE__HIRED, 'MM/DD/YY')	Converts a character string to its corresponding date value. The template indicates the format of the character version. Similar to the dBASE CTOD() function.

due, and you used a date function to select only those people who've been around for more than 90 days. Keep this up, and you'll be on network television some day."

MORE FUNCTIONS

The functions used in these exercises are only a few of those available. A more complete list is shown in Table 8-2.

USING DATES IN COMMANDS

As the previous exercise demonstrates, you can use date functions in any element of a SQL command.

A DATE AS A CONDITION

This example uses a date function to set the conditions for the SELECT command, then it uses the same function in a GROUP BY command:

```
SQL> SELECT TO_CHAR(DATE_HIRED, 'YYYY') "DATE
      HIRED",
2     COUNT (*) NUMBER
3     FROM ROSTER
4     GROUP BY TO_CHAR(DATE_HIRED, 'YYYY');
```

This command creates a two-column report. The first column extracts the year from each employee's hiring date. The second column reports the number of employees hired during that year. The entire report is grouped in chronological order:

```
DATE HIRED  NUMBER
-----------  ----------------
1978                1
1979                2
1981                1
1985                3
1986                1
1987                2
```

6 records selected.

THE TO_DATE CONVERSION

Another way to use a date function in a command occurred in Chapter 2. You probably didn't notice, and if you did you may have been confused.

Chapter 2 presented a linked pair of dBASE and SQL command files that converted a dBASE file into a SQL table. Each INSERT command that created a new record included this sequence:

```
TO_DATE('01/09/49','MM/DD/YY')
```

TO_DATE is just the reverse of TO_CHAR. During the conversion process, dBASE records its date entries as character values. In the SQL command file, TO_DATE converts these characters into the SQL date format.

TO_DATE uses a template just as TO_CHAR does, but, again, the process works in reverse. A template in TO_DATE describes the form in which the program will find the date value.

Once it knows what kind of format to look for, ORACLE knows what it must to do make the change.

REVIEW QUESTIONS

1. What is the SQL equivalent of the dBASE DTOC( ) function?
2. Name an important use of TO__CHAR.
3. If you were going to give an argument to a SQL date function, what would you give it?
4. How would the date December 7, 1941 appear if you specified the format "DD Dy. YY".
5. How about the same date in this format: "DDth of Day, YYYY'?
6. The DUMMY table supplied with ORACLE contains hardly anything; still, it must be good for something. What is it good for?
7. The formula TODAY + 365 should give you the same date next year. It works only about 75 percent of the time. Explain why, and tell what you can do about it.
8. The command used in this chapter to count employees according to the years in which they were hired can be adapted to a common research use. For extra credit, can you identify this use? HINT: It doesn't have to be done with dates.

ANSWERS

1. TO__CHAR().
2. Establish a custom format for date displays. Give yourself credit if you thought of another important use.
3. Effective arguments would consist of two parameters: the date to be displayed and a format for the display.
4. 12 Dec. 41.
5. 7th of December, 1941.
6. DUMMY is a vehicle for displaying a value defined completely in the SQL command and not taken from any table.
7. Adding 365 days does not allow for leap years. ADD-MONTHS(TODAY, 12) makes all necessary allowances.
8. The count-by-date exercise was a simple example of cross-tabulation.

Working with Null Values

WHAT IS A NULL VALUE?

USING NULL VALUES

NVL( ): SOMETHING FROM NOTHING

"Curiouser and curiouser," muttered David Madison as he mulled over a list of UnderFed customers. "I find our regional manager, Ms. Allison Wunderland, on our customer list. But I find no entry for her income classification."

The customer table that caused Madison so much confusion is shown in Figure 9-1. It lists typical directory information. It also includes five columns of codes that represent demographic information about the customers. The codes represent certain income brackets, occupational class, and so on. The official titles of these five columns are INCOME, PROFESSION, RESIDENCE, HOME_OWNER, and AGE_GROUP. Because SQL truncates column headings to any designated column width, these appear as I, P, R, H and A.

WHAT IS A NULL VALUE?

"Oh, that's easily explained," said Addie Davidson. "Of course, Ms. Wunderland is entitled to have an account with us. After all, we do work for the same bank."

"Yes, but why the blank for her income class?"

"Do you think she likes the idea that people in her own organization could look up this file and find out how much she makes? Even though we only list customers' incomes in broad classes?"

"No, I guess she wouldn't."

"You remember what happened when somebody put my salary on the internal computer bulletin board."

FIGURE 9-1   The Customer Table with a Few Null Values

```
SSNO          LAST         FIRST     I STREET           CITY        ST ZIP   I P R H A
-----------   -----------  --------  - ---------------  ---------   -- ----- - - - - -

222-33-4444   BUNNY        ESTHER    C 2813 N. THIRD    ELSIE       NB 69134 1 3 3 2 1
333-44-4444   HAMMERSTEIN  ROGER     A 117 W. TARGET    BOWSTRING   MN 56631 4 2 2 1 3
666-77-8888   BUNNY        BUD       B 2813 N. THIRD    ELSIE       NB 69134 2 3 3 1 1
777-88-9999   STARR        WOODY     A 603 E. PINE      FOSSIL      OR 97830 0   1 1 2
888-99-0000   BENJAMIN     FRANKLIN  X 1627 CHEW ST.    WYSOX       PA 18854 3 2 2 2 3
999-00-1111   DRIVER       SCROOGE   Q 121 GOLIAD       SANDY       TX 78665 3 4 2 1 3
111-22-3333   WUNDERLAND   ALLISON   N 2 ROYAL WAY      GLENCOE     AR 72539   1 1 1 2

7 records selected.
```

"Yeah. You lost two friends and four casual acquaintances. Then, how about this Starr fella? He shows an income of zero, whereas our courageous leader has a blank, and Starr has a blank for his occupation."

"When he took out the account, Mr. Starr was unemployed, so when we created his record, we entered a zero for his income class."

"Well, that's how much he was earning at the time."

"Then, we left a null value for his occupation. Shouldn't that be a zero as well?"

"No, we don't have an occupational code of zero."

"So you left it empty instead."

"Right. When you leave something empty, that's a null value. We did the same thing when we left Ms. Wunderland's salary out of the table. She does get paid, you know."

"So zero is zero, and null is empty."

"That's a very good way of looking at it."

WHEN SOMETHING IS MISSING

Thus did Dennis Madison encounter the concept of a null value. In SQL, a null value may be missing, unknown or irrelevant. It may be omitted on purpose, as with Wunderland's income class. If a table were to contain the responses to a marketing survey, there would be nulls to indicate questions that the respondents did not answer.

However, a null value is not the same as zero. A null value is a value that isn't there. Starr had an income of zero. There *was* a value to be entered, no matter how minimal it was. Wunderland had an income, but it was not entered. Thus, Wunderland had a null value in her income column and Starr did not.

SEARCHING FOR NULLS

The difference between a null and a zero will be apparent when you include them in a search term. A search for a zero might be this:

```
SQL> SELECT LAST, PROFESSION
  2    FROM CUSTOMER
  3    WHERE INCOME = 0;
```

The result is:

```
LAST              P
------------------ -
STARR
```

This query retrieved Starr's record because its income value is zero. However, there is no visible value in the profession display, because that column contains a null value for Starr.

Now, conduct the same search with one exception. Instead of searching for the zero value, search for the SQL condition called IS NULL:

```
SQL> SELECT LAST, PROFESSION
  2   FROM CUSTOMER
  3   WHERE INCOME IS NULL;
```

This command results in:

```
LAST              P
------------------ -
WUNDERLAND    1
```

HARD TO SATISFY

A null will satisfy only one search condition: IS NULL. Of course, in addition to searching for records that meet this condition, you can also search for records that do not:

```
SQL> SELECT LAST, INCOME
  2   FROM CUSTOMER
  3   WHERE INCOME IS NOT NULL;
```

The result is:

```
LAST              I
------------------ -
BUNNY            1
HAMMERSTEIN   4
BUNNY            2
STARR            0
BENJAMIN        3
DRIVER           3
```

6 records selected.

This query retrieved all the records whose income value was not null, including Starr's zero. You should notice, though, that Wunderland, with a null in her income figure, does not appear in this list.

OTHER COMPARISONS

To further demonstrate that a null is nothing at all, enter this query:

```
SQL> SELECT LAST, INCOME
   2    FROM CUSTOMER
   3    WHERE INCOME < 2;
```

If a null is less than 2, Allison Wunderland's record should appear. This, however, is not the case. A null is nothing. It has no value, either greater than, or less than, 2:

```
LAST                I
----------------- -
BUNNY               1
STARR               0
```

NULLS AND CHARACTER VALUES

Any type of value, not just a number, can be a null. Here's the command to add the record of a new customer. This particular customer happens to have no middle initial. He also currently lacks a home address:

```
SQL> INSERT INTO CUSTOMER VALUES
   2    ('012-12-1212', 'BONGO', 'BING', ' ', ' ',
   3    'NEW YORK', 'NY', '10000',
   4    3,2,2,2,2)
```

In Line 2, there are two sets of paired apostrophes. The two apostrophes with nothing between them indicate a string with nothing in it. As far as SQL is concerned, this is a null value. Were there a space between the apostrophes, the resulting entry would be a space, such as that between two words. The space would not be a null value; it would be a one-letter Char value. Be careful, too, not to confuse these paired apostrophes with quotations marks, which are something else entirely.

To see the effect of the null values on the table, enter the query:

```
SQL> SELECT LAST, FIRST, INIT,
  2    STREET, CITY, STATE
  3    FROM CUSTOMER;
```

The resulting display is shown in Figure 9-2. In the last row appear null values.

USING NULL VALUES

The presence of a null value has an effect on most SQL operations. The best way to predict what those effects might be is to remember that a null has no particular place in any normal ordering system. Because it is a nonentity, it cannot be sorted or calculated.

IN ORDER

Ordering is a major case in point. When you use an ORDER BY clause and display the records in ascending order, the nulls will appear first:

```
SQL> SELECT LAST, INCOME
  2    FROM CUSTOMER
  3    ORDER BY INCOME;
```

FIGURE 9-2   Null Char Values Appear as Blanks

```
    LAST              FIRST            I  STREET             CITY              ST
    ---------------   ---------------  -  ---------------    ---------------   --
    BUNNY             ESTHER           C  2813 N. THIRD      ELSIE             NB
    HAMMERSTEIN       ROGER            A  117 W. TARGET      BOWSTRING         MN
    BUNNY             BUD              B  2813 N. THIRD      ELSIE             NB
    STARR             WOODY            A  603 E. PINE        FOSSIL            OR
    BENJAMIN          FRANKLIN         X  1627 CHEW ST.      WYSOX             PA
    DRIVER            SCROOGE          Q  121 GOLIAD         SANDY             TX
    WUNDERLAND        ALLISON          N  2 ROYAL WAY        GLENCOE           AR
    BONGO             BING                                   NEW YORK          NY

    8 records selected.
```

Allison Wunderland, because of her null income value, will appear first, followed by Woody Starr with his income value of zero:

```
LAST              I
----------------- -
WUNDERLAND
STARR             0
BUNNY             1
BUNNY             2
BENJAMIN          3
DRIVER            3
BONGO             3
HAMMERSTEIN       4
```

8 records selected.

However, when you put the same results in descending rather than in ascending order, you'll find that the null values still come first. That puts Wunderland ahead even of the wealthy Roger Hammerstein:

```
SQL> SELECT LAST, INCOME
  2    FROM CUSTOMER
  3    ORDER BY INCOME DESC;

LAST              I
----------------- -
WUNDERLAND
HAMMERSTEIN       4
BENJAMIN          3
DRIVER            3
BONGO             3
BUNNY             2
BUNNY             1
STARR             0
```

8 records selected.

NULLS IN EXPRESSIONS AND FUNCTIONS

When a SQL function or expression refers to a null value, the result will also be null. Say, for example, that UnderFed should decide to alter the income scales it uses in its customer demographic records. The scheme will begin by increasing every existing class by one digit. Income group 1 will become group 2 and so on. This query will test the results of such a change before you actually commit yourself:

```
SQL> SELECT LAST, INCOME, INCOME+1
   2    FROM CUSTOMER;

LAST                 I   INCOME+1
-----------------    -   ----------
BUNNY                1       2
HAMMERSTEIN          4       5
BUNNY                2       3
STARR                0       1
BENJAMIN             3       4
DRIVER               3       4
WUNDERLAND
BONGO                3       4

8 records selected.
```

This result should confirm the power of ranking executives to cause awkward moments. Everyone's income class was increased by one except Allison Wunderland's. Her entry started as a null, and it remains a null.

NO-COUNT NULLS

Whenever it's possible to ignore a null value, a SQL function will do so. This command uses the COUNT( ) function in two ways:

```
SQL> SELECT COUNT(SSNO), COUNT(INCOME)
   2    FROM CUSTOMER;
```

The function first counts the number of entries in a column in which we know there are no null values. The second counts the number of values in INCOME, in which there is one null value. The results show that COUNT( ) ignored the null:

```
COUNT(SSNO)    COUNT(INCOME)
---------------   ------------------
      8                7
```

AVERAGES AND MISSING VALUES

SQL's ability to record but ignore null values can be valuable in applications such as scientific or market research. There, it is often necessary to identify a missing value, such as a survey question that the respondent did not answer, and to separate it from actual responses. You can record the missing values as nulls, so that they won't show up in your averages or in other calculations unless you want them to. Lack of this ability has been criticized as a major shortcoming in dBASE.

To demonstrate, use the AVG( ) function to compute an otherwise meaningless figure—the mean income class from the CUSTOMER table:

```
SQL> SELECT AVG(INCOME)
  2    FROM CUSTOMER;

AVG(INCOME)
---------------
       2.28571
```

There are eight rows in this sample database; seven of them have non-null values. An average that includes the null value can be calculated like this:

```
SQL> SELECT SUM(INCOME)/8
  2    FROM CUSTOMER;

SUM(INCOME)/8
-----------------
            2
```

The result is, only by chance, a round number. The significant fact is that the number is smaller than it was before. The same calculation using only the non-null values would be:

```
SQL> SELECT SUM(INCOME)/7
  2    FROM CUSTOMER;

SUM(INCOME)/7
-----------------
       2.28571
```

This is the same fraction that AVG( ) produced. It's obvious that the function also restricted itself to the non-null values.

NVL( ): SOMETHING FROM NOTHING

There may be times that you want to treat a null value as a real value in your queries or calculations. This is the purpose of the null value, or NVL( ), function. It temporarily turns a null value into the real value of your choice.

NVL( ) requires two arguments. The first is the name of the column in which the null value or values appear. The second is the value that you want to assign to each null for this occasion. When NVL( ) encounters a non-null value, it will accept that value. When it finds a null, it will use, instead, the value you assigned in the second argument.

EVERYONE MOVES UP

Here's a variation on the earlier exercise that increased the income class by one. This time, it uses NVL( ) to treat the null value as a zero:

```
SQL> SELECT LAST, NVL(INCOME,0)+1
  2    FROM CUSTOMER;
```

In this version, even Allison Wunderland moves up a class. Because she started from zero instead of from a null value, the program added one, just as it did for everyone else:

LAST	NVL(INCOME,0)+1
BUNNY	2
HAMMERSTEIN	5
BUNNY	3
STARR	1
BENJAMIN	4
DRIVER	4
WUNDERLAND	1
BONGO	4

8 records selected.

IT DOESN'T HAVE TO BE ZERO

Your natural instinct in using NVL( ) would be to assign to a null a value of zero. Actually, you can use any value that SQL will recognize. Say, for instance, that you want to flag null entries by assigning them a value that is clearly outside the normal range:

```
SQL> SELECT LAST, NVL(INCOME,99)
  2   FROM CUSTOMER;
```

Normal values fall in the range of 0 to 4, but the null shows itself as a 99:

LAST	NVL(INCOME,99)
BUNNY	1
HAMMERSTEIN	4
BUNNY	2
STARR	0
BENJAMIN	3
DRIVER	3
WUNDERLAND	99
BONGO	3

8 records selected.

PRESENT AND ACCOUNTED FOR

In queries and calculations in which SQL normally treats a null as the nonentity it is, a null converted with NVL() can be readily included.

```
SQL> SELECT LAST, PROFESSION
  2   FROM CUSTOMER
  3   WHERE NVL(INCOME,99) > 2;
```

The result proves that 99 is indeed larger than 2:

LAST	P
HAMMERSTEIN	2
BENJAMIN	2
DRIVER	4
WUNDERLAND	1
BONGO	2

AWARENESS COUNTS

As the averaging exercise demonstrated, it pays to keep track of the nulls in your database. If you don't acknowledge their presence, they could have an unintended effect on your results. In other words, your output will be wrong. Use NVL( ) when you want to include nulls; otherwise, SQL will assume you want to ignore them.

Any type of value can be a null. In addition, you can use NVL( ) to temporarily assign to a null any type of non-null value. The only requirement is that the type match that of the values in the rest of the column.

For example, you could use NVL( ) to assign a string value that would specifically identify a value as missing. To do this with the missing street address in CUSTOMER, the format would be:

```
NVL(STREET, 'MISSING')
```

You could apply this to the query that produced Figure 9-2:

```
SQL> SELECT LAST, FIRST, INIT,
   2    NVL(STREET, 'MISSING') CITY, STATE
   3    FROM CUSTOMER;
```

Instead of the blank street address in Mr. Bongo's row, the resulting output will display the word MISSING.

REVIEW QUESTIONS

1. A null value is literally nothing; of what possible use can it be?
2. Write a WHERE clause that searches for a null value.
3. Write a WHERE clause that searches for all values except nulls or zeros.
4. You cannot sort on the basis of null values; where, then, will they inevitably appear in an ordered output?
5. When a SQL function or expression refers to a null value, what will be the inevitable result?
6. SQL normally does its best to ignore null values. What can you do to overcome this tendency?
7. Say that, for some reason, you want your null values to appear as 10s. How would you make them do this?

ANSWERS

1. A null value is usually the best way to handle data that are missing or omitted. It will not be included in averages, counts, or similar calculations, unless you specify that it should be.

2.   WHERE <value> IS NULL.
3.   WHERE <value> > 0 AND <value> IS NOT NULL.

4. At the beginning, regardless of the sorting order.
5. The result will also be null.
6. There are at least two possibilities: Construct a WHERE clause to search for NULL or NOT NULL, or use the NVL() function.
7. Use the function NVL(<value>,10).

Up Periscope: Using the View

The view is an unimportant part of dBASE III Plus. Few serious dBASE users have found much use for it. That's unfortunate, because proper use of views can make your database both more secure and easier to use. The view is a very important part of SQL.

WHAT IS A VIEW, ANYWAY?

Many commentators have compared the view to a window. When you look through a window, you can see certain things; there are other things that you can't see from that particular vantage point. A view can be more than just a window. It can be a telescope that zooms in on one critical section of your data. It can be a periscope that lets you see things from a new direction. It can even be a kaleidoscope that combines bits and pieces into interesting new patterns.

The ORACLE manual presents another kind of visual image: think of your data as a piece of sculpture. The book suggests you look at it from many different angles. Each slant provides a new perspective. When you look at your data through a view, each angle also offers a new perspective.

THE VIRTUAL TABLE PLUS

C. J. Date avoids metaphors and goes straight to the facts of the matter: a view is a kind of virtual table.

There was a brief introduction to virtual tables in Chapter 1; a virtual table is any table other than a real one. It can be a selected group of rows and columns from an existing table. It can be a collection of selected data from two or more tables. Any time you issue a query other than SELECT * from a single table, you create a virtual table. The results will appear to be a single table, made up of parts of one or more larger wholes.

The view is a virtual table that's lost its transient status. If you use a query to create a virtual table, that table will exist within the computer only for as long as it remains on the screen. However, you can use a very similar command to create a view. The view will have a name, and its specifications will be stored in the database. Once you've done that, you can query the view as though it were a real table. Actually, the only thing the database will store is a set of specifications which recreate the view, at your command, from tables that do exist.

CREATING A SIMPLE VIEW

The case load at McKnife, Tawdry has fleshed out quite a bit since last time you saw it. Allen Tawdry's impromptu compensation study may have lacked scientific precision, but it convinced members of the firm they must do more to earn their pay. Many of them now have substantial caseloads. The expanded CASES table is shown in Figure 10-1.

Among the cases are two that involve a major client. If you want to isolate these from the full table, you could command;

```
SQL> SELECT CASE, COUNSEL
   2   FROM CASES
   3   WHERE CLIENT = 'CLOVERHOUSE';
```

FIGURE 10-1   The Expanded CASES Table

```
CASE                             CLIENT            COUNSEL
------------------------------   ---------------   ---------------
MICHIGAN V. NORTHWESTERN         MULLER            COSSACK
PEASE V. QUIETTE                 QUIETTE           BOYSENBERRY
KATELEY V. ELLISON               ELLISON           BUNSEN
PEOPLE V. CLOVERHOUSE            CLOVERHOUSE       MUKLUK
GREENHEAD V. CLOVERHOUSE         CLOVERHOUSE       COSSACK
HAMMER V. BELL                   BELL              BUNSEN
NOTTINGHAM V. KINGSFIELD         NOTTINGHAM        TUCKER
CROWE V. MAGNON                  MAGNON            BOYSENBERRY
SUTCLIFFE V. TUDOR               SUTCLIFFE         MASON
CANNERY V. ROWE                  ROWE              BAILEY
ASHTON V. TATE                   ASHTON            HARTLESS
WILEY V. COYOTE                  WILEY             MUKLUK
ASKEW V. ELLE                    ASKEW             BUNSEN
IRVING V. BYRD                   BYRD              TUCKER
DEE V. BASIE                     DEE               MASON
REALE V. STATE                   REALE             BAILEY
LONG V. ISLANDER                 LONG              HARTLESS
LABOR V. PAYNE                   PAYNE             MUKLUK
WARD V. PREFECT                  WARD              COSSACK
LEVITT V. BEAVERS                BEAVERS           BUNSEN
QUICK V. SILVER                  SILVER            TUCKER
FRONTERO V. PAGE                 PAGE              BOYSENBERRY
COMMONER V. STOCK                STOCK             MASON
AXEL V. RODD                     AXEL              BAILEY
ANDREA V. CHEEVER                CHEEVER           HARTLESS
MANUEL V. STILES                 STILES            MUKLUK

26 records selected.
```

This command will produce a virtual table consisting only of two selected rows and two selected columns from the actual table:

```
CASE                                         COUNSEL
-------------------------------------        ----------
PEOPLE V. CLOVERHOUSE                         MUKLUK
GREENHEAD V. CLOVERHOUSE                      COSSACK
```

You can create a view that presents the same information. The command is:

```
SQL> CREATE VIEW RETAINER
   2         AS SELECT CASE, COUNSEL
   3         FROM CASES
   4         WHERE CLIENT = 'CLOVERHOUSE';
```

This is the same query, except that it creates a view. This view has the name RETAINER. An AS precedes a query that describes the contents of the view. Unless you receive an error message, you should see nothing new on your screen except the confirmation:

```
View created.
```

Now that you've created the view, you can pretend it's a table. You can even issue a query command to it:

```
SQL> SELECT *
   2    FROM RETAINER;
```

The results:

```
CASE                                         COUNSEL
-------------------------------------        ----------
PEOPLE V. CLOVERHOUSE                         MUKLUK
GREENHEAD V. CLOVERHOUSE                      COSSACK
```

These are exactly the same as the results achieved previously, with one significant exception. RETAINER is in your database, ready to be used just like a real table would be. You can do anything you would with a real table, including killing it with DROP VIEW RETAINER.

RULES FOR CREATING A VIEW

A CREATE VIEW command has two main elements. The first is:

```
CREATE  VIEW  <name>  AS
```

The second element is the query that creates the view. Like most other queries, this should have three elements of its own:

- The columns to be displayed in the view. These can retain the names they have been given in the source table(s), or you can assign aliases to them.
- The rows to be displayed. These are specified by a WHERE clause.
- The table or tables from which the data are to be selected. This can include other existing views.

The query that creates a view can contain any valid query expression, with one exception. You may not use ORDER BY to create the view. If you want your display in a certain order, use ORDER BY when you query the view.

WHY DO THIS?

There are two main reasons to use views. The first is that views can help you *secure your data*. The two main tables being used in this book both contain salary data. You wouldn't want just anyone to be able to call up this information on the screen. Therefore, you restrict access to the full table. Those who need information such as names and addresses can be given access to views that display only the "safe" columns.

The second reason to use views is to *make things easier*. A SQL query can sometimes be a convoluted exercise. Must you type it every time you want to retrieve the data it describes? No. Turn the query into a view. That way you can store the query until next time you need it. Then, instead of executing the full query again, you can simply SELECT * from the view.

HOW dBASE DOES IT

The view is a subject of some disdain among dBASE users, who often write command files to serve the same purpose. Just as a SQL view does, a dBASE view gives you an isolated look at a particular body of data.

To create a dBASE version of RETAINER you would issue the command:

- CREATE VIEW RETAINER

You would then be presented with several menu selections that would let you:

- Select one or more files from which the view is to be extracted. In this case, it would be the single file CASES.
- Establish the relationships between multiple files, if any.
- Select the fields or columns to be displayed. To duplicate the SQL CASES view, these would be CASE and COUNSEL.
- Write a filter formula to select the records you want. In the current example, that formula would be CLIENT = 'CLOVER-HOUSE.'

In short, you would do almost exactly the same thing in either dBASE or SQL. As a dBASE user, you then could SET VIEW TO RETAINER and proceed as though there were a dBASE file of that name and configuration. If you were using the security features of dBASE's network version, you could control access to both the view and the table from which it sprang.

HOW SQL DOES IT

A dBASE view is basically a collection of filters. The commands that make up a dBASE view filter out certain database files, certain fields, and certain records. SQL does much the same thing, but by means of a different process.

When you query a SQL view, the program binds your query to the query that created the view in the first place. Binding is also used in artificial intelligence languages such as Prolog. In fact, SQL has much in common with AI.

When two SQL queries are bound, the query you issue acts in tandem with the query that formed the view. The command:

```
SELECT * FROM RETAINER
```

. . . has the same effect as:

```
SELECT * FROM CASES
WHERE CLIENT = 'CLOVERHOUSE'
```

A MORE COMPLEX VIEW

The good folks at McKnife, Tawdry might be interested in calling up separate records of their civil and criminal cases. This query will list their pending civil cases:

```
SQL> SELECT * FROM CASES
   2    WHERE COUNSEL IN
   3      (SELECT LAST
   4       FROM LA__FLAW
   5       WHERE ASSIGN = 'CIVIL');
```

The subquery in this command uses the LA__FLAW table to identify those professional staff members who are assigned to civil cases. ORACLE will first scan LA__FLAW for the civil attorneys and will pass their last names to the outer query. The outer query then will look in the CASES table for rows in which the selected names appear. The result is shown in Figure 10-2.

SOME CASES AREN'T CIVIL

Now edit this query to select the criminal instead of the civil laywers:

```
SQL> LIST 5
   5*        WHERE ASSIGN = 'CIVIL')
SQL> CHANGE/CIVIL/CRIMINAL/
   5*        WHERE ASSIGN = 'CRIMINAL')
SQL> RUN
   1    SELECT * FROM CASES
   2    WHERE COUNSEL IN
```

FIGURE 10-2 The Civil Cases Selected

```
CASE                          CLIENT             COUNSEL
----------------------------  -----------------  -------------
PEASE V. QUIETTE              QUIETTE            BOYSENBERRY
FRONTERO V. PAGE              PAGE               BOYSENBERRY
CROWE V. MAGNON               MAGNON             BOYSENBERRY
KATELEY V. ELLISON            ELLISON            BUNSEN
LEVITT V. BEAVERS             BEAVERS            BUNSEN
ASKEW V. ELLE                 ASKEW              BUNSEN
HAMMER V. BELL                BELL               BUNSEN
ASHTON V. TATE                ASHTON             HARTLESS
LONG V. ISLANDER              LONG               HARTLESS
ANDREA V. CHEEVER             CHEEVER            HARTLESS
NOTTINGHAM V. KINGSFIELD      NOTTINGHAM         TUCKER
QUICK V. SILVER               SILVER             TUCKER
IRVING V. BYRD                BYRD               TUCKER

13 records selected.
```

```
3               (SELECT LAST
4               FROM LA__FLAW
5*              WHERE ASSIGN = 'CRIMINAL')
```

This screens out an entirely different list of cases, as shown in Figure 10-3.

FROM QUERY TO VIEW

Both the civil and criminal case tables are transient. They exist only until the computer moves on to some other task. A slight change in the command, however, will turn the temporary table of civil cases into a permanently stored view:

```
SQL> CREATE VIEW CIVIL__CASES AS
2               SELECT * FROM CASES
3               WHERE COUNSEL IN
4                   (SELECT LAST
5                   FROM LA__FLAW
6                   WHERE ASSIGN = 'CIVIL');
```

The only thing added is the CREATE VIEW command in Line 1. The original query now begins in Line 2. Because it still is the outer query, there is no need to put it in parentheses. The subquery does appear in brackets, just as it did in the earlier command.

FIGURE 10-3 Filtering Out the Criminal Cases

```
CASE                            CLIENT           COUNSEL
------------------------------  ---------------  -------------
CANNERY V. ROWE                 ROWE             BAILEY
AXEL V. RODD                    AXEL             BAILEY
REALE V. STATE                  REALE            BAILEY
MICHIGAN V. NORTHWESTERN        MULLER           COSSACK
GREENHEAD V. CLOVERHOUSE        CLOVERHOUSE      COSSACK
WARD V. PREFECT                 WARD             COSSACK
SUTCLIFFE V. TUDOR              SUTCLIFFE        MASON
COMMONER V. STOCK               STOCK            MASON
DEE V. BASIE                    DEE              MASON
PEOPLE V. CLOVERHOUSE           CLOVERHOUSE      MUKLUK
WILEY V. COYOTE                 WILEY            MUKLUK
LABOR V. PAYNE                  PAYNE            MUKLUK
MANUEL V. STILES                STILES           MUKLUK

13 records selected.
```

You have created a view called CIVIL__CASES. As with all views, you can issue a command as though the view were a table:

```
SQL> SELECT *
   2   FROM CIVIL__CASES;
```

That's a lot easier than the earlier query, but it gets the same results. It also lets a user who is interested only in case records retrieve these without getting near the confidential information in LA__FLAW.

TABLE HOPPING

You also can issue a query that creates a new virtual table from the CIVIL__CASES view:

```
SQL> SELECT CASE
   2   FROM CIVIL__CASES
   3   WHERE COUNSEL = 'BUNSEN';
```

This query retrieves the cases Bunsen is handling at the moment:

```
CASE
-------------------------------------------
KATELEY V. ELIASON
ASKEW V. ELLE
LEVITT V. BEAVERS
HAMMER V. BELL
```

USING AN ALIAS IN CRIMINAL CASES

The column headings in a view need not duplicate those in the source tables. You can assign them aliases, just as you can in a normal query:

```
SQL> CREATE VIEW CRIMINAL__CASES
   2   (MATTER, PARTY, ATTY)
   3     AS SELECT *
   4     FROM CASES
   5     WHERE COUNSEL IN
   6           (SELECT LAST
   7           FROM LA__FLAW
   8           WHERE ASSIGN = 'CRIMINAL');
```

Line 2 does the job of assigning the new aliases. The three columns taken from the CASES table will have, in order, the three headings specified in Line 2. To retrieve the contents of the new view, issue the query:

```
SQL> SELECT *
   2    FROM CRIMINAL__CASES;
```

The outcome is shown in Figure 10-4.

MAINTAINING AND UPDATING VIEWS

A view has another handy feature: flexible updating. You can add, drop, or alter a row in the underlying table, and your change automatically will be reflected the next time you query the view. This works the other way around, too. If you update a view, you also update the underlying table.

UPDATING THE TABLE

The retirement of Percy Mason and the hiring of Ben Mukluk means that all Mason's cases should be assigned to Mukluk. You can UPDATE the CASES table to reflect this:

```
SQL> UPDATE CASES
   2    SET COUNSEL = 'MUKLUK'
   3    WHERE COUNSEL = 'MASON';
```

FIGURE 10-4 Criminal Cases and Aliases Go Together Somehow

```
MATTER                          PARTY             ATTY
-------------------------------- ----------------- ----------------
CANNERY V. ROWE                 ROWE              BAILEY
AXEL V. RODD                    AXEL              BAILEY
REALE V. STATE                  REALE             BAILEY
MICHIGAN V. NORTHWESTERN        MULLER            COSSACK
GREENHEAD V. CLOVERHOUSE        CLOVERHOUSE       COSSACK
WARD V. PREFECT                 WARD              COSSACK
SUTCLIFFE V. TUDOR              SUTCLIFFE         MASON
COMMONER V. STOCK               STOCK             MASON
DEE V. BASIE                    DEE               MASON
PEOPLE V. CLOVERHOUSE           CLOVERHOUSE       MUKLUK
WILEY V. COYOTE                 WILEY             MUKLUK
LABOR V. PAYNE                  PAYNE             MUKLUK
MANUEL V. STILES                STILES            MUKLUK

13 records selected.
```

Now, take a look at how this affects the view CRIM-INAL_CASES:

SQL> SELECT *
   2   FROM CRIMINAL_CASES;

The results are shown in Figure 10-5. You have updated the CASES table. The reassigned cases are now reflected in the view based on that table. Also note that the column headings you assigned when you created the view are still in place.

UPDATING THE VIEW

Client Sutcliffe objects to being represented by Mukluk. "I signed on with Mason, and I want to stick with Mason," the client said.

Mason agrees to stick with this case until completion, so it's necessary to correct the file to indicate that he's still handling it. You can update the view this way:

SQL> UPDATE CRIMINAL_CASES
   2   SET ATTY = 'MASON'
   3   WHERE PARTY = 'SUTCLIFFE';

To check your work:

SQL> SELECT *
   2   FROM CRIMINAL_CASES
   3   WHERE PARTY = 'SUTCLIFFE';

FIGURE 10-5   The New View of the Reassigned Cases

```
    MATTER                          PARTY              ATTY
    ----------------------------    ----------------   -------------
    CANNERY V. ROWE                 ROWE               BAILEY
    AXEL V. RODD                    AXEL               BAILEY
    REALE V. STATE                  REALE              BAILEY
    MICHIGAN V. NORTHWESTERN        MULLER             COSSACK
    GREENHEAD V. CLOVERHOUSE        CLOVERHOUSE        COSSACK
    WARD V. PREFECT                 WARD               COSSACK
    PEOPLE V. CLOVERHOUSE           CLOVERHOUSE        MUKLUK
    WILEY V. COYOTE                 WILEY              MUKLUK
    LABOR V. PAYNE                  PAYNE              MUKLUK
    MANUEL V. STILES                STILES             MUKLUK
    COMMONER V. STOCK               STOCK              MUKLUK
    DEE V. BASIE                    DEE                MUKLUK
    SUTCLIFFE V. TUDOR              SUTCLIFFE          MUKLUK

    13 records selected.
```

MATTER	PARTY	ATTY
SUTCLIFFE V. TUDOR	SUTCLIFFE	MASON

AUTOMATIC TABLE-SETTING

This is the right idea, but you updated the view CRIMINAL
_CASES instead of the CASES table, which provides the source
material for the view. What has this done to CASES? To find out,
enter:

```
SQL> SELECT * FROM CASES
   2   WHERE CLIENT = 'SUTCLIFFE';
```

The update *did* alter the base table. In fact, it even managed to
allow for the differences in column names between the table and
the view:

CASE	CLIENT	COUNSEL
SUTCLIFFE V. TUDOR	SUTCLIFFE	MASON

UPDATE RESTRICTIONS

There are some limits you must observe when using a view to
update a table. You can delete one or more rows only if you
observe these two rules:

- You must select rows from only one table.
- You must not use the GROUP BY or DISTINCT clauses or a
group function. You must also avoid functions that refer to row
numbers.

These restrictions also apply when you are updating existing
rows, as does this additional requirement:

- You may not use an expression to define the columns to be
updated.

There is another restriction, in addition to the previous limits,
that apply when you insert a new row:

- Any columns identified as NOT NULL in the table must be
represented in the view.

None of these restrictions applies when you directly update the table. It is not safe to add a column to a table on which a view depends. Otherwise, when you update the table, the view will adjust itself to reflect your work.

VIEWS FROM MULTIPLE TABLES

In Chapter 5, you saw Allen Tawdry busily looking for staff members whose pay exceeded his. He also wanted to know in which cases these salaries were justified because the attorneys were handling active cases. To find out, he used a JOIN command:

```
SQL> SELECT L.LAST, L.SALARY, C.CASE, C.CLIENT
  2    FROM LA__FLAW L, CASES C
  3    WHERE C.COUNSEL = L.LAST
  4    AND L.SALARY >=
  5       (SELECT SALARY
  6        FROM LA__FLAW
  7        WHERE LA__FLAW.LAST = 'TAWDRY');
```

This is a fairly complex effort on ORACLE's part, not to mention Tawdry's. The subquery in the last three lines identifies his salary. It then feeds that figure into the WHERE clause of the main query. Using the criteria thus established, the query selects columns from two different tables.

The result was hardly worth the work. The query returned only three cases, and one attorney was handling two of those.

FROM QUERY TO VIEW

Now, Tawdry wants to run that query again to see how things have improved recently. He also wants this to be the last time he has to bother with such a complex command. He decides to turn it into the view WORTH__IT.

The process is the same as creating a view from a less complex query:

```
SQL> CREATE VIEW WORTH__IT
  2    AS SELECT L.LAST, L.SALARY,
  3    C.CASE, C.CLIENT
```

```
4    FROM LA__FLAW L, CASES C
5    WHERE C.COUNSEL = L.LAST
6    AND L.SALARY >=
7         (SELECT SALARY
8          FROM LA__FLAW
9          WHERE LA__FLAW.LAST = 'TAWDRY');
```

Tawdry can now treat WORTH__IT as though he had a table by that name, including:

```
SQL> SELECT *
2    FROM WORTH__IT;
```

With the firm's increased caseload, this should produce the healthier output shown in Figure 10-6.

EXPRESSIONS AND FUNCTIONS IN VIEWS

The ability to use a view as though it were a table extends to using expressions and functions. In fact, you can give a view a pseudo-column, just like the one you can add to a base table, to display the results of mathematical expressions and functions.

FIGURE 10-6   The Contents of the WORTH__IT View

```
     LAST              SALARY CASE                                 CLIENT
     ---------------   ------- ----------------------------------  ---------------
     BAILEY               4800 CANNERY V. ROWE                     ROWE
     BAILEY               4800 AXEL V. RODD                        AXEL
     BAILEY               4800 REALE V. STATE                      REALE
     COSSACK              4500 MICHIGAN V. NORTHWESTERN            MULLER
     COSSACK              4500 GREENHEAD V. CLOVERHOUSE            CLOVERHOUSE
     COSSACK              4500 WARD V. PREFECT                     WARD
     HARTLESS             7500 ASHTON V. TATE                      ASHTON
     HARTLESS             7500 LONG V. ISLANDER                    LONG
     HARTLESS             7500 ANDREA V. CHEEVER                   CHEEVER
     MUKLUK               4700 PEOPLE V. CLOVERHOUSE               CLOVERHOUSE
     MUKLUK               4700 LABOR V. PAYNE                      PAYNE
     MUKLUK               4700 MANUEL V. STILES                    STILES
     MUKLUK               4700 COMMONER V. STOCK                   STOCK
     MUKLUK               4700 DEE V. BASIE                        DEE
     MUKLUK               4700 WILEY V. COYOTE                     WILEY

     15 records selected.
```

COMPUTING ANNUAL SALARIES

This view takes the monthly salary figures from LA_FLAW and calculates the equivalent annual figures:

```
SQL> CREATE VIEW ANNUAL_PAY
  2    AS SELECT LAST, ASSIGN,
  3    SALARY MONTHLY,
  4    SALARY * 12 ANNUAL
  5    FROM  LA_FLAW;
```

This command creates the new view ANNUAL_PAY. It then selects the last name, assignment, and monthly salary from LA_FLAW. In a fourth column, it computes the annual pay and gives it the heading ANNUAL. When you SELECT 8 from ANNUAL PAY, you get these results:

LAST	ASSIGN	MONTHLY	ANNUAL
MCKNIFE	PARTNER	5000	60000
TAWDRY	PARTNER	4000	48000
COSSACK	CRIMINAL	4500	54000
BUNSEN	CIVIL	2975	35700
TUCKER	CIVIL	2850	34200
BOYSENBERRY	CIVIL	2450	29400
ROX	SECRETARY	1300	15600
MASON	CRIMINAL	3850	46200
BAILEY	CRIMINAL	4800	57600
BORQUE	PARALEGAL	950	11400
HARTLESS	CIVIL	7500	90000
MUKLUK	CRIMINAL	4700	56400

12 records selected.

USING GROUP FUNCTIONS

The difference between the pseudocolumns you create with a query and those you create in a view is that, in the latter, the columns and their calculated contents will be available whenever you query the view. You can also create a view that repeatedly reports the outcome of group functions. For example, this command creates a view that finds the low, mean, and high salaries in each of three branch offices:

```
SQL> CREATE VIEW PAY__RANGE
  2    (BRANCH, LOW, MEAN, HIGH)
  3        AS SELECT BRANCH,
  4        MIN(SALARY), AVG(SALARY), MAX(SALARY)
  5        FROM LA__FLAW
  6    GROUP BY BRANCH
```

The first two lines create the view, with columns headed BRANCH, LOW, MEAN, and HIGH. Lines 3 through 5 comprise the query that defines the view. It calls for the branch numbers plus the results of three functions as applied to the salary figures. Line 6 instructs ORACLE to report the results in order of the branch numbers.

Now this query will retrieve the contents of the new view:

```
SQL> SELECT *
  2    FROM PAY__RANGE;
```

The results should look like this:

BRANCH	LOW	MEDIAN	HIGH
1	950	3425	5000
2	1300	4095	7500
3	3850	3850	3850

REPEATING THE QUERY

Once you have established the functions and their output as components of the view, you need not repeat the calculations to run another query of the view. You can refer, instead, to the column headings you assigned to each function. For example, this query:

```
SQL> SELECT BRANCH, HIGH
  2    FROM PAY__RANGE;
```

. . . would retrieve this result:

BRANCH	HIGH
1	5000
2	7500
3	3850

REVIEW QUESTIONS

1. What is the main difference between a view and a virtual table?
2. What's the main difference between a command that creates a view and an ordinary SELECT command?
3. What is the one command you can use in a query but not in creating a view?
4. What are the two main reasons to use views?
5. Explain the use of the term *bind* in creating a view.
6. In Chapter 5, Dennis Madison created a new table consisting only of customer service representatives. Why would he have been better off creating a view?
7. Help Madison rewrite this command to create a view instead of a new table:

```
SQL> INSERT INTO REPS (LAST, FIRST, DEPT_NO)
   2    SELECT LAST, FIRST, DEPT_NO
   3    FROM ROSTER
   4    WHERE DEPT_NO = 2;
```

8. When you update a table, what happens to any views based on that table?
9. Can you also update a table by updating a view derived from that table?

ANSWERS

1. A view can be saved, retrieved, and treated like an actual table.
2. To create a view, simply precede the SELECT command with the phrase "CREATE VIEW <name> AS."
3. ORDER BY.
4. To protect data by restricting access and to make it easier to execute frequently repeated queries.
5. When you query a view, SQL binds your query to the query that originally set the specifications for the view. In effect, your query executes the original.
6. A view could have been created from the same sources, but would not have put duplicate information in a separate table.

7.   SQL> CREATE VIEW REPS AS
        2   SELECT LAST, FIRST, DEPT__NO
        3   FROM ROSTER
        4   WHERE DEPT__NO = 2;

8. They are automatically updated, too.
9. Yes, but use care and observe the many restrictions on which commands you can use. It usually is better to update from the table.

3 MANAGING A SQL DATABASE

11

Managing Multiple Access

THE ADMINISTRATOR'S TASK

ACCESS AND OWNERSHIP

PRINCIPLES OF PRIVILEGES

USING THE VIEW FOR ACCESS CONTROL

SHARING DATA PEACEFULLY

LOCKING IN SQL

USING MULTIPLE DATABASES

dBASE began life as a single-user database system for the truly "personal" computers of a few years ago. It accommodates multiple users and multiple computers only when you superimpose accessories and programming techniques on the original product.

ORACLE, on the other hand, began life as a multi-user product. It was designed from the start to be used on larger computers, with which the cost could be justified only if it were spread among significant numbers of users. Even in its personal computer embodiments, ORACLE is best viewed as a multi-user tool.

ORACLE's advantage over dBASE in such an environment is that its multi-user features are built in rather than added on. You need ORACLE's Networkstation version to put ORACLE on a network, but you won't need much else you do not already have. You don't need to learn any programming tricks, either. ORACLE handles most multi-user needs internally.

There is one big difference between ORACLE in one-person use and ORACLE in a shared system. A network must be managed. It requires someone's regular attention. We're going to assume from here on that this someone is you. Congratulations. You have just become the network administrator (or network manager as the position might also be called).

THE ADMINISTRATOR'S TASK

An ORACLE database administrator, or DBA, is responsible for nearly every facet of managing the database. As an administrator, your duties include:

- *Data security,* which includes access control and other activities that prevent loss or corruption of important data.
- *Network and file management,* which includes installation, memory management, maintaining a data dictionary, and providing for regular backups.
- *Improving database performance,* including performance tuning and customizing the installation.

Multi-user access, security, and operations will be the main topics of this chapter. Subsequent chapters will cover network management and performance.

ACCESS AND OWNERSHIP

The user name and password are at the heart of ORACLE's access control system. They dictate *who* has access to the computer. At least as important, they also determine *what* each user may see and do.

The network version of dBASE includes a utility called Protect, with which you can identify users and control the access each has to data within the system.

The ORACLE system of access control is based on a concept of ownership. Each user of the system has both a name and a password; some may have more than one of each. Each user "owns" the tables or views he or she has created. For example, in my database, the user identified as System holds title to the ROSTER table shown in Figure 11-1. User Baker also owns a ROSTER table, shown in Figure 11-2. There tables are very different. As a matter of fact, the ROSTER that belongs to System is an early version that was used in the first chapter in this book. The current version is filed under my own name.

If you own a particular asset, you may grant other users the *privilege* of access to your data. You can tailor a privilege to give particular users access to specified tables or views. You also can grant this access in varying degrees, including no access at all, look-but-don't touch access, authority to add or alter data, and authority to alter the database system itself.

FIGURE 11-1 The ROSTER Table as Owned by System

EMPNO	LAST	FIRST	M	DEPT_NO	POSITION	SALARY
1	MAYS	ADDIE	H	1	MANAGER	24000
2	MADISON	DENNIS	W	1	ASST MGR	21000
3	PEST	ANGIE	D	1	RECEPTION	42500
4	TUBA	HUBERT	G	2	NEW ACCT	11000
5	SUTTON	WILSON	W	3	TELLER	12500
6	MAHONEY	SUZANNE	S	3	TELLER	12400
7	BUCHINSKY	CHARLES	B	4	SECURITY	15000
8	PALMER	VERA	M	3	TELLER	13450
9	COLLINS	KATHLEEN	D	2	NEW ACCT	13300
9	ZIMMERMAN	ROBERT	D	2	NEW ACCT	18000

10 records selected.

FIGURE 11-2   Under New Management

```
EMP  LAST          FIRST      I DEP POSITION    SS_NO         DATE_HIRE SALARY EXTE
---  ------------  ---------  - --- ----------  ------------  --------- ------ ----
AD   DAVIDSON      ADDIE      H  1  MANAGER     123-45-6789   09-SEP-79  24000 101
DM   MADISON       DENNIS     W  1  ASST MGR    234-56-7890   07-JUL-81  21000 102
MP   PRESTO        MISTY      D  1  RECEPTION   456-78-9012   19-JUN-78  42500 100
HT   TUBA          HUBERT     G  2  NEW ACCT    567-89-0123   17-MAY-87  11000 109
SM   MAHONEY       SUZANNE    S  3  TELLER      789-01-2345   18-JAN-79  12400 107
CB   BUCHINSKY     CHARLES    B  4  SECURITY    890-12-3456   18-DEC-86  15000 108
VP   PALMER        VERA       M  3  TELLER      901-23-4567   23-SEP-85  13450 106
KC   COLLINS       KATHLEEN   D  2  NEW ACCT    987-65-4321   15-OCT-85  13300 105
RZ   ZIMMERMAN     ROBERT     D  2  SUPERVISOR  876-54-3210   14-OCT-85  13400 104
PR   ROWE-HATTON   PHYLLIS    F  2  NEW ACCT    765-43-2109   07-NOV-8   11250 103

10 records selected.
```

The view is a particularly useful access control feature. By using a carefully constructed view and the right access controls, you can give an individual access only to the specific data items you want to let that user see or change.

GRANTING PRIVILEGES

Except for the stray table under the System user name, the tables and views created for this book so far have all been under the user name Baker. There's nothing exceptional about this. There is a problem, though.

Because I own all these tables, the good people at UnderFed must rely on me whenever they need data for the voluminous reports they must file with their corporate superiors at Marinecorp. The same is true of the far-flung law offices of McKnife, Tawdry, Diver, and Brown. Surely Addie Davidson should have the privilege of seeing and using data about her own shop. In my role as system manager, therefore, I'll do this:

```
SQL> GRANT RESOURCE
  2    TO ADDIE
  3    IDENTIFIED BY SHEPHERD
```

Davidson can now log onto ORACLE and use any of its facilities by stating the user name Addie and the password Shepherd. Her log-on command for SQL*Plus would be:

```
C> SQLPLUS ADDIE/SHEPHERD
```

Actually, this password is a poor choice. As Addie's many friends know, she is fond of photos and knickknacks that depict sheep. It isn't wise to select a password that is so clearly connected to its holder.

ACCESS TO TABLES

Now that the system recognizes Addie as an authorized user, I can grant her whatever privileges I choose over the tables, view, and other assets I have been superintending on her behalf. Feeling magnanimous, I decide to let her do anything she'd like with the ROSTER table. I log on as Baker and give ORACLE this command:

```
SQL> GRANT ALL
   2    ON ROSTER
   3    TO ADDIE;
```

Because I know Ms. Davidson's user name and password I can log on in her behalf to see whether the GRANT command did what I expected. I am already logged onto the system, therefore I can use this command to operate under another user name:

```
SQL> CONNECT ADDIE/SHEPHERD;
```

This is simply a shortcut that saves me from having to sign off and log on again under the new name. Now, as far as the computer is concerned, I'm Addie. Should I want to see the ROSTER table, I would enter:

```
SQL> SELECT *
   2    FROM BAKER.ROSTER;
```

This command will cause the system to display ROSTER's full contents as shown in Figure 11-2.

PRINCIPLES OF PRIVILEGES

If you own a table, view, or other asset, your name becomes part of its name. When Addie Davidson wants to see my version of the ROSTER table, she has to prefix it with my name: BAKER.ROSTER. Otherwise, ORACLE would simply have become confused about whether Addie wanted to see my version of ROSTER or the older one owned by System.

The basic format for specifying someone else's file is the owner's name, a period, and the name of the table or view.

BY ANY OTHER NAME

This can sometimes be awkward. If you use such a table regularly, you can establish a *synonym* for the other user's table. A synonym is much like an alias. For example, Addie Davidson might want to refer to BAKER.ROSTER as NEWLIST. If so, she could issue these instructions:

```
SQL> CREATE SYNONYM NEWLIST
   2    FOR BAKER.ROSTER;
```

Then, the command:

```
SQL> SELECT *
   2    FROM NEWLIST;
```

would have the same effect as:

```
SQL> SELECT *
   2    FROM BAKER.ROSTER;
```

THE SYNTAX OF PRIVILEGE

The basic syntax of a GRANT command is:

```
SQL> GRANT <privilege>
   2    ON <table, view or synonym>
   3    TO <user);
```

It then becomes your fond hope that you will see the message:

Grant succeeded

There is an optional fourth line. If you want the user to be allowed to pass on the privileges you have granted, the command is:

```
SQL> GRANT <privilege>
   2    ON <table, view or synonym>
   3    TO <user)
   4    WITH GRANT OPTION;
```

The user could then delegate someone else who could also exercise his or her privileges. This power to delegate is limited to the privileges you have granted in the first place. Use GRANT OPTION with care, because you have little control over what the user will do with the authority you have bestowed.

MANY KINDS OF PRIVILEGES

Because Addie Davidson is the office manager, it makes sense to give her a wide range of privileges over the data that concern her office. These privileges come in several varieties:

- *Select* lets the newly privileged user see, but not alter, the data in a table or view.
- *Insert* lets the user add new rows or records to the file.
- *Update* grants permission to edit existing data.
- *Delete* confers authority to delete existing rows or records.
- *Alter* gives the user permission to change the structure of a table, including new column definitions.
- *Index* grants the authority to create an index, which will be described in Chapter 13.

You often will want to give a user only a single, limited privilege. For example, the command:

```
SQL> GRANT SELECT
   2   ON DEPT
   3   TO MISTY;
```

would give Misty Presto the right to see, but not change, the data in the DEPT table. Her privileges are limited to those designated by SELECT. This assumes that she has previously been assigned this user name and password.

Often you will want to give a user a limited list of privileges. For example, a customer service representative should have the ability to add new customers to the CUSTOMER file and to update the records of existing customers. However, not all employees should be able to delete existing customers. You wish to reserve this privilege for the department supervisor. At the same time, you do not want to give anyone the power to alter the table's column structure. To do this, list the privileges you do want to confer, such as:

```
SQL> GRANT INSERT, UPDATE
  2    ON CUSTOMER
  3    TO TUBA, COLLINS, ROWE-HATTON;
```

Again, this assumes that these people have previously been granted CONNECT privileges under these user names. Another command will grant the additional DELETE privilege to the supervisor:

```
SQL> GRANT INSERT, UPDATE, DELETE
  2    ON CUSTOMER
  3    TO ZIMMERMAN;
```

ADMITTING THE PUBLIC

Some kinds of data are so innocuous that you can let any member of the network have access to them. SQL*Plus maintains the dummy user Public for this purpose. You can grant Public the particular kinds of privileges you are willing to grant to everyone:

```
SQL> GRANT SELECT
  2    ON DEPT
  3    TO PUBLIC;
```

You still can determine the type of privileges you grant with this command. Make good use of this ability. You probably do not want to grant everyone the power to do anything they want to do—that way lies chaos. If you grant a privilege to Public, make sure it is a carefully defined privilege. The previous command, for example, grants just read-only access.

TRAPPING THE UNAUTHORIZED

ORACLE has two ways to trap unauthorized users who try to gain access to your data, whether they do so deliberately or by mistake.

If someone tries to perform an operation that exceeds his or her authorized privileges, ORACLE will simply refuse to participate. For example, if a user with SELECT privileges tries to change the data in a table, ORACLE will flash the error message "insufficient privileges."

MAINTAINING DENIABILITY

Something a little bit different happens when a user tries to manipulate a table or view for which he or she has no privileges at all. In this case, the error message will read "table or view does not exist."

The table does exist, yet ORACLE has proclaimed that it does not. Why the deception? It helps maintain the security and integrity of your data. The program keeps unauthorized users out while telling them as little as possible. Should the error message confirm that the table does exist, then the unauthorized user would have some new knowledge of your system. He or she might make use of it to try again. Instead, the program simply denies that the table exists—whether or not it actually does.

REVOKING PRIVILEGES

The privileges you grant, you can also revoke. This is an essential tool that can be used when someone leaves the organization or moves to a new assignment and no longer should have access to all the data that were available before. When this happens, use the REVOKE command in just the way that you previously used GRANT. For example, should Addie Davidson leave UnderFed to work for a competing bank, you would want to revoke her access to UnderFed data—immediately if not sooner. To cancel her access to ROSTER the command would be:

```
SQL> REVOKE ALL
  2    ON ROSTER
  3    FROM ADDIE;
```

Take careful note of what this command does and does not do. It revokes Addie's access to the ROSTER table. It also revokes any privileges she might have passed along under the grant option. It does not revoke any privileges you might have granted her to use any other table or view. You must revoke those separately.

USING THE VIEW FOR ACCESS CONTROL

To repeat a point from Chapter 10, the most important reason for using a view is to secure your data. You need not grant access privileges for an entire table, such as the salary columns in ROS-TER or LA_FLAW. Instead, you can create a view which omits sensitive information, then grant access privileges to the view.

CREATING A PHONE BOOK

Suppose you want to create an internal telephone directory from the ROSTER table. You would make this available to everyone on the system. The names and extension numbers are all in the table, but so are the salary figures, which you don't want to publicize. The solution is:

```
SQL> CREATE VIEW PHONEBOOK
  2   AS      SELECT LAST, FIRST, MI, DEPT_NO, EXT
  3           FROM ROSTER;
```

The results are shown in Figure 11-3.

A LITTLE ACCESS FOR EVERYONE

Now you can grant everyone the right to read the phone directory, but not to change it or to see anything that lies outside the view:

```
SQL> GRANT SELECT
  2   ON PHONEBOOK
  3   TO PUBLIC;
```

FIGURE 11-3 The PHONEBOOK View

```
LAST           FIRST     I DEP EXTE
-------------  --------  - --- ----
DAVIDSON       ADDIE     H  1  101
MADISON        DENNIS    W  1  102
PRESTO         MISTY     D  1  100
TUBA           HUBERT    G  2  109
MAHONEY        SUZANNE   S  3  107
BUCHINSKY      CHARLES   B  4  108
PALMER         VERA      M  3  106
COLLINS        KATHLEEN  D  2  105
ZIMMERMAN      ROBERT    D  2  104
ROWE-HATTON    PHYLLIS   F  2  103
```

CONTROLLING ACCESS TO ROWS

You can use a view to control which rows, as well as which columns, a user can see or manipulate. For example, it might be a good idea to let each department head have access to the information in ROSTER, including the salaries. Each, however, should be able to see only the data that apply to the members of his or her own department.

Departmental Rosters

It is for occasions such as this that SQL provides a pseudocolumn called USER. You can use it in a WHERE clause to identify the user who is querying the database at the moment. A view that uses USER could look like this:

```
SQL>  CREATE VIEW STAFF AS
   2     SELECT *
   3     FROM ROSTER
   4     WHERE DEPT__NO IN
   5           (SELECT DEPT__NO
   6           FROM ROSTER
   7           WHERE LAST = USER
   8           AND POSITION = 'SUPERVISOR');
```

The next step is:

```
SQL>  GRANT SELECT
   2     ON STAFF
   3     TO PUBLIC;
```

How This View Works

At first glance, it might seem as if the GRANT command will let anyone look at the information in this file, including the sensitive salaries. This would indeed be the case if access were controlled by the grant alone, but grant is only the first level of control.

The second level is in the CREATE VIEW command. As usual, the best way to analyze a complex query such as this is to work from the inside out, starting with the subquery.

Here, the WHERE clause sets up two conditions. The first is that the entry in the LAST column must match the name under which the user has signed on. The second condition is that the individual must have the title of supervisor. There are only two people whose last names appear in ROSTER and who are listed as supervisors. If the current user is anyone else, this query will fail. This assures that only the two supervisors will have access to this view.

Yet Another Control

There is also a third level of control. The WHERE clause in the outer main query specifies that the rows to be retrieved must match the department number of the supervisor who retrieves them. Thus, if Zimmerman issues the command:

```
SQL> SELECT *
   2    FROM STAFF;
```

the view will present only the records of members of Zimmerman's department (Figure 11-4).

MANAGING THE PASSWORD SYSTEM

Computer security experts recommend that passwords be changed often. The more sensitive the data the passwords protect, the more often you should change the passwords that protect it. A monthly change is not too frequent for highly sensitive data.

Change a password, too, any time you think it might have been compromised.

You can use GRANT to make the changes. The syntax is:

```
SQL> GRANT CONNECT
   2    TO <user>
   3    IDENTIFIED BY <new password>;
```

There's a good reason to change passwords frequently. Inventive "hackers" who obtain access to computerized files have gen-

FIGURE 11-4 A Restricted Roster Selected with a View

```
EMP LAST           FIRST     I DEP POSITION    SS_NO        DATE_HIRE  SALARY EXTE
--- ------------   --------- - --- ----------- ------------ ---------- ------ ----
HT  TUBA           HUBERT    G 2   NEW ACCT    567-89-0123  17-MAY-87  11000  109
KC  COLLINS        KATHLEEN  D 2   NEW ACCT    987-65-4321  15-OCT-85  13300  105
RZ  ZIMMERMAN      ROBERT    D 2   SUPERVISOR  876-54-3210  14-OCT-85  13400  104
PR  ROWE-HATTON    PHYLLIS   F 2   NEW ACCT    765-43-2109  07-NOV-87  11250  103
```

erated heavy publicity over the years. Experience shows, however, that your risk of loss from this source is remote. You face a far greater danger from within. The person most likely to seek improper access to your data is the greedy or disgruntled employee. This employee is also likely to know a password or two.

SHARING DATA PEACEFULLY

Passwords, privileges, and other access control measures protect the security of your data. If the system works as planned—always an important condition—your data will be unavailable to people who are not supposed to enjoy access to them.

There is a second kind of control, called *concurrency control.* Its purpose is to protect your data from people who do have legitimate access. You must control who can do what to the database, and when. Otherwise, any of four things can happen, all of them bad:

- The *lost update,* in which one user's change to the data overwrites someone else's change before anyone even knows it is there. In the classic case, Joe checks an inventory record, finds twenty-five of a particular item in stock, and promises to ship twenty of them to his customer. Before Joe can record that change, Les finds the twenty-five items still on record and promises fifteen of them to one of his customers.
- The *uncommitted update,* in which one user acts on the basis of a second user's update; then, the second user decides for some reason not to make the change. This is the reverse of the lost record. Joe's customer decides not to make the purchase, so instead of issuing a COMMIT to remove the items from inventory Joe restores them with a ROLLBACK. Les checks the record between these two actions, believes only five items are in stock, and loses the sale.
- The *instantly outdated analysis,* in which a change in the data alters the figures some other employee is currently using. Sally issues a command to total the value of the current inventory. Joe makes his sale while she is doing that; the figures are out of date before Sally even sees them.
- The *deadly embrace,* in which two users simultaneously each lay exclusive claim to a resource urgently needed by the other.

CONCURRENCY CONTROL IN dBASE

The network version of dBASE uses a system of file and record *locks* to monitor simultaneous use. When a user applies a lock to a resource, no one else can use that resource until the lock is released.

For example, when Joe receives the order and checks the inventory, he can apply a lock to the database record that records the stock levels of the item in question. Les can not gain access to the same record until Joe has completed his transaction, whatever it might be. If Sally is totalling inventory figures, she can lock the entire inventory file until her calculations are complete.

In some cases, dBASE will automatically lock a file. It will do so in operations such as APPEND and JOIN (which change the size or structure of the file) and COPY and REPLACE (which work with multiple records) and in calculations such as SUM and AVERAGE.

In addition, dBASE programmers can apply locks to individual records for such purposes as recording the sales from inventory. The two main dBASE resources are FLOCK( ), a function that locks a file, and RLOCK( ), which locks a single record.

The obvious drawback to dBASE locking is that while data is locked, no one else can make use of it. When using dBASE in multi-user service, the best advice is to lock as little as possible and to release the lock as soon as possible. Don't lock an entire file if you can serve the same purpose by locking a single record. Release the lock the instant the transaction is completed. Usually, locking should be done through dBASE command-file programs. This helps to keep users from applying locks too expansively or for too long.

AVOIDING THE EMBRACE

Even then, there is nothing in the dBASE system that allows you to avoid the deadly embrace. Here, Joe has locked the inventory record to record his pending sale. Because he is selling to a new customer, he wants to add a record to the separate customer file. Meanwhile, Sally is preparing a report of purchases by major customers. She has locked the customer file and now needs access to the inventory file for details of what the customers have purchased. Joe and Sally sit, each waiting for the other to release the lock, both probably unaware of the real reason they can't complete their transactions.

There is no built-in dBASE facility for avoiding the deadly embrace. The best solution is a dBASE programming practice. Establish a pecking order of all the files in your database, and make sure your programs always apply locks in that order.

LOCKING IN SQL

ORACLE's locking system is similar to that of dBASE, but it is more sophisticated and, thus, more versatile. As with dBASE, you can let ORACLE apply its locks automatically, or you can override the automatic system to issue your own locking commands. In automatic mode, ORACLE offers a greater variety of locks, including one that automatically will resolve a deadly embrace.

TYPES OF ORACLE LOCKS

ORACLE offers these types of locks:

- A *share* lock lets other users see the locked data, but they cannot alter them. This lock is useful when you want to query a table but don't plan to change it. A share lock makes sure no one else will change the data while you are trying to work with them. It would be a useful solution to the outdated analysis problem.
- A *share update* lock will let other users lock the data as well as query them. It is a counterpart to dBASE record locking. Other users have full access to the rest of the table. However, they may be able to establish locks that keep you from completing an update.
- A *table definition* lock is comparable to the automatic file locks dBASE applies when the file itself is being changed. ORACLE applies this lock automatically whenever it receives an ALTER TABLE command or some other command that would change the table's structure.
- An *exclusive lock* is much like a share lock in that other users can issue queries that allow them to examine data but not change them. Unlike a share lock, an exclusive lock prevents them from applying locks of their own. An exclusive lock is most useful when you plan a series of multiple updates, and you

want to keep other users from entering other changes until you have finished your work.

Once you have established a lock, it will remain in effect until you issue a COMMIT or a ROLLBACK.

ORACLE also has an automatic deadlock detector. When two users become entangled in a deadly embrace, the program will resolve matters by terminating one or the other of the commands that created the situation.

TYPES OF AUTOMATIC LOCKS

As with dBASE, SQL commands that alter the size or structure of a table automatically lock the entire table. UPDATE, INSERT, and DELETE create exclusive locks that allow others to view the table's contents but not to alter them while you are at work.

Three other commands create table definition locks. They are CREATE TABLE, ALTER TABLE, and DROP TABLE. When you issue these commands, no one else can do anything with the table until your action is complete. The good side to this is that, once any of these commands has been completed, ORACLE automatically issues a COMMIT. This means that others almost immediately can gain access to a table you have created or altered. A dropped table no longer exists, so you need not worry about it.

LOCKING A TABLE

If you don't wish to rely on the automatic locking service, you can apply your own locks, either by issuing direct commands or through a SQL command file. As with dBASE and the automatic SQL locks, you can lock an entire table or a selected part of it.

The basic command to lock a table takes this form:

```
SQL> LOCK <table> IN <type> MODE
```

To lock the ROSTER table in a SHARE mode, the command is:

```
SQL> LOCK TABLE ROSTER
   2   IN SHARE MODE;
```

To use other modes, instead, the command is:

```
SQL> LOCK TABLE ROSTER
   2   IN SHARE UPDATE MODE;
```

or:

```
SQL> LOCK TABLE ROSTER
   2   IN EXCLUSIVE MODE;
```

If another user already has applied a lock that interferes with yours, ORACLE will wait until the other lock has been released with a COMMIT or ROLLBACK. Then, it will apply your lock.

You may not want to wait that long. If so, you can prevent the delay with a command like:

```
SQL> LOCK TABLE ROSTER
   2   IN SHARE MODE NOWAIT;
```

Then, should the program encounter another lock, it will simply report this fact and return matters to your control.

LOCKING INDIVIDUAL ELEMENTS

In SQL, as in dBASE, you can lock the individual records of your choice. You can do so with a variation of the SELECT command. Basically, you can lock whatever you can SELECT.

Perhaps Addie Davidson will decide to give Dennis Madison a raise for all his hard work in developing a sales tracking database. She does not want someone else, even another authorized party, to be able to retrieve Madison's salary figure while she is trying to change it. Before beginning the update, she could establish a lock this way:

```
SQL> SELECT SALARY
   2   FROM ROSTER
   3   WHERE LAST = 'MADISON'
   4   FOR UPDATE OF SALARY;
```

Then she would issue an UPDATE command to change Madison's salary to the new figure.

The SELECT . . . FOR UPDATE combination applies a lock to the specified row or rows for the purposes stated. Although the query specified SALARY as the column to be selected, ORACLE will lock Madison's entire record, just as the dBASE RLOCK( ) would do.

Unlike RLOCK( ), SELECT . . . FOR UPDATE will lock more than one row at a time. Suppose there were a general cost-of-living raise for the people in Department 3. The locking command would be:

```
SQL> SELECT *
  2    FROM ROSTER
  3    WHERE DEPT_NO = 3
  4    FOR UPDATE OF SALARY;
```

Then, to grant a 5 percent raise, the command would be:

```
SQL> UPDATE ROSTER
  2    SET SALARY = SALARY * 1.05
  3    WHERE DEPT_NO = 3;
```

There is one potential problem here. SELECT . . . FOR UPDATE locks only specified rows of the table. It keeps others from changing the selected rows until you have completed the update. The UPDATE command itself places an exclusive lock on the entire table. The lock will remain in effect until you release it. Therefore, you should issue a COMMIT or ROLLBACK as soon as your update is completed.

MINIMIZE LOCKING TIME

In SQL, dBASE, or any other database system, it is best to minimize the time a lock remains in place. A lock is a valuable and necessary tool while you are working with the locked data. The instant you are finished, the lock becomes an unnecessary obstruction to others' productive use of the data.

To minimize the delays your locks cause to others, lock only the rows you expect to update. Don't use LOCK TABLE when SELECT . . . FOR UPDATE will do. Use automatic locking whenever possible; it releases locks as expeditiously as it creates them. If you must rely on manual locking, issue a COMMIT or ROLLBACK as soon as you have finished your task. This will release the lock and let others have access to the file.

USING MULTIPLE DATABASES

A small to midsize ORACLE installation will probably run a single copy of SQL, although multiple users may have access to it. A larger installation may have copies of ORACLE running on several different computers. In fact, SQL*Net, the ORACLE add-on for network users, requires that there be at least two copies of ORACLE on the network. Each must run its own independent database.

Just as you can link multiple users in a database, you can link multiple databases in a network. As a member of the network, you can log onto another computer's database, query another computer's database and copy tables from the other computer to your database.

CREATING A DATABASE LINK

When you start SQL*Plus, it normally logs onto the database in your own computer. In network terms, this is called the *local database*. You can also gain access to a *remote database* on another computer.

To reach the remote database, you create a *database link,* which specifies the database and the tables within that database to which you want access.

Creating a database link is much like creating a table or a view. Suppose that Goldie Rox in Denver regularly needs access to McKnife, Tawdry's personnel records. These are the contents of the LA__FLAW table. However, that table is part of a database maintained on a computer in the Los Angeles office.

Rox does have a telephone connection with the West Coast computer. She can create a database link that will give her simple, repeated access to LA__FLAW and other tables in the Los Angeles database. The command would be this:

```
SQL>  CREATE DATABASE LINK HOME__OFFICE
    2    CONNECT TO MCKNIFE
    3    IDENTIFIED BY BIG__MACK
    4    USING 'LA__FILES';
```

CREATE DATABASE LINK must identify three objects:

- The name of a remote database. Here, the database that includes LA_FLAW and its related tables has been named LA_FILES.
- A user name authorized to use that database. This command uses the name of senior partner Darren McKnife.
- The password associated with that user name.

In effect, this command gives Rox access to everything to which McKnife has access, which is, presumably, just about everything. All she must do is invoke the database link named HOME_OFFICE. If you want to grant only limited access, substitute the user name of someone who has the appropriate degree of access. You even can create a fictional user and tailor that person's access privileges for use by the remote user.

USING THE DATABASE LINK

To make use of this link, Rox must include it in her queries of the remote database. To retrieve everything from LA_FLAW, she would say:

```
SQL> SELECT *
  2    FROM LA_FLAW@HOME_OFFICE;
```

The @ in Line 2 means roughly "by way of." This command, then, tells ORACLE to retrieve every column from LA_FLAW by way of the database link HOME_OFFICE.

Rox can use @HOME_OFFICE to identify a remote table in the FROM clause of nearly any query. In effect, the computer will think she is Darren McKnife and will process her query under his access privileges.

CREATING SYNONYMS

Rox can also create a shortcut for herself. Instead of typing out LA_FLAW@HOME_OFFICE every time she wants to access LA_FLAW, she can create a synonym that will automatically call for that table and the database link. It's done this way:

```
SQL> CREATE SYNONYM PERSONNEL
  2    FOR LA_FLAW@HOME_OFFICE;
```

Then she can retrieve the full contents of LA__FLAW with:

```
SQL> SELECT *
  2    FROM PERSONNEL;
```

REMOTE ACCESS BY WAY OF A VIEW

Instead of a synonym, Rox can create a view to retrieve all or part of the remote table. To make PERSONNEL a view instead of a synonym, the command is:

```
SQL> CREATE VIEW PERSONNEL
  2          AS SELECT *
  3          FROM LA__FLAW@HOME__OFFICE;
```

The advantage of a view in this instance is that Rox then could query this view as though it were a table in her own database. For example:

```
SQL> SELECT LAST
  2    FROM PERSONNEL
  3    WHERE BRANCH = 1;
```

would give her the last names of the employees in Branch 1.

RULES FOR USING LINKS

In ORACLE's standard form, you can have only four database links in effect at one time. You can change this default by entering a new OPEN__LINKS value in the CONFIG.ORA file. If you try to open more links than the program allows, ORACLE will stubbornly refuse your request. Repeated use of the same link does not count against the limit.

You can use a database link in the FROM clause of a CREATE TABLE, CREATE VIEW, SELECT, or INSERT command. You also can use it in subqueries that begin with the same phrases.

You also can drop a database link as though it were a table or view with a command such as:

```
SQL> DROP DATABASE LINK HOME__OFFICE;
```

COPYING DATA

With the SQL*Plus command COPY, you can move data from a remote database to your own, send data from your database to a remote database, or even move data between two remote databases.

To copy data, you need to specify the same things about the remote database that you would specify to create a database link. You must know the name applied to the remote database, and you must be able to invoke a user name and password with the access privileges you require.

The simplest COPY command is to retrieve selected data from a remote database and place it in a file on your own computer, where you can manipulate it further. If Rox wants the full contents of LA__FLAW she can enter:

```
SQL> COPY FROM MCKNIFE/BIG__MACK@HOME__OFFICE—
2     CREATE STAFFPEOPLE
3     USING SELECT * FROM LA__FLAW;
```

If Rox did not already have a file called STAFFPEOPLE in her database, ORACLE would create such a file and fill it with the contents of LA__FLAW. If Rox already has such a file in her database, ORACLE will report the error and stop. This, then, is the command to use when you want to make sure you do not accidentally overwrite an existing table.

In the future, Rox may simply want to replace her version of LA__FLAW with a current version from the Los Angeles database. In this case, the second line of the command would read REPLACE STAFFPEOPLE. REPLACE will drop any table of the same name that it finds and will then create a new table.

There are two other alternatives. INSERT will place the retrieved data within an existing database but will not create a new table. APPEND will insert the data into a table if one exists; otherwise, it will create one.

USING introduces a query which specifies the information to be moved. It is as selective as any other SELECT command is, allowing you to import only specified rows and columns.

EXPORTING DATA

Rox also can copy the information in her file to the remote database. To do this, she can issue this slightly modified version of the earlier COPY command:

```
SQL> COPY TO MCKNIFE/BIG__MACK@HOME__OFFICE—
  2    CREATE STAFFPEOPLE—
  3    USING SELECT * FROM LA__FLAW;
```

Instead of copying from the remote table, this command copies to it. The CREATE, REPLACE, INSERT, and APPEND alternatives work in the same manner in both directions.

Because COPY is a SQL*Plus command, it requires hyphens at the ends of continued lines. The line numbers and concluding semicolons are not required.

You can copy data between any pair of databases to which you have access. Simply indicate the source database with FROM and the destination database with TO. If both tables are in remote databases, you must identify each with a database link.

DIRECT CONNECTION TO A REMOTE DATABASE

Once you have established a database link, you can use it to make a direct connection to a remote database. Then, you can use it as if it were a local database on your own computer.

You must specify the database link when you invoke SQL from DOS. The command is this:

```
C> SQLPLUS <user name>/<password>@<database link>.
```

REVIEW QUESTIONS

1. If a table called DOWNTIME is created under the user name MADISON, what must Addie Davidson call that table in order to gain access to it? (Assume she has the necessary authorization and privileges.)
2. What's wrong with this command?

```
SQL> GRANT CONNECT
  2    TO HART
  3    IDENTIFIED BY MONKEY__BUSINESS;
```

3. You have been working in ORACLE under the user name Roger. Now, you want to gain access to a separate set of files, to which you have a different set of privileges under the user name Wilco. As Wilco, you have the password OVER__OUT. What's the quickest way to make the switch?

4. In light of recent monkey business, you decide to let Hart see, but not alter, a table called POLL__RESULTS. Write a command that will do that.

5. Earlier, this command granted certain privileges to the supervisor of Department 2 at UnderFed:

```
SQL> GRANT INSERT, UPDATE, DELETE
  2   ON CUSTOMER
  3   TO ZIMMERMAN;
```

Revise this command so that, after Zimmerman moves on and someone else takes over his position, the new supervisor can use the file.

6. You see the error message "Table does not exist." What does this mean? What else might it mean?

7. Early in this chapter, Addie Davidson gained access to the ROSTER file under the user name Addie. Later, a view was created with this command:

```
SQL> CREATE VIEW STAFF AS
  2   SELECT *
  3   FROM ROSTER
  4   WHERE DEPT__NO IN
  5        (SELECT DEPT__NO
  6        FROM ROSTER
  7        WHERE LAST = USER
  8        AND POSITION = 'SUPERVISOR');
```

Davidson cannot gain access to this view. Why not, and what can you do about it?

8. Access control helps protect you against damage caused by people who are not authorized for access to your database. What kind of control helps prevent damage caused by people who *are* authorized?

9. What's the difference between a Share lock and a Share Update lock?

10. Allison Wunderland, the Marinecorp regional manager, has established a database link called BRANCH__69, which gives her the same access as Addie Davidson has to the UnderFed database. How would she use this link to retrieve the full contents of the ROSTER table?

ANSWERS

1. MADISON.DOWNTIME

2. The password is too readily connected with its holder.

3.   SQL> CONNECT WILCO/OVER__OUT
4.   SQL> GRANT SELECT
         2   ON POLL__RESULTS
         3   TO HART;
5.   SQL> GRANT INSERT, UPDATE, DELETE
         2   ON CUSTOMER
         3   TO (SELECT LAST
         4   FROM ROSTER
         5   WHERE DEPT__NO = 2
         6   AND POSITION = 'SUPERVISOR');

6. The error message may mean that the table does not exist. It may also mean that you have tried to gain access to a table for which you have no access privileges of any kind.

7. The USER assignment in Line 7 grants access only to those whose user names match last names recorded in ROSTER. Addie could gain access to this view by signing on as Davidson, or you could rewrite Line 7 to read:

         7   WHERE LAST = USER OR FIRST = USER

8. Concurrency control.

9. A Share lock lets others look but not touch. A Share Update lock lets users also apply their own locks to the same data.

10.   SQL> SELECT *
         2   FROM ROSTER@BRANCH__69;

12

Database Maintenance and Repair

An ORACLE database can become a massive collection of data. Multiple databases created by multiple users can become multiply massive. If you have assumed the role of database administrator, you will need some tools to manage the system. Otherwise, it will become a massive collection of data that can't be efficiently used because no one knows what's there or where to find it.

The *data dictionary* is a database administrator's repair and maintenance toolkit. It is a set of tables and views that record user names, the privileges these users hold, the names and definitions of tables and views, and similar information. ORACLE maintains this dictionary automatically.

The dictonary provides most of the tools you'll need to keep from violating a key element of the definition of a database: that it is an *organized* system of information. Many of these features come in the forms of database tables and views. This chapter will describe several of them, including additional means to control access plus auditing facilities to keep track of who does what. There also are several nondictionary utilities, including a means to back up your data.

This chapter will also tell you how to install ORACLE for use on a network, as opposed to the single-user installation described in Chapter 2.

dBASE DATA MANAGEMENT

The dBASE designers have adopted many features of SQL and other mainframe data management packages in their most recent products. The users of dBASE have not done the same. For example, the dBASE view is an idea taken directly from SQL, but few serious dBASE users seem to have adopted it. The Protect utility is an attempt to add to dBASE the kind of access control that SQL has. Like most dBASE multi-user features, it is an addition to what was originally a single-user program. The dBASE catalog is equally obscure.

DICTIONARY VERSUS CATALOG

The catalog in dBASE serves much the same purpose as the dictionary in SQL does. This creates some unnecessary confusion between two kinds of reference works. More to the point, dBASE features such as the view and the catalog appear to have been victims of the condescension so many skilled people in so many fields hold for the less knowledgeable. The view and catalog in dBASE have become associated with the menu-driven Assist accessory. Because "real" dBASE users don't use menus, those of us who know a little something about dBASE have done less than an excellent job of informing others about how to use these features. It's no accident that the view and catalog have only recently begun to appear in the high-speed dBASE substitutes favored by professional application developers.

These oversights and omissions make things difficult when the object is to explain SQL in terms of familiar dBASE commands and operations. It's now become necessary to explain the SQL data dictionary in terms of an unfamiliar dBASE facility—and one with a confusingly different name to boot.

CREATING A CATALOG

The basic command to activate a dBASE catalog is:

. SET CATALOG TO <catalog name>

The name must be appropriate for a .DBF file. In fact, a catalog file has the same type of structure as a database file. The main difference is its .CAT extension. If there is no catalog by that name, dBASE will create one for you. If you've lost track of your available catalogs, you can get a menu of them with this command, called a *catalog query:*

. SET CATALOG TO ?

Once you have activated a catalog, any database you use or create will be added to the catalog. In general, one catalog should record all the linked .DBF files that make up a single database. A user who wants to select this database from what might be a host of possibilities need only activate the catalog. The catalog will also keep track of any associated format, index, label, query, or report files.

A catalog file has this standard structure:

Field	Field Name	Type	Width	Dec
1	PATH	Character	70	
2	FILE_NAME	Character	12	

3	ALIAS	Character	8
4	TYPE	Character	3
5	TITLE	Character	80
6	CODE	Numeric	3
7	TAG	Numeric	4
** Total **			181

Figure 12-1 lists the varied contents of a catalog file. This one happens to be the travel agency database supplied as a dBASE training exercise. The last three entries might be a little confusing. The *title* is actually a description you can supply. It will appear in the Catalog Query display. The code and tag are numerical indexes assigned by dBASE. Since they don't mean much to human readers, you won't see them here.

THE SQL DATA DICTIONARY

Like dBASE, ORACLE maintains its own data dictionary. The dictionary maintains records about a single database, in most cases the tables and views you have created under your own user name. Whenever you create a new table or view, ORACLE updates the collection of its own tables and views that makes up the dictionary. The same thing happens when you drop or alter a table or view.

FIGURE 12-1   A Look Inside a dBASE Catalog

```
Record#  PATH          FILE_NAME     ALIAS    TYPE TITLE
      1  tours.dbf     tours.dbf     TOURS    dbf  Description of Available Tours
      2  clients.dbf   clients.dbf   CLIENTS  dbf  Client Address and Phone Entry
      3  travel.dbf    travel.dbf    TRAVEL   dbf  Trip Reservation Entry
      4  traveler.frm  traveler.frm  TRAVEL   frm  Report of firstname, lastname...
      5  address.lbl   address.lbl   CLIENTS  lbl  address labels (for clients)
      6  notpaid.qry   notpaid.qry   TRAVEL   qry  ((Cost>1500 or departure < 10/15 ) and paid false)
and not 'Garnett'
      7  trips.ndx     trips.ndx     TRAVEL   ndx  Travel file index on 'Travelcode + Lastname'
      8  tourdate.ndx  tourdate.ndx  TOURS    ndx  Tours file index on 'Departure'
      9  zipcode.ndx   zipcode.ndx   CLIENTS  ndx  Clients file index on 'zipcode'
     10  reserve.fmt   reserve.fmt   TRAVEL   fmt  Format file for Reserve view file (Travel and
Clients - lastname)
     11  travel.fmt    travel.fmt    TRAVEL   fmt  Format file for Travel db file
     12  tours.fmt     tours.fmt     TOURS    fmt  Format file for Tours dbf file
     13  clients.fmt   clients.fmt   CLIENTS  fmt  Format file for Clients db file
     14  cnames.ndx    cnames.ndx    CLIENTS  ndx  clients file index on 'lastname + firstname'
     15  reserve.vue   reserve.vue   TRAVEL   vue  View file linking TRAVEL and CLIENTS file by common
last names
     16  triplog.cat   triplog.cat            cat  Bon Voyage Travel Agency File Catalog
     17  travel.scr    travel.scr    TRAVEL   scr  Screen Format file for Travel Database file
     18  tours.scr     tours.scr     TOURS    scr  Screen Format file for Tours database file
     19  clients.scr   clients.scr   CLIENTS  scr  Screen format file for Clients database file
```

The dictionary describes tables, columns, user access privileges, and other elements of the database. It also describes some features you won't encounter until the next chapter: indexes and clusters.

As a database administrator you should be authorized to act under two user names, SYSTEM and SYS. Only the person who holds the authority of SYSTEM has the power to alter the dictionary, and only SYS can change its most critical elements.

Now that you know that, forget it. ORACLE does a good job of maintaining its own dictionary. For the most part, the operation is automatic and totally reliable. Don't even think about human intervention, particularly in the SYS resources, unless you are clearly on the edge of disaster, and you've literally already tried everything else.

Even without SYS, you have read-only access to the dictionary's contents. A variety of tables and views make up the dictionary. You can read any of them with a standard SQL query. You can read even the tables that describe other tables in the dictionary. You don't even need to know whether you are querying a table or a view.

EXAMINING THE DICTIONARY

The dictionary table DTAB holds the names and descriptions of the tables that make up the dictionary itself. To see it, enter the simple query:

SQL> SELECT * FROM DTAB;

The results will be the extensive display shown in Figure 12-2. You should be able to note the similarities between this display and the dBASE output shown in Figure 12-1. In fact, dBASE has a nearly exact counterpart to DTAB. It's a file called:

CATALOG.CAT (a catalog of other catalogs.)

EXAMINING OTHER TABLES

Of the forty-two possibilities in Figure 12-2, there are three that describe the tables, views, and clusters to which you have access:

- TAB displays all the tables and views that you own. If you create clusters as a way to improve performance and space allo-

FIGURE 12-2 The Standard Dictionary Tables

```
TNAME               REMARKS
--------------      ----------------------------------------------------------------
Reference Date      ORACLE catalog as of 10-Oct-85, installed on 24-APR-87 11:17:25.
AUDIT_ACCESS        Audit entries for accesses to user's tables/views (DBA sees all)
AUDIT_ACTIONS       Maps auditing action numbers to action names
AUDIT_CONNECT       Audit trail entries for user logon/logoff (DBA sees all users)
AUDIT_DBA           Audit trail entries for DBA activities -- for DBA use only
AUDIT_EXISTS        Audit trail entries for objects which do NOT EXIST -- DBA's only
AUDIT_TRAIL         Audit trail entries relevant to the user (DBA sees all)
CATALOG             Tables and views accessible to user (excluding data dictionary)
CLUSTERS            Clusters and their tables (either must be accessible to user)
CLUSTERCOLUMNS      Maps cluster columns to clustered table columns
COL                 Specifications of columns in tables created by the user
COLUMNS             Columns in tables accessible to user (excluding data dictionary)
DEFAULT_AUDIT       Default table auditing options
DTAB                Description of tables and views in Oracle Data Dictionary
EXTENTS             Data structure of extents within tables
INDEXES             Indexes created by user and indexes on tables created by user
PARTITIONS          File structure of files within partitions -- for DBA use only
PRIVATESYN          Private synonyms created by the user
PUBLICSYN           Public synonyms
SESSIONS            Audit trail entries for the user's sessions (DBA sees all)
SPACES              Selection of space definitions for creating tables and clusters
STORAGE             Data and Index storage allocation for user's own tables
SYNONYMS            Synonyms, private and public
SYSAUDIT_TRAIL      Synonym for sys.audit_trail -- for DBA use only
SYSCATALOG          Profile of tables and views accessible to the user
SYSCOLAUTH          Directory of column update access granted by or to the user
SYSCOLUMNS          Specifications of columns in accessible tables and views
SYSEXTENTS          Data structure of tables throughout system -- for DBA use only
SYSINDEXES          List of indexes, underlying columns, creator, and options
SYSPROGS            List of programs precompiled by user
SYSSTORAGE          Summary of all database storage -- for DBA use only
SYSTABALLOC         Data and index space allocations for all tables -- for DBA's
SYSTABAUTH          Directory of access authorization granted by or to the user
SYSTEM_AUDIT        System auditing options -- for DBA use only
SYSUSERAUTH         Master list of Oracle users -- for DBA use only
SYSUSERLIST         List of Oracle users
SYSVIEWS            List of accessible views
TAB                 List of tables, views, clusters and synonyms created by the user
TABALLOC            Data and index space allocations for all user's tables
TABQUOTAS           Table allocation (space) parameters for tables created by user
TABLE_AUDIT         Auditing options of user's tables and views (DBA sees all)
VIEWS               Defining SQL statements for views created by the user

42 records selected.
```

cations (as discussed in Chapter 13) TAB will display all these as well.

- CATALOG describes both the tables you own and those to which you have been granted access. It is limited to working tables and does not include those that are part of the dictionary.

- SYSCATALOG is a complete catalog listing of database assets that you own, that you have access to, or that are in your data dictionary.

You can see the structure of TAB with this command:

SQL> DESCRIBE TAB;

The results:

Name	Null?	Type
TNAME	NOT NULL	CHAR(30)
TABTYPE	NOT NULL	CHAR(7)
CLUSTERID		NUMBER

These three columns contain, in order, the name of the item, whether it is a table, view, or cluster; and, in the case of a cluster, an identification. Figure 12-3 shows how TAB looks as a result of the operations conducted to produce this book so far. Essentially, it lists everything associated with the user name Baker.

FIGURE 12-3 The Author's Tables Displayed in TAB

```
TNAME                                 TABTYPE CLUSTERID
------------------------------------  ------- ---------
ANNUAL_PAY                            VIEW
BONUS                                 TABLE
BRANCHES                              TABLE
CASES                                 TABLE
CIVIL_CASES                           VIEW
CLIENTS                               TABLE
CRIMINAL_CASES                        VIEW
CUSTOMER                              TABLE
DEPT                                  TABLE
DUMMY                                 TABLE
EMP                                   TABLE
LA_FLAW                               TABLE
NEW_ACCT                              TABLE
PAYGRADES                             TABLE
PAY_RANGE                             VIEW
PRODUCTS                              TABLE
PROJ                                  TABLE
REPS                                  TABLE
RETAINER                              VIEW
ROSTER                                TABLE
SALES                                 TABLE
SALGRADE                              TABLE
TRACKING                              TABLE
WORTH_IT                              VIEW

24 records selected.
```

The SQL data dictionary does include a table called CATA-LOG. A query of CATALOG would show approximately the same thing as a query of TAB would show. To the tables and views I own, it would add other peoples' databases to which I have access. In my case, there are none. CATALOG also has a few extra columns:

```
SQL> DESCRIBE CATALOG;

Name            Null?         Type
--------------  ------------  -------
TNAME           NOT NULL      CHAR(30)
CREATOR                       CHAR(30)
TABLETYPE       NOT NULL      CHAR(7)
CLUSTERID                     NUMBER
LOGBLK                        NUMBER
REQBLK                        NUMBER
IXCOMP                        CHAR(10)
REMARKS                       CHAR(240)
```

The numerical columns reflect memory allocations. RE-MARKS provides room for a description. A full display of this table would spread over more real estate than the standard terminal or printer could readily handle. For most purposes, you probably will want to limit your query to specific columns and rows.

SYSCATALOG inclues those tables to which I have access and all the dictionary entries that affect me. Its structure is the same as CATALOG's. Figure 12-4 is the result of this query:

```
SQL> SELECT TNAME, CREATOR, TABLETYPE
   2   FROM SYSCATALOG;
```

Among other things, SYSTEM, the database manager's user name, owns one group of dictionary files. Others are held under the more restrictive name SYS. The SYS files are classified because, short of extreme circumstances, it is important to leave them alone.

Use these commands occasionally to check on the status of your database. For example, I once found a mysterious table called PROJ in my database. It turned out to be a stray from the ORACLE tutorial. Get rid of unwanted material like this with the DROP TABLE command.

FIGURE 12-4   The Fill-Line Display of SYSCATALOG

TNAME	CREATOR	TABLETY
ANNUAL_PAY	BAKER	VIEW
AUDIT_ACCESS	SYSTEM	VIEW
AUDIT_ACTIONS	SYSTEM	TABLE
AUDIT_CONNECT	SYSTEM	VIEW
AUDIT_TRAIL	SYSTEM	VIEW
BONUS	BAKER	TABLE
BRANCHES	BAKER	TABLE
CASES	BAKER	TABLE
CATALOG	SYSTEM	VIEW
CIVIL_CASES	BAKER	VIEW
CLIENTS	BAKER	TABLE
CLUSTERCOLUMNS	SYSTEM	VIEW
CLUSTERS	SYSTEM	VIEW
COL	SYSTEM	VIEW
COLUMNS	SYSTEM	VIEW
CRIMINAL_CASES	BAKER	VIEW
CUSTOMER	BAKER	TABLE
DEFAULT_AUDIT	SYSTEM	VIEW
DEPT	BAKER	TABLE
DTAB	SYSTEM	TABLE
DUAL	SYSTEM	TABLE
DUMMY	BAKER	TABLE
EMP	BAKER	TABLE
EXPTAB	SYSTEM	VIEW
EXPVEW	SYSTEM	VIEW
EXTENTS	SYSTEM	VIEW
HELP	SYSTEM	TABLE
IAPAPP	SYSTEM	TABLE
IAPBLK	SYSTEM	TABLE
IAPCOMMENT	SYSTEM	TABLE
IAPFLD	SYSTEM	TABLE
IAPMAP	SYSTEM	TABLE
IAPSQLTXT	SYSTEM	TABLE
IAPTRG	SYSTEM	TABLE
IAPTRIGGER	SYSTEM	TABLE
INDEXES	SYSTEM	VIEW
LA_FLAW	BAKER	TABLE
NEW_ACCT	BAKER	TABLE
PAYGRADES	BAKER	TABLE
PAY_RANGE	BAKER	VIEW
PRIVATESYN	SYSTEM	VIEW
PRODUCTS	BAKER	TABLE
PROJ	BAKER	TABLE
PUBLICSYN	SYSTEM	VIEW
REPS	BAKER	TABLE
RETAINER	BAKER	VIEW
ROSTER	BAKER	TABLE
SALES	BAKER	TABLE
SALGRADE	BAKER	TABLE
SESSIONS	SYSTEM	VIEW
SPACES	SYSTEM	VIEW
STORAGE	SYSTEM	VIEW
SYNONYMS	SYSTEM	VIEW
SYSCATALOG	SYSTEM	VIEW
SYSCOLAUTH	SYSTEM	VIEW

```
SYSCOLUMNS          SYSTEM              VIEW
SYSINDEXES          SYSTEM              VIEW
SYSPROGS            SYSTEM              VIEW
SYSTABAUTH          SYSTEM              VIEW
SYSUSERLIST         SYSTEM              VIEW
SYSVIEWS            SYSTEM              VIEW
TAB                 SYSTEM              VIEW
TABALLOC            SYSTEM              VIEW
TABLE_AUDIT         SYSTEM              VIEW
TABQUOTAS           SYSTEM              VIEW
TRACKING            BAKER               TABLE
V4EXPCLUS           SYS                 VIEW
V4EXPCOL            SYS                 VIEW
V4EXPEXTENTS        SYS                 VIEW
V4EXPINDEX          SYS                 VIEW
V4EXPSPACE          SYS                 VIEW
V4EXPSYN            SYS                 VIEW
V4EXPTAB            SYS                 VIEW
V4EXPTABAUTH        SYS                 VIEW
V4EXPUSER           SYS                 VIEW
V4EXPVIEW           SYS                 VIEW
VIEWS               SYSTEM              VIEW
WORTH_IT            BAKER               VIEW

78 records selected.
```

DEFINING COLUMNS

The SQL dictionary can go one step further than the dBASE catalog can. The dictionary also has three tables that describe the columns within your tables and views. The three are counterparts to the three table description files:

- COL displays the column specifications in the assets you own.
- COLUMN adds column data for others' assets to which you have access.
- SYSCOLUMN also adds column descriptions from the dictionary tables.

The COL table, simplest of the three, has a structure that is still expansive:

Name	Null?	Type
TNAME	NOT NULL	CHAR(30)
COLNO	NOT NULL	NUMBER
CNAME	NOT NULL	CHAR(30)
COLTYPE	NOT NULL	CHAR(6)

WIDTH	NOT NULL	NUMBER
SCALE		NUMBER
NULLS	NOT NULL	CHAR(8)
REMARKS		CHAR(240)
DEFAULTVAL		CHAR(240)

TNAME is the table's name; COLNO is the column's position in the table, similar to the record number in dBASE. Subsequent columns record the column's name, type, width and default value and whether it accepts nulls. REMARKS lets you include a description. Less obviously, SCALE records the number of decimal points in a Number column.

The display of every column in every table—even in my own small database—can require a hefty amount of space. Again, selective queries are in order when you examine these tables. Usually, you can SELECT only the columns in a single table. It also pays to use the COLUMN command to keep the width of the display within manageable limits.

In this series of commands, the widths of several columns have been limited. Two have designated as nonprinting. This lets you designate the columns you don't want to display, sometimes a useful alternative to the usual practice of specifying those you do want.

```
SQL> COLUMN TNAME FORMAT A15;
SQL> COLUMN CNAME FORMAT A15;
SQL> COLUMN REMARKS NOPRINT;
SQL> COLUMN DEFAULTVAL NOPRINT;
```

You then can use the wild-card asterisk and see everything but the NOPRINT columns:

```
SQL> SELECT *
  2   FROM COL
  3   WHERE TNAME = 'LA_FLAW';
```

The result is shown in Figure 12-5, a description of the columns in LA_FLAW.

COLUMNS and SYSCOLUMNS will give you the same kind of display. They could extend further, though, to include columns in outside-access tables and the data dictionary as well as in your

FIGURE 12-5   Column Descriptions from the COL Table

```
TNAME               COLNO  CNAME              COLTYP   WIDTH   SCALE  NULLS
---------------     -----  ---------------    ------   -----   -----  --------
LA_FLAW                 1  LAST               CHAR        15          NULL
LA_FLAW                 2  FIRST              CHAR        15          NULL
LA_FLAW                 3  BRANCH             NUMBER       1       0  NULL
LA_FLAW                 4  ASSIGN             CHAR        10          NULL
LA_FLAW                 5  SPECIALTY          CHAR        15          NULL
LA_FLAW                 6  HIRED              DATE         7          NULL
LA_FLAW                 7  SALARY             NUMBER       9       2  NULL

7 records selected.
```

personal database. They both have the same structure, similar, but not identical, to COL:

Name	Null?	Type
CNAME	NOT NULL	CHAR(30)
TNAME	NOT NULL	CHAR(30)
CREATOR		CHAR(30)
COLNO	NOT NULL	NUMBER
COLTYPE	NOT NULL	CHAR(6)
WIDTH	NOT NULL	NUMBER
SCALE		NUMBER
NULLS	NOT NULL	CHAR(8)
REMARKS		CHAR(240)
DEFAULTVAL		CHAR(240)

The CREATOR in this case is the owner's user name. You can use either COLUMNS or SYSCOLUMNS to examine the structure of someone else's table—assuming, of course, that you have legitimate access to it. For example, after I gave Addie Davidson access to my database in the last chapter, she could issue this query:

```
SQL> SELECT CNAME, COLNO, COLTYPE, WIDTH, SCALE
     NULLS
   2     FROM COLUMNS
   3     WHERE CREATOR = 'BAKER' AND TNAME =
        'ROSTER';
```

The results would be similar to those shown in Figure 12-5 but with my name added in the omnipotent position of CREATOR. It's not often you get an honor like that.

ADDING COMMENTS

Most of the table and column description tables have extensive room for REMARKS. The DTAB table in Figure 12-2 shows some extensive remarks, as does its dBASE equivalent in Figure 12-1. You, too, can make remarks about the tables you own.

COMMENTING ON TABLES

For example, you can write description of the table LA__FLAW. It will appear in response to queries of the CATALOG or SYSCATALOG. Some people speak worse English than SQL does in this command:

```
SQL> COMMENT ON TABLE LA__FLAW
   2    IS 'MASTER PERSONNEL ROSTER';
```

This comment will be added automatically to the REMARKS columns of both catalog files. To check, enter:

```
SQL> COLUMN REMARKS FORMAT A35;
SQL> SELECT TNAME, REMARKS
   2    FROM CATALOG
   3    WHERE TNAME = 'LA__FLAW'
```

You should see:

```
TNAME       REMARKS
----------- -----------------------------------
LA__FLAW    MASTER PERSONNEL ROSTER
```

In fact, you should see the same thing whether you issued this query to CATALOG or SYSCATALOG.

COMMENTING ON COLUMNS

You can use the same technique to help identify the columns listed in any of the three column definition tables. I entered:

```
SQL> COMMENT ON COLUMN LA__FLAW.LAST
   2    IS 'EMPLOYEE'S LAST NAME';
```

Instead of getting confirmation that the comment was added, I got this error message instead:

```
IS 'EMPLOYEE'S LAST NAME'
            *
ERROR at line 2: ORA-0933:  SQL command not properly
ended
```

This error is included as a reminder that you must remember the lessons of earlier chapters—particularly if it was you who wrote those earlier chapters. SQL has its own way of interpreting apostrophes. The way to get around that tendency in this case is:

```
SQL> COMMENT ON COLUMN LA__FLAW.LAST
   2    IS 'EMPLOYEE' 'S LAST NAME';
```

The double apostrophe does the trick. Now it's possible to enter:

```
SQL> SELECT CNAME, REMARKS
   2    FROM COL
   3    WHERE TNAME = 'LA__FLAW';
```

You should get these results:

```
CNAME          REMARKS
-------------- ----------------------------
LAST           EMPLOYEE'S LAST NAME
FIRST
BRANCH
ASSIGN
SPECIALTY
HIRED
SALARY

7 records selected.
```

You can add your own comments to the other column descriptions.

MORE KINDS OF MONITORING

There are other commands that let you monitor storage space, indexes, views, and database privileges. As you might expect, ORACLE maintains a table or two in the dictionary for this purpose.

MAINTAINING STORAGE

ORACLE doesn't manage its disk and memory storage the way DOS does. It does have a means, though, to keep track of the amount of disk space that each table occupies. A table called STORAGE, naturally enough, keeps track of each table's storage requirements in units that ORACLE calls *blocks*.

This term means many things to many different types of computer operations. In ORACLE, a block is simply a standard unit of disk storage. It's also known as a *page*.

Just how large a page is depends on the host computer and its operating system. In DOS, a page or block is 512 bytes.

The STORAGE table is built like this:

Name	Null?	Type
NAME		CHAR(30)
TYPE		CHAR(7)
WHICH		CHAR(5)
STORAGE		NUMBER
EXTENTS		NUMBER

Along with the table's name, this dictionary records its type (table or view) and whether it contains data or is an index (which is what WHICH is for). The STORAGE column gives the storage space in blocks.

EXTENTS helps you identify fragmented tables whose pieces are scattered all over a disk. It reports the number of separate disk areas the file occupies. If the number becomes too large, the computer must search widely for all the pieces, and the operation will be unnecessarily slow. More to the point, DOS allows a maximum of about 110 extents. If you crowd that limit, you may run out of storage space.

There's no such problem with the table LA__FLAW, as this query reveals:

```
SQL> SELECT *
  2    FROM STORAGE
  3    WHERE NAME = 'LA__FLAW';
```

The results are:

NAME	TYPE	WHICH	STORAGE	EXTENTS
LA__FLAW	TABLE	DATA	5	1
LA__FLAW	TABLE	INDEX	5	1

The biggest surprise here is that LA__FLAW has an index as well as its data table. The index will be discussed in the next chapter. For the purposes of the storage check, there's no problem with these modestly sized entities. Each unit occupies five blocks, or 2,560 bytes. Each is also able to confine itself within a single extent.

KEEPING TRACK OF INDEXES

Once you begin to create indexes, there will also be a table, called INDEXES, that keeps track of these indexes. It includes columns to record such items as the index name, its associated table, the creator of each, the column indexed, and whether or not the index requires a unique value in that column. dBASE users might recognize that these specifications are similar to the indexing that dBASE uses.

A VIEW TO A VIEW

Another logically named dictionary table is VIEWS. It lists the views in your database along with the queries that created them.

This is a database whose contents tend to sprawl, so it is helpful to precede a query with a couple of COLUMN commands to keep things under control:

```
SQL> COLUMN VIEWNAME FORMAT A24;
SQL> COLUMN VIEWTEXT FORMAT A50 WORD__WRAPPED;
SET LONG 255;
```

This introduces you to the WORD__WRAPPED option of COLUMN. When the contents of the column are too long, it will wrap them to the next line, breaking the lines between words rather than randomly between letters. The SET LONG command tries to make sure you allow enough space to retrieve the entire query. Otherwise, you might find several of the long queries that appear in this table to be lopped off at awkward places. Now you can:

```
SQL> SELECT *
   2   FROM VIEWS;
```

The results are shown in Figure 12-6.

FIGURE 12-6   The Details of Current Views

```
VIEWNAME                   VIEWTEXT
------------------------   ---------------------------------------------------
ANNUAL_PAY                 SELECT LAST, ASSIGN,
                           SALARY MONTHLY,
                           SALARY * 12 ANNUAL
                           FROM LA_FLAW

CIVIL_CASES                SELECT * FROM CASES
                           WHERE COUNSEL IN
                           (SELECT LAST
                           FROM LA_FLAW
                           WHERE ASSIGN = 'CIVIL'

CRIMINAL_CASES             SELECT *
                           FROM CASES
                           WHERE COUNSEL IN
                           (SELECT LAST
                           FROM LA_FLAW
                           WHERE ASSIGN = 'CRIMINAL'

PAY_RANGE                  SELECT BRANCH,
                           MIN(SALARY), AVG(SALARY), MAX(SALARY)
                           FROM LA_FLAW
                           GROUP BY BRANCH

RETAINER                   SELECT *
                           FROM CASES
                           WHERE CLIENT = 'CLOVERHOUSE'

WORTH_IT                   SELECT L.LAST, L.SALARY,
                           C.CASE, C.CLIENT
                           FROM LA_FLAW L, CASES C
                           WHERE C.COUNSEL = L.LAST
                           AND L.SALARY >=
                                   (SELECT SALARY
                                   FROM LA_FLAW
                                   WHERE LA_FLAW.LAST = 'TAWDRY'


6 records selected.
```

KEEPING TRACK OF PRIVILEGES

You can easily lose track of who has granted what kinds of privileges to whom. When this happens, the table SYSBAUTH places its elephantine power of recall at your disposal. It looks like this:

Name	Null?	Type
GRANTOR	NOT NULL	CHAR(30)
GRANTEE	NOT NULL	CHAR(30)
CREATOR	NOT NULL	CHAR(30)
TNAME	NOT NULL	CHAR(30)
TIMESTAMP	NOT NULL	DATE
ALT	NOT NULL	CHAR(1)
DEL	NOT NULL	CHAR(1)
NDX	NOT NULL	CHAR(1)
INS	NOT NULL	CHAR(1)
SEL	NOT NULL	CHAR(1)
UPD	NOT NULL	CHAR(1)

The first five items identify, in order, who has granted the privilege, to whom, over whose creation, the creation's name, and the time all this happened. The last six identify the types of access granted; in order, ALTER, DELETE, INDEX, INSERT, SELECT, and UPDATE. Either a Y or a G in this column indicates the privilege has been granted.

To find out which privileges I have conferred:

```
SQL> SELECT *
   2    FROM SYSTABAUTH
   3    WHERE GRANTOR = 'BAKER';
```

The results are shown in Figure 12-7. First, you'll find, ORACLE automatically has me granting many privileges to myself. In the last two rows, though, you'll see the two privileges I granted in the last chapter: to Addie for the ROSTER table and to the public for DEPT. If you want to screen out the long list of self-bestowed privileges, change Line 3 of the last query to read:

```
   3    WHERE GRANTOR = USER AND GRANTEE < > USER;
```

FIGURE 12-7   A List of Privileges—and One Privileged Character

GRANTOR	GRANTEE	CREATOR	TNAME	TIMESTAMP	A	D	N	I	S	U
BAKER	BAKER	BAKER	EMP	21-OCT-87	G	G	G	G	G	G
BAKER	BAKER	BAKER	DEPT	21-OCT-87	G	G	G	G	G	G
BAKER	BAKER	BAKER	BONUS	21-OCT-87	G	G	G	G	G	G
BAKER	BAKER	BAKER	SALGRADE	21-OCT-87	G	G	G	G	G	G
BAKER	BAKER	BAKER	DUMMY	21-OCT-87	G	G	G	G	G	G
BAKER	BAKER	BAKER	PROJ	03-NOV-87	G	G	G	G	G	G
BAKER	BAKER	BAKER	TRACKING	05-NOV-87	G	G	G	G	G	G
BAKER	BAKER	BAKER	NEW_ACCT	07-NOV-87	G	G	G	G	G	G
BAKER	BAKER	BAKER	REPS	10-NOV-87	G	G	G	G	G	G
BAKER	BAKER	BAKER	PAYGRADES	23-NOV-87	G	G	G	G	G	G
BAKER	BAKER	BAKER	PRODUCTS	30-NOV-87	G	G	G	G	G	G
BAKER	BAKER	BAKER	CUSTOMER	30-NOV-87	G	G	G	G	G	G
BAKER	BAKER	BAKER	SALES	30-NOV-87	G	G	G	G	G	G
BAKER	BAKER	BAKER	ROSTER	30-NOV-87	G	G	G	G	G	G
BAKER	BAKER	BAKER	LA_FLAW	30-NOV-87	G	G	G	G	G	G
BAKER	BAKER	BAKER	BRANCHES	30-NOV-87	G	G	G	G	G	G
BAKER	BAKER	BAKER	CLIENTS	30-NOV-87	G	G	G	G	G	G
BAKER	BAKER	BAKER	CASES	17-DEC-87	G	G	G	G	G	G
BAKER	BAKER	BAKER	CIVIL_CASE S	17-DEC-87	G	G	G	G	G	G
BAKER	BAKER	BAKER	CRIMINAL_C ASES	17-DEC-87	G	G	G	G	G	G
BAKER	BAKER	BAKER	RETAINER	17-DEC-87	G	G	G	G	G	G
BAKER	BAKER	BAKER	WORTH_IT	17-DEC-87	G	G	G	G	G	G
BAKER	BAKER	BAKER	ANNUAL_PAY	17-DEC-87	G	G	G	G	G	G
BAKER	BAKER	BAKER	PAY_RANGE	17-DEC-87	G	G	G	G	G	G
BAKER	ADDIE	BAKER	ROSTER	31-DEC-87	Y	Y	Y	Y	Y	Y
BAKER	PUBLIC	BAKER	DEPT	31-DEC-87					Y	

26 records selected.

This command will give you only the last two rows, identifying privileges you have granted to someone else rather than to yourself.

At one point in this display, you'll find an example of what happens without WORD_WRAP. ORACLE split a word clean in two and bumped the tail end to the next line.

Also, note the distinctions between the privileges I granted in the last two lines. I gave Addie the right to do anything with the data for her own office. However, the Public has only the right to read the departmental table.

CONTROLLING OUTSIDE ACCESS

The access control described in the previous chapter is only one of two available levels. At this level, owners of tables, views, and other database resources use the GRANT command to authorize controlled access to these resources. The database manager under the user name SYSTEM has the authority to grant or deny another kind of access: that to ORACLE itself.

A couple of times in previous chapters you made some brief, unmemorable contact with commands that began GRANT CONNECT. In Chapter 2, that command was used to give you access to the ORACLE database. In Chapter 11, you, as administrator, granted similar privileges to the fictional Addie Davidson.

Both instances used a variety of GRANT that is intended to let database managers control access to the system itself. If you are in that position, your power to do this is derived from your ownership of the tables in the data dictionary. You hold title to most of them in your guise as SYSTEM. You own a few others under the alter ego of SYS.

DEAN OF ADMISSIONS

Of the many hats you wear as DBA, one is a mortarboard. You are in charge of admissions to the database. You control it with this version of the GRANT command:

```
SQL> GRANT <privilege> TO <user name> IDENTIFIED BY
<password>
```

There are two main differences between this use of GRANT and that used by database owners:

- Instead of granting privileges to a specified table, view or other resource, you grant access to the entire ORACLE system. There is no ON <resource> clause.
- The types of privileges you can grant are different from those a database owner can confer, but they serve similar functions.

The BY <password> clause is optional. You must use it only if you are signing on a new user who does not yet have an assigned password. You can use it, too, to change passwords.

This command will place the user name and password in the data dictionary. Whenever someone tries to log on, his or her identity is checked against the dictionary entries. The user will be admitted only if the name and password appear in the same row.

LEVELS OF ACCESS

There are three levels of system-access privileges. In ascending order of authority, they are CONNECT, RESOURCE, and DBA.

CONNECT is the basic level of access, the one you should assign to most ordinary users. These users can log onto the system and exercise any privileges the owners of particular resources have granted to them. They may also create their own views and synonyms, but not new tables.

A user with RESOURCE authority has all the CONNECT user's privileges, plus the ability to create new tables and to grant and revoke privileges for their use. This user also has access to the auditing features that will be described shortly.

DBA is the privilege level intended for database administrators. It is automatically granted to SYSTEM. In addition to the privileges granted at lower levels, the DBA can do anything he or she wants with anyone's data. You also can grant or revoke access to the database, create PUBLIC resources, manage memory, and audit the system.

DROPPING USERS

You can drop a user just as you can drop a table or view. The command is:

```
SQL> REVOKE CONNECT FROM <user name>
```

It's not necessary to know what level of access the user has. When you revoke CONNECT, you automatically revoke any higher-level privileges as well.

CHANGING PASSWORDS

To change a user's password, use the same command you would use to admit an individual as a new user:

```
SQL> GRANT <privilege> TO <user name> IDENTIFIED BY <password>
```

AUDITING ORACLE USE

ORACLE's auditing features are intended primarily for security. They let the DBA examine records of who has gained access to what resources and for what purposes. They also let the owners of individual resources monitor the use of these resources.

Anyone who has use of the auditing facility can activate it with the SQL AUDIT command. This command is a bit complex, but the complexity comes from its great variety of available options. Any authorized user can select from these options to:

- Keep track of attempts—successful or otherwise—to gain access to a table or a view.
- Monitor particular types of SQL operations. You have the option of monitoring only operations such as INSERT, UPDATE, and DELETE, which change the shape of the database, or you can also keep track of SELECT commands.
- Control the amount of detail included in the audit report.

In addition, a DBA can:

- Monitor attempts to gain access to the system and to grant or revoke access privileges.
- Enable or disable writing to an audit trail table called SYS.AUDIT_TRAIL.
- Set the default auditing options for database tables.

START AUDITING

By default, ORACLE's auditing facility is turned off. To activate it, you must edit the file INIT.ORA, which you should find in the ORACLE5\DBS directory. Look for a parameter called AUDIT_TRAIL. The correct entry to activate the auditing feature is:

AUDIT_TRAIL 1

If this parameter is set to 0, or if you find no AUDIT_TRAIL entry at all, auditing is turned off, and you must provide the above command to activate it. Any changes you make will take effect the next time you load ORACLE or issue the command:

IOR W

THE AUDIT COMMAND

A typical AUDIT command is:

SQL> AUDIT ALTER ON ROSTER BY ACCESS WHENEVER
      SUCCESSFUL

To examine the many available options, it's best to break this command into its individual components. The first is:

AUDIT ALTER

ALTER is one of eleven operations, including AUDIT itself, that you can monitor. The others are COMMENT, DELETE, GRANT, INDEX, INSERT, LOCK, RENAME, SELECT, and UPDATE. You can choose any combination of your choice, as in:

SQL> AUDIT ALTER, SELECT, UPDATE

If you want to oversee all these operations, you can say:

SQL> AUDIT ALL

The next phrase, ON ROSTER, is the simplest. It identifies the table or view to be audited. Then, you come to:

BY ACCESS

This command specifies the kinds of activities that will place new entries in the audit trail. Under BY ACCESS, a new record will be created any time a user attempts one of the operations specified in the ALTER command. The alternative is BY SESSION. It will lay down only one new bread crumb in the audit trail every time a user begins a new ORACLE session. If you make no specification here, BY SESSION is the default.

With this specification:

WHENEVER SUCCESSFUL

the audit trail will record only successful access attempts. The alternative, WHENEVER NOT SUCCESSFUL, records only unsuccessful attempts. If you omit this specification, both will be recorded.

AUDIT REPORTS

The dictionary tables listed in Figure 12-2 include several records that contain the term AUDIT. As you might suspect, these are the tables that maintain the audit trail.

AUDIT_TRAIL is the main record. The DBA can examine the entire table. Other users can examine the results of their own auditing activities. Others can record particular types of activities.

AUDIT_EXISTS is particularly interesting. It records any

activity that results in a "Does not exist" error message. Because some types of unauthorized access produce this message even when the table does exist, this file is a useful log of attempts to use your data improperly. A few random entries in this table will probably reflect only an occasional error. A large number of entries, particularly if they have anything in common, indicates that someone may be systematically trying to gain unauthorized access. Check this and the other auditing tables for details that can tell you more about who it is and what they have accomplished.

FOR THE ADVANCED DBA

The ORACLE documentation package includes a separate manual for database administrators. It starts with the material discussed in this chapter and proceeds into highly advanced database management techniques.

Most of these techniques are not for the beginning user, or even the beginning DBA. The contents of the DBA manual can become valuable, though, as you gain experience—and as your database system gains weight.

BACKUP AND RESTORATION

Much has been said about the importance of backing up your data regularly. Much less has been done about it. Backup is one of those activities in which even the most self-disciplined computer users develop virulent cases of procrastination.

Perhaps this is because backing up data is like doing paperwork in that it consumes a lot of time and seems unproductive to the person who's doing it. These are probably the reasons that both are so widely resisted.

A timely backup can be highly productive—in exactly those situations for which it was intended. Consider the lost labor, not to mention lost knowledge, that can result when some on-disk disaster wipes out the only copy of an important database. Saving that amount of work is truly a productive activity. In a network, a backup could save the work of many people—and failure to back up could be disastrous. Regular backups are not just productive—they're vital.

How often is regular? You must answer this question yourself, considering the nature of your operation, the number of users, and how frequently your database is modified. The basic rule is if you can't afford to lose it, back it up.

BACKUP METHODS

A DOS backup program, including the one supplied with DOS itself, would back up an ORACLE database by creating copies of the ORACLE files that contain the tables in ORACLE's own storage format. This approach is effective in the same way a sledgehammer is effective.

ORACLE comes with its own pair of backup utilities. One exports your data to backup files; the other imports backup material when you need it. They are called EXP and IMP. You should be able to figure out which does which.

EXP and IMP can manage files on any of three levels. An administrator who has access to the SYSTEM name and password can back up or restore an entire database, every table assigned to a particular user, or specified tables. Those who have limited access to the database can process the files to which they claim title.

EXP creates a text file that can be edited for use in dBASE or a word processor, but only if you are inventive, desperate, or both. (Children should not try this at home and adults should not try this with the only copy of the backup file.) If you look closely, you'll see that it's similar to the SQL command file used in Chapter 2 to create a new table. In effect, IMP will run that command file if you need to restore data from the backup.

EXP and IMP do tend to be slow when asked to handle large databases. A faster alternative is simply to copy the files that contain your database tables to a backup disk. You can use the DOS COPY function, or you can use BACKUP or some equivalent backup utility. The names of the database files begin with DBA and carry the suffix .ORA. Also, include any database files that might have been created with different types of names, plus any "before image" files whose names begin with BI.

OTHER UTILITIES

Another utility, called the ORACLE Data Loader (or ODL), does load straight text files into an ORACLE table. ODL requires that you first create a control file that specifies the structure of a table to receive the imported data and then use a variation of the INSERT command to import data. It will handle binary or text files at your option.

A CRT utility lets you switch to a new screen display, replacing the one you specified when you installed ORACLE.

INSTALLING NETWORK ORACLE

Networks come in a bewildering variety of forms. A more or less typical configuration these days is the local area network, or LAN, in which personal computers are connected to each other and, possibly, to a larger mainframe or minicomputer.

Any one of the linked computers can hold ORACLE RDBMS, the central ORACLE database. This central computer is designated as a database server. In some LAN installations, it is also known as a *file server*. For any kind of serious database management, this server should be a heavyweight personal computer in the 286 or 386 class. If you connect with a larger computer, that's probably where the database should be. One of ORACLE's great strengths is that it can reach a SQL database on nearly any kind of computer.

The computers assigned to individual users in the network are called *work stations*. They can gain access to the central database by way of Networkstation ORACLE and its most important component, SQL*Net. These networking facilities are optional accessories to the basic ORACLE package.

REVIEW QUESTIONS

1. Which user of the database system automatically has more than one user name?
2. Both the table and column definition tables in the data dictionary are available in three different versions. What is the purpose of each?
3. In some of the column definition tables, you will find a column called SCALE. What does it hold?
4. Write a command that would describe the column ASSIGN in the table LA__FLAW wherever that column appears in the column definition tables.
5. What's the difference between a block and a page in managing SQL data storage?

6. You want to display a column called BLURB that may have as many as 200 characters. Your screen has room for only forty characters after other data is displayed. Write the commands that will cut the display down to size.
7. Write a command that anyone can use to display the privileges he or she has granted to other users.
8. If you want a user to be able to create new tables, what's the minimum access level that this person should have?
9. You suspect that someone has repeatedly been trying to gain access to a table but so far has been unable to determine the password. In what dictionary table would you find a log of these attempts?
10. Be honest. Do you back up your data often enough to prevent any kind of loss?

ANSWERS

1. The database administrator, who has access to some tables under the user name SYS and general access to the data dictionary as SYSTEM.
2. In each case, one table describes assets you own, a second adds assets to which you have access, and a third adds system assets that relate to yours.
3. The number of decimal places in a number column.
4. One possibility:

```
SQL> COMMENT ON COLUMN LA_FLAW.LAST
  2    IS 'JOB ASSIGNMENT';
```

5. Nothing.

6.
```
SQL> COLUMN BLURB FORMAT A40 WORD_WRAPPED;
SQL> SET LONG 200;
```

7.
```
SQL> SELECT *
  2    FROM SYSTABAUTH
  3    WHERE GRANTOR = USER
  4    AND GRANTEE <> USER;
```

8. RESOURCE

9. AUDIT_EXISTS

10. No. No one can do that. You should back up often enough to avoid any loss you can't afford.

Tuning for Mileage and Performance

"You know, Hubert," said Dennis Madison, "sometimes it pays to think big. How many people do we have in this office?"

"Ten, sir."

"That's right, ten. How big would you say Marinecorp is?"

"There's the regional office, the state office, the district office, the national office, the North American office . . . "

"I think you've got the picture. Now, did you ever stop to think that the database you create for this little office someday might be used to hold records for the great vast bulk of Marinecorp? As I think you can readily appreciate, both dBASE and ORACLE do a very good job of retrieving data from the tables that list our small roster of employees and our puny customer list. But what if we grow larger? What if headquarters wants to combine data and create a really big database? Would the same methods be adequate? I don't think so. We must be prepared with the better methods we'll need in a better future. We have to find out what we can do to handle really big databases. I want you and Misty Presto to see what you can do."

THE ART OF INDEXING

In both dBASE and ORACLE, indexing is the key to improved performance. In both programs, you can use an index to speed up a query. You also can use an index to help make sure a column or field contains a unique value for each entry. Indexing is mandatory if you are going to link two dBASE files. In SQL, an index isn't required, but it helps speed up the joining of SQL tables.

WHAT IS AN INDEX?

A database index is like an index to a book. If you want to look up every reference to the join command that appears in this book, you would turn to the back and look up that topic in the index. The indexed terms are in alphabetical order, so it should be fairly easy to find. The index will then tell on what pages you can find something about joining. If there were no index, or if your chosen term were not indexed, you would have to read the whole book page by page to make sure you didn't miss some vital piece of information on how to be a joiner.

In database operations, an index holds the same kind of

information. For every item in the indexed field, an index file holds a key to its location in the table or database file. The key is like the page number in a printed index—it leads you directly to the proper place. If you are searching for a particular term, and there is no index for that term, the computer must search the entire file, item by item.

Indexing can make a database search vastly quicker, particularly when the table is large. It will do little to speed up the search of a smaller database, however. In the case of a very small table, indexing might even slow you down. The computer must first search the index file for the address of the term you seek then find that address in the main table.

As your tables grow, however, the time needed for this two-step search will become much less than the time needed to scan the entire file without benefit of an index.

CREATING A dBASE INDEX

In dBASE, the command to create an index takes this form:

```
. USE ROSTER
. INDEX ON SS__NO TO ROS__NO
```

After the index has been created, you can call the indexed file with:

```
. USE ROSTER INDEX ROS__NO
```

A display of selected fields from the indexed file then might look like this:

```
. LIST SS__NO, LAST
```

Record#	SS__NO	LAST
1	123-45-6789	DAVIDSON
2	234-56-7890	MADISON
3	456-78-9012	PRESTO
4	567-89-0123	TUBA
10	765-43-2109	ROWE-HATTON
5	789-01-2345	MAHONEY
9	876-54-3210	ZIMMERMAN
6	890-12-3456	BUCHINSKY
7	901-23-4567	PALMER
8	987-65-4321	COLLINS

The display is no longer in order of the record numbers; it is instead organized by Social Security numbers. This is the order determined by the keys in the index file.

CREATING A SQL INDEX

In SQL, the command to create a comparable index is:

```
SQL> CREATE INDEX ROSTER__SSNO
  2   ON ROSTER (SS__NO);
```

One advantage to ORACLE is that the index name is not bound by the eight-character limit imposed by DOS. You can use this expansive feature to avoid abbreviations and make your name a little more descriptive. The title of this index file means that the table ROSTER has been indexed on the Social Security number. If some other title is more meaningful to you, by all means use it.

One difference between a dBASE and a SQL index is that a SQL table is not necessarily displayed in its index order:

```
SQL> SELECT SS__NO, LAST
  2   FROM ROSTER;
```

SS__NO	LAST
123-45-6789	DAVIDSON
234-56-7890	MADISON
456-78-9012	PRESTO
567-89-0123	TUBA
789-01-2345	MAHONEY
890-12-3456	BUCHINSKY
901-23-4567	PALMER
987-65-4321	COLLINS
876-54-3210	ZIMMERMAN
765-43-2109	ROWE-HATTON

10 records selected.

The fact that the table appears *almost* in order of the Social Security numbers is a coincidence. This table really appears in the order in which the rows were created. If you want your query results to appear in some particular order, you must use an ORDER BY clause to state your intentions.

The standard format for a simple indexing command is:

```
SQL> CREATE INDEX <name>
   2   ON <table name> (<column name(s)>);
```

INDEXING ON MULTIPLE VALUES

It also probably would be useful to index a table such as Roster on the names of the people listed there. This requires that you index on more than one field. The last name should be the primary index. People with the same last name should be indexed in alphabetical order of their first names. The middle initial is a third level of indexing.

In dBASE, you would index the ROSTER file this way:

```
. INDEX ON LAST + FIRST + INITIAL TO EMP__NAME
```

The SQL equivalent is:

```
SQL> CREATE INDEX EMP__NAME
   2   ON ROSTER (LAST, FIRST, INIT);
```

When you want to index on more than one column, simply list the columns in order as was done in Line 2.

Again, dBASE will display its contents in the indexed order:

```
. LIST LAST, FIRST, INITIAL
```

Record#	LAST	FIRST	INITIAL
6	BUCHINSKY	CHARLES	B
8	COLLINS	KATHLEEN	D
1	DAVIDSON	ADDIE	H
2	MADISON	DENNIS	W
5	MAHONEY	SUZANNE	S
7	PALMER	VERA	M
3	PRESTO	MISTY	D
10	ROWE-HATTON	PHYLLIS	F
4	TUBA	HUBERT	G
9	ZIMMERMAN	ROBERT	D

and again, ORACLE will not.

TIME IS OF THE ESSENCE

"I have one question," said Tuba. "If ORACLE doesn't display its output in an indexed order, what on earth is indexing good for?"

"Indexing," said Madison, "speeds up queries. Oh, it won't do that on the small tables we manage in this office, but when you get into searching the world-class databases we were talking about earlier, you'll be glad you have an index to do it with."

The simplest example of how indexing can speed up a search comes from dBASE. If you have the index ROSTER.DBF in order of the employees' names and you issue the command SEEK 'PALMER', dBASE will zip into the index file, find the location of Vera Palmer's record, and take you right to it. SEEK, which works only in indexed fields, is noticeably faster than any other searching command.

In SQL, indexing makes SELECT work faster, at least when large tables are involved. This command:

```
SQL>  SELECT LAST, FIRST, INIT, SS_NO
   2     FROM ROSTER
   3     WHERE LAST = 'PALMER';
```

takes much the same route through an index file as SEEK does in dBASE. It leads you speedily to these results:

```
LAST        FIRST    I    SS_NO
----------  -------  --   -----------
PALMER      VERA     M    901-23-4567
```

AUTOMATIC INDEXING

Any time you enter a WHERE clause that refers to an indexed column, ORACLE will automatically make use of the index. In a large database, this will almost always be a quicker and more efficient search method than scanning the entire file without benefit of indexing.

You don't have to identify an index file. You don't even have to know whether one exists.

There is one limitation on searching with indexes. ORACLE will take advantage of an index only when your query refers directly to the column by name. If you use the name in an expression, the index will not be activated. For example, you would not get an indexed query in response to the clause:

WHERE UPPER (LAST) = 'PALMER.'

INDEXING FOR UNIQUE VALUES

The Social Security number is a useful identifier in any table of employees, customers, or other groups of people. It is unique to the individual it identifies. For that reason, it is often used (and sometimes misused) for personal identification.

One reason this number is so frequently used is that it makes an ideal database key. It is a unique identifier that directly identifies the person to whom it is attached. No one else on earth has your Social Security number—at least, no one is supposed to.

In indexing ROSTER on the Social Security numbers, you can use UNIQUE to help screen out errors in data entry. Use this version of the earlier command:

```
SQL> CREATE UNIQUE INDEX EMP_NO
  2    ON ROSTER (SS_NO);
```

TESTING UNIQUENESS

Now, imagine that you are adding a new employee to the table. This command will have several nulls in columns that aren't relevant to the present discussion. It will include two important things, though. First, the new employee to be added has the same last name as a current employee. Second, this command duplicates a Social Security number that already is in the table:

```
SQL> INSERT INTO ROSTER
  2    VALUES ('JP', 'PALMER', 'JANE', 'T',
  3    NULL, NULL, '123-45-6789', NULL, NULL, NULL);
```

ORACLE's response is:

```
INSERT INTO ROSTER
          *
ERROR at line 1: ORA-0001: duplicate value in index
```

This error message is a bit misleading. The error is not in Line 1; it is in line 3, in the duplicate Social Security number. To prove it, edit the third line and run this version:

```
SQL> INSERT INTO ROSTER
  2    VALUES ('JP', 'PALMER', 'JANE', 'T',
  3    NULL, NULL, '111-11-1111', NULL, NULL, NULL)
```

You should be rewarded with the announcement:

1 record created.

MOMENTS TO REMEMBER

At this point, a little review might be in order. The table is indexed uniquely on the Social Security number. It is also indexed, but without the unique requirement, on the columns that make up the employee's name.

You've just seen a demonstration of a computer's sometimes-perverse proclivity to do exactly what you tell it to do. ORACLE rejected the duplicate Social Security number, because that field was under the influence of a unique index. After the offending number was changed, the program accepted the new entry, including the duplicate last name. That index was not specified as unique.

SOME dBASED BEHAVIOR

dBASE also has a UNIQUE option to its index command, but in the exercises for this section it exhibited some unusual behavior.

First, even though it was indexed uniquely on the Social Security number, dBASE readily accepted an APPEND that included the duplicate number. When asked to LIST the altered file, dBASE produced:

```
. USE ROSTER INDEX ROS_NO
. LIST LAST, SS_NO
```

Record#	LAST	SS_NO
1	DAVIDSON	123-45-6789
2	MADISON	234-56-7890
3	PRESTO	456-78-9012
4	TUBA	567-89-0123
10	ROWE-HATTON	765-43-2109
5	MAHONEY	789-01-2345
9	ZIMMERMAN	876-54-3210

```
6   BUCHINSKY      890-12-3456
7   PALMER         901-23-4567
8   COLLINS        987-65-4321
```

The newly added record is not there—or, at least, it does not seem to be. However, when you remove the index or apply some other index, the suspect record will reappear:

```
Record#   LAST          SS__NO
   1      DAVIDSON      123-45-6789
   2      MADISON       234-56-7890
   3      PRESTO        456-78-9012
   4      TUBA          567-89-0123
   5      MAHONEY       789-01-2345
   6      BUCHINSKY     890-12-3456
   7      PALMER        901-23-4567
   8      COLLINS       987-65-4321
   9      ZIMMERMAN     876-54-3210
  10      ROWE-HATTON   765-43-2109
  11      PALMER        123-45-6789
```

The dBASE UNIQUE appears to have a hole in it. Under a UNIQUE condition, the program will accept a duplicating entry but will not display it. The danger is that the record has been added to the file, and it could reappear when you change indexing. If you are not very, very careful, these reappearances can be particularly ill-timed. ORACLE does it better, refusing to accept the duplicate entry in the first place.

MAKING GOOD USE OF INDEXES

An index can be a time-saver, particularly when you use a join command. A join is like the dBASE SET RELATION—it links two tables on a common field. dBASE insists that you create indexes for this purpose. ORACLE doesn't insist, but it shows its appreciation by working much faster.

The reason for this improved performance is that a join command requires multiple database searches. Every time the computer finds a new key field in one table, it must search through the other file for a match. Indexing makes each of these many searches much faster.

PICK A FIELD, ANY FIELD

You can create an index on any of the common fields. For example, you can precede a join of LA__FLAW and its associated BRANCHES table by indexing the common field, the branch number, in LA__FLAW:

```
SQL> CREATE INDEX BRANCH__NO
   2    ON LA__FLAW (BRANCH);
```

Then, you could issue this join query:

```
SQL> SELECT LAST, LOCATION
   2    FROM LA__FLAW, BRANCHES
   3    WHERE LA__FLAW.BRANCH = BRANCHES.BRANCH;
```

That is a fairly simple query. You may even find it familiar, with these equally routine results:

LAST	LOCATION
MCKNIFE	LOS ANGELES
COSSACK	LOS ANGELES
TUCKER	LOS ANGELES
BOYSENBERRY	LOS ANGELES
BAILEY	LOS ANGELES
BORQUE	LOS ANGELES
TAWDRY	DENVER
BUNSEN	DENVER
ROX	DENVER
HARTLESS	DENVER
MUKLUK	DENVER
MASON	ATLANTA

12 records selected.

Again, because a small file is being used, the time saved here may be negligible. The advantage would be greater with larger files, in which the number of searches required would rapidly multiply.

WHEN MULTIPLE INDEXES ARE NECESSARY

Sometimes you must index both columns in the join condition to get the improved performance you seek. Take this query, for example:

```
SQL> SELECT LAST, LOCATION
   2    FROM LA__FLAW, BRANCHES
   3    WHERE LA__FLAW.BRANCH = BRANCHES.BRANCH
   4    AND LAST = 'HARTLESS';
```

As usual, analyze this query from the bottom up. The first thing it looks for is the last name Hartless in LA__FLAW. Then, it reads the department number in that row and searches for a match in BRANCHES. The important point is that it never searches for the department number in LA__FLAW. This means that the index on LA__FLAW.BRANCH does you absolutely no good.

There are two other indexes that will help. The first is:

```
SQL> CREATE INDEX LAST__NAME
   2    ON LA__FLAW (LAST);
```

and the second is:

```
SQL> CREATE INDEX OFFICE
   2    ON BRANCHES (BRANCH);
```

Each of these will help speed up your query. The first will make it easier for ORACLE to find the last name. The second will pave the path to the branch number column in BRANCHES.

PRINCIPLES OF INDEXING

There is no fixed formula that can help you determine the right way to index in any given situation. You must think through the query step by step. Determine exactly what the program will search for at each step. The best way to improve performance is to index the object of each search.

INDEXING AND TABLE SIZE

Indexing is of little help, and may be of some harm, when you are working with small tables. The makers of ORACLE suggest that a table should have several hundred rows before you consider an index.

The more indexes available, the better ORACLE's chances of finding a direct route to the data you request. There are limits to this, however.

LIMIT THE NUMBER OF INDEXES

Indexing is subject to a few diminishing returns. Two or three indexes per table should usually be your maximum. Having too many indexes simply creates too many diversions that inhibit rather than enhance the search process. An index also takes up disk space you might need for something else.

An even bigger drawback to indexing, though, is that although it improves one kind of operation—the query—you must trade that improvement for reduced speed in some other operations. These are operations such as INSERT, UPDATE, and DELETE that alter a table's size. Whenever you make such a change, the program must also alter any accompanying indexes. This takes time. The more indexes you have, the more time it takes.

Striking a Balance

Between too many indexes and too few indexes, there is useful middle ground—to apply indexes to the columns for which you search most often.

To find these, keep track of the WHERE clauses you use. A WHERE clause specifies the type of data to take from a particular column. The more you find yourself searching a given column, the better candidate that column is for an index.

You'll often have to experiment. Establish an index and see whether it improves things. If not, you can DROP it, just as you can DROP a table or view.

CLUSTERING FOR HIGHER PERFORMANCE

If you're in New York and want to go shopping, it makes sense to go shopping in New York. If the item is available in New York, it makes little sense to look for it in Cleveland or Omaha. For most purchases, it's easier and quicker to shop close to home.

Database searching works in much the same way. It's easier and quicker to search close to home. This is the idea behind the performance-boosting technique called *clustering*.

When you give DOS new data to be recorded on the disk, DOS picks the most convenient spot—most convenient for DOS at that particular moment. It may not be the most convenient spot for you. Later, it may not be convenient even for DOS. The result is that, for example, the piece of data you save today in an ORACLE database may be on one part of the disk. Another few bites that you stored last week are in another location, and some of last month's data are stored somewhere else. When you need to retrieve these far-flung data, DOS must try to remember where it put everything, get it all back together in the right order, and, only then, present it for your approval.

Needless to say, this takes time. By comparison, gathering nuts in May is a simple process.

The object of clustering is to overcome this shortsighted tendency. It puts related data in nearby storage spots on your disk. This way, DOS need not search as far, and it can retrieve your data faster.

HOW CLUSTERING WORKS

Clustering works by doing the same thing on a disk that a view or a join can do on your terminal screen. It takes related data, even from separate tables, and puts them all in the same place.

A cluster ordinarily consists of a group of related tables, linked as they would be in a join. The first thing you need is a common column that is of the same type, length, and meaning in both tables. In other words, you need the same kind of common field you would use to link tables in any other kind of operation. In this query:

```
SQL> SELECT LAST, LOCATION
  2    FROM LA__FLAW, BRANCHES
  3    WHERE LA__FLAW.BRANCH = BRANCHES.BRANCH;
```

the two BRANCHES columns provide that common link.

When used in clustering, this column-in-common is called a *cluster column*. It need not have the same name in every clustered table, but there must be enough in common to form a link between the two.

WHAT A CLUSTER DOES

A cluster does three things to improve performance:

- It stores all the related data from the clustered files in the same place, making disk access easier and quicker.

- When two tables share the same type of value, such as the branch numbers, these values appear only once in the database. This saves space and retrieval time.
- The program creates an index on the cluster column. This index is called—surprisingly—the *cluster index*.

Clustering affects only the way your data are physically stored on disk. It has no effect on the appearance of your data when you retrieve or display them. All the usual SQL commands will do all the usual things.

It's possible to have more than one cluster column in a single cluster. As a rule of thumb, you can establish cluster columns in much the same way, and for much the same reasons, as you would establish indexes on the same columns.

CREATING A CLUSTER

You can create a cluster with the command CREATE CLUSTER, which seems sensible enough. The standard format is:

```
SQL> CREATE CLUSTER <cluster name>
  2    (<cluster column specifications>);
```

The specifications for one or more cluster columns include the column name and its data type. Also, specify the width if you are using something other than the SQL default. The cluster column need not bear the name of any existing column in the clustered tables, although in practice it often does.

To create a cluster for LA__FLAW and its related BRANCHES table, the command is:

```
SQL> CREATE CLUSTER LA__DEPT
  2    (BRANCH NUMBER);
```

This command names the cluster LA__DEPT and establishes the number column BRANCH as the cluster column.

INSTALLING TABLES

You cannot move existing tables into a cluster. You can create new tables, though, including tables with the same contents as existing tables.

To originate a new cluster table, use the CREATE TABLE command with a few added specifications and requirements:

- You must identify the cluster and the cluster column or columns. Do this with a CLUSTER clause which will be demonstrated.
- At least one of each table's cluster columns must carry the NOT NULL restriction. ORACLE will look for common data in the cluster column. These will be hard to find if any of the entries in that column are blank.

To create a new clustered table, the general format is:

```
SQL>  CREATE TABLE (<column specifications>)
   2    CLUSTER <cluster name> (<cluster column>);
```

The cluster column in this command is the column within the newly created table that will become the cluster column in the completed cluster.

ADDING AN EXISTING TABLE

You can create duplicates of LA__FLAW and BRANCHES in a cluster linked on their common element, the branch numbers. First, you must make sure that each table has a NOT NULL specification in its BRANCH column:

```
SQL>  ALTER TABLE LA__FLAW
   2    MODIFY (BRANCH NOT NULL);
```

Table altered.

```
SQL>  ALTER TABLE BRANCHES
   2    MODIFY (BRANCH NOT NULL);
```

Table altered.

If you want to remove this specification after the exercise is completed, the command is:

```
SQL>  ALTER TABLE LA__FLAW
   2    MODIFY (BRANCH NULL);
```

Now, to create the clustered version of LA__FLAW, enter:

```
SQL> CREATE TABLE CL__FLAW
   2    CLUSTER LA__DEPT (BRANCH)
   3    AS SELECT *
   4        FROM LA__FLAW;
```

Here, you need no column specifications for the new table; it will take them from the original. The CLUSTER command identifies the BRANCH column as LA__FLAW's contribution to the cluster column. The AS clause directs the system to, in effect, copy everything from the original table, including its contents and column specifications.

The comparable command for BRANCHES is:

```
SQL> CREATE TABLE CL__BRANCH
   2    CLUSTER LA__DEPT (BRANCH)
   3    AS SELECT *
   4        FROM BRANCHES;
```

USING CLUSTERED TABLES

A query of the clustered tables might be this:

```
SQL> SELECT LAST, LOCATION
   2    FROM CL__FLAW, CL__BRANCH
   3    WHERE CL__FLAW.BRANCH = CL__BRANCH.BRANCH;
```

The only difference is in the third line, in which you specify the clustered tables instead of the originals. This command should function just as it did earlier—but more quickly.

It is also possible to create a cluster that holds only a single table. This will do nothing to improve searching performance, but it will promote more efficient use of your disk space. This will be particularly true if the table holds many duplicate values. All these will be condensed into smaller storage spaces.

REMOVING CLUSTERED TABLES

You can use the DROP command to get rid of a clustered table just as you can wipe out its conventional counterparts.

If you want to keep an unclustered version of the table, the process requires two steps: first you copy, then you DROP.

If you did not already have an unclustered copy of LA__FLAW, or if you have DROPped the original, you could use these commands to create a new, unclustered version.:

```
SQL> CREATE TABLE LA__FLAW
   2    AS (SELECT *
   3        FROM CL__FLAW);
```

Then you could enter:

```
SQL> DROP TABLE CL__FLAW;
```

You will be left with only the original unclustered version of LA__FLAW. You must then recreate any indexes you may want to apply.

DROP CLUSTER is the command to eliminate an existing cluster. First, you must DROP all the tables which make up the cluster.

TAKING INVENTORY

The database table CLUSTERS contains a list of active clusters and their component tables. The command to display your current selections is:

```
SQL> SELECT CLNAME, TNAME
   2    FROM CLUSTERS;
```

As with indexes, clusters work better in some situations than in others. You'll have to experiment to see how well clustering improves ORACLE's usual performance, and whether it performs better than indexing.

REVIEW QUESTIONS

1. Write a SQL command that will do the same thing as these dBASE commands will do:

```
. USE JUNK
. INDEX ON FENDERS TO PARTS
```

2. If a SQL database column appears in this order:

```
ABLE
BAKER
```

CHARLIE
DOG

what does this indicate about its indexing?
3. How do you invoke an ORACLE index?
4. Name three factors that determine the performance increase you can obtain from indexing.
5. What do clustering and joining have in common?

ANSWERS

1. SQL> CREATE INDEX PARTS
    2   ON JUNK(FENDERS);

2. Nothing. A SQL index affects only searching, not the data display.
3. Include an indexed column in a WHERE clause.
4. Pick any three of these four: the table size, the number of other indexes, whether you make frequent changes, and how often you make queries on the indexed column.
5. A common field to link more than one table.

4 DEVELOPING SQL APPLICATIONS

Designing a Database

"I've just had a truly inspiring idea," Hubert Tuba told Dennis Madison. "It's part of the customer relations tracking system. I've created a data entry form in dBASE. We could put one in each of the personal computers. I've set up this data entry screen," said Tuba, presenting a copy of Figure 14-1. "When we sign up a new account, we just enter the pertinent data into the blank spots. You'll notice that where we use codes for the marketing data, I've included lists of the codes to use."

"Very nicely done," Madison said. "I suppose you also have designed a database file to accept all this information."

"Yes, I've adapted it from some of those we put together for the earlier chapters. I hope this meets with your approval."

```
Structure for database  : D:TRACKING.dbf
Number of data records:
Date of last update      :
Field   Field Name       Type       Width   Dec
    1   EMP__CODE        Character     3
    2   SALES__REP       Character    20
    3   BRANCH__NO       Character     3
    4   TODAY            Date          8
    5   SSNO             Character    11
```

FIGURE 14-1   Data Entry Screen for Sales Tracking

```
                    SALES TRACKING RECORD

Rep. Code: ███  Sales Rep: ███████████  Branch: ██  Date: ██████
CUSTOMER INFORMATION:
Social Sec. No: ████████  Last: ████████  First: █████████  Initial:█
New Customer? █  No. Existing Accounts: ██
Source: █  1: Newspaper  2: Walk-in  3: Customer  4: Radio  5: Empl. 6: Other
Initated by: █  1: Customer  2: FSR  3: Teller  4: Other
Income: █1: To $12M  2: $12M-$25M  3: $25M-$55M  4: Over $55M
Profession: █  1: Professional  2: Self-Employed  3: Trades  4: Retired
Residence: █1: Permanent  2: Seasonal  3: Non-resident
Home Ownership: █  1: Owns  2: Rents
Age:█  1: To 35  2: 35-55  3: Over 55

SALES INFORMATION:
Product Code ██████  Account No. ████████  Amount: ████████
New Funds? █  Cross Sale? █
```

6	CUST__LAST	Character	12	
7	CUST__FIRST	Character	12	
8	CUST__INIT	Character	1	
9	NEW__CUST	Logical	1	
10	NO__ACCT	Numeric	2	
11	SOURCE	Character	2	
12	INITIATED	Character	1	
13	INCOME	Character	1	
14	PROFESSION	Character	1	
15	RESIDENCE	Character	1	
16	HOME__OWNER	Character	1	
17	AGE	Character	1	
18	PROD__CODE	Character	7	
19	PRODUCT	Character	20	
20	ACCT__NO	Character	10	
21	AMOUNT	Numeric	12	2
22	NEW__MONEY	Logical	1	
23	CROSS__SOLD	Logical	1	

** Total **   132

"Well, it's long," said Madison, "but it certainly does cover everything. I'd say you've done a capital job here. Misty Presto, though, is also working on this project, and I think it's only fair that we give her a chance to comment."

Soon, their coworker was inspecting the data entry screen and its related database file. After a period of anxious silence, Presto announced, "It's got too many things in it."

"Well, I realize it has twenty-three separate fields that fill 132 spaces," said Madison, "but we really do need all that information."

"Oh, that's not the problem," Presto explained. "It's that all this information is about too many *different* things. First, you have something about the employee. Then, you have something about the customer. Then, you have something about the product you sold. They're all in the same list."

"That's what it's all about, though—which employee sold what product to which customer."

"Sure, but put them in separate tables. You can still get them together for a screen display."

A PLACE FOR EVERYTHING

Presto is right. Tuba has designed a comprehensive database. It records exactly the information the company needs to know to meet the particular goal of this exercise: assessing its performance at signing up customers for more than one kind of account.

The problem is that the suggested database tries to cover too many subjects at once. As Presto noted, it includes data on three separate entities:

- The *customer service representative* who makes the sale.
- The *customer* who signs up for the account.
- The *product*. In this case it's a bank account, but it could be anything a business has to sell.

Each of these entities should be represented in a table of its own. There should be one table with the data on the employees, another that describes the customers, and a third with descriptions of the products. Take advantage of the relational technology available in both dBASE and SQL to link these files for entering data through the screen display.

WHY BOTHER WITH THIS?

It probably seems logical to figure that everything you record in a single sales transaction would go into a single record of that transaction. Everything's neat and simple. If you think about breaking the data into separate files your next thought may be, "Why bother?"

The reason to maintain separate files for separate entities is tied to the reason you enter the data in the first place. The reason you enter data is, quite simply, so your data will be there when you want to get them out again. Retrieval is the cardinal reason to maintain a database.

What you put in, then, is directly related to what you want to retrieve. The need to enter data in the first place is one thing you naturally should consider when you design a database system. It's more important, though, to think about what will happen when you try to get the data out again.

MULTIPLE RETRIEVAL PROBLEMS

Consider the system Tuba suggested. Not only does the database cover a multiplicity of subjects, but there is to be a separate copy in each sales representative's computer. Consider the following scenario.

Customer Bud Bunny walks in one day and wants to open a certificate of deposit. Tuba is glad to accommodate, of course. Tuba is also anxious to know whether the Bunny household already has an account with the bank. If so, Hubert will get credit for signing up a multiple account. He therefore searches the database for Bunny's name. He is disappointed to find nothing.

Tuba would be even more chagrined to learn that Bunny's account could indeed have qualified him for the multiple-relationship points. It seems that a few months ago, Katie Collins had opened a new checking account for Bud's wife, Esther. That transaction, however, was on Katie's version of the database; Bud's business was recorded on Tuba's hard disk. The twain aren't likely to meet any time soon. In other words, Tuba can't retrieve the data that would support his claim.

There are a couple of ways to overcome this problem. A rollup report that consolidated the individual databases could flag the two Bunny accounts. A multi-user database kept on a network server or some other central computer would place the Bunnys as close to one another in the business records as they are at home. However, the existence of two Bunny records is nothing compared with the existence of hundreds of records that all contain the name Hubert Tuba.

Over and Over Again

When Tuba opened the second Bunny account, he filled in the data entry screen of his own design. As usual, he entered his initials, which the system uses as a code, plus his name and branch number. If Tuba signs up 100 accounts, this data will appear in the file 100 times. Since there's only one Hubert Tuba, to have 100 records of his existence seems a bit much.

There is much the same problem with the product information entered at the end of the form. Like many service-oriented businesses, a bank sells only a limited range of products and services. These, too, will be repeated throughout Tuba's 100 transactions.

This database design is equally inadequate for a more commonplace type of business that must maintain a long inventory list. It may record many sales of some items and no sales at all of some slow-moving lines. This certainly is not a useful or comprehensive record of your inventory.

A BETTER DESIGN

The solution is to divide this multi-subject database into separate tables: one to keep track of the employees, another to record the customer data, and a third to maintain inventory records. When Madison and Tuba challenged Misty Presto to produce a better database design in SQL, she responded with precisely those three tables.

The largest is the CUSTOMER file as it's been used in several previous chapters. It reappears in Figure 14-2 for your reading convenience.

The table of the customer service representatives has been presented earlier as either a table or a view. The view is the better choice, since this listing duplicates information already in ROSTER. It appears in Figure 14-3 in a slightly modified form. It includes the initial codes, the employees' names, and their branch assignments. The branch numbers are of little value within the UnderFed office, of course, but they could be significant in consolidated reports of activity from several offices.

FIGURE 14-2 The CUSTOMER Table for Your Rereading Pleasure

SSNO	LAST	FIRST	I	STREET	CITY	ST	ZIP	I	P	R	H	A
222-33-4444	BUNNY	ESTHER	C	2813 N. THIRD	ELSIE	NB	69134	1	3	3	2	1
333-44-4444	HAMMERSTEIN	ROGER	A	117 W. TARGET	BOWSTRING	MN	56631	4	2	2	1	3
666-77-8888	BUNNY	BUD	B	2813 N. THIRD	ELSIE	NB	69134	2	3	3	1	1
777-88-9999	STARR	WOODY	A	603 E. PINE	FOSSIL	OR	97830	0		1	1	2
888-99-0000	BENJAMIN	FRANKLIN	X	1627 CHEW ST.	WYSOX	PA	18854	3	2	2	2	3
999-00-1111	DRIVER	SCROOGE	Q	121 GOLIAD	SANDY	TX	78665	3	4	2	1	3
111-22-3333	WUNDERLAND	ALLISON	N	2 ROYAL WAY	GLENCOE	AR	72539		1	1	1	2

FIGURE 14-3 The REPS View Updated

```
        EMP  LAST           FIRST      I  DEP
        ---  -------------  ---------  -  ---
        HT   TUBA           HUBERT     G   2
        KC   COLLINS        KATHLEEN   D   2
        RZ   ZIMMERMAN      ROBERT     D   2
        PR   ROWE-HATTON    PHYLLIS    F   2
```

A FOURTH FOR TWO BRIDGES

Presto also designed a fourth table. It holds three columns: ACCT__NO, SSNO, and PROD__CODE. The justification for this file is that an account is an entity in its own right. Some customers will have several, which, after all, is the object. The accounts in any household will represent an unpredictable assortment of products. To avoid duplication, the accounts should be in a table of their own.

The other two columns link these account records to other tables. The Social Security number connects the account with its owner in the CUSTOMER table. PROD__CODE is a link to the descriptions in PRODUCTS.

SEARCHING MULTIPLE FILES

Tuba's search for other Bunny accounts could take the form:

```
SQL>  SELECT C.LAST, P.PRODUCT
   2     FROM CUSTOMER C, ACCOUNTS A, PRODUCTS P
   3     WHERE C.SSNO = A.SSNO
   4     AND A.PROD__CODE = P.PROD__CODE
   5     AND C.LAST = 'BUNNY'
```

Starting in CUSTOMER, this query finds the two rows which record the Bunnys. It finds their Social Security numbers and searches for matching links in ACCOUNTS. It then records the product codes that match the selected accounts and looks up the full product description in PRODUCTS. If there's another Bunny in this database, Tuba will find it and get due credit.

TECHNICAL DATABASE DESIGN

There are two reasons to design a database system as a collection of single-subject tables. One is the efficient use of searching techniques and storage space. In an ideal system, the only duplicated data would be the keys that link one table with another. This saves storage space. At the same time, the data you need will be conveniently stored in one, well-marked place. This makes searching more efficient.

ORACLE and other relational databases work this way because this is precisely what the inventors of the relational system set out to accomplish. A product almost always works best when you use it as it was designed to be used; a race car would be a poor choice to carry a basketball team, and a van would be unlikely to win a race.

A relational system such as ORACLE is designed primarily for systems of interrelated blocks of data. If your aim is only to maintain a mailing list, you probably would do best with one of the modestly priced flat file databases that are widely available for personal computers. One of those products can use one data file—comparable to a single SQL table—at a time. A spreadsheet is also much like a SQL table. Some of the three-dimensional spreadsheets now available have taken on relational characteristics, though.

HIGHER MATH

The relational database theory is a product of higher mathematics. A simplified explanation is that relational theory takes the mathematical concept of a *relation* and uses it to describe data. You don't have to understand all this to use SQL. If you hope to be a serious database user, though, it helps to know a little about how the system works.

The smallest unit of data in a relational system is, basically, the smallest unit of data there can be. For example, many databases describe certain classes of people, such as customers or employees. Short of surgery or horror movies, a person is the smallest possible subdivision of this particular kind of data.

An *attribute* is one characteristic of each individual, such as height, last name, or Social Security number. In a database, an attribute is represented as a field or column. An attribute is taken from a *domain,* which consists of all possible values for the attribute. Unless that range is small—the names of the fifty states, for example—you won't usually find a full domain stored in a database.

Each record or row in a database represents what advanced scholars call a *tuple.* This is a set of the listed attributes of a particular data unit. This is the last you'll hear of the tuple in this book.

A relation is a fixed set of attributes that corresponds with the values in their underlying domain. For each person in the table, there is one height, one Social Security number, and so on. A relation is a mathematical set. The SQL table is a visible representation of the relation. A SELECT query that calls for certain rows or columns calls for a subset of the relation.

THEORY TO PRACTICE

Those who want to know more about this subject should consult a textbook on mathematics or relational database theory. Those who want to know less need not worry. For most purposes, it's enough to recognize that a relation is just one syllable short of a relation*ship*.

Several times in this chapter, a table has been called an *entity*. That is not by accident. An entity is any distinguishable object, such as Joe Smith, Los Angeles, or (813)555-6789. It is the noun of database design. In database use, an entity is the object about which we want to store information in the database.

A *property* is a single fact about an entity. That could be Smith's salary, the latitude of Los Angeles, or the state in which you would find the 813 area code. A property is like an adjective: It describes things.

A *relationship* is a connection among two or more entities. You can compare a relationship with a verb. It shows an active connection. Relationships can come in several types:

- A *one-to-one* relationship, such as that between Smith and his Social Security number.
- A *one-to-many* relationship. Hubert Tuba has such a relationship with all the accounts he has opened.

- A *many-to-many* relationship. This would exist between the UnderFed staff and all the people on the office's customer list.

TYPES OF ENTITIES

There are also three types of entities:

- A *kernel* is an entity that can exist independently. You could address Joe Smith as "kernel." You can even salute him if you'd like.
- A *characteristic* describes another entity. The line items on an invoice are characteristics of that invoice. A characteristic cannot exist independently of the entity it describes. Hubert Tuba is an individual in his own right, not a characteristic of UnderFed.
- An *association* is a many-to-many relationship and can become very complex. An inventory of items obtained from a varied list of suppliers would be an example.

Because characteristics cannot be independent, it might seem they should not be the subjects of database tables. The fact that they should, though, is one thing many database designers miss. This is why they often end up with databases that are simultaneously overcrowded and underused.

ASSESSING MANY PROPERTIES

An entity usually has many properties. Each customer uses a distinctive combination of banking services. That's why it's best to maintain separate tables for the customers and the services. Otherwise, you'd have to include in the customer database a series of columns called ACCOUNT_1, ACCOUNT_2, and ACCOUNT_3. This does a poor job of accommodating the customer who has only one account, and it's even worse when a customer wants to open a fourth account.

It works much better to treat each account as a characteristic of the account-holder and to keep these characteristics in a table of their own.

UNLOCKING KEYS

The most important aspect of an entity is that it can be distinguished in some way from every other entity. A single property that distinguishes this entity from all others is called a *key*.

Consider, for example, the UnderFed customer table. People use their names to distinguish themselves from other people. It doesn't always work as well as we'd like. Pity the honest citizen who happens to bear the same name as a notorious serial killer. The last names in the UnderFed table don't fully distinguish every member of even this tiny group.

However, there is also the Social Security number. It distinctly identifies each individual. A person is an independent entity. We cannot be further subdivided, we do not serve as descriptions of something else. When an entity has these traits, it should be identified by a distinctive *primary key*. The Social Security number serves that purpose here.

LEGAL ALIENS

The Social Security number also appears in the ACCOUNTS table. Here, though, it doesn't identify the account—the account number does that. The account number, then, becomes the primary key to this table. The Social Security number is a link to the CUSTOMER table. In the same way, the product code provides a a link to PRODUCTS.

These two columns are both *foreign keys*. They do not distinctly identify an entity in their own table. They can be linked, though, with matching primary keys in other tables. You would do so with clauses such as this:

WHERE ACCOUNTS.SSNO = CUSTOMER.SSNO

. . . or:

WHERE ACCOUNTS.PROD__CODE = PRODUCTS.PROD__CODE

Figure 14-4 shows how the three are connected.

GUIDELINES FOR DATABASE DESIGN

You won't always design the perfect database. Theoreticians in the relational field have a concept called *normalization:* The more completely a design meets the rules of relational database design, the higher its *normal form*. The first normal form is pretty good. You can seek increasingly higher levels of perfection until you reach database nirvana at the fifth normal form, or NF5 for short.

FIGURE 14-4   Primary and Foreign Keys

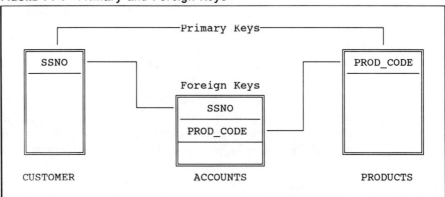

Above NF5 are a few higher forms named for those rare individuals who have achieved them.

A database can achieve at least the first normal form when each table has these characteristics:

- A *primary key* uniquely identifies each row or record.
- All additional fields identify properties of the entity type that is identified by the primary key.

If a table identifies employees or customers, each would be identified by a primary key, such as the Social Security number. Each additional field would identify some property of that individual, such as his or her last name. It would not identify properties of some other identity type, such as an employee's department.

You don't need to worry much about which level of normalization you achieve. It's more important that you recognize which traits a database must have in order to get there. If a database satisfies these theoretical requirements, it should satisfy your practical needs as well.

For most day-to-day purposes, Misty Presto's level of perception is good enough: A single table should have a single subject. If you can understand this idea and put it to use, you are well on your way to database enlightenment. Everything within a given table should have a one-to-one relationship with the primary subject of that database. To put it a bit more technically, each entity should be the subject of a separate data table.

The specific form of the table depends on which type of data it contains:

- Represent each *kernel* as a single table. Designate one column as a primary key that uniquely identifies each row.
- Represent each *characteristic* as a separate table. Use foreign keys to link the descriptive material in the characteristic table with the objects being described in the kernel table.
- Represent each *association* as a separate table, using foreign keys to link the various members.
- Represent each *property* of a given entity as a column within the table which represents that entity.

When you think you have it right, go back and try again. You'll almost always find room for improvement. This includes the database designs in this book. In fact, the designs you've encountered in the last few pages will have been improved by the time you reach the end of the chapter.

PRACTICAL DATABASE DESIGN

The design that works well in theory should also work well in practice. That's the theory, anyway. A theoretically correct database isn't enough, though, unless it also meets the practical needs of the people who will have to use it. Presumably, you are designing a database system to be used. Otherwise, why are you doing it? One reason might be to design a database for instructional purposes, as for this book, for example. Most likely, though, you have some practical purpose in mind.

This leads to the obvious good test of a database design: how well it serves the purposes it is intended to serve. There also is a less obvious, but even better, test: how well the database serves predictable future needs as well as those that exist now.

There are several yardsticks you can use, both to plan in the initial phases of database design and to judge your completed product. Factors to consider include:

- The basic *purpose* the system is supposed to serve
- The level of *safety and security* you want to build in
- The type of people who will *use* the system
- The level of *performance* you require

There is one good way to determine these factors. Talk to the people who will use the system, including those who depend on its reports and other output. Determine who they are, what they can do, and what they expect. Find out what they need, and design the system to meet their needs.

SERVING A PURPOSE

Nearly anyone who gives advice on how to design a database system will agree on this first step: Turn the computer off.

Don't sit at the keyboard and start to create something for the sake of creating something. Instead, get a legal pad or some similar "blunt instrument" and begin to make a few notes on what the new system is supposed to accomplish.

At this stage of development, don't worry too much about the contents of a particular table or the appearance of a screen display. Pay attention, instead, to the objectives you are trying to meet.

At UnderFed, the main objective is to provide a way to track sales activity. The company has adopted a strategy of getting maximum benefit from its existing customer base by selling multiple services to individual account-holders.

The purpose of the sales tracking system is to monitor the success of individual customer service representatives at making multiple sales. At the branch office level, supervisors can use the output to appraise the employees' performance in terms of a company-wide goal.

Of course, there's another purpose, too: The system serves as an instructional tool in this book. The two purposes aren't always compatible; the elements you need to demonstrate a particular database management technique aren't always the elements you need to track employees' sales performance. This is one reason you'll probably notice a few variations between the system presented in this chapter and the versions you saw earlier. You may also have figured out that the value of LA_FLAW and its related tables is more instructional than practical.

SAFETY AND SECURITY

As Chapter 11 pointed out, securing a database requires much more than protecting it against youthful hackers from outside.

You must fight crime and data corruption wherever they are likely to occur.

Early in your planning, you should assess the security needs of the database. Determine what should be protected and from whom. In the case of the UnderFed tracking system, there is a great deal of information that should remain confidential. The salary figures have been mentioned before. You should also protect individual performance appraisals from outside disclosure. Such matters should be kept strictly confidential, available only to the employee and those supervisors who need to know them.

You should also determine how badly you need to maintain an audit trail to record individual transactions that alter the database contents. Auditing is vital to any accounting system. It is less necessary when tracking sales, although individual transactions will automatically be recorded.

Validation is a third major concern. You want to be as sure as you can that the information you enter into your system is correct. Validation can't prevent every mistake, but it can trap many that otherwise would corrupt your data. Validation usually involves checking the data input against a list of correct entries, much as the spelling checker in a word processor does.

One standard validation technique is to check the entry against the contents of another table. A common example is a list of standard state abbreviations. If an operator makes an entry that is not in the table, the program should refuse the input and call attention to the error. At UnderFed, you might want to check each sales transaction to make sure the employee codes and customer identification match your current employee and customer records respectively.

Another standard validation method is a test to determine whether an entered value falls within a certain range. At UnderFed, for example, some types of accounts require minimum balances. There is also a maximum amount that will qualify for federal insurance. A validation test could determine whether the entry falls between those two figures.

The Cost of Security

No security system is free of cost. A validation process in particular almost certainly requires that you embed SQL commands in a program (a subject to be discussed in later chapters). Access controls and audit trails also require extra effort to establish and maintain.

Except for validation, SQL requires less programming effort than do most other forms of database management, including dBASE. Access controls are built in, and ORACLE automatically maintains a set of auditing tables. Still, someone must maintain the password system, and someone must find the time to check and interpret the audit records.

The trade-off between secure data and the effort needed to keep it that way is one other important consideration in any database plan.

WHO USES THE SYSTEM?

Another major consideration is the level of sophistication of the people who will use the system. Some employees know little about database operations. They require extensive help screens, full documentation, and other features that used to be described as "user friendly." To a grizzled database veteran, the same features that are necessary to a beginner simply slow down the system and get in the way. To compound the problem, some beginners learn well and soon attain veteran status. Others don't really want to master the computer and are content with their prompts, menus, and help screens.

The new account representatives at UnderFed combine something of all these characteristics. They will be filling out records as they deal with customers. Sometimes they'll be in a hurry. They should be able to answer on-screen questions by filling in blanks, without having to resort to outside references.

At higher levels of Marinecorp, the organization will probably have the benefit of knowledgeable people to assemble and consolidate data from operating locations, such as UnderFed. They'll need less on-screen help, but a complete procedure manual might be in order.

Along with the beginner-versus-veteran trade-off, there is another consideration: the time it takes to develop a system. The fancier a display screen or a printed report, the more time is required to produce it. It also takes the computer more time to generate this fancier output.

Against this cost in computer time there is a possible savings in human time. An attractive, easy-to-use screen can help computer-shy employees overcome their reluctance. If the form can guide these employees through the data entry process, they may also make fewer mistakes.

HOW MUCH PERFORMANCE?

How fast should the system operate and how many features should it have? A database system's performance is a combination of speed and ability.

Certainly, no employee should unnecessarily have to keep a customer waiting while the computer flashes a "please be patient" signal. At the same time, no employee should be forced to wait or adapt because the system will not perform some necessary operation.

The ideal system, then, should be fast but versatile—offering a wide range of functions and performing them quickly. Often the two halves of this goal conflict with one another. The more features you include in a system, the more programming effort you must exert to provide them. Often, extra features will also cut into the system's speed.

The earlier comparison between a race car and a van is again apt. One offers speed but Spartan comfort; the other is much slower but can be equipped for the plush life. No wonder there's such a market for so-called sports sedans that combine some elements of both.

Your database may require a similar compromise. You may have to sacrifice some speed and devote extra development time to provide a useful extra feature or two. You may also have to sacrifice a few less essential features on the altar of speedier performance.

Marinecorp's management undoubtedly can think of all manner of reports they could derive from a comprehensive database system. As Dennis Madison perceived back when the project first started, though, it is possible to go to extremes. People cannot spend so much time reporting their activities that they are left with little time to conduct those activities. If management allows this to happen, it soon will find itself with a corps of overpaid research assistants.

Capacity is another aspect of database performance. Consider the sheer number of records you will expect your database system to accommodate. There is the usual trade: the more records, the slower the system. Indexing and clustering can help, but sheer volume will always manage to make itself felt.

PRACTICAL PLANNING STEPS

Creating a good database design requires reams of paper. The prediction that the computer would produce the "paperless office" could not have been farther off the mark. Here's one small example: Electronic mail systems have never really caught on, but there's a growing market in facsimile transmission machines. The "fax" works just like electronic mail, but it uses a readable piece of paper at each end. Users seem much more comfortable with this tangible input and output.

Likewise, the paper documents you now use provide invaluable input into your planning process. You should not try to duplicate existing forms in the output of your system, but, to a large extent, you still will be working from paper to paper, with the computer as a go-between.

COLLECT DOCUMENTS

Among the first papers you'll want to see are the reports the organization is now producing. Obtain samples of everything. It doesn't matter whether the report is produced by computer, by quill pen, or by any other medium. Just get a copy of every type of report.

Systems analysts long have observed the principle of looking at the output you desire—from that, you can determine the input you require. The current report forms are your first step in examining the output.

Then, have a look at the current input. Get copies of every data entry document. These are not necessarily on paper. Run screen dumps of all data entry screens. Make logs of those communications such as telephone calls or electronic mail transmissions that don't ordinarily leave paper traces. These probably will be few, even in the "paperless office."

A third class of documents to obtain reflects the transactions, calculations, and other activities that take place within the system—between input and output.

Whenever you can, get a few filled-in samples of each document plus a blank copy or two that you can run through your own copier for experimentation. Try to get related documents. If you obtain a data entry sample that records a particular transaction, try to obtain reporting documents that reflect that same transaction.

MAKE IMPROVEMENTS

It doesn't make much sense to build a new database if you cannot improve on what already exists. Go over the existing documents and look for ways to make things better. Perhaps a better layout would make them less intimidating and easier to use. Perhaps there is too much or too little information presented.

Database development is largely a process of naming things. You must name tables, views, columns, and many other things. You can start by naming the documents.

As you refine each existing document for use in the new system, give it a code name—something you'll find easy to use and remember. Name each data element, too. Start thinking about the type of table in which each element could be found. If you anticipate that a particular element will become the last name in a customer file, give it a tentative name like CUSTOMER.LAST. Do this in pencil. You'll probably make many changes.

SHOOTING TROUBLES

You'll probably find some problems. Perhaps a report calls for data, but none of the data entry documents provides it. Perhaps you find a problem like the one that arose in the documents used to develop UnderFed's sales tracking system. There were two different forms, each with a list of products and a system of codes to identify each product.

Each document used a different set of product codes. Not only that, but each also used a different list of products. There were a couple of items on each that did not appear in the other. Reconciling conflicts such as these will be a big part of your development work. This is particularly true if a department responsible for one of the variant coding schemes refuses to adapt to a uniform system. It happens often.

Whatever problems you encounter, be glad when you can learn about them early. The wrong time is after the system has been designed, developed, and put into operation.

DEVELOPING THE TRACKING SYSTEM

Having learned these lessons, sometimes through trial and error, sometimes through error and trial, the crew at UnderFed was about to apply them to the final design of its sales tracking database.

As head of the project, Dennis Madison determined that each sales transaction brought together three significant entities: a customer, a product, and a sales representative. The tables describing each should be treated as kernel-type entities.

The result of this coming together is, one hopes, a sale. A sale does not qualify as an identifying characteristic of any one of the three kernels, but it does represent an association. It is the common ground by which all the other entities were linked. Accordingly, Madison set out to modify the earlier experimental tables.

THE CUSTOMER TABLE

The CUSTOMER table was already well-conceived, Madison decided. The Social Security number would be a primary key to this table. It was the obvious unique identifier. Checking the columns, Madison determined that each legitimately described the primary subject, the customer. One group of columns recorded each customer's address and telephone number; another group recorded demographic data, such as income and home ownership.

It would be tempting here also to record account numbers for each customer, Madison acknowledged. It would be a mistake, though. An account number identifies an account, not a customer. It properly belongs in a table of account information; consider that a customer can have more than one account. In fact, this was the object of the entire marketing campaign.

The table could use some fine-tuning, though. Since the column SSNO was to serve as this table's primary key, it should not be allowed to contain null values. Madison took care of the situation with this command:

```
SQL> ALTER TABLE CUSTOMER
  2   MODIFY (SSNO NOT NULL);
```

Another consideration also arose: The customer table would soon be quite large, or so everyone hoped. Searching it for existing customers could be a time-consuming process, unless an index were created to help. With this in mind, Madison created an index:

```
SQL> CREATE INDEX CUS_SSNO
  2   ON CUSTOMER (SSNO);
```

The resulting CUSTOMER table in its final form:

Name	Null?	Type
SSNO	NOT NULL	CHAR(11)
LAST		CHAR(15)
FIRST		CHAR(15)
INIT		CHAR(1)
STREET		CHAR(15)
CITY		CHAR(15)
STATE		CHAR(2)
ZIP		CHAR(5)
INCOME		CHAR(1)
PROFESSION		CHAR(1)
RESIDENCE		CHAR(1)
HOME_OWNER		CHAR(1)
AGE_GROUP		CHAR(1)

THE ROSTER TABLE

The ROSTER table was also in reasonably good shape. Granted, it contained some information that was extraneous to sales tracking. Both a view and a separate table had been created earlier to restrict access by unauthorized users. In any event, this table contained sensitive data that would require strict access control.

For the sake of the tracking system, though, Madison decided to use the base ROSTER table. The system would be designed to retrieve only relevant information from ROSTER. In addition, ROSTER also had the basic qualities of a good, clean table. Every item in it described the employee who was to be the main subject.

Madison did spot one awkward situation. Each employee

record has two unique identifiers: one is the employee code, based on each employee's inititals, the other is the familiar Social Security number.

"Someone else's Social Security number doesn't exactly trip off one's tongue," Madison mused. "We included the initials so that there would be something that is easy to remember." Accordingly, the employee code would be the primary key for sales tracking purposes. ROSTER was also constructed so it could be used in a personnel management system. In that kind of service, the Social Security number probably would be the key.

Madison decided to require that both potential keys be designated NOT NULL. ROSTER would always be a rather small table, though, so Madison decided it would not need an index. "If the folks in Personnel want an index for their use, they can create one," he reasoned. The commands to tune up ROSTER:

```
SQL> ALTER TABLE ROSTER
  2    MODIFY (EMP_CODE NOT NULL);

SQL> ALTER TABLE ROSTER
  2    MODIFY (SS_NO NOT NULL);
```

As Madison learned the hard way, each modification requires a separate command; there is no way to combine them into one. The final version of the ROSTER table:

Name	Null?	Type
EMP_CODE	NOT NULL	CHAR(3)
LAST		CHAR(12)
FIRST		CHAR(12)
INIT		CHAR(1)
BRANCH_NO		NUMBER(3)
DEPT_NO		NUMBER(2)
POSITION		CHAR(10)
SS_NO	NOT NULL	CHAR(11)
DATE_HIRED		DATE
SALARY		NUMBER(8,2)
EXTENSION		CHAR(4)

LISTING PRODUCTS

The two-column PRODUCTS table should have been simple. Madison remembered, though, that there was one complication:

the two separate lists of product codes, and even different product lists, used in different versions of the resource forms.

For a while, Madison considered a translation table that would convert each department's codes into a uniform style for use in the sales tracking system. He decided against it. The effort required to establish it couldn't be justified in terms of a better-performing system. "This is where I get stubborn," Madison decided. There would be one list of products and one set of codes. Everyone who used this system would simply have to go along. It was too expensive to accommodate variations.

Because the column PROD__CODE would be the primary key to this table, it should be designated NOT NULL, Madison decided. This, too, probably always would be a small table, so it need not be indexed. The completed version:

Name	Null?	Type
PROD__CODE	NOT NULL	CHAR(4)
PRODUCT		CHAR(20)

THE SALES CONNECTION

Misty Presto had originally designed an ACCOUNTS table to record basic data about each newly opened account. Madison soon became aware, though, that this idea had some drawbacks. One was that such a table would duplicate information already in the bank's master account records. If these are themselves kept in a SQL database, some future system designer could arrange access to them.

The other was that the tracking system didn't really need data that specifically referred to an account. What it really needed was data about each individual *sale*. With this in mind, Madison decided to expand the material he had originally planned for an ACCOUNTS table to record SALES, instead. This would include data on the source of the account, whether the customer already had existing business with the bank, and details such as the amount borrowed or deposited.

The SALES table also would need enough foreign keys to link the sales records to the three kernel databases. These links would serve two purposes. Initially, they could be used to relate the sales data to the individual customers, employees, and products involved with each sales transaction.

Later, the same links could meet this table's many needs for validation. The system should be set up to make sure each customer was properly recorded in CUSTOMER, that the entered EMP_CODE was actually the initials of a listed employee, and that the PROD_CODE reflected an actual product.

With an eye to the future, Madison also recognized that the account number represents a potential link to the main account files. This meant that four different columns in this table would be possible links to other tables. All would be foreign keys: SSNO to the matching CUSTOMER records, EMP_CODE to the employees listed in ROSTER, and PROD_CODE to the list of PRODUCTS. In addition, ACCT_NO could be used some day either as a link to the account records or as a primary key to the SALES itself. All would be NOT NULL:

```
SQL> ALTER TABLE SALES
  2    MODIFY (EMP_CODE NOT NULL);

SQL> ALTER TABLE SALES
  2    MODIFY (SSNO NOT NULL);

SQL> ALTER TABLE SALES
  2    MODIFY (PROD_CODE NOT NULL);

SQL> ALTER TABLE SALES
  2    MODIFY (ACCT_NO NOT NULL);
```

Two indexes also would be required. This would become another large table. Madison anticipated that there would be many searches for sales made by particular employees. An index on the employee code would speed up those operations. Other searches would look for individual customers' accounts. An index on their Social Security numbers would help here. This led to two index commands:

```
SQL> CREATE INDEX SALES_REP
  2    ON SALES (EMP_CODE);

SQL> CREATE INDEX SALES_SSNO
  2    ON SALES (SSNO);
```

The final structure of SALES:

Name	Null?	Type
TODAY		DATE
EMP__CODE	NOT NULL	CHAR(3)
SSNO	NOT NULL	CHAR(11)
SOURCE		CHAR(1)
REFERRAL		CHAR(30)
INITIATED		CHAR(1)
NEW__CUST		CHAR(1)
NEW__MONEY		CHAR(1)
PROD__CODE	NOT NULL	CHAR(7)
ACCT__NO	NOT NULL	CHAR(10)
AMOUNT		NUMBER(12,2)

A diagram of the completed system is shown in Figure 14-5.

FIGURE 14-5   A Diagram of the Completed Database

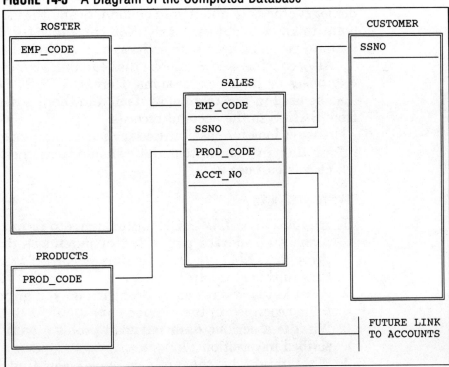

ADAPTING THE SYSTEM

Although this system was devised for banking, it can be adapted to other types of business, particularly service industries. The first adaptation probably would be to establish a customer code to replace the Social Security number as a key to the customer file. Banks routinely obtain their customers' Social Security numbers for tax purposes; most other types of businesses do not.

PRODUCTS would have to be modified to suit your particular line of offerings. If yours is a service-oriented business, the only thing necessary would be to place your own products within the existing framework. A retail business that must manage a large inventory probably would have to establish a more sophisticated PRODUCTS table. You might need columns for stock numbers, colors, sizes, or similar descriptive data, plus a column to contain a code that identifies the vendor. This code would be a foreign key, linked to a separate table that listed the vendors, their addresses, and similar information.

You probably also would want to maintain your own set of demographic data about your customers and the information you want to know about each sale. You can tailor the database contents to your marketing objectives, just as UnderFed did.

Also, consider adding hooks that can link your system to other databases or future expansions. Here, the ROSTER table could also be used in a personnel system, and there is a potential link from SALES to the account records.

Always look for possibilities such as these. Once you have the information in your system, there should be no end to the ways in which you can use it.

REVIEW QUESTIONS

1. A table called INVOICE has columns to record a customer's name and address and a list of purchases titled ITEM__1 through ITEM__10. How would you correct the most serious flaw in this structure?
2. What kinds of data entry problems do you anticipate for the table described in the previous question?
3. What is a serious data retrieval problem with the table described in question 1?
4. What might be the problem when you find a table that

repeatedly records detailed information about one of your employees?

5. What is the difference between a primary key and a foreign key?

6. What is a relation, and what does it have to do with database design?

7. What type of SQL command would link a foreign key with a primary key?

8. Whare are the two characteristics a table must have to meet at least the entry-level requirements of normalization?

9. Translate the preceding answer into everyday terms.

10. List the major practical criteria you should consider when planning a database.

11. What is validation, and why should you consider it in database design?

12. The person who's asked to design a database system for a truly paperless office would be in a very difficult situation. Why?

ANSWERS

1. Put the customer information in one table and the list of items purchased in another.

2. A customer may not make exactly ten purchases. Someone may want to buy 11 or more items.

3. It would be difficult to retrieve a record of sales using any key but the customer's name.

4. The table probably contains information about two entities, the employee and something else.

5. A primary key directly identifies a record in the table in which it appears. A foreign key refers to a corresponding column in another table.

6. A relation is a fixed set of attributes that describe the single subject of a table. In a relational database, each table is a single relation.

7. The WHERE clause of a JOIN. For example:

    WHERE SALES.SSNO = CUSTOMER.SSNO

8. A primary key uniquely identifies each row or record. All additional fields identify properties of the entity type that is identified by the primary key.

9. A single table should have a single subject.
10. The purpose it will serve, the degree of safety and security you require, the type of people who will use the system, and the level of performance you must achieve.
11. Validation compares a data entry with an established list or range of correct values. It is a valuable way to screen out errors.
12. There would be a shortage of existing documents with which to work.

15

SQL Command Files

"That's a wonderful database," said Addie Davidson when Madison made his grand presentation, "but how are our employees ever going to be able to use it?"

"Simple. They can type in the new data for every new account they sign up."

"Not so simple. Can you imagine Misty Presto typing in a command like this:

```
SQL> INSERT INTO SALES VALUES
  2    (SYSDATE, 'HT','777-88-9999',
  3    '2',NULL,'1','Y','Y','N',
  4    'MM','69-0000001',759);
```

I don't think we can install this system unless we make it a great deal easier to use," Davidson declared. "Why don't you go back and see what you can do to improve the user interface?"

"I agree. It's time we start presenting a better face to the users."

COMMAND FILE PROGRAMMING

SQL can barely exist without some kind of external support. The standard SQL command set is versatile but small. It's designed to be included within a larger system like ORACLE or embedded in a programming language such as C. It is possible, though, to write some simple programs in SQL itself.

If you've had any exposure to the dBASE programming language, you probably have figured out that, at its heart, it's fairly simple. You can easily write out a list of dBASE commands, run the list as a program—called a *command file*—and dBASE will execute the commands one by one. The authors of the dBASE language have fleshed out this ability by adding programming features such as control loops, which repeat an operation a certain number of times, and conditional logic (through commands that begin with IF).

SQL starts with the same capacity. You can write a list of commands and execute them in order, just as in dBASE. Here, though, there are no control loops, conditional logic, or other programming additions. A SQL command file conducts only the simplest of all programming operations. It issues SQL commands, one by one, in order. Even this limited capacity can be useful, though.

ONE WAY TO PROGRAM

There are two ways to create a SQL program. The first is simply to write it. Use any word processor or text editor that will produce straight, unadorned ASCII text. Just type the commands in order. That's how VIEWSET.SQL (Listing 15-1) was created.

```
REM      Listing 15-1
REM      VIEWSET.SQL
REM      Creates view for new account transactions

CREATE VIEW SIGNUP AS
        SELECT S.EMP_CODE, R.BRANCH_NO,
               C.SSNO, C.LAST, C.FIRST, C.INIT,
               S.SOURCE, S.INITIATED,
               C.INCOME, C.PROFESSION,
               C.RESIDENCE, C.HOME_OWNER, C.AGE_GROUP,
               S.PROD_CODE, S.ACCT_NO, S.AMOUNT,
               S.NEW_CUST, S.NEW_MONEY,S.REFERRAL
        FROM SALES S, ROSTER R, CUSTOMER C
        WHERE S.EMP_CODE = R.EMP_CODE AND
               S.SSNO = C.SSNO;
```

This is just a single SQL command, although an intricate one. It creates a view with which to query the sales tracking system. It uses most of the files and relationships set up in the previous chapter, and it corresponds roughly to the data entry screen shown in Figure 14-1.

This one command is highly complex, though, and it can be a bear to write and edit. So, instead of trying to use the SQL command editor, I made use of a word processor to put it together. Then, I saved it under a name that bore the .SQL suffix.

RUNNING THE PROGRAM

To run this program, load SQL*Plus and issue:

    SQL> @VIEWSET

or:

    SQL> START VIEWSET

or this pair:

    SQL> GET VIEWSET
    SQL> RUN

All will run the command file. When you use the @ or START versions, you may get a message that there's nothing in the buffer. If so, just repeat the command. These commands process the command file through the same buffer ORACLE uses to store and repeat direct commands from the SQL> prompt. The final pair formalizes this process by doing it a step at a time. GET loads the command file into the buffer; RUN then executes it.

You may want to develop the habit of using the START alternative. It has some extra capacity, as you'll see shortly.

The purpose of creating this view is to let users query the database without having access to the personal data in ROSTER. You can assign a more relaxed access level to this view, while maintaining strong controls over the rest of the ROSTER table.

What you cannot do with this view is update the sales records. Although it often is possible to add or alter records by way of a view, it cannot be done when the relationships are as complex as those in this view. Should you try, ORACLE will simply refuse to participate.

ANOTHER WAY TO PROGRAM

The second way to program is to use the command buffer in reverse. Consider the query at the beginning of this chapter:

```
SQL> INSERT INTO SALES VALUES
  2    (SYSDATE, 'HT','777-88-9999',
  3    '2',NULL,'1','Y','Y','N',
  4    'MM','69-0000001',759);
```

This command adds a record to the SALES table. It, too, can be a bit difficult to enter, particularly when you must get all the punctuation marks just right. Suppose for the sake of this demonstration that you expect you will have to use this command fairly often. Once you've managed to enter it correctly, you'd be really happy if you did not have to go through the same process again.

You don't have to. Once you have written and executed this command—and before you do anything else—enter:

```
SQL> SAVE NSERT
```

ORACLE will save the contents of the buffer—this command—in a file named NSERT. Of course, you can pick your own file name and add the disk and directory designations of your choice. The saved NSERT.SQL looks like this:

```
INSERT INTO SALES VALUES
(SYSDATE, 'HT','777-88-9999',
'2',NULL,'1','Y','Y','N',
'MM','69-0000001',759,)
/
```

There are a few modest differences in format and punctuation from the original command, but it is essentially the same thing. When you run this file, you should get exactly the same results as those the direct command produced.

Those results are in Figure 15-1. The SYSDATE command inserts today's date into the record. The null entry is a place to enter a referral by another employee, if there is one. The single-letter headings contain codes to record details of the transaction.

MORE ADVANCED PROGRAMMING

When you restrict yourself to standard SQL, a command file still has only limited usefulness. You can take advantage of a text editor to construct a command, or you can store a command you've already written for future use.

Things begin to open up, though, when you go beyond standard SQL. In ORACLE, the extended features of SQL*Plus add flexibility to the process. Other SQL-based programs offer added facilities of their own.

EXPANDING THE BUFFER

When you expand the command set into SQL*Plus, you also must expand the capacity of the command buffer. As Chapter 2 discussed, the standard buffer holds only standard SQL commands; it does not store SQL*Plus commands.

FIGURE 15-1 A Record of the First Sale

```
    TODAY      EMP SSNO          S REFERRAL I N N X PROD_CO ACCT_NO    AMOUNT
    ---------  --- -----------   - -------- - - - - ------- ---------- -------
    22-JAN-88  HT  777-88-9999 2               1 Y Y N MM      69-0000001    759
```

There's an easy way around this: Create another buffer. When you create your own buffer, it will store any command you issue, including those from SQL*Plus. This means you can work within ORACLE to write and define a series of commands. Once you have them perfected, you can use the SAVE command to record them all on disk.

The command to establish a new buffer is:

```
SQL> SET BUFFER <name>
```

The name can be anything you choose, as long as you comply with the rules for naming a SQL table. You'll never have to refer to it in any other command. The only purpose in giving it a name is to distinguish your self-created buffer from the normal SQL buffer. Suppose that you decide to:

```
SQL> SET BUFFER X
```

X now becomes the *current buffer.* As long as that setting remains in effect, every command you enter will be recorded in Buffer X. This includes SQL*Plus commands. When you issue a SAVE command, ORACLE will save the contents of the current buffer. This means that, in this case, it will save the contents of X, including all the SQL*Plus commands.

Once you SAVE the comments, ORACLE will close Buffer X, and the SQL buffer will again become the current buffer. There's nothing to prevent you, though, from issuing a new SET BUFFER command.

USING PARAMETERS

Suppose that you'd like to examine the demographic data of the UnderFed customers in a certain income bracket. A command to do that might be:

```
SQL> SELECT LAST, PROFESSION, RESIDENCE,
  2   HOME_OWNER, AGE_GROUP
  3   FROM CUSTOMER
  4   WHERE INCOME = 2
```

The results are:

LAST	P	R	H	A
BUNNY	3	3	1	1

The least you could say about this one qualifying entry is that it is a representative sample. Having seen this response, you'd now like to look at every other income group. Does this mean you must write a new query for each group?

You need not. Instead, you can write a version of this command to retrieve any income level you select. The first step is to edit the query:

```
SQL> LIST 3
   3*  WHERE INCOME = 2
SQL> CHANGE /2/&1/
   3*  WHERE INCOME = &1
```

These are editing commands you might remember from Chapter 2. Instead of a specific income level, this command now is prepared to use something akin to dBASE's macro substitution. In fact, both SQL and dBASE use the & symbol. The &1 also operates as does the %1 you might encounter in an advanced DOS batch file.

Now, save the command to the file specification of your choice, such as:

```
SQL> SAVE D:MONEY
```

ORACLE should respond with:

```
Wrote file D:MONEY
```

The confirmation is reassuring, if a bit ungrammatical.

STARTING THE COMMAND

Now, if you run the saved program using the START command (but only START) you can add a parameter to specify the value that will be substituted in place of &1. For example:

```
SQL> START D:MONEY 3
```

ORACLE's first response will be to explain the substitutions it is about to make:

```
old   3: WHERE INCOME = &1
new   3: WHERE INCOME = 3
```

The command now will run as though it had the "new" Line 3, producing:

```
LAST          P  R  H  A
-------------  -  -  -  -
BENJAMIN      2  2  2  3
DRIVER        4  2  1  3
BONGO         2  2  2  2
```

You can try it with other values, too:

```
SQL> START D:MONEY 4
old   3: WHERE INCOME = &1
new   3: WHERE INCOME = 4

LAST             P  R  H  A
-----------------  -  -  -  -
HAMMERSTEIN      2  2  1  3

SQL> START D:MONEY 1
old   3: WHERE INCOME = &1
new   3: WHERE INCOME = 1

LAST             P  R  H  A
-----------------  -  -  -  -
BUNNY            3  3  2  1
```

You can even try to make a deliberate mistake, calling for a value that doesn't exist:

```
SQL> START D:MONEY 5
old   3: WHERE INCOME = &1
new   3: WHERE INCOME = 5

no records selected
```

USING MULTIPLE PARAMETERS

You can use as many as nine parameters in this way. The first parameter in the START command will replace &1 in the command file, the second parameter will replace &2, and so on, through &9. For example, this could be an even more versatile version of MONEY.SQL.:

```
SQL> SELECT LAST, INCOME, PROFESSION, RESIDENCE,
  2    HOME_OWNER, AGE_GROUP
  3    FROM CUSTOMER
  4    WHERE &1 = $2
```

Then, this command:

SQL> START D:MONEY PROFESSION 2

would have the same effect as:

```
SQL> SELECT LAST, INCOME, PROFESSION, RESIDENCE,
  2    HOME__OWNER, AGE__GROUP
  3    FROM CUSTOMER
  4    WHERE PROFESSION = 2
```

PROGRAMMED INPUT

One of the big advantages of a dBASE command file over dot-command data entry is the control a programmer can establish. A well-written dBASE command file can set formats, validate entries, and generally filter out many types of errors.

dBASE programmers usually do this with a system of @ ... SAY ... GET commands, with which they can lay out data entry screens and call for the results in a certain format. Less used, because they are much less versatile, are ACCEPT and INPUT. Both accept data at whatever point on the screen they happen to fall. In either case, standard dBASE practice is to store the input in memory variables. Then, once everything has been entered and confirmed, the contents of the variables are copied to a new database record.

THE ORACLE VERSION

You can write a SQL command file that will do much the same thing. As you'll soon see, though, the results will be on, or even a bit below, the level of dBASE's relatively primitive ACCEPT and INPUT.

In SQL*Plus, the basic data entry command is ACCEPT. INPUT is one of the editing commands discussed in Chapter 2. As in dBASE, the response to an ACCEPT command is stored as a variable, called a *user variable* in ORACLE. You then can use macro substitution to INSERT these variables into the database.

A SIMPLE DATA ENTRY PROGRAM

A basic data entry program is SIGNUP.SQL, shown in Listing 15-2. It runs through the basic techniques of ACCEPTing data for

```
REM Listing 15-2
REM SIGNUP.SQL
REM Data input for SALES table.

CLEAR BUFFER;
CLEAR BREAKS;
CLEAR COLUMNS;
CLEAR COMPUTES;
ACCEPT M_EMP_CODE PROMPT 'Employee Code: ';
ACCEPT M_SSNO PROMPT 'Customer''s Social Security Number: ';
ACCEPT M_SOURCE PROMPT 'What brought customer here? ';
ACCEPT M_REFERRAL PROMPT 'Employee who referred customer: ';
ACCEPT M_INITIATED PROMPT 'Who initiated this contact? ';
ACCEPT M_NEW_CUST PROMPT 'New Customer? (Y/N) ';
ACCEPT M_NEW_MONEY PROMPT 'Are new funds being deposited? ';
ACCEPT M_PROD_CODE PROMPT 'Type of new account: ';
ACCEPT M_ACCT_NO PROMPT 'Account No.: ';
ACCEPT M_AMOUNT PROMPT 'Amount deposited: ';
INSERT INTO SALES VALUES
(SYSDATE, '&M_EMP_CODE', '&M_SSNO',
'&M_SOURCE', '&M_REFERRAL', '&M_INITIATED',
'&M_NEW_CUST', '&M_NEW_MONEY',
'&M_PROD_CODE', '&M_ACCT_NO', &M_AMOUNT)
/
```

a new SALES record, then inserting the values into the table. As most good programs do, this one starts by clearing the decks of any nonstandard settings that might be in force at the time:

CLEAR BUFFER;
CLEAR BREAKS;
CLEAR COLUMNS;
CLEAR COMPUTES;

Just as dBASE programs usually start with a series of SET commands to clear the air, this program begins by clearing the buffer and eliminating several definitions. For example, CLEAR COLUMNS gets rid of any column format definitions that might have been in effect. The other commands clear some things you probably haven't encountered before, but you will shortly.

Next comes a series of ACCEPT commands beginning with:

ACCEPT M_EMP_CODE PROMPT 'Employee Code: ';

This command will store the operator's response in the variable M_EMP_CODE. It corresponds to the EMP_CODE column in SALES. The M_ prefix is a dBASE convention that identifies memory variables as such while also associating them with their related database fields. It works just as well in SQL.

PROMPT is an optional command. To no one's surprise, it states a prompt to be displayed for the operator.

INSERTING THE NEW VALUES

The remaining ACCEPT commands create variables to match the remaining columns of SALES. Then, the program reaches an INSERT command that installs the newly entered values in a new row of the table. In dBASE, the same thing would be done with APPEND BLANK followed by a series of commands such as REPLACE EMP_CODE WITH M_EMP_CODE.

ORACLE uses macro substitution, instead. SYSDATE, the first item on the list of values, places the current date in the file. The next item adds the employee code. Take a close look at its form and format:

'&M_EMP_CODE'

SQL uses the ampersand to extract the contents of a variable just as it did to extract the contents of parameters. This convention is also the same as in dBASE. The ampersand refers to the contents of a variable, as opposed to the variable's name. Here, the command in effect is to insert the contents of M_EMP_CODE. Its order among the values indicates that it should go into the second column, which is EMP_CODE.

There is one detail that easily could frustrate an experienced dBASE user. When the macro-substituted variable contains Char data, the entire expression must be in single quotes, as you see here. SQL insists that these quotes surround Char data. Here, they surround the ampersand and the variable name that refers to that character. Don't put quotes around Number data such as AMOUNT.

You can also create an ORACLE variable with the DEFINE command. It works only with Char variables, though. The basic format:

DEFINE <variable> = <value>

RUNNING STARTUP

The command to run this program is:

SQL> START SIGNUP

It should walk you through the series of on-screen prompts and responses shown in Figure 15-2.

Then, you'll get a line-by-line report, as ORACLE plugs the

FIGURE 15-2   SIGNUP Creates This Data Entry Display

```
Employee Code: KC
Customer's Social Security Number: 111-22-3333
Employee Code: 5
Employee who referred customer: WUNDERLAND
Who initiated this contact? : 1
New Customer? (Y/N) N
Are new funds being deposited? (Y/N) Y
Does this customer have another type of  account? (Y/N) Y
Type of new account: CK
Account No.: 69-0000006
Amount deposited: 45.67
```

variables into the INSERT command then INSERTs them into the table (Figure 15-3). The line numbers are those SQL would display if you wrote the INSERT command directly.

IMPROVING THE BREED

You certainly could say there is room for improvement—particularly if you are prone to understatement. The best way to trap an error is to prevent it in the first place. This program does next to nothing to help the operator determine what is a correct entry.

Particularly awkward are the several entries like those that describe the source of the business. They require coded answers: 1 for a response to a newspaper ad, 2 for a walk-in, and so on. You should give the operator some guidance as to how to use the coding system. Not only is there a danger that someone will enter a 2 where there should be a 1, but someone else might enter a 7, which is not used as a code for anything.

FIGURE 15-3   A Blow-by-Blow Report of the Conversions

```
old    2: (SYSDATE, '&M_EMP_CODE', '&M_SSNO',
new    2: (SYSDATE, 'KC', '111-22-3333',
old    3: '&M_SOURCE', '&M_REFERRAL', '&M_INITIATED',
new    3: '5', 'WUNDERLAND', '1',
old    4: '&M_NEW_CUST', '&M_NEW_MONEY',
new    4: 'N', 'Y',
old    5: '&M_PROD_CODE', '&M_ACCT_NO', &M_AMOUNT)
new    5: 'CK', '69-0000006', 45.67)
```

PROVIDING A PROMPTER

A revised version of SIGNUP.SQL, Listing 15-3, has some additions to remind the operator of the proper codes.

```
REM Listing 15-3
REM SIGNUP.SQL
REM Revised version with prompts.

 CLEAR BUFFER;
 CLEAR BREAKS
 CLEAR COLUMNS
 CLEAR COMPUTES
 ACCEPT M_EMP_CODE PROMPT 'Employee Code: (your initials) ';
 ACCEPT M_SSNO PROMPT 'Customer''s Social Security Number: ';
DOCUMENT
What brought customer here? Codes:
1: Newspaper     2: Walk-in      3: Other Customer
4: Radio         5: Employee Recommended        6: Other
#
 ACCEPT M_SOURCE PROMPT  'Enter code: ';
 ACCEPT M_REFERRAL PROMPT 'Employee who referred customer: ';
DOCUMENT
Who initiated this contact? Codes:
1: Customer      2: Service Rep. 3. Teller       4. Other
#
 ACCEPT M_INITIATED PROMPT 'Enter code: ';
 ACCEPT M_NEW_CUST PROMPT 'New Customer? (Y/N) ';
 ACCEPT M_NEW_MONEY PROMPT 'Are new funds being deposited? (Y/N) ';
 ACCEPT M_PROD_CODE PROMPT 'Type of new account: ';
 ACCEPT M_ACCT_NO PROMPT 'Account No.: ';
 ACCEPT M_AMOUNT PROMPT 'Amount deposited: ';
INSERT INTO SALES VALUES
(SYSDATE, '&M_EMP_CODE', '&M_SSNO',
'&M_SOURCE', '&M_REFERRAL', '&M_INITIATED',
'&M_NEW_CUST', '&M_NEW_MONEY',
'&M_PROD_CODE', '&M_ACCT_NO', &M_AMOUNT)
/
```

An example:

DOCUMENT
What brought customer here? Codes:
1: Newspaper   2: Walk-in   3: Other Customer
4: Radio   5: Employee Recommended   6:
Other
#
ACCEPT M_SOURCE PROMPT   'Enter code: ';

DOCUMENT is a command to display the ensuing text on screen. A # on a line by itself is the signal to end the display. It works something like the dBASE commands TEXT and ENDTEXT.

FIGURE 15-4 New Prompts

```
Employee Code: (your initials) KC
Customer's Social Security Number: 111-22-3333
DOC>'What brought customer here? Codes:
DOC>1: Newspaper     2: Walk-in        3: Other Customer
DOC>4: Radio         5: Employee Recommended          6: Other
DOC>#
Enter code: 5
Employee who referred customer: WUNDERLAND
DOC>Who initiated this contact? Codes:
DOC>1: Customer      2: Service Rep. 3. Teller         4. Other
DOC>#
Enter code: 1
New Customer? (Y/N) N
Are new funds being deposited? (Y/N) Y
Does this customer have another type of  account? (Y/N) Y
Type of new account: CK
Account No.: 69-0000006
Amount deposited: 45.67
```

This is not to say it works very well. The new screen display does help the operator with the coding system, but it has its awkward moments, as Figure 15-4 reveals. For the record, the ORACLE manual describes DOCUMENT as an obsolete command, but the suggested substitutes aren't entirely adequate for multi-line text displays.

VALIDATION AND VERIFICATION

Even this revised command file is short on validation. The program should determine, for example, whether the customer who is opening the account is already listed in the CUSTOMER table. It should also be able to verify that the entered product code actually represents an item in the PRODUCTS table.

An expanded SIGNUP.SQL (Listing 15-4) adds these lines to make those two checks:

```
SELECT LAST, FIRST   FROM CUSTOMER
        WHERE SSNO = '&M_SSNO';
DOCUMENT
If no records found, make sure number is correct.
If so, enter new customer record.
#
PAUSE Press <Return> to Continue;
SELECT PROD_CODE, PRODUCT FROM PRODUCTS
        WHERE PROD_CODE = '&M_PROD_CODE';
```

DOCUMENT
If no records found, the product code you entered is incorrect.
#
PAUSE Press <Return> to Continue;

The two SELECT commands use macro substitutions and variables to search the CUSTOMER and PRODUCTS tables for matching entries. The prompts tell the operator what to do if there's no match. The PAUSE command is similar to the dBASE WAIT. It lets the operator read the message before it scrolls out of sight. The UNDEFINE commands remove the variables from memory, much as RELEASE commands do in dBASE.

```
REM Listing 15-4
REM SIGNUP.SQL
REM Data input for SALES table.

 CLEAR BUFFER;
 CLEAR BREAKS
 CLEAR COLUMNS
 CLEAR COMPUTES
 ACCEPT M_EMP_CODE PROMPT 'Employee Code: (your initials) ';
 ACCEPT M_SSNO PROMPT 'Customer''s Social Security Number: ';
DOCUMENT
'What brought customer here? Codes:
1: Newspaper    2: Walk-in      3: Other Customer
4: Radio        5: Employee Recommended         6: Other
#
 ACCEPT M_SOURCE PROMPT  'Enter code: ';
 ACCEPT M_REFERRAL PROMPT 'Employee who referred customer: ';
DOCUMENT
Who initiated this contact? Codes:
1: Customer     2: Service Rep. 3. Teller       4. Other
#
 ACCEPT M_INITIATED PROMPT 'Enter code: ';
 ACCEPT M_NEW_CUST PROMPT 'New Customer? (Y/N) ';
 ACCEPT M_NEW_MONEY PROMPT 'Are new funds being deposited? (Y/N) ';
 ACCEPT M_PROD_CODE PROMPT 'Type of new account: ';
 ACCEPT M_ACCT_NO PROMPT 'Account No.: ';
 ACCEPT M_AMOUNT PROMPT 'Amount deposited: ';
SELECT LAST, FIRST  FROM CUSTOMER
        WHERE SSNO = '&M_SSNO';
DOCUMENT
If no records found, make sure number is correct.
If so, enter new customer record.
#
PAUSE Press <Return> to Continue;
SELECT PROD_CODE, PRODUCT FROM PRODUCTS
        WHERE PROD_CODE = '&M_PROD_CODE';
DOCUMENT
If no records found, the product code you entered
is incorrect.
#
PAUSE Press <Return> to Continue;
```

```
INSERT INTO SALES VALUES
(SYSDATE, '&M_EMP_CODE', '&M_SSNO',
'&M_SOURCE', '&M_REFERRAL', '&M_INITIATED',
'&M_NEW_CUST', '&M_NEW_MONEY',
'&M_PROD_CODE', '&M_ACCT_NO', &M_AMOUNT);
UNDEFINE M_EMP_CODE
UNDEFINE M_SSNO
UNDEFINE M_SOURCE
UNDEFINE M_REFERRAL
UNDEFINE M_INITIATED
UNDEFINE M_NEW_CUST
UNDEFINE M_NEW_MONEY
UNDEFINE M_PROD_CODE
UNDEFINE M_ACCT_NO
UNDEFINE M_AMOUNT
/
```

RUNNING THE REVISED VERSION

Running this version of the command file produces results like those shown in Figure 15-5.

After reporting on the substitutions, the program checks CUSTOMER for a SSNO entry that matches M_SSNO. Then, it makes a similar check of PRODUCTS. In this case, both entries were verified as correct.

FIGURE 15-5   Results of the Validation Checks

```
    old   2:        WHERE SSNO = '&M_SSNO'
    new   2:        WHERE SSNO = '111-22-3333'

    LAST            FIRST
    --------------- ---------------
    WUNDERLAND      ALLISON

    DOC>If no records found, make sure number is correct.
    DOC>If so, enter new customer record.
    DOC>#
    'Press <Return> to Continue'

    old   2:        WHERE PROD_CODE = '&M_PROD_CODE'
    new   2:        WHERE PROD_CODE = 'CK'

    PROD PRODUCT
    ---- --------------------
    CK   CHECKING

    DOC>If no records found, the product code you entered
    DOC>is incorrect.
    DOC>#
    'Press <Return> to Continue'
```

A LITTLE SURPRISE

Then comes something that wasn't expected. ORACLE presents the prompt:

Enter value for m__prod__code:

The program apparently has done some validation of its own, beyond that provided in SIGNUP.SQL. Nothing in the command file itself is designed to produce such a prompt. ORACLE came up with that one itself. I hit <Enter>, and the program again checked the null response against the PRODUCTS table. The entire routine went like this:

```
Enter value for m__prod__code:
old    2:    WHERE PROD__CODE = '&M__PROD__CODE'
new    2:    WHERE PROD__CODE = ' '

no records selected
```

I wasn't able to find an explanation for this anywhere in ORACLE's vast documentation, although that doesn't necessarily mean it isn't there. My own experiments determined that this is a one-time-only opportunity to correct an entry that fails to pass the validation test. The program will not repeat the validation search a second time, and it apparently will conduct only one validation test in any command file. It always checks the last validation routine, never any that came before.

CUSTOMER DATA ENTRY

Listing 15-5 creates a data entry display for the CUSTOMER file. It sticks to the basic ACCEPT and INSERT commands. You can embellish it if you wish.

```
REM Listing 15-5
REM NEWCUST.SQL
REM Data input for CUSTOMER table.

 CLEAR BUFFER;
 CLEAR BREAKS;
 CLEAR COLUMNS;
 CLEAR COMPUTES;
ACCEPT M_SSNO PROMPT 'Customer Social Security No.: ';
ACCEPT M_LAST PROMPT 'Last name: ';
ACCEPT M_FIRST PROMPT 'First: ';
ACCEPT M_INIT PROMPT 'Middle initial: ';
ACCEPT M_STREET PROMPT 'Street : ';
```

```
ACCEPT M_CITY PROMPT 'City: ';
ACCEPT M_STATE PROMPT 'State: ';
ACCEPT M_ZIP PROMPT 'ZIP Code: ';
ACCEPT M_INCOME PROMPT 'Income class (1-4) ';
ACCEPT M_PROFESSION PROMPT 'Job class (1-4) ';
ACCEPT M_RESIDENCE PROMPT 'Permanent resident? (Y/N) ';
ACCEPT M_HOME_OWNER PROMPT 'Home owner? (Y/N) ';
ACCEPT M_AGE_GROUP PROMPT 'Age group: (1-3) ';
INSERT INTO CUSTOMER VALUES(
       'M_SSNO', 'M_LAST', 'M_FIRST', 'M_INIT',
       'M_STREET', 'M_CITY', 'M_STATE', 'M_ZIP',
       'M_INCOME', 'M_PROFESSION', 'M_RESIDENCE',
       'M_HOME_OWNER', 'M_AGE_GROUP');
```

There is no need to validate these entries against another file. Where the entries call for codes, a range of proper values has been suggested. If you see fit, you can add prompts to explain the codes more completely.

REVIEW QUESTIONS

1. What's the difference between a command file and a program?
2. What happens when you write a SQL command from the SQL> prompt? What's the difference when you write a SQL*Plus command?
3. What's the exception to the previous answer?
4. Name three ways to start a command file from within SQL.
5. Some views cannot be used to update their underlying table. If this is the case, why create one?
6. What does the command SAVE do in SQL*Plus?
7. What does the ampersand mean in dBASE? In ORACLE?
8. Name two ways to create a user variable in ORACLE.

ANSWERS

1. Not much. Both are simply lists of commands for the computer to execute in order.
2. A SQL command is stored in the current buffer; a SQL*Plus command is not.
3. When you have specified your own current buffer.
4.   @, START or GET . . . RUN.
5. To control access. You can leave sensitive information out of a view that is widely accessible.

6. It saves the contents of the current buffer in a disk file.
7. In both cases, the ampersand directs the program to the contents of the indicated variable rather than the variable's name.
8. Through an ASSIGN command, or by accepting keyboard input with ACCEPT.

CHAPTER

16

Reporting in SQL

A SQL command file does only a bare-bones job of providing for data entry, even with enhancements such as those in SQL*Plus. The combination seems better-suited to producing reports. Reporting in ORACLE is really just a matter of putting SQL and SQL*Plus commands to good use. You've already encountered most of what you need.

Basically, an ORACLE report is just the heavily formatted output of a query. The tabular display produced by standard SQL is a kind of report. ORACLE adds several SQL*Plus enhancements for flexibility and to produce a better-looking result. The enhancements are available only in ORACLE; they aren't part of standard SQL. Nevertheless, they are examples of what you can do with a few simple additions to the standard package.

The additional SQL*Plus commands can become complex. There are commands to format columns, create titles, and lay out pages. There are enough of these that you probably will want to save the most frequently used command sets in a SQL command file. You can do this as described in the previous chapter, either by writing the program in advance or by capturing your session in a buffer of your own making.

BUILDING A BASIC REPORT

It's said with irony that with a few commands you can build a report from SQL that matches one produced by the dBASE report generator. The irony is that dBASE reports have long been noted for their limited features and flexibility.

Less ironically, and with a few more commands, you can build a much better report from a SQL database.

THE STANDARD dBASE REPORT

This may not be obvious at the outset. Figure 16-1 shows a typical dBASE report, taken from the dBASE version of ROSTER. It shows the employees' names and salaries, and includes a computed column that derives monthly salaries from the annual figures. Each column has its own expansive heading, and there's a heading for the report itself. The totals are broken down by department.

FIGURE 16-1 A Typical dBASE Report

```
Page No.      1
01/24/88
                        UNDERWOOD FEDERAL SALARY REPORT

LAST NAME       ANNUAL    MONTHLY
                SALARY    SALARY


**    1
DAVIDSON      24000.00    2000.00
MADISON       21000.00    1750.00
PRESTO        42500.00    3541.67
** Subtotal **
              87500.00    7291.67

**    2
TUBA          11000.00     916.67
COLLINS       13300.00    1108.33
ZIMMERMAN     13400.00    1116.67
ROWE-HATTON   11250.00     937.50
** Subtotal **
              48950.00    4079.17

**    3
MAHONEY       12400.00    1033.33
PALMER        13450.00    1120.83
** Subtotal **
              25850.00    2154.17

**    4
BUCHINSKY     15000.00    1250.00
** Subtotal **
              15000.00    1250.00
*** Total ***
              177300.0   14775.00
```

Compare this with Figure 16-2. This is the standard result of a SQL query seeking the same type of information:

```
SQL> SELECT DEPT_NO, LAST, SALARY, SALARY/12
  2   FROM ROSTER;
```

Compared with even the much-maligned dBASE version, it does look a little Spartan.

Step by step, you can burnish this rough display until it becomes a polished report. The first of those steps is to make use of a command you encountered in earlier chapters.

FIGURE 16-2   The Beginnings of a SQL Report

```
        DEPT_NO LAST            SALARY SALARY/12
        ------- ------------    ------- ---------
              1 DAVIDSON         24000      2000
              1 MADISON          21000      1750
              1 PRESTO           42500    3541.67
              2 TUBA             11000    916.667
              3 MAHONEY          12400    1033.33
              4 BUCHINSKY        15000      1250
              3 PALMER           13450    1120.83
              2 COLLINS          13300    1108.33
              2 ZIMMERMAN        13400    1116.67
              2 ROWE-HATTON      11250     937.5
```

REVIEWING COLUMN

This is the COLUMN command, used earlier to format numerical displays and to add titles to columns. It now will be called upon to perform these services again.

By way of review, here's a COLUMN head that replaces the cryptic DEPT_NO, a column in the ROSTER table, with something that more closely resembles the English language:

SQL> COLUMN DEPT_NO HEADING DEPARTMENT;

Now the same SQL command that was used before will produce the display shown in Figure 16-3.

FIGURE 16-3   A Departmental Improvement

```
      DEPARTMENT LAST            SALARY SALARY/12
      ---------- ------------    ------- ---------
               1 DAVIDSON         24000      2000
               1 MADISON          21000      1750
               1 PRESTO           42500    3541.67
               2 TUBA             11000    916.667
               3 MAHONEY          12400    1033.33
               4 BUCHINSKY        15000      1250
               3 PALMER           13450    1120.83
               2 COLLINS          13300    1108.33
               2 ZIMMERMAN        13400    1116.67
               2 ROWE-HATTON      11250     937.5

      10 records selected.
```

This is a little more presentable. You can improve the group of names by providing a more complete heading and a little more width:

SQL> COLUMN LAST HEADING 'LAST NAME' FORMAT A20;

Now the display looks like Figure 16-4.

FORMATTING FIGURES

Things still are awkward, though, in the two salary columns. The formatting there leaves almost everything to be desired.

As you no doubt recall with sparkling clarity, COLUMN can take care of that, too. Here's one way:

SQL> COLUMN SALARY HEADING 'ANNUAL|SALARY' FORMAT $99,999.99;

The vertical bar between ANNUAL and SALARY puts these two words on separate lines. The FORMAT clause provides an outline for the numerical display, much like PICTURE in dBASE. Now we have a display that looks like Figure 16-5.

This still leaves the figures in the last column. You probably want to format them the same way as you did the other stack of salaries. If so, COLUMN has a LIKE option for you:

SQL> COLUMN SALARY/12 LIKE SALARY HEADING 'MONTHLY|SALARY'

FIGURE 16-4 The Names Get Some Elbow Room

```
       DEPARTMENT LAST NAME                SALARY SALARY/12
       ---------- --------------------     ------ ---------
                1 DAVIDSON                   24000      2000
                1 MADISON                    21000      1750
                1 PRESTO                     42500   3541.67
                2 TUBA                       11000   916.667
                3 MAHONEY                    12400   1033.33
                4 BUCHINSKY                  15000      1250
                3 PALMER                     13450   1120.83
                2 COLLINS                    13300   1108.33
                2 ZIMMERMAN                  13400   1116.67
                2 ROWE-HATTON                11250     937.5

       10 records selected.
```

FIGURE 16-5   Better-Looking Salaries

```
                                      ANNUAL
           DEPARTMENT LAST NAME       SALARY  SALARY/12
           ---------- -------------------- ----------- ---------
                    1 DAVIDSON       $24,000.00      2000
                    1 MADISON        $21,000.00      1750
                    1 PRESTO         $42,500.00   3541.67
                    2 TUBA           $11,000.00   916.667
                    3 MAHONEY        $12,400.00   1033.33
                    4 BUCHINSKY      $15,000.00      1250
                    3 PALMER         $13,450.00   1120.83
                    2 COLLINS        $13,300.00   1108.33
                    2 ZIMMERMAN      $13,400.00   1116.67
                    2 ROWE-HATTON    $11,250.00     937.5

           10 records selected.
```

The LIKE SALARY means this column should be formatted just as SALARY is (Figure 16-6). The LIKE clause will duplicate the format and heading of the specified column except for any changes you make in the same command. That was done here with the column heading.

TAKING TITLE TO A PAGE

Most word processors can install headers at the top of each page—usually something with a title and a page number. They also can install footers, at the bottom of each page.

FIGURE 16-6   Even Better-Looking Salaries

```
                                      ANNUAL     MONTHLY
           DEPARTMENT LAST NAME       SALARY      SALARY
           ---------- -------------------- ----------- -----------
                    1 DAVIDSON       $24,000.00  $2,000.00
                    1 MADISON        $21,000.00  $1,750.00
                    1 PRESTO         $42,500.00  $3,541.67
                    2 TUBA           $11,000.00    $916.67
                    3 MAHONEY        $12,400.00  $1,033.33
                    4 BUCHINSKY      $15,000.00  $1,250.00
                    3 PALMER         $13,450.00  $1,120.83
                    2 COLLINS        $13,300.00  $1,108.33
                    2 ZIMMERMAN      $13,400.00  $1,116.67
                    2 ROWE-HATTON    $11,250.00    $937.50

           10 records selected.
```

ORACLE can also create headers and footers, but it gives them different names. At the top of the page is a TTITLE; at the bottom is a BTITLE. The TTITLE comes with a standard format, but you can create your own custom layout.

USING THE STANDARD FORMAT

Veterans of dBASE reporting will probably find the standard format familiar. The command to create a TTITLE in the standard format is simply TTITLE followed by the text you want in the title. For example:

SQL> TTITLE 'UNDERWOOD FEDERAL SALARY REPORT'

In the standard format, the date will appear at the upper left and a page number at the upper right. The title you entered will be centered on the next line. Figure 16-7 shows the report with the standard title.

FORMATTING YOUR OWN

If ORACLE discerns a string of text immediately after a TTITLE command, it will give you the standard format. If it finds another formatting command, it will presume you want a custom format and will proceed to follow your instructions.

FIGURE 16-7   The Standard Title Format

```
Mon Jan 25                                                     page    1
                      UNDERWOOD FEDERAL SALARY REPORT

                                          ANNUAL      MONTHLY
DEPARTMENT LAST NAME                       SALARY       SALARY
---------- --------------------      ------------  -----------
         1 DAVIDSON                    $24,000.00   $2,000.00
         1 MADISON                     $21,000.00   $1,750.00
         1 PRESTO                      $42,500.00   $3,541.67
         2 TUBA                        $11,000.00     $916.67
         3 MAHONEY                     $12,400.00   $1,033.33
         4 BUCHINSKY                   $15,000.00   $1,250.00
         3 PALMER                      $13,450.00   $1,120.83
         2 COLLINS                     $13,300.00   $1,108.33
         2 ZIMMERMAN                   $13,400.00   $1,116.67
         2 ROWE-HATTON                 $11,250.00     $937.50

10 records selected.
```

Available title formatting commands include LEFT, RIGHT, and CENTER, to place entries at those positions on the page, and COL to begin the entry at a particular column. SKIP produces a blank line. To demonstrate:

SQL> TTITLE LEFT 'UNDERWOOD FEDERAL SALARY
REPORT' SKIP;

This command calls for a flush-left title, then a blank line before the body of the report begins (Figure 16-8).

BRINGING UP THE BOTTOM

BTITLE works in a similar fashion at the nether end of the page. This command produces a centered bottom title, or footer:

SQL> BTITLE CENTER 'CONFIDENTIAL: INTERNAL
USE ONLY';

The results are shown in Figure 16-9. This title is centered on ORACLE's default column width of 80. If you wish to change it you can:

SET LINESIZE = <width>;

If neither the left, the right, nor the center satisfies you, you can make use of the COL option. COL with a number immediately afterward states the column at which you want the text entry to

FIGURE 16-8   A Title Set Flush Left

```
UNDERWOOD FEDERAL SALARY REPORT
                                     ANNUAL      MONTHLY
DEPARTMENT LAST NAME                 SALARY       SALARY
---------- -------------------- ----------- -----------
         1 DAVIDSON              $24,000.00   $2,000.00
         1 MADISON               $21,000.00   $1,750.00
         1 PRESTO                $42,500.00   $3,541.67
         2 TUBA                  $11,000.00     $916.67
         3 MAHONEY               $12,400.00   $1,033.33
         4 BUCHINSKY             $15,000.00   $1,250.00
         3 PALMER                $13,450.00   $1,120.83
         2 COLLINS               $13,300.00   $1,108.33
         2 ZIMMERMAN             $13,400.00   $1,116.67
         2 ROWE-HATTON           $11,250.00     $937.50

10 records selected.
```

FIGURE 16-9 A Bottom Title Added

```
UNDERWOOD FEDERAL SALARY REPORT
                                   ANNUAL      MONTHLY
DEPARTMENT LAST NAME               SALARY       SALARY
---------- --------------------- ----------- -----------
         1 DAVIDSON              $24,000.00   $2,000.00
         1 MADISON               $21,000.00   $1,750.00
         1 PRESTO                $42,500.00   $3,541.67
         2 TUBA                  $11,000.00     $916.67
         3 MAHONEY               $12,400.00   $1,033.33
         4 BUCHINSKY             $15,000.00   $1,250.00
         3 PALMER                $13,450.00   $1,120.83
         2 COLLINS               $13,300.00   $1,108.33
         2 ZIMMERMAN             $13,400.00   $1,116.67
         2 ROWE-HATTON           $11,250.00     $937.50

              CONFIDENTIAL: INTERNAL USE ONLY

10 records selected.
```

begin. COL 10 begins the entry in column 10. The toughest thing about this is to distinguish between the eighty columns on the screen, to which COL refers, and the very different columns in a SQL table.

CUSTOM DATE HEADINGS

As if to make up for the simplicity of COL, trying to enter a date in a custom title format can send you screaming back to the standard format, which prints the data automatically. To get the date into a header or footer you must first fool ORACLE into thinking the date is in a column. Here goes:

SQL> COLUMN TODAY NOPRINT NEW_VAL DATEVAR;

This is a COLUMN command that sets the specifications for a column called TODAY. If you remember from your earlier encounters with COLUMN, it sets specifications for the columns to be produced by later queries. Such a column need not exist at the time COLUMN sets the specifications.

In this case, TODAY will not be printed. It will bear the special designation NEW_VAL, which tells COLUMN to expect a new value presently. DATEVAR identifies that value.

Now to use all this in a TTITLE command:

```
SQL> TTITLE COL 10 'UNDERWOOD FEDERAL SALARY
REPORT'–
  > SKIP–
  > COL 20 DATEVAR–
  > SKIP;
```

This delightful sequence starts the main heading at column 10 of the first line. Then, it skips a line and moves to column 20. There, it will insert the value you previously identified as DATEVAR. Then, it skips a line to begin the body of the report.

Wait, there's more. ORACLE still has no idea what DATEVAR is supposed to be. However, if you provide a value TODAY, which is the phony column created a few moments ago, it will travel the length of the COLUMN command to lodge in DATEVAR.

First, another detail: The hyphens at the ends of the lines mean the command continues on the next line. This is standard form for a SQL*Plus command, which doesn't really need the concluding semicolon.

Meanwhile, you still must get a value into the phony column TODAY. You do that by rewriting the query to include it:

```
SQL> SELECT TO_CHAR(SYSDATE) TODAY,
  2    DEPT_NO, LAST, SALARY, SALARY/12
  3    FROM ROSTER;
```

Along with the information that actually comes from the ROSTER table, this query picks up the current date as stored in the computer, converts it to characters, and gives it the label TODAY. With that, it can travel across the COLUMN command, into DATEVAR, and to the header of your report. Figure 16-10 shows what happened at the end of the line.

BREAK DANCING

The dBASE report subtotals the salary figures by department. ORACLE can do this too, with a BREAK instruction.

BREAK sorts a report into groups and specifies some action to be taken at the end of each group. A group can be a column, a row,

FIGURE 16-10 The Header with a Date Added

```
              UNDERWOOD FEDERAL SALARY REPORT
                       25-JAN-88
                                    ANNUAL        MONTHLY
DEPARTMENT  LAST NAME               SALARY         SALARY
----------  ----------------     ----------     ----------
         1  DAVIDSON             $24,000.00      $2,000.00
         1  MADISON              $21,000.00      $1,750.00
         1  PRESTO               $42,500.00      $3,541.67
         2  TUBA                 $11,000.00        $916.67
         3  MAHONEY              $12,400.00      $1,033.33
         4  BUCHINSKY            $15,000.00      $1,250.00
         3  PALMER               $13,450.00      $1,120.83
         2  COLLINS              $13,300.00      $1,108.33
         2  ZIMMERMAN            $13,400.00      $1,116.67
         2  ROWE-HATTON          $11,250.00        $937.50

              CONFIDENTIAL: INTERNAL USE ONLY

10 records selected.
```

a page or even the whole report. The usual action is a total or some other computation for the group.

FORMS OF BREAK COMMANDS

BREAK comes in several variations. To duplicate the dBASE breaks in ORACLE, use:

BREAK ON DEPT__NO;

When you specify a break on a column, as in this example, ORACLE will put all rows with the same value into one group—within limits, as you'll see shortly.

You can specify more than one column for a break, as in:

BREAK ON BRANCH__NO ON DEPT__NO;

You can also call for breaks between each row:

BREAK ON ROW;

. . . or at the bottom of each page:

BREAK ON PAGE;

. . . and at the end of the report:

BREAK ON REPORT;

CALLS FOR ACTION

An additional clause determines what is to happen at each break. To skip a line between each group:

SQL> BREAK ON DEPT__NO SKIP;

You can also specify more than one line between groups, as in SKIP 2. If you don't call for lines to be skipped, none will be. You must specify this if you want it, unlike in dBASE, in which this part of the formatting is fairly automatic.

You can also put each group on a separate page with:

SQL> BREAK ON DEPT__NO PAGE;

When you specify a column for the breaks, ORACLE will normally print the name of that column once for each break. This format is shown in Figure 16-11. If you want that value in every row, add DUPLICATES to the BREAK command.

ONE SLIGHT PROBLEM

Now it's time to remember the important point that BREAK will gather only consecutive groups of like column values. In the

FIGURE 16-11   Results of a BREAK Command

```
            UNDERWOOD FEDERAL SALARY REPORT
                    25-JAN-88
                                    ANNUAL      MONTHLY
       DEPARTMENT LAST NAME         SALARY       SALARY
       ---------- -------------------- ----------- -----------
                1 DAVIDSON         $24,000.00   $2,000.00
                  MADISON          $21,000.00   $1,750.00
                  PRESTO           $42,500.00   $3,541.67

                2 TUBA             $11,000.00     $916.67

                3 MAHONEY          $12,400.00   $1,033.33

                4 BUCHINSKY        $15,000.00   $1,250.00

                3 PALMER           $13,450.00   $1,120.83

                2 COLLINS          $13,300.00   $1,108.33
                  ZIMMERMAN        $13,400.00   $1,116.67
                  ROWE-HATTON      $11,250.00     $937.50

       10 records selected.
```

ROSTER table, members of Departments 2 and 3 are scattered in different places. In dBASE, you can avoid that situation by sorting the file or, usually better, indexing it on the field that is to be the basis of the breaks.

To get the same effect with SQL, add an ORDER BY clause to the query:

```
SQL> SELECT TO_DATE (SYSDATE) TODAY,
  2    DEPT_NO, LAST, SALARY, SALARY/12
  3    FROM ROSTER
  4    ORDER BY DEPT_NO;
```

This should produce the neater output shown in Figure 16-12.

COMPUTING SUBTOTALS

Setting the break points is only the first step in computing departmental subtotals. You now must tell ORACLE what computations to make at each break. You do so with the command called COMPUTE. The basic syntax is:

```
COMPUTE <numerical function> OF <column to be
calculated> ON <break column>
```

FIGURE 16-12 Better Results of a BREAK Command

```
                UNDERWOOD FEDERAL SALARY REPORT
                        25-JAN-88
                                         ANNUAL      MONTHLY
           DEPARTMENT LAST NAME           SALARY       SALARY
           ---------- --------------------- ----------- -----------
                    1 DAVIDSON           $24,000.00   $2,000.00
                      PRESTO             $42,500.00   $3,541.67
                      MADISON            $21,000.00   $1,750.00

                    2 TUBA               $11,000.00     $916.67
                      ZIMMERMAN          $13,400.00   $1,116.67
                      ROWE-HATTON        $11,250.00     $937.50
                      COLLINS            $13,300.00   $1,108.33

                    3 MAHONEY            $12,400.00   $1,033.33
                      PALMER             $13,450.00   $1,120.83

                    4 BUCHINSKY          $15,000.00   $1,250.00
           10 records selected.
```

INCLUDING SUBTOTALS

Every time the program encounters a break, it will execute the COMPUTE command on every row after the last break, or, in the case of the first break, after the beginning of the report. COMPUTE and BREAK both are necessary for any calculations within an ORACLE report. One won't work without the other.

This command computes a total of the monthly salary column at every break based on the department number:

SQL> COMPUTE SUM OF SALARY/12 ON DEPT__NO;

The results are shown in Figure 16-13.

When you specify a computation on a different column, it takes effect in addition to any existing COMPUTE commands on other columns. For example, the monthly salary computation will remain in effect when you also give this command:

SQL> COMPUTE SUM OF SALARY ON DEPT__NO;

Both columns are now subtotaled, as Figure 16-14 illustrates.

FIGURE 16-13   Subtotals on the Monthly Salaries

```
              UNDERWOOD FEDERAL SALARY REPORT
                      25-JAN-88
                                         ANNUAL      MONTHLY
           DEPARTMENT LAST NAME          SALARY       SALARY
           ---------- --------------------  -----------  -----------
                    1 DAVIDSON          $24,000.00   $2,000.00
                      PRESTO            $42,500.00   $3,541.67
                      MADISON           $21,000.00   $1,750.00
           **********                               -----------
           sum                                       $7,291.67

                    2 TUBA              $11,000.00     $916.67
                      ZIMMERMAN         $13,400.00   $1,116.67
                      ROWE-HATTON       $11,250.00     $937.50
                      COLLINS           $13,300.00   $1,108.33
           **********                               -----------
           sum                                       $4,079.17

                    3 MAHONEY           $12,400.00   $1,033.33
                      PALMER            $13,450.00   $1,120.83
           **********                               -----------
           sum                                       $2,154.17

                    4 BUCHINSKY         $15,000.00   $1,250.00
           **********                               -----------
           sum                                       $1,250.00

           10 records selected.
```

FIGURE 16-14 Subtotals on an Additional Column

```
                    UNDERWOOD FEDERAL SALARY REPORT
                              25-JAN-88
                                          ANNUAL       MONTHLY
        DEPARTMENT  LAST NAME             SALARY        SALARY
        ----------  --------------------  -----------  -----------
                 1  DAVIDSON             $24,000.00   $2,000.00
                    PRESTO               $42,500.00   $3,541.67
                    MADISON              $21,000.00   $1,750.00
        **********                       -----------  -----------
        sum                              $87,500.00   $7,291.67

                 2  TUBA                 $11,000.00     $916.67
                    ZIMMERMAN            $13,400.00   $1,116.67
                    ROWE-HATTON          $11,250.00     $937.50
                    COLLINS              $13,300.00   $1,108.33
        **********                       -----------  -----------
        sum                              $48,950.00   $4,079.17

                 3  MAHONEY              $12,400.00   $1,033.33
                    PALMER               $13,450.00   $1,120.83
        **********                       -----------  -----------
        sum                              $25,850.00   $2,154.17

                 4  BUCHINSKY            $15,000.00   $1,250.00
        **********                       -----------  -----------
        sum                              $15,000.00   $1,250.00

        10 records selected.
```

OTHER CALCULATIONS

You can use other numerical functions as well. For example, this command will calculate the average annual salary for each break:

SQL> COMPUTE AVG OF SALARY ON DEPT_NO;

As Figure 16-15 illustrates, this command supersedes the earlier COMPUTE command on the same column.

If you would like a count to go with the present averages and totals, try:

SQL> COMPUTE COUNT OF LAST ON DEPT_NO;

The results are shown in Figure 16-16. Other mathematical functions you can use in a COMPUTE command are MAX, which returns the maximum value; MIN, which returns the minimum value; AVG, which produces the mean; STD, which produces the standard deviation; and VAR, which produces the variance.

FIGURE 16-15 An Average Instead of a Total

```
                UNDERWOOD FEDERAL SALARY REPORT
                        25-JAN-88
                                           ANNUAL      MONTHLY
            DEPARTMENT LAST NAME            SALARY       SALARY
            ---------- --------------------  -----------  -----------
                    1 DAVIDSON             $24,000.00   $2,000.00
                      PRESTO               $42,500.00   $3,541.67
                      MADISON              $21,000.00   $1,750.00
            **********                     -----------  -----------
            avg                            $29,166.67
            sum                                         $7,291.67

                    2 TUBA                 $11,000.00     $916.67
                      ZIMMERMAN            $13,400.00   $1,116.67
                      ROWE-HATTON          $11,250.00     $937.50
                      COLLINS              $13,300.00   $1,108.33
            **********                     -----------  -----------
            avg                            $12,237.50
            sum                                         $4,079.17

                    3 MAHONEY              $12,400.00   $1,033.33
                      PALMER               $13,450.00   $1,120.83
            **********                     -----------  -----------
            avg                            $12,925.00
            sum                                         $2,154.17

                    4 BUCHINSKY            $15,000.00   $1,250.00
            **********                     -----------  -----------
            avg                            $15,000.00
            sum                                         $1,250.00

            10 records selected.
```

FORMATTING THE PAGE

You may have noticed that, in the previous example, there is an extra set of titles and column headings about midway through the report. (Actually, all the demonstration reports for this chapter came out that way; the extra headings were edited out of the earlier displays for the sake of clarity.) This is because ORACLE assumes that a new page begins every twenty-four lines. That's enough room to display one page on each CRT screen. This default setting certainly is too short for a printed report.

SETTING THE PAGE LENGTH

You can set a page length of your own choice with SET PAGE-SIZE. SET PAGESIZE 66 specifies the length of a standard sheet

FIGURE 16-16 Three Functions with One Report

```
              UNDERWOOD FEDERAL SALARY REPORT
                       25-JAN-88
                                          ANNUAL        MONTHLY
DEPARTMENT LAST NAME                      SALARY        SALARY
---------- --------------------      -----------    -----------
         1 DAVIDSON                   $24,000.00     $2,000.00
           PRESTO                     $42,500.00     $3,541.67
           MADISON                    $21,000.00     $1,750.00
********** --------------------      -----------    -----------
avg                                   $29,166.67
count                    3
sum                                                  $7,291.67

         2 TUBA                       $11,000.00       $916.67
           ZIMMERMAN                  $13,400.00     $1,116.67
           ROWE-HATTON                $11,250.00       $937.50
           COLLINS                    $13,300.00     $1,108.33
********** --------------------      -----------    -----------
avg                                   $12,237.50
count                    4
sum                                                  $4,079.17

         3 MAHONEY                    $12,400.00     $1,033.33
           PALMER                     $13,450.00     $1,120.83
              UNDERWOOD FEDERAL SALARY REPORT
                       25-JAN-88
                                          ANNUAL        MONTHLY
DEPARTMENT LAST NAME                      SALARY        SALARY
---------- --------------------      -----------    -----------
********** --------------------      -----------    -----------
avg                                   $12,925.00
count                    2
sum                                                  $2,154.17

         4 BUCHINSKY                  $15,000.00     $1,250.00
********** --------------------      -----------    -----------
avg                                   $15,000.00
count                    1
sum                                                  $1,250.00

10 records selected.
```

of typing paper at the standard six lines per inch. Most laser printers prefer the page length used in this demonstration:

SQL> SET PAGESIZE 60

SETTING THE TOP MARGIN

A companion command, SET NEWPAGE, sets the width of the top margin, between the top of the page and the first line of the top title. To set a top margin of one inch:

SQL> SET NEWPAGE 6

Figure 16-17 shows the effects of these two commands.

If you set NEWPAGE at zero, the program will insert a form feed character at the beginning of the report's first line.

A STATUS REPORT

If you are planning to save your commands from the buffer to a command file, it's a good idea to make sure first that the specifications you now have in force are those you intend.

The commands COLUMN, TTITLE, BTITLE, AND COMPUTE, with nothing else, will display the current values associated with those commands. SHOW PAGESIZE and SHOW

FIGURE 16-17 Page Size Specifications Set

```
              UNDERWOOD FEDERAL SALARY REPORT
                      25-JAN-88
                                      ANNUAL        MONTHLY
          DEPARTMENT LAST NAME        SALARY         SALARY
          ---------- ----------      ----------    ----------
                   1 DAVIDSON        $24,000.00    $2,000.00
                     PRESTO          $42,500.00    $3,541.67
                     MADISON         $21,000.00    $1,750.00
          ********** ----------      ----------    ----------
          avg                        $29,166.67
          count               3
          sum                                      $7,291.67

                   2 TUBA            $11,000.00      $916.67
                     ZIMMERMAN       $13,400.00    $1,116.67
                     ROWE-HATTON     $11,250.00      $937.50
                     COLLINS         $13,300.00    $1,108.33
          ********** ----------      ----------    ----------
          avg                        $12,237.50
          count               4
          sum                                      $4,079.17

                   3 MAHONEY         $12,400.00    $1,033.33
                     PALMER          $13,450.00    $1,120.83
          ********** ----------      ----------    ----------
          avg                        $12,925.00
          count               2
          sum                                      $2,154.17

                   4 BUCHINSKY       $15,000.00    $1,250.00
          ********** ----------      ----------    ----------
          avg                        $15,000.00
          count               1
          sum                                      $1,250.00

          10 records selected.
```

FIGURE 16-18   The Status Reported

```
SQL> COLUMN
column    SALARY/12 ON
heading   'MONTHLY|SALARY' headsep '|'
format    $99,999.99

column    SALARY ON
heading   'ANNUAL|SALARY' headsep '|'
format    $99,999.99

column    LAST ON
heading   'LAST NAME'
format    A20

column    DEPT_NO ON
heading   'DEPARTMENT'

column    TODAY ON
new_value DATEVAR
noprint
SQL> TTITLE
ttitle ON and is the following 65 characters:
COL 10 'UNDERWOOD FEDERAL SALARY REPORT' SKIP COL 20 DATEVAR SKIP
SQL> COMPUTE
COMPUTE sum OF SALARY, ON DEPT_NO
COMPUTE sum OF SALARY/12 ON DEPT_NO
COMPUTE avg OF SALARY ON DEPT_NO
COMPUTE count OF LAST ON DEPT_NO
SHOW PAGESIZE
pagesize 60
SHOW NEWPAGE
newpage 6
```

NEWPAGE will report the status of these commands. Figure 16-18 shows these specifications as of the most recent report.

ADVANCED CALCULATION AND REPORT

"What's Madison up to now?" Allen Tawdry asked suspiciously. "Looks like he's been playing around again with the salary figures in his organization. If he's going to write a salary report, I'll write an even better salary report!"

To refresh himself on the firm's salary data, Tawdry entered a quick:

```
SQL> SELECT LAST, SALARY
   2   FROM LA_FLAW;
```

The usual result came rolling up the screen:

LAST	SALARY
MCKNIFE	5000
TAWDRY	4000
COSSACK	4500
BUNSEN	2975
TUCKER	2850
BOYSENBERRY	2450
ROX	1300
MASON	3850
BAILEY	4800
BORQUE	950
HARTLESS	7500
MUKLUK	4700

"Now, what can I do with these?" Tawdry mused. "I know. I'll do a percentage analysis. That'll show Madison what kind of analytical mind he's up against."

Tawdry decided he would create a report that contained not only the salary figures, but also their percentages of the total payroll. What's more, there should be percentages and subtotals broken down by each of the firm's three offices.

CREATING A VIEW

First, Tawdry needed a vehicle to hold the office's total payroll. He assembled this command:

```
SQL> CREATE VIEW FIRM_PAY (FPAY) AS
  2    SELECT SUM(SALARY)
  3    FROM LA_FLAW;
```

The result is a simple one-column, one-row view that holds the firm's total payroll:

```
SQL> SELECT * FROM FIRM_PAY;

FPAY
-------
44875
```

To check the results, Tawdry first set up the format he wanted for the SALARY column:

SQL> COLUMN SALARY FORMAT $99,999.99;

Then, he issued a command that joined LA__FLAW with the newly created FIRM__PAY:

```
SQL> SELECT LAST, SALARY,
  2     SALARY/FPAY * 100 "% FIRM"
  3     FROM LA_FLAW, FIRM_PAY;
```

Because this query has no WHERE clause to specify a condition for the join, every row of LA__FLAW is joined to every row of FIRM__PAY. FIRM__PAY has only one row, so every row of LA__FLAW is joined to that row. The expression in Line 2 returns each employee's salary as a percentage of the figure FPAY in FIRM__PAY. It will appear under the column heading "% FIRM" (Figure 16-19).

A MORE COMPLEX VIEW

Now Tawdry needs a second view to record the salary totals broken down by department. This is a little more complicated:

```
SQL> CREATE VIEW OFFICE__PAY
  2     (BRANCH, OPAY) AS
  3     SELECT BRANCH, SUM(SALARY)
  4     FROM LA__FLAW
  5     GROUP BY BRANCH;
```

FIGURE 16-19 The Salary Figures Joined to the Total Salary View

```
LAST                  SALARY  % FIRM
----------------  ----------  -------
MCKNIFE           $5,000.00   11.1421
TAWDRY            $4,000.00   8.91365
COSSACK           $4,500.00   10.0279
BUNSEN            $2,975.00   6.62953
TUCKER            $2,850.00   6.35097
BOYSENBERRY       $2,450.00   5.45961
ROX               $1,300.00   2.89694
MASON             $3,850.00   8.57939
BAILEY            $4,800.00   10.6964
BORQUE              $950.00   2.11699
HARTLESS          $7,500.00   16.7131
MUKLUK            $4,700.00   10.4735

12 records selected.
```

A look at that view reveals:

BRANCH	OPAY
1	20550
2	20475
3	3850

To compute each employee's salary as a percentage of the departmental total, Tawdry must join each row of LA__FLAW to the appropriate departmental row in OFFICE__PAY. He must also calculate the percentages and list the results in departmental order:

```
SQL> SELECT LA__FLAW.BRANCH, LAST, SALARY,
   2    SALARY/OPAY * 100 "% OFFICE",
   3    SALARY/FPAY * 100 "% FIRM"
   4    FROM LA__FLAW, FIRM__PAY, OFFICE__PAY
   5    WHERE LA__FLAW.BRANCH = OFFICE__PAY.BRANCH
   6    ORDER BY LA__FLAW.BRANCH
```

This time there are two percentage figures, as shown in Figure 16-20.

NAMES INSTEAD OF NUMBERS

"Not bad, but it still needs some finishing touches," Tawdry mused. "I sure could impress Bruce Banker if I could display the

FIGURE 16-20 Departmental Percentages Added

BRANCH	LAST	SALARY	% OFFICE	% FIRM
1	MCKNIFE	$5,000.00	24.3309	11.1421
1	TUCKER	$2,850.00	13.8686	6.35097
1	BAILEY	$4,800.00	23.3577	10.6964
1	BORQUE	$950.00	4.62287	2.11699
1	BOYSENBERRY	$2,450.00	11.9221	5.45961
1	COSSACK	$4,500.00	21.8978	10.0279
2	TAWDRY	$4,000.00	19.536	8.91365
2	HARTLESS	$7,500.00	36.63	16.7131
2	MUKLUK	$4,700.00	22.9548	10.4735
2	ROX	$1,300.00	6.34921	2.89694
2	BUNSEN	$2,975.00	14.5299	6.62953
3	MASON	$3,850.00	100	8.57939

12 records selected.

office locations instead of just their numbers. I'm sure he doesn't know how to do that."

Tawdry did. He expanded the JOIN command to include the BRANCHES table, which lists the office numbers and their locations. Then, he could extract the location that matched the number. He could even change the ORDER command to list the offices in alphabetical order. The query now read:

```
SQL> SELECT LOCATION, LAST, SALARY,
     2    SALARY/OPAY * 100 "% OFFICE",
     3    SALARY/FPAY * 100 "% FIRM"
     4    FROM LA_FLAW, FIRM_PAY, OFFICE_PAY, BRANCHES
     5    WHERE LA_FLAW.BRANCH = OFFICE_PAY.BRANCH
     6    AND BRANCHES.BRANCH = LA_FLAW.BRANCH
     7    ORDER BY LOCATION
```

The new output (Figure 16-21) did indeed report the branch locations in order.

FINISHING TOUCHES

All Tawdry needed now was to present the display in an attractive format with more descriptive column headings and breaks with subtotals for each office. The first commands established

FIGURE 16-21   Names Instead of Numbers

```
LOCATION            LAST                   SALARY % OFFICE   % FIRM
----------------    ----------------    -----------  --------   -------
ATLANTA             MASON               $3,850.00       100  8.57939
DENVER              TAWDRY              $4,000.00    19.536  8.91365
DENVER              BUNSEN              $2,975.00   14.5299  6.62953
DENVER              MUKLUK              $4,700.00   22.9548  10.4735
DENVER              HARTLESS            $7,500.00     36.63  16.7131
DENVER              ROX                 $1,300.00   6.34921  2.89694
LOS ANGELES         MCKNIFE             $5,000.00   24.3309  11.1421
LOS ANGELES         TUCKER              $2,850.00   13.8686  6.35097
LOS ANGELES         BAILEY              $4,800.00   23.3577  10.6964
LOS ANGELES         BORQUE                $950.00   4.62287  2.11699
LOS ANGELES         BOYSENBERRY         $2,450.00   11.9221  5.45961
LOS ANGELES         COSSACK             $4,500.00   21.8978  10.0279

12 records selected.
```

breaks at each location and subtotals of the salary figures and the two percentages:

```
SQL> BREAK ON LOCATION SKIP
   2  COMPUTE SUM OF SALARY ON LOCATION;
   3  COMPUTE SUM OF "% FIRM" ON LOCATION
   4  COMPUTE SUM OF "% OFFICE" ON LOCATION;
```

The headings "% FIRM" and "% OFFICE" are not only column headings; they are aliases for the two percentage columns. Because they contain spaces and start with punctuation marks, they must appear within quotation marks. When you do that, though, ORACLE will treat these terms as column names.

Then came COLUMN commands to establish new headings and display formats for the percentage columns. A format for the salary figures was set earlier, as you no doubt recall:

```
SQL> COLUMN "% FIRM" FORMAT 999.99 HEADING—
SQL> "PERCENT|FIRM"
SQL> COLUMN "% OFFICE" FORMAT 999.99 HEADING—
SQL> "PERCENT|OFFICE"
SQL> COLUMN LAST HEADING "EMPLOYEE|NAME"
SQL> COLUMN SALARY HEADING "MONTHLY|SALARY"
SQL> COLUMN LOCATION HEADING "OFFICE"
```

A third set of commands established the page size and heading:

```
SQL> SET PAGESIZE 60
SQL> TTITLE CENTER "McKnife, Tawdry, Diver and Brown"—
> SKIP—
> CENTER "Salary Analysis"—
> SKIP;
```

Now the report took on the more polished look of Figure 16-22.

ROOM FOR MORE IMPROVEMENT

Word of Tawdry's efforts eventually reached Dennis Madison. "That TV lawyer thinks he can compete with me," Madison bragged. "Well, I know something he doesn't—he doesn't know how to get rid of those asterisks and little 'sums' in the first column," said Madison. "I do."

FIGURE 16-22 Breaks, Subtotals, and New Headings

```
                        McKnife, Tawdry, Diver and Brown
                                Salary Analysis

                      EMPLOYEE           MONTHLY PERCENT PERCENT
          OFFICE      NAME                SALARY  OFFICE    FIRM
          --------------- ---------------- ------------ ------- -------
          ATLANTA     MASON              $3,850.00  100.00    8.58
          ***************                ------------ ------- -------
          sum                            $3,850.00  100.00    8.58

          DENVER      TAWDRY             $4,000.00   19.54    8.91
                      BUNSEN             $2,975.00   14.53    6.63
                      MUKLUK             $4,700.00   22.95   10.47
                      HARTLESS           $7,500.00   36.63   16.71
                      ROX                $1,300.00    6.35    2.90
          ***************                ------------ ------- -------
          sum                           $20,475.00  100.00   45.63

          LOS ANGELES MCKNIFE           $5,000.00   24.33   11.14
                      TUCKER            $2,850.00   13.87    6.35
                      BAILEY            $4,800.00   23.36   10.70
                      BORQUE              $950.00    4.62    2.12
                      BOYSENBERRY       $2,450.00   11.92    5.46
                      COSSACK           $4,500.00   21.90   10.03
          ***************                ------------ ------- -------
          sum                          $20,550.00  100.00   45.79

          12 records selected.
```

"How do you do it?"

"With a dummy column; you take this column, call it Column X. Then, you call for breaks on *both* the department number and on Column X. You compute all the totals on Column X. Then, though, you use the COLUMN command so X won't print.

"You SELECT the LOCATION column twice. The first time, you just select LOCATION as you ordinarily would. Then, you SELECT it again, only you give it an alias. And guess what that alias is?"

"I guess X."

"That's exactly what you do. Now, let's go over this again. Here's how you set up the breaks and computations:

```
SQL> BREAK ON LOCATION ON X SKIP
SQL> COMPUTE SUM OF SALARY ON X;
SQL> COMPUTE SUM OF "% FIRM" ON X;
SQL> COMPUTE SUM OF "% OFFICE" ON X;
```

"Then, you call for the nonprinting column:

COLUMN X NOPRINT

"Then, you add it to the SELECT command as an alias for LOCATION:

SELECT LOCATION, LOCATION X, LAST, SALARY,

"All the rest of the commands are used just as Tawdry used them. Now, if you'll kindly direct your attention to Figure 16-23 you'll see what I can do. Keep in mind, please, that I'm even doing this with the other guy's personnel roster."

"Not bad," said Davidson.

"I'm glad you think so, because I think I'll make a command file of this and send it to Mr. Tawdry." Madison did, and his file is now enshrined in Listing 16-1.

FIGURE 16-23   Some Distracting Elements Removed

```
                        McKnife, Tawdry, Diver and Brown
                                Salary Analysis

                   EMPLOYEE           MONTHLY PERCENT PERCENT
    OFFICE         NAME                SALARY  OFFICE    FIRM
    --------------- ------------------ ------------ ------- -------
    ATLANTA        MASON              $3,850.00  100.00    8.58
                                      ------------ ------- -------
                                      $3,850.00  100.00    8.58

    DENVER         TAWDRY             $4,000.00   19.54    8.91
                   BUNSEN             $2,975.00   14.53    6.63
                   MUKLUK             $4,700.00   22.95   10.47
                   HARTLESS           $7,500.00   36.63   16.71
                   ROX                $1,300.00    6.35    2.90
                                      ------------ ------- -------
                                      $20,475.00  100.00   45.63

    LOS ANGELES    MCKNIFE            $5,000.00   24.33   11.14
                   TUCKER             $2,850.00   13.87    6.35
                   BAILEY             $4,800.00   23.36   10.70
                   BORQUE               $950.00    4.62    2.12
                   BOYSENBERRY        $2,450.00   11.92    5.46
                   COSSACK            $4,500.00   21.90   10.03
                                      ------------ ------- -------
                                      $20,550.00  100.00   45.79

    12 records selected.
```

```
REM Listing 16-1
REM SALARY.SQL
REM Salary analysis report form.

 CLEAR BUFFER;
 CLEAR BREAKS;
 CLEAR COLUMNS;
 CLEAR COMPUTES;
BREAK ON LOCATION ON X SKIP
COMPUTE SUM OF SALARY ON X;
COMPUTE SUM OF "% FIRM" ON X;
COMPUTE SUM OF "% OFFICE" ON X;
COLUMN "% FIRM" FORMAT 999.99 HEADING "PERCENT|FIRM"
COLUMN "% OFFICE" FORMAT 999.99 HEADING "PERCENT|OFFICE"
COLUMN LAST HEADING "EMPLOYEE|NAME"
COLUMN SALARY HEADING "MONTHLY|SALARY";
COLUMN LOCATION HEADING "OFFICE"
COLUMN X NOPRINT
SET PAGESIZE 60;
TTITLE CENTER "McKnife, Tawdry, Diver and Brown"-
SKIP-
CENTER "Salary Analysis"-
SKIP;
SELECT LOCATION, LOCATION X, LAST, SALARY,
SALARY/OPAY * 100 "% OFFICE",
SALARY/FPAY * 100 "% FIRM"
FROM LA_FLAW  FIRM_PAY, OFFICE_PAY, BRANCHES
WHERE LA_FLAW.BRANCH = OFFICE_PAY.BRANCH
AND BRANCHES.BRANCH = LA_FLAW.BRANCH
ORDER BY LOCATION
/
```

THE CROSS-SELLING REPORT

"After you've mailed off your epic," Davidson suggested, "perhaps you could prepare that cross-selling report—you know, the one for which we created this whole database? The one that tells us how many new accounts we opened for existing customers? Do you think it could possibly be done before the Marinecorp MIS people out in Black Hole start screaming for it?"

"Yes, I think that can be done."

A DIFFERENT APPROACH

Madison noted that he could probably take an approach similar to Tawdry's. In the spirit of competition, though, he decided to see if he could do better. He started with a preliminary query for the relevant data in the SALES table:

```
SQL> SELECT EMP_CODE, COUNT(*), SUM(AMOUNT)
   2   FROM SALES
```

```
3    WHERE NEW__MONEY = 'Y'
4    AND NEW__CUST = 'N'
5    GROUP BY EMP__CODE;
```

This query called for those sales in which new money was taken in from an existing customer. It counted the number of new accounts, summed their amounts, and grouped the results by employee code. When applied to an expanded SALES table it produced:

```
EMP   COUNT(*)   SUM(AMOUNT)
----  ---------- -----------------
HT        2            898
KC        4          13414
PR        5         183799
RZ        3         882726
```

"Not bad for a start," Madison decided. "I can already tell that Robbie Zimmerman may not have landed too many repeat accounts, but when he did, they must have been big ones. Poor Hubie, though, seems to be having some trouble."

THE FIRST REFINEMENTS

Madison decided, without much hesitation, that the display could use some meaningful column headings. So he provided them:

```
SQL> COLUMN COUNT(*) HEADING NUMBER|OPENED;
SQL> COLUMN SUM(AMOUNT) HEADING TOTAL|AMOUNT;
```

Then, instead of displaying only the initials that made up the employee codes, he decided to let the ROSTER table join in the action and provide the employees' last names. The new query was:

```
SQL> SELECT LAST, COUNT(*), SUM(AMOUNT)
2    FROM SALES, ROSTER
3    WHERE SALES.EMP__CODE = ROSTER.EMP__CODE
4    AND NEW__MONEY = 'Y'
5    AND NEW__CUST = 'N'
6    GROUP BY LAST
```

Not only would this query retrieve the last names, but it would group the results in alphabetical order. It would also display the new column headings:

LAST	NUMBER OPENED	TOTAL AMOUNT
COLLINS	4	13414
ROWE-HATTON	5	183799
TUBA	2	898
ZIMMERMAN	3	882726

MAKING COMPARISONS

"That sure was simple," Madison congratulated himself. As he looked at the results, though, he began to wonder. "I know how many cross-sales we had," he mused. "I wonder how that compares with these people's total sales. Two views would be nice," he said. "One could record the total sales. The other could record the sales to existing customers. Then, we could put both into the report."

The first view used the WHERE specifications of the previous query to search for cross-sales. It also had similar columns to record each employee code, the number of sales and the dollar total.

```
SQL> CREATE VIEW XSOLD (EMP_CODE, NO, AMT) AS
   2    SELECT EMP_CODE, COUNT(*), SUM(AMOUNT)
   3    FROM SALES
   4    WHERE NEW_MONEY = 'Y'
   5    AND NEW_CUST = 'N'
   6    GROUP BY EMP_CODE
```

A check of its contents revealed that it had the same contents as the earlier query response did, but in order of the employee code instead of the last name. Madison knew he could fix the order later.

EMP	NO	AMT
HT	2	898
KC	4	13414
PR	5	183799
RZ	3	882726

The second view was a simpler version of the first. It called for similar comments, but this time it recorded all sales instead of just cross-sales:

```
SQL> CREATE VIEW SOLD (EMP__CODE, NO, AMT) AS
   2    SELECT EMP__CODE, COUNT(*), SUM(AMOUNT)
   3    FROM SALES
   4    GROUP BY EMP__CODE;
```

This view looked like:

```
EMP   NO    AMT
----- ---  -------
HT    11  275004
KC    10   24855
PR     9  234124
RZ     9  931366
```

PUTTING THEM TOGETHER

To test a joining of the two tables, Madison ran this query:

```
SQL> RUN
   1    SELECT SOLD.EMP__CODE,
   2    SOLD.NO, XSOLD.NO,
   3    SOLD.AMT, XSOLD.AMT
   4    FROM SOLD, XSOLD
   5    WHERE SOLD.EMP__CODE = XSOLD.EMP__CODE
  6*    ORDER BY SOLD.EMP__CODE
```

It produced:

```
EMP   NO   NO    AMT      AMT
----  ---  ---  ------   ------
HT    11    2  275004      898
KC    10    4   24855    13414
PR     9    5  234124   183799
RZ     9    3  931366   882726
```

Now that he knew he had this much under control, Madison brought in the ROSTER table, again to retrieve the last names. The combining of three tables (actually a table and two views) required two JOIN clauses:

```
SQL> RUN
   1    SELECT ROSTER.LAST,
   2    SOLD.NO, XSOLD.NO,
   3    SOLD.AMT, XSOLD.AMT
   4    FROM SOLD, XSOLD, ROSTER
```

```
5    WHERE SOLD.EMP__CODE = XSOLD.EMP__CODE
6    AND SOLD.EMP__CODE = ROSTER.EMP__CODE
7*   ORDER BY SOLD.EMP__CODE
```

Again there were last names instead of codes:

LAST	NO	NO	AMT	AMT
TUBA	11	2	275004	898
COLLINS	10	4	24855	13414
ROWE-HATTON	9	5	234124	183799
ZIMMERMAN	9	3	931366	882726

WHOOPS

It again was time to begin assigning column headings and formats. When he began to try, though, Madison found that the use of the same column headings in the two views was a major source of trouble. Sometimes a COLUMN command would affect both of two like-named columns; at other times it would affect neither.

That problem was solved by restructuring the query to provide aliases for the four columns:

```
SQL> RUN
    1    SELECT ROSTER.LAST,
    2    SOLD.NO NO__SOLD, XSOLD.NO NO__XSOLD,
    3    SOLD.AMT AMT__SOLD, XSOLD.AMT AMT__XSOLD
    4    FROM SOLD, XSOLD, ROSTER
    5    WHERE SOLD.EMP__CODE = XSOLD.EMP__CODE
    6    AND SOLD.EMP__CODE = ROSTER.EMP__CODE
    7*   ORDER BY SOLD.EMP__CODE
```

This time when Madison ran the query the display showed a group of unique aliases he could use in COLUMN commands:

```
SQL> RUN
    1    SELECT ROSTER.LAST,
    2    SOLD.NO NO__SOLD, XSOLD.NO NO__XSOLD,
    3    SOLD.AMT AMT__SOLD, XSOLD.AMT AMT__XSOLD
    4    FROM SOLD, XSOLD, ROSTER
    5    WHERE SOLD.EMP__CODE = XSOLD.EMP__CODE
    6    AND SOLD.EMP__CODE = ROSTER.EMP__CODE
    7*   ORDER BY SOLD.EMP__CODE
```

He also corrected the last line to put the display in last-name order. The results:

LAST	NO_SOLD	NO_XSOLD	AMT_SOLD	AMT_XSOLD
COLLINS	10	4	24855	13414
ROWE-HATTON	9	5	234124	183799
TUBA	11	2	275004	898
ZIMMERMAN	9	3	931366	882726

NOW THE COLUMN HEADINGS

By this time, he had created a basis for using COLUMN to assign headings and formats:

```
COLUMN LAST HEADING 'LAST NAME'
SQL> COLUMN NO_SOLD HEADING 'NUMBER|OPENED'
SQL> COLUMN NO_XSOLD HEADING 'CROSS-|SOLD'
SQL> COLUMN AMT_SOLD HEADING 'TOTAL|AMOUNT'
SQL> COLUMN AMT_XSOLD HEADING 'CROSS-|SOLD'
```

The display was beginning to look more and more civilized:

LAST NAME	NUMBER OPENED	CROSS- SOLD	TOTAL AMOUNT	CROSS- SOLD
COLLINS	10	4	24855	13414
ROWE-HATTON	9	5	234124	183799
TUBA	11	2	275004	898
ZIMMERMAN	9	3	931366	882726

FORMATTING NUMBERS

The two dollar-amount columns could have been assigned a format with the same COLUMN commands that created their headings. This was a correctable omission, though, because it is entirely possible to assign the formats with a second command:

```
SQL> COLUMN AMT_SOLD FORMAT $999,999
SQL> COLUMN AMT_XSOLD FORMAT $999,999
```

With the aid of these new formats, the report becomes:

LAST NAME	NUMBER OPENED	CROSS-SOLD	TOTAL AMOUNT	CROSS-SOLD
COLLINS	10	4	$24,855	$13,414
ROWE-HATTON	9	5	$234,124	$183,799
TUBA	11	2	$275,004	$898
ZIMMERMAN	9	3	$931,366	$882,726

A TITLE TO COMPLETE THINGS

Now the report needs only a title. Madison decided the standard SQL*Plus format would do the job:

SQL> TTITLE 'Underwood Federal Cross-Sales Report'

The finished product is shown in Figure 16-24. With a larger work force, of course, it would cover substantially more territory, but the basic task of creating it is the same.

CUSTOMERS AND CROSS-TABULATION

Having completed his major assignment, Madison became curious about the other kinds of knowledge he could glean from this database.

"I think it would be a great idea to work up a profile of our customers," said Davidson. "Find out what ages, income groups and other demographic characteristics our customers have."

"Capital idea," said Madison. "I think it's called cross-tabulation."

FIGURE 16-24 The Completed Cross-Sales Report

```
Tue Jan 26                                                      page    1
                    Underwood Federal Cross-Sales Report

             NUMBER  CROSS-      TOTAL    CROSS-
LAST NAME    OPENED   SOLD      AMOUNT     SOLD
-----------  ------  ------   ---------  ---------
COLLINS          10       4     $24,855    $13,414
ROWE-HATTON       9       5    $234,124   $183,799
TUBA             11       2    $275,004       $898
ZIMMERMAN         9       3    $931,366   $882,726
```

DECODE-ING THE DATA

Madison went about creating a cross-tabulation with the DECODE( ) function. That's the function, described in Chapter 7, that translates one value into another. In the exercise Madison was about to try, DECODE( ) would translate the numerical codes used in CUSTOMER to indicate age and income brackets, and translate them into verbal descriptions of these ranges.

As an initial experiment, he tried:

```
SQL>   SELECT AGE__GROUP,
     2     DECODE(INCOME, '1', 1, 0) "To $12,000",
     3     DECODE(INCOME, '2', 1, 0) "$12,001-$25,000",
     4     DECODE (INCOME, '3', 1, 0) "25,001-$55,000",
     5     DECODE (INCOME, '4', 1, 0) "$55,001 and up"
     6   FROM CUSTOMER;
```

To understand this, you may need a refresher course on DECODE( ). Within the brackets are four elements:

- The name of the column to be decoded
- The value for which to search in that column
- The value to return if the value sought is found
- The value to return if the value sought is not found

The second and third items on this list can be repeated as often as necessary.

It might be helpful to think of the elements of these DECODE( ) statements as IF-THEN-ELSE options. If you're familiar with these options' abbreviated forms in the dBASE IIF( ) function, you're in even better shape.

Here, each line that begins with DECODE( ) will become a separate column in the report. Each line also provides a heading for that column. In Line 2, the program would search for an income value of 1 (remember, these codes were inserted as Char values, so they must be in single quotes). If found, the program will return a 1 in that row of the report. If not, the row will contain a 0.

Running this command produces an expansive output. For each of the four age brackets, the command returned either a 1 or a 0 for each customer. Part of the output is shown in Figure 16-25. It's too long and too meaningless to reproduce in full.

FIGURE 16-25 Sample Output of the Initial DECODE( ) Test

A	To $12,000	$12,001-$25,000	25,001-$55,000	$55,001 and up
2	0	1	0	0
1	1	0	0	0
3	0	0	0	1
1	0	1	0	0
2	0	1	0	0
3	0	0	1	0
3	0	0	1	0
3	0	0	0	1
3	0	0	0	0
2	0	0	1	0
3	0	0	1	0
3	0	0	1	0
1	0	1	0	0
2	0	1	0	0

ADDING MORE FUNCTION

The results convinced Madison he was on the right track. His next step was to add a function to the query. Instead of simply listing the 1s and 0s, he would count them. A GROUP BY statement at the end of the command would count the DECODEd values by age group:

```
SQL> SELECT AGE_GROUP,
  2    COUNT(DECODE(INCOME, '1', 1, 0)) "TO $12,000",
  3    COUNT(DECODE(INCOME, '2', 1, 0)) "$12,001-$25,000",
  4    COUNT(DECODE(INCOME, '3', 1, 0)) "$25,001-$55,000",
  5    COUNT (DECODE(INCOME, '4', 1, 0)) "$55,001 and up"
  6    FROM CUSTOMER
  7    GROUP BY AGE_GROUP
```

A GLITCH IN TIME

The results (Figure 16-26) weren't quite what he had expected.

What Madison really wanted to do was count all the 1s, which indicated found values. What the program had done was count every non-null value, 1 or 0.

There are two ways out of this. If Madison had used SUM( ) instead of COUNT( ), the program would have added up all the 1s, skipping the 0s and producing the results he wanted. Madison chose the other method because that's the one he thought of first.

FIGURE 16-26   Unexpected Results

```
A To $12,000 $12,001-$25,000 $25,001-$55,000 $55,001 and up
- ---------- ---------------- ---------------- ---------------
1         10               10               10              10
2         13               13               13              13
3         20               20               20              20
4          1                1                1               1
```

It is based on the fact that a SQL function will consider only non-null values. He changed the final option in the DECODE( ) sequence to NULL. Instead of returning a zero for an unfound value, the program would return a NULL. The revised command:

```
SQL> SELECT AGE__GROUP,
   2    COUNT(DECODE(INCOME, '1', 1, NULL)) "To $12,000",
   3    COUNT(DECODE(INCOME, '2', 1, NULL)) "$12,001-$25,000",
   4    COUNT(DECODE(INCOME, '3', 1, NULL)) "$25,001-$55,000",
   5    COUNT(DECODE(INCOME, '4', 1, NULL)) "$55,001 and up"
   6  FROM CUSTOMER
   7  GROUP BY AGE__GROUP
```

BACK TO THE CODE BOOK

This time the results looked more like Figure 16-27. At least the figures were right. At this point, Madison had created column headings to identify the income brackets. The age brackets down the left side of the report still were only numerical codes. Correcting that called for more use of DECODE( )

FIGURE 16-27   Expected Results

```
A To $12,000 $12,001-$25,000 $25,001-$55,000 $55,001 and up
- ---------- ---------------- ---------------- ---------------
1          5                3                1               1
2          1                6                3               3
3          4                2                6               7
4          0                0                0               1
```

In the next version of his command, Madison used another DECODE( ) statement to provide text explanations for the age brackets as well as the income groups:

```
SQL> RUN
   1   SELECT DECODE(AGE_GROUP,
   2   '1', 'Under 35',
   3   '2', '35-55',
   4   '3', 'Over 55',
   5   'Unlisted') AGE,
   6   COUNT(DECODE(INCOME, '1', 1, NULL)) "TO12",
   7   COUNT(DECODE(INCOME, '2', 1, NULL)) "12-25",
   8   COUNT(DECODE(INCOME, '3', 1, NULL)) "25-55",
   9   COUNT(DECODE(INCOME, '4', 1, NULL)) "OVER55"
  10   FROM CUSTOMER
  11*  GROUP BY AGE_GROUP
```

"I suppose you're wondering," he said to Addie Davidson, "how I got one DECODE( ) statement to put columns across the page and another to put rows running down."

"It had crossed my mind."

"These aren't just your ordinary statements," Madison explained. "Check out the first five lines. They're all one statement. It starts with the item to be decoded. Then, it gives a value to search for. Then, it tells what to do if you find it. Then, it gives another value to search for—then, what to do if you find *that* one—and so on, back and forth, until you run out of values. At the end you tell the program what to do if it didn't find anything— none of the above, so to speak."

"I still don't get how one of these commands goes up and down while the others go sideways,"

"Look again. When I decoded the age groups, I decoded several values with one command. That's the first column. Then, I decoded just one of the income groups. That's the next column. Then, I decoded another one of the income groups, and it's the column after that . . . "

"I get it, I get it."

"Well, I hope the readers do by now. Perhaps it would be better if we referred them to Figure 16-28."

FIGURE 16-28   The Age Groups Decoded

```
AGE         TO12    12-25   25-55   OVER55
--------  -------  -------  ------  -------
Under 35     5        3       1        1
35-55        1        6       3        3
Over 55      4        2       6        7
Unlisted     0        0       0        1
```

SOMETHING DECORATIVE

"Oh, I forgot to tell you," Madison continued, "I changed the column headings to something simpler. That's because I'm about to write some COLUMN commands for them."

These are the commands he wrote:

SQL> COLUMN AGE HEADING "Age|Group";
SQL> COLUMN 12-25 HEADING "$12,001-|$25,000";
SQL> COLUMN 25-55 HEADING "$25,001-|$55,000";
SQL> COLUMN OVER55 HEADING "$55,001|and up";

At this point, the report was beginning to take on a finished look (Figure 16-29).

A TITLE FINISHES UP

All that was left was to give the report a title. Madison accomplished this with:

SQL> TTITLE LEFT 'Underwood Federal Customer Profile'—
> SKIP 2—
> COL 16 'Income Bracket'—
> SKIP 2;

FIGURE 16-29   Nearly Finished

```
Age       $12,000  $12,001- $25,001- $55,001
Group     or Less  $25,000  $55,000  and up
--------  -------  -------  --------  -------
Under 35     5        3        1         1
35-55        1        6        3         3
Over 55      4        2        6         7
Unlisted     0        0        0         1
```

FIGURE 16-30 Finished at Last

```
        Underwood Federal Customer Profile

                 Income Bracket

Age         $12,000 $12,001- $25,001- $55,001
Group       or Less $25,000 $55,000 and up
-------     ------- ------- ------- -------
Under 35          5       3       1       1
35-55             1       6       3       3
Over 55           4       2       6       7
Unlisted          0       0       0       1
```

He ran the query again; the finished report is shown in Figure 16-30.

REVIEW QUESTIONS

1. The COLUMN command does two main things. What are they?
2. What will this command do?

   COLUMN LAST HEADING 'LAST|NAME' FORMAT A20

3. You've written a command that assigns a format to a column called PRIME. You want to duplicate that format in a column called CHOICE. Do this without repeating the format specifications.
4. How would the output of these two commands differ?

   TTITLE 'Top Gun Sales Contest'
   TTITLE CENTER 'Top Gun Sales Contest'

5. You need two separate commands to produce subtotals on a break. What are they?
6. What kind of DECODE( ) command would you use to produce the row designation of a cross-tabulation?
7. What kind of COLUMN( ) command would you use to produce the columns in the same crosstab?

ANSWERS

1. They format columns and add headings.
2. It will display text data in a format that is 20 columns wide. The heading will have LAST and NAME on separate lines.

3.   COLUMN CHOICE LIKE PRIME

4. The command without formatting instructions will produce ORACLE's standard heading format. The one with the CEN-TER specifications will produce a centered heading with nothing else.
5. BREAK and COMPUTE.
6. A single command translating each row value.
7. A separate command translating a single value for each column.

Programming with SQL

All but the simplest of SQL commands can seem formidable to write. A SQL command describes data. Sometimes it must provide a very detailed description. A SQL command file can help reduce the command-writing workload, particularly when it can repeat a frequently-used query or an intricate report format. A command file will even accept data entries, although somewhat crudely and with few ways to screen out errors.

Even so, a SQL command file does not come close to the full-featured programming facilities of a dBASE command file—in reality, a broad-featured program. Serious dBASE programmers probably will not warm to the much more limited SQL command file. The convert from dBASE to SQL will often want a programming facility to match the one that was left behind.

Indirectly, SQL does offer the frustrated ex-dBASE programmer an alternative. In fact, it's a very powerful and full-featured alternative that runs right past dBASE to achieve new heights of its own. This alternative is to incorporate SQL commands into the C programming language.

Actually, you can embed SQL into other languages, too, including Pascal and COBOL. Any of these programs can give the descriptive commands of the SQL the procedural support they badly need. With these languages you can do loops, exercise conditional logic, and trap errors, just as you can in dBASE. You can do graphics, advanced statistical operations, or whatever else you'd like. If you can program in one of these languages, you can incorporate SQL into your program.

This chapter will illustrate how to include SQL commands in C programs. C is a popular and versatile language that is widely available to PC users and includes several inexpensive versions. A C interface is standard equipment in the ORACLE package for PC users. Links to other languages are optional extras.

Officially, the ORACLE-C link, called Pro*C, is compatible with either Microsoft or Lattice C. The short programs you are about to see were compiled with Microsoft's QuickC. This lower-priced compiler is compatible with Microsoft's senior product at the level on which C and SQL interact. The programs here ran with no apparent problems—with emphasis on the *apparent*.

HOW SQL AND C INTERACT

Here's a data entry sequence from a sample C program that's supplied with the PC version of ORACLE. The first thing you see is:

```
Enter employee name   :
```

As the prompt suggests, enter a name and hit <Return>. Then follow the other prompts as they appear. Soon you should see something like this:

```
Enter employee name : BAKER
Enter employee job    : CUSTODIAN
Enter employee salary: 7500
Enter employee dept  :   20
```

So far, this is unspectacular. The screen display and data entries are not much different from those done with a command file in Chapter 15. You're about to see some differences, though. When you hit <Return> after the department number, the program will pause for a moment, then report:

```
BAKER added to the RESEARCH department as employee
number 7964
```

ONE STEP BEYOND

Good custodians are always research experts. That's how I justify my high salary. Note that the program has translated the department number into the department name. That's a fairly standard SQL operation using joined files.

The program has also assigned me an employee number. This should be evidence that the level of sophistication has advanced at least a small notch over the last couple of chapters.

ERROR CHECKING

A real sign of this program's advancement over a simple SQL command file is this sequence:

```
Enter employee name : BAKER
Enter employee job    : CHM OF BD
```

Enter employee salary: 100
Enter employee dept : 99

With my salary as a janitor I can afford this kind of self-indulgent moonlighting. However, all is not right with the world. The program's response to this entry is:

No such department
Enter employee dept :

It appears that this program provides for some validation. It checks the entry against a list of known department numbers. If the number you entered is not on the list, you'll be asked to provide a corrected entry. Do this, and you should see:

BAKER added to the ACCOUNTING department as employee number 7974

Again, the program translated the department number into a department name. It also assigned me a second employee number which, by no coincidence, is the previous employee number plus 10. Why 10? I don't know. I didn't write the program. It's designed to assign numbers in increments of 10, and that's what it did.

THE RESULTS OF THIS EFFORT

To accomplish all this, I compiled and linked the sample C program, which appears on an ORACLE disk as SAMPLE.PC. The resulting program is SAMPLE.EXE. Then, from the DOS prompt, I issued the simple command SAMPLE. The program opened the ORACLE database, accepted the data entries and inserted them into the EMP table, which is also part of the ORACLE demonstration package.

Then a search for my name in EMP yielded:

EMPNO	ENAME	JOB	SAL
7964	BAKER	CUSTODIAN	7500
7974	BAKER	CHM OF BD	100

This exercise was only a small taste of the potential. SQL does a great job at its specialty of describing data and extracting it from a database. It does a lousy job of almost anything else.

Enhanced command sets such as SQL*Plus and the ability to create command files give SQL a minimal sort of usefulness. SQL was originally intended, though, to be operated from a procedural language such as COBOL, FORTRAN, or, more recently, C. That gives you all the flexibility of the dBASE programming language, plus a great deal more.

This single chapter can't offer more than cursory instruction in C programming, or more than a basic view of how C and SQL can interact. It will demonstrate, though, how you can incorporate SQL into the language. Then you will be limited only by your ability to accomplish things in C.

HOW C AND SQL GET TOGETHER

Compiling a program in most versions of C is a two-step process. You compile the text version of the program into an object file. You then link the object file, plus any external files you plan to include, into an executable program.

Compiling a C program for use with SQL is a three-step process. The first is to precompile the text program using the PCC precompiler that comes with ORACLE. Then, you compile and link the program as usual.

IMPORTANT DETAILS

There are a few things to remember when you go through this process. SQL requires that you specify a large memory model. A full ORACLE database simply won't fit in the small, compact, and midsize models also offered in various versions of C.

In the linking stage you must be sure to include the library file SQLMSC.LIB, which comes with ORACLE.

COMPILER COMMANDS

The commands to execute the three steps in Microsoft C are, in order:

```
pcc iname=<input file> host=c
Cl −AL −c <input file>
link <object file>,,,sqlmsc /se:512 /stack:15000
```

PCC is the command that activates ORACLE's precompiler. The variable iname accepts the name of the C file you wish to compile. If you don't specify a suffix for the input file, the program will assume it bears the suffix .PC. The output file will carry the .C suffix, which is favored by the C compiler. Since ORACLE supports several languages, host identifies the language you plan to use.

The next line activates the C compiler. If you are using QuickC, the command is QCL instead of CL. The −AL flag specifies the large memory model; −c is the signal to create an object file on disk to be linked later. Finally, there is the name of the input file. The input file will usually have the −C extension; the output file will have the same base name but with the extension .OBJ.

The linker commands on the third line identify, first, the object file, then, after a few omitted parameters, the SQLMSC library file. The se: (for segment) and stack: entries are for the sake of the large-scale memory management to come. ORACLE actually specifies a stack size of 10000; in practice I found I needed more. An optional final addition to the link command is /map. This addition creates a text file, called a map file, to track your success, or lack of it, in creating a runable file. The /map command is strictly optional. Advanced programmers probably will find it indispensable; beginners will find it useless.

SQL IN THE PROGRAM FILE

Using these three steps, you can create a file that includes SQL commands along with those native to C. The basic idea is to use the descriptive commands of SQL to input or extract data. Then use the procedural commands of C to manipulate the data.

The SQL commands within C come in two basic types:

- *Declarations,* which establish the specifications for variables, much as you would do in C itself or in a dBASE command file.
- *SQL statements,* which are the SQL commands you've come to know and, perhaps, to love. Within a C program, they are usually preceded by EXEC SQL.

DECLARATIONS OF DEPENDENCE

The declarations are the major part of the *prologue* you must provide near the beginning of the program. Don't confuse a prologue with the Prolog language. They have nothing to do with one another. Most of the statements in a prologue usually declare host variables. These will accept values from SQL databases as these values are read into the program.

The general rule for a prologue is that is must appear early in the C program. The specific rule is that it must precede any other SQL statements.

There should be two other SQL statements within the prologue:

- *INCLUDE SQLCA* incorporates a C program that sets up an entity known as the SQL Communications Area. This statement serves the same purpose as the #INCLUDE statement in C, but in a slightly different format. When included, SQLCA translates the SQL statements in your program into terms both C and ORACLE can understand.
- *CONNECT*, which establishes a user name and password, and, if these are acceptable, logs onto the ORACLE database.

STATEMENTS OF INTENT

After the prologue, you can include any number of SQL statements. These are just like the SQL statements that should be familiar to you by now, with two differences:

- The commands must be preceded by EXEC SQL. For example, instead of saying SELECT say EXEC SQL SELECT. This will notify SQLCA to a coming SQL statement it must interpret.
- The results of the command should be stored in *host variables* that the C program then can process.

THE PROLOGUE

The challenge of writing a C program to execute SQL commands is that of writing in two languages at once. You'll be using some commands from C and some from SQL. Then there are the names of host variables, which appear in both.

To the extent that it can be done, the samples in this chapter will present SQL commands in capital letters and elements of the

C language in lower case. Keep in mind when writing these programs, though, that C is a very case-sensitive language. A lowercase variable name won't work if it is uppercased elsewhere. This will inevitably result in a few instances in which you must capitalize for the computer and not for the sake of the reader.

DO YOUR DECLARATIONS EARLY

A C program traditionally begins with one or more #include commands. The best place to begin the SQL prologue is right after that.

The declaration section is the first part of the prologue. In it you must declare the names and types of all the host variables you expect to use. If you don't identify them here, you'll be out of luck later.

Listing 17-1 is a simple program called LOGON.PC. It gives access to ORACLE under the user name BAKER and the password BLACK_HOLE (or it would give access if that actually were my password).

```
/*Listing 17-1
  LOGON.PC
  C language file to log onto an SQL database. */

#include <stdio.h>

/* declare host variables */
EXEC SQL BEGIN DECLARE SECTION;
        VARCHAR user_name[20];
        VARCHAR pass_go[20];
EXEC SQL END DECLARE SECTION;
EXEC SQL INCLUDE SQLCA;

main()
{

/* accept name and password into host variables */
strcpy(user_name.arr,"BAKER");
user_name.len=strlen(user_name.arr);
strcpy(pass_go.arr,"BLACK_HOLE");
pass_go.len=strlen(pass_go.arr);

/* log onto Oracle */
EXEC SQL CONNECT :user_name IDENTIFIED BY :pass_go;

/* confirm logon */
printf("Connected to Oracle as user %s\n", user_name.arr);

/* leave SQL (nothing yet to commit) */
EXEC SQL COMMIT WORK RELEASE;
return;
}
```

Because this is a simple program, it has a simple declaration section. It begins with:

EXEC SQL BEGIN DECLARE SECTION;

Actually, that's how you always begin a SQL declaration section. After you have declared a list of variables, end the section with:

EXEC SQL END DECLARE SECTION;

Between these two lines a pair of host variables are designated:

VARCHAR user__name[20];
VARCHAR pass__go[20];

VARCHAR is a special data type that will be explained more fully in a moment. The effect of these declarations is to establish two character variables of variable length to a maximum of twenty. One, called user__name, will hold my user name; the other, pass__go, will hold the password.

ETIQUETTE FOR HOST VARIABLES

You use host variables much as you use what dBASE calls *memory variables*. For example, to store the contents of a field called LAST into a variable called M__LAST you would:

STORE LAST TO M__LAST

The equivalent SQL command within a C program would be:

SELECT LAST INTO :m__last

When used within a SQL command, the variable's name must be preceded by a colon. Its type in the declaration section need not match its type in the SQL table. ORACLE will perform what its manual calls "all reasonable conversions."

When using a host variable, follow these rules:

- You must explicitly declare it in the declaration section.
- You must declare it in the same combination of uppercase and lowercase letters as it will appear later in the program.
- You must precede the name with a colon in a SQL statement.
- You must never precede the name with a colon in a C statement.
- You can use the variable only where it is proper to use a constant.

THE VARCHAR TYPE

The VARCHAR data type is strictly a product of the declaration section. It is not recognized anywhere else. In essence, it is a variable-length character string. When the precompiler processes the declarations, it will convert the VARCHAR into a character array accompanied by a separate variable to hold its current length.

When a VARCHAR variable accepts a value from a SQL table, ORACLE will set its length. When using a VARCHAR variable as an input medium, as in the password sequence, you must establish its length in the declaration.

WHAT YOU CANNOT DO IN A DECLARATION

Don't use the declaration section to refer to a variable that also is declared in a typedef statement in C. Don't refer to previously named structures, either, or include a structure type within the declarations. ORACLE will only get confused.

INCLUDING THE TRANSLATOR

The second main part of the prologue is:

EXEC SQL INCLUDE SQLCA;

The file SQLCA.H is what ORACLE calls a communications area. What it really does is translate the SQL commands in a C program into language both C and SQL can understand. The first stage of this translation takes place during the precompiling phase. Listing 17-2 is what LOGON.C looks like after it has been through the precompiler. The SQL commands have been surrounded by comment brackets. They've been supplanted by code that is only barely fit for human consumption.

```
/* Listing 17-2
   LOGON.C
   Precompiled version.

#include <stdio.h>

/* SQL stmt #1
EXEC SQL BEGIN DECLARE SECTION;
        VARCHAR user_name[20];
*/
struct {
  unsigned short len;
```

```
        unsigned char arr[20];
        } user_name;
/*
        VARCHAR pass_go[20];
*/
struct {
  unsigned short len;
  unsigned char arr[20];
  } pass_go;
/* SQL stmt #2
EXEC SQL END DECLARE SECTION;
*/
static struct {
int          sq001N;
unsigned char *sq001V[4];
unsigned long  sq001L[4];
unsigned short sq001T[4];
unsigned short *sq001I[4];
} sq001 = {4};
static struct {
int          sq002N;
unsigned char *sq002V[1];
unsigned long  sq002L[1];
unsigned short sq002T[1];
unsigned short *sq002I[1];
} sq002 = {1};
static int SQLTM[8];
static int sqlusi[1] = {
0};
static unsigned long sqlami = 0;
static int SQLBT0 = 1;
static int SQLBT1 = 2;
static int SQLBT2 = 4;
static int SQLBT3 = 9;
static unsigned long sqlvsn = 10109;
extern    sqlbs2();
extern    sqlcom();
extern    sqllo2();
extern    sqlsca();
extern    sqlsch();
/* SQL stmt #3
EXEC SQL INCLUDE SQLCA;
*/
/* Copyright (c) 1985,1986 by Oracle Corporation. */

/*
  SQLCA : SQL Communications Area.
FUNCTION
  Contains no code. Oracle fills in the SQLCA with status info
  during the execution of a SQL stmt.
*/

#ifndef SQLCA
#define SQLCA 1

struct   sqlca
        {
        /* ub1 */ char    sqlcaid[8];
        /* b4  */ long    sqlabc;
        /* b4  */ long    sqlcode;
```

```
        struct
          {
          /* ub2 */ unsigned short sqlerrml;
          /* ub1 */ char           sqlerrmc[70];
          } sqlerrm;
        /* ub1 */ char     sqlerrp[8];
        /* b4  */ long     sqlerrd[6];
        /* ub1 */ char     sqlwarn[8];
        /* ub1 */ char     sqlext[8];
        };

#ifdef    SQLCA_STORAGE_CLASS
SQLCA_STORAGE_CLASS struct sqlca sqlca
#else
        struct sqlca sqlca
#endif

#ifdef    SQLCA_INIT
        = {
        {'S', 'Q', 'L', 'C', 'A', ' ', ' ', ' '},
        sizeof(struct sqlca),
        0,
        {  0, {0}},
        {'N', 'O', 'T', ' ', 'S', 'E', 'T', ' '},
        {0, 0, 0, 0, 0, 0},
        {0, 0, 0, 0, 0, 0, 0, 0},
        {0, 0, 0, 0, 0, 0, 0, 0}
        }
#endif

        ;

#endif

/* end SQLCA */

main()
{
strcpy(user_name.arr,"BAKER");
user_name.len=strlen(user_name.arr);
strcpy(pass_go.arr,"BLACK_HOLE");
pass_go.len=strlen(pass_go.arr);

/* SQL stmt #4
EXEC SQL CONNECT :user_name IDENTIFIED BY :pass_go;
*/
sqlsca(&sqlca);
sq001.sq001V[0] = (unsigned char *)&user_name.len;
sq001.sq001L[0] = (unsigned long)22;
sq001.sq001T[0] = (unsigned short)9;
sq001.sq001I[0] = (unsigned short *)0;
sq001.sq001V[1] = (unsigned char *)&pass_go.len;
sq001.sq001L[1] = (unsigned long)22;
sq001.sq001T[1] = (unsigned short)9;
sq001.sq001I[1] = (unsigned short *)0;
sq001.sq001T[2] = (unsigned short)10;
sq001.sq001T[3] = (unsigned short)10;
SQLTM[0] = (int)0;
SQLTM[1] = (int)10;
sqllo2(
  &sq001.sq001N,sq001.sq001V,sq001.sq001L,sq001.sq001T,
  &sqlami, &SQLTM[0], &SQLTM[1], &sqlvsn);
```

```
printf("Connected to Oracle as user %s\n", user_name.arr);
/* SQL stmt #5
EXEC SQL COMMIT WORK RELEASE;
*/
sqlsca(&sqlca);
if ( !sqlusi[0] )
  {  /* OPEN SCOPE */
sq002.sq002T[0] = (unsigned short)10;
SQLTM[0] = (int)4;
sqlbs2(&sq002.sq002N, sq002.sq002V,
  sq002.sq002L, sq002.sq002T, sq002.sq002I,
  &SQLTM[0], &sqlusi[0]);
  }  /* CLOSE SCOPE */
sqlsch(&sqlusi[0]);
SQLTM[0] = (int)1;
sqlcom(&SQLTM[0]);
return;
}
```

An experienced C programmer can probably understand it. Essentially, it translates the SQL commands into an assortment of arrays and variables, most of them with numbers for names. SQLCA thus becomes part of the C program. As the program runs, it will read these statements and convert them into commands SQL can interpret.

SQL PROGRAM STATEMENTS

The body of the program contains both C and SQL statements. For example, LOGON goes through a series of statements that accept the user name and password into the host variables that were the subjects of the earlier declarations:

```
strcpy(user__name.arr,"BAKER");
user__name.len=strlen(user__name.arr);
strcpy(pass__go.arr,"BLACK__HOLE");
pass__go.len=strlen(pass__go.arr);
```

As you will find in future encounters with VARCHAR variables, separate variables are created to hold the string's contents and its length.

USING THE VARIABLES

Then the program uses these variables in a SQL command:

```
EXEC SQL CONNECT :user__name IDENTIFIED BY :pass__go;
```

Pay attention to the colons. Using the variables assigned to the two variables, this line effectively says:

EXEC SQL CONNECT BAKER IDENTIFIED BY BLACK__HOLE;

This program assumes the attempt will be successful, because it provides nothing to do in any other event. If the attempt is successful, the program displays the message:

Connected to ORACLE as user BAKER

SIGNING OFF

There's one more SQL command in this program:

EXEC SQL COMMIT WORK RELEASE;

This probably sounds like something out of the criminal justice system. Actually, it commands SQL to COMMIT any work that might have been done (here, there was none), then release any resources that have been devoted to that process and log off ORACLE.

SIMPLE SELECTIONS

NEWTABLE.PC (Listing 17-3) starts with the basic framework of LOGON and does some useful work. It contains this SQL command:

```
EXEC SQL CREATE TABLE SALES
    (TODAY          DATE,
    EMP__CODE       CHAR(3),
    SSNO            CHAR(11),
    SOURCE          CHAR(1),
    REFERRAL        CHAR(3),
    INITIATED       CHAR(1),
    NEW__CUST       CHAR(1),
    NEW__MONEY      CHAR(1),
    PROD__CODE      CHAR(7),
    ACCT__NO        CHAR(10),
    AMOUNT          NUMBER(12,2));
```

As you should recognize by now, this is a SQL command to create a table, namely a duplicate of the SALES table that's been used in previous chapters. (I conveniently renamed the older ver-

```
/* Listing 17-3
   NEWTABLE.PC
   Executes SQL commands to create new table */

#include <stdio.h>

EXEC SQL BEGIN DECLARE SECTION;
        VARCHAR user_name[20];
        VARCHAR pass_go[20];
EXEC SQL END DECLARE SECTION;
EXEC SQL INCLUDE SQLCA;

main()
{
strcpy(user_name.arr,"BAKER");
user_name.len=strlen(user_name.arr);
strcpy(pass_go.arr,"BLACK_HOLE");
pass_go.len=strlen(pass_go.arr);

EXEC SQL CONNECT :user_name IDENTIFIED BY :pass_go;

printf("Connected to Oracle as user %s\n", user_name.arr);

printf("Creating table SALES ...\n");

/* create table */
EXEC SQL CREATE TABLE SALES
        (TODAY           DATE,
         EMP_CODE        CHAR(3),
         SSNO            CHAR(11),
         SOURCE          CHAR(1),
         REFERRAL        CHAR(3),
         INITIATED       CHAR(1),
         NEW_CUST        CHAR(1),
         NEW_MONEY       CHAR(1),
         PROD_CODE       CHAR(7),
         ACCT_NO         CHAR(10),
         AMOUNT          NUMBER(12,2));

/* commit work, leave SQL */
EXEC SQL COMMIT WORK RELEASE;

/* confirm action */
printf("Table SALES created.\n");

return;
}
```

sion before running this program.) Before and after this command are a pair of messages for the user. As the work is being done, you see:

Creating table SALES . . .

Then, when the table has been created and the program goes back on work release, you should get this confirmation:

Table SALES created.

A DATA ENTRY ROUTINE

A program to enter data into this newly created table will take you one step upward from the simple routines you've seen so far. It requires that you establish a set of host variables to accept the new entries. This is similar to initializing dBASE variables. For use with SQL, these variables must be established in the declarations.

A second step is to enter data into these variables. In the program you are about to see, this is done in the way dBASE would do it with ACCEPT or INPUT. Formatted screens, such as those that use the dBASE @ . . . SAY . . . GET sequence, require functions found only in extensions to standard C. These are much like the SQL*Plus extensions to standard SQL and are, sad to say, beyond the scope of this chapter.

The third step involves a direct SQL command. It inserts the values stored by the host variables into a row of the SALES table.

The program ADDROW.PC (Listing 17-4) illustrates all these steps in turn.

```
/* Listing 17-4
   ADDROW.PC
   Adds a new role to SALES */

#include <stdio.h>

/* declare host variables */
EXEC SQL BEGIN DECLARE SECTION;
    VARCHAR user_name[20];
    VARCHAR pass_go[20];
    VARCHAR emp_code[3];
    VARCHAR ssno[11];
    VARCHAR source[1];
    VARCHAR referral[3];
    VARCHAR initiated[1];
    VARCHAR new_cust[1];
    VARCHAR new_money[1];
    VARCHAR prod_code[7];
    VARCHAR acct_no[10];
    float    amount;
EXEC SQL END DECLARE SECTION;
EXEC SQL INCLUDE SQLCA;

main()
{
strcpy(user_name.arr,"BAKER");
user_name.len=strlen(user_name.arr);
strcpy(pass_go.arr,"BLACK_HOLE");
pass_go.len=strlen(pass_go.arr);

EXEC SQL CONNECT :user_name IDENTIFIED BY :pass_go;
```

```
printf("Connected to Oracle as user %s\n", user_name.arr);
while(1) /* In dBASE: DO WHILE .T. */
{
    printf("New Account Record\n");
    printf("Enter each item and press <Return>\n");

    /* accept first entry /*
    printf("Enter your employee code (or Q to quit): ");
    scanf("%s",emp_code.arr);

    /* record length of variable string */
    emp_code.len=strlen(emp_code.arr);

    /* if only one character, leave loop */
    if (emp_code.len < 2)
        break;
    printf("Customer Social Security Number (99-99-9999): ");
    scanf("%s",ssno.arr);
    ssno.len=strlen(ssno.arr);
    printf("Source codes:\n");
    printf("\t1=Newspaper\t2=Walk-in\t3=Customer\n");
    printf("\t4=Radio\t5=Employee\t6=Other\n");
    printf("Enter code: ");
    scanf("%s",source.arr);
    source.len=strlen(source.arr);
    printf("If employee referral, enter employee code\n");
    printf("Enter 0 for no referral: ");
    scanf("%s",referral.arr);
    referral.len=strlen(referral.arr);
    printf("Who initiated this contact? Codes:\n");
    printf("\t1=Customer\t2=Service Rep.\n");
    printf("\t3=Teller\t4=Other\n");
    printf("Enter code: ");
    scanf("%s",initiated.arr);
    initiated.len=strlen(initiated.arr);
    printf("New Customer (Y/N): ");
    scanf("%s",new_cust.arr);
    new_cust.len=strlen(new_cust.arr);
    printf("Addition to this customer's deposits? (Y/N): ");
    scanf("%s",new_money.arr);
    new_money.len=strlen(new_money.arr);
    printf("Product code: ");
    scanf("%s",prod_code.arr);
    prod_code.len=strlen(prod_code.arr);
    printf("Account number: ");
    scanf("%s",acct_no.arr);
    acct_no.len=strlen(acct_no.arr);
    printf("Amount: ");
    scanf("%f",&amount);

    /* insert new data into table */
    EXEC SQL INSERT INTO SALES
        (TODAY, EMP_CODE, SSNO, SOURCE,
        REFERRAL, INITIATED, NEW_CUST, NEW_MONEY,
        PROD_CODE, ACCT_NO, AMOUNT)
        VALUES
            (SYSDATE, :emp_code, :ssno, :source,
            :referral, :initiated, :new_cust, :new_money,
            :prod_code, :acct_no,:amount);
```

```
        /* commit changes; leave SQL */
        EXEC SQL COMMIT WORK RELEASE;

        /* confirm action */
        printf("New Account Entered\n");
        }
return;
}
```

DECLARING THE VARIABLES

The declaration section has been fattened considerably from the earlier examples. Now you must declare a variable in this section for each of the columns in the database:

```
EXEC SQL BEGIN DECLARE SECTION;
    VARCHAR user__name[20];
    VARCHAR pass__go[20];
    VARCHAR emp__code[3];
    VARCHAR ssno[11];
    VARCHAR source[1];
    VARCHAR referral[3];
    VARCHAR initiated[1];
    VARCHAR new__cust[1];
    VARCHAR new__money[1];
    VARCHAR prod__code[7];
    VARCHAR acct__no[10];
    float    amount;
EXEC SQL END DECLARE SECTION;
```

For all but the one numerical column, the variables are declared as VARCHAR types. This facilitates data entry, since, short of the maximum length, the program will make no assumptions about the length and will insist that the operator hit <Return> to close out an entry.

The lone numerical entry is the amount that, being money, will have the usual two decimal places. When you are not using a type like VARCHAR, which is unique to the Pro*C environment, these declarations should be in the standard C types. Here, then, the two-decimal figure is designated as the float type (for floating decimal point).

DATA ENTRY DETAILS

After logging on with the same routine used in earlier programs, this program swings into a loop controlled by the statement **while(1).** Like the dBASE loop that begins with DO WHILE .T., this loop will let you make new entries until you deliberately break out of it.

Within the loop, the C **printf( )** statement displays prompts similar to the dBASE question mark or SAY. Then **scanf( )** will accept input much like ACCEPT, INPUT or GET. A \n at the end of a **printf( )** indicates a carriage return; **scanf( )** will issue a carriage return when you issue a carriage return.

When using a VARCHAR variable, the data entry process takes three lines. The first is a prompt to call for the entry:

```
printf("Enter your employee code (or Q to quit): ");
```

The second line will accept the entry, not just as a variable but in a string of characters SQLCQ will maintain as an array:

```
scanf("%s",emp__code.arr);
```

For those not familiar with C, the %s indicates the entry will become a string variable. Then, a third command makes a record of the length of that array:

```
emp__code.len=strlen(emp__code.arr);
```

EXIT LINES

The "Q to quit" line in the prompt is a clue that the departure point from the loop is nigh. After it has processed one new record, the program will return to the top again and ask for a new employee code. If the operator is finished, entering Q at that point will break out of the loop and bring the program to an end. It's done with these lines:

```
if (emp__code.len < 2)
   break;
```

Here you have a demonstration that the length variable really does store the length of the entry. Normally, UnderFed employees use two or three initials for their employee codes. If the operator enters a Q—or for that matter, any other single letter or digit—the value of **emp__code.len** will fall below 2. This is the program's signal to take a break.

GETTING THE NUMBER

The succeeding lines repeat the process of prompt, entry, and length calculation for each VARCHAR value. Some of the prompts are more elaborate than others. All are designed to suggest correct entries to the operators, within the limits of screen space and a very simple program.

The non-VARCHAR entry is somewhat different:

```
printf("Amount: ");
scanf("%f", &amount);
```

Here, the **%f** calls for a **float** entry. The ampersand indicates the contents of the amount variable, much as it does in dBASE.

FROM VARIABLES TO COLUMNS

To a large extent, this program duplicates a standard dBASE technique. The routine accepts input into variables, then adds the contents of the variables to the file. In dBASE this is done with REPLACE commands. In SQL, INSERT does the same job.

The INSERT command in this program is structured much like its conventional SQL counterpart:

```
EXEC SQL INSERT INTO SALES
    (TODAY, EMP__CODE, SSNO, SOURCE,
    REFERRAL, INITIATED, NEW__CUST, NEW__MONEY,
    PROD__CODE, ACCT__NO, AMOUNT)
VALUES
    (SYSDATE, :emp__code, :ssno, :source,
    :referral, :initiated, :new__cust, :new__money,
    :prod__code, :acct__no, :amount);
```

There's the EXEC SQL part, of course. The other main difference is in the list of values. Within the SQL command, these values are preceded by colons. These actually are the variable names; their values will be transferred to the corresponding columns in the table.

There is one exception. SYSDATE automatically records the

date of the transaction in the table in the column TODAY. Since it's not involved in the rest of the program, there's no need to deal with SYSDATE outside of the SQL command.

FREE SAMPLES

A sample of the program's screen display is shown along with its output in Figure 17-1. It's nothing fancy—the main purpose has been to illustrate SQL techniques, not to paint screens.

UPDATING A RECORD

The sales tracking program at UnderFed had been such a success it was decided to give substantial raises to two of the main contributors, Hubert Tuba and Misty Presto. Even Allison Wunderland, the district manager, went along with the idea.

FIGURE 17-1   Input and Output of ADDROW

```
C:\ORACLE5\PRO>addrow
Connected to Oracle as user BAKER
New Account Record
Enter each item and press <Return>
Enter your employee code (or Q to quit): HT
Customer Social Security Number (99-99-9999): 666-66-6666
Source codes:
        1=Newspaper      2=Walk-in        3=Customer
        4=Radio 5=Employee       6=Other
Enter code: 2
If employee referral, enter employee code
Enter 0 for no referral: 0
Who initiated this contact? Codes:
        1=Customer       2=Service Rep.
        3=Teller         4=Other
Enter code: 1
New Customer (Y/N): N
Addition to this customer's deposits? (Y/N): Y
Product code: IRA
Account number: 2500
Amount: 12500
New Account Entered
New Account Record
Enter each item and press <Return>
Enter your employee code (or Q to quit):
TODAY       EMP SSNO         S REF I N N PROD_CO ACCT_NO      AMOUNT
---------   --- ----------- - --- - - - ------- ---------- ----------
01-FEB-88 HT   666-66-6666 2 0   1 N Y IRA      2500            12500
```

At first, Madison felt a bit grumpy because, not only was he
not included, but he also had to write a program that would give
the raises to his two assistants. Only after being assured he would
receive his reward later did Madison create PAYRAISE.PC
(Listing 17-5).

```
/* Listing 17-5
   PAYRAISE.PC
   Locates and updates a record */

#include <stdio.h>

EXEC SQL BEGIN DECLARE SECTION;
        VARCHAR user_name[20]; /* host variables */
        VARCHAR pass_go[20];
        VARCHAR last[12];
        float   salary;
        short   i_salary; /* indicator variable */
EXEC SQL END DECLARE SECTION;
EXEC SQL INCLUDE SQLCA;

main()
{
int     salcheck;

strcpy(user_name.arr,"BAKER");
user_name.len=strlen(user_name.arr);
strcpy(pass_go.arr,"BLACK_HOLE");
pass_go.len=strlen(pass_go.arr);


/* Halt program if error trapped */
EXEC SQL WHENEVER SQLERROR STOP;
EXEC SQL WHENEVER NOT FOUND STOP;
EXEC SQL CONNECT :user_name IDENTIFIED BY :pass_go;

printf("Connected to Oracle as user %s\n\n", user_name.arr);

/* Enter query condition */
printf("Enter employee's name: ");
scanf("%s",last.arr);
last.len=strlen(last.arr);

/* Retrieve salary for specified employee */
EXEC SQL SELECT SALARY
        INTO :salary:i_salary
        FROM ROSTER
        WHERE LAST=:last;

/* Display employee and salary;
   prompt for change */
printf("Employee: %s. Current salary: %8.2f\n\n", last.arr, salary);
printf("Enter new salary: ");

/* Accept salary into host and checking variables */
salcheck=scanf("%f",&salary);
```

```
/* set indicator variable to 0 */
i_salary=0;

/* declare error if end of file or
   entry is zero */
if(salcheck == EOF || salcheck == 0)
        i_salary = -1;

/* update the table*/
EXEC SQL UPDATE ROSTER
        SET SALARY = :salary :i_salary
        WHERE LAST = :last;

/* confirm the change*/
printf("\n%s salary updated to %8.2f\n", last.arr, salary);

EXEC SQL COMMIT WORK RELEASE;
return;
}
```

PROMPTS AND NEW DATA

In its basic operation, this program is again about as simple as those that have come before. First, it declares two host variables to house an employee's last name and the associated salary:

```
VARCHAR    last[12]
float      salary;
```

Then, it prompts the operator to enter the employee's name. This entry is accepted into the host variable **last.arr** just as in the previous example:

```
printf("Enter employee's name: ");
scanf("%s",last.arr);
last.len=strlen(last.arr);
```

The next step is to locate the entered last name and retrieve that employee's current salary:

```
EXEC SQL SELECT SALARY
    INTO :salary:i__salary
    FROM ROSTER
    WHERE LAST=:last;
```

The employee's name and current salary are displayed, and the operator is prompted to enter a new salary:

```
printf("Employee: %s. Current salary: %8.2f\n\n", last.arr, salary);
```

```
printf("Enter new salary: ");
salcheck=scanf("%f",&salary);
```

The **%8.2f** calls for a float-type number that is eight digits wide and has two decimal places. This matches the specifications for the SALARY column in ROSTER.

Another SQL command then inserts the revised value into the table:

```
EXEC SQL UPDATE ROSTER
    SET SALARY = :salary :i__salary
    WHERE LAST = :last;
```

A final report then confirms the update:

```
printf("\n%s salary updated to %8.2f\n", last.arr, salary);
```

PAYRAISE IN OPERATION

The program first stops to accept the name of the employee whose pay is to be changed:

Enter employee's name:

After entering a name you should see:

Enter employee's name: TUBA
Employee: TUBA. Current salary: 11000.00
Enter new salary:

Enter a figure $500 higher:

Enter new salary: 11500.00

The program will then display the new values. If they are not correct you can run the program again and change them:

TUBA salary updated to 11500.00

Likewise, you'll get this screen display when you increase Presto's salary by the same amount:

Enter employee's name: PRESTO
Employee: PRESTO. Current salary: 42500.00

Enter new salary: 43000

PRESTO salary updated to 43000.00

Notice how the formatting commands display the salary with the specified two decimal points, even though they were not entered. Now, try this and see what happens:

Enter employee's name: BAKER

You'll see nothing but:

C:>

My name isn't in ROSTER. The program simply shut itself off and returned to the DOS prompt.

TRAPPING ERRORS

This program contains two error-trapping mechanisms. You may have noticed one: a variable called **i_salary** sort of floating around the place. This is an *indicator variable* that attaches itself to the host variable **salary.** It contains flags that will signify an error such as the failure to find my name in the table.

The other mechanism is contained in these two commands:

```
EXEC SQL WHENEVER SQLERROR STOP;
EXEC SQL WHENEVER NOT FOUND STOP;
```

These are special SQL commands that tell the program what to do when it encounters an error in a SQL command or when a search does not succeed. To some extent, these commands and the indicator variables do overlap.

THE EXTRA VARIABLE

The indicator variable in this program was included, as it must be, in the declarations:

```
short      i_salary;
```

Then, whenever **salary** is used in a SQL command, **i_salary** tags along. For instance, in the SELECT command to retrieve the employee's salary, the variable appears this way:

```
EXEC SQL SELECT SALARY
    INTO :salary:i_salary
```

The same form appears again in the update command:

```
EXEC SQL UPDATE ROSTER
    SET SALARY = :salary :i__salary
```

When two variables trail each other this way, with colons but no intervening comma, the program assumes that the second is an indicator value. We all hope this value will just be an extra passenger on a smooth ride. Should there be trouble, though, the indicator variable will go to work and help you bail out of it.

Usually, the indicator cruises along with a value of 0. If you encounter a null value or a string that's too long for the host variable, its value will change. If the program encounters a null value, the indicator will change its own value to -1. If the value is too large for the variable, the indicator will take on the *original length* of the string.

Someone with a little facility in C could then write a function (in C, functions and procedures are the same) that would use the indicator variable's value to alert the operator to the problem and see what the operator wants to do about it.

This program also sets the indicator variable to -1 to flag a couple of other errors:

```
if(salcheck = EOF | | salcheck == 0)
    i__salary = -1;
```

The flag will go up if the search reaches the end of the file, or if the operator enters 0 for the employee's name.

There's one restriction: You can't use an indicator variable as a condition in a WHERE clause. If you want to search for a null value, use IS NULL as you would in a direct SQL query.

WHENEVER

The C programs you write to use with ORACLE will have one salient characteristic. They will doggedly try to complete their appointed rounds no matter what goes wrong. Although this is an admirable tendency, sometimes it can go to extremes—such as when the program stubbornly inserts corrupted data into your pristine SQL tables.

This program uses two clauses that are designed to curb its zeal when an error crops up:

```
EXEC SQL WHENEVER SQLERROR STOP;
EXEC SQL WHENEVER NOT FOUND STOP;
```

The first command of this pair is triggered whenever an error is encountered in a SQL operation. In this case, such an error will simply halt the program. The second does the same thing if a search is unsuccessful. A third option, WHENEVER SQLWARNING, cuts in if the program encounters a warning flag, as long as the error is not fatal.

For any of these three events, you can predict any of three outcomes. STOP simply halts the program in its tracks. CONTINUE is just the opposite—it tells the program to go on despite the error. A third option is GOTO, followed by a label. This instructs the program, in case of an error, to go to that label within the C program and execute the instructions it finds there.

Quite often, these instructions will be:

```
EXEC SQL ROLLBACK WORK
```

ROLLBACK here works just as it does in a direct command. It does not COMMIT pending changes to the database. In the case of an error, this information would often be suspect in any event. Optionally you can add RELEASE to close down the SQL part of the operation.

USING WHENEVER IN VALIDATION

You can use WHENEVER to validate a data entry, too. For example, in ADDROW, you want to make sure that an operator enters a valid code to identify the product whose sale is being recorded. After the program accepts the entry, you could include a sequence like this:

```
EXEC SQL WHENEVER NOT FOUND GOTO el_wrongo;
EXEC SQL SELECT PRODUCT
    FROM PRODUCTS
    WHERE PROD_CODE = :prod_code;
EXEC SQL WHENEVER NOT FOUND CONTINUE;
```

For the duration of the SELECT command, a failure will direct the program to a section labeled **el_wrongo.** Once the query has been completed, the second WHENEVER command provides instructions for handling the next error that arises. The GOTO command could divert the program to something like this:

```
el_wrongo:
    printf("Improper department number");
return
```

MULTIPLE-CHOICE QUERIES

The programs so far have worked with a limited type of database query. When you search for a single employee or even for a single product code, you can be reasonably sure there is only one row in the table that will satisfy your query.

What if you aren't sure, though? What happens if more than one row meets your query specifications? In particular, what happens if you aren't expecting more than one row? When in doubt, put a cursor in your program.

CURSES: THE CURSOR

The word *cursor* brings to mind for most readers the blinking block that moves around the screen and marks your place. A cursor in SQL is somewhat different.

People with scientific minds have a frustrating habit of applying familiar words to unfamiliar concepts. In the current context, a cursor is certainly an example. In ORACLE, a cursor is a work area that is used to store the results of a query. dBASE people are used to thinking of a work area as a place to gather related files and such. An ORACLE work area, though, is a place where query results are stored. This is one way in which the two concepts have just enough similarity to cause confusion.

Here's another: The ORACLE cursor does have something in common with its on-screen namesake. As a cursor operation begins, the cursor is positioned at the first row that satisfies the query. It will make its way downward as the program progresses. This idea doesn't seem to square very well with the concept of the cursor as a work area. However, it does make a cursor seem similar to the pointer in dBASE. That doesn't help much, though, because we're working in C. There, a pointer indicates the memory position of a variable. It all goes to show how much damage you can do when you muck about with the language.

Fortunately, explaining how to use a cursor is a whole lot easier than trying to explain what it is. Start with the program CURSES.PC (Listing 17-6).

```
/* Listing 17-6
   CURSES.PC
   Uses cursor to retrieve a group of records */

#include <stdio.h>

EXEC SQL BEGIN DECLARE SECTION;
        VARCHAR user_name[20];
        VARCHAR pass_go[20];
        char    last[12];
        char    first[12];
        char    init[1];
        int     dept_no;
EXEC SQL END DECLARE SECTION;
EXEC SQL INCLUDE SQLCA;

main()
{
strcpy(user_name.arr,"BAKER");
user_name.len=strlen(user_name.arr);
strcpy(pass_go.arr,"CUBS_WIN");
pass_go.len=strlen(pass_go.arr);

EXEC SQL CONNECT :user_name IDENTIFIED BY :pass_go;

printf("Connected to Oracle as user %s\n", user_name.arr);

/* declare cursor; link to query */
EXEC SQL DECLARE C_ROSTER CURSOR FOR
        SELECT LAST, FIRST, INIT, DEPT_NO
        FROM ROSTER;

/* open cursor; position at first record */
EXEC SQL OPEN C_ROSTER;

/* in dBASE: DO WHILE .NOT. EOF() */
EXEC SQL WHENEVER NOT FOUND STOP;

/* display headings separated by tabs */
printf ("Last Name\tFirst Name\tInitial\tDept. No.\n");
printf ("------------ \t------------ \t------- ---------\n");
```

```
/* loop without specifications spools through file */
for( ; ; )
{
        EXEC SQL FETCH C_ROSTER INTO
                :last, :first, :init, :dept_no;
        /* display one row */
        printf("%-12s \t%-12s \t%-1s \t%2d\n",last, first, init, dept_no);
}  /*end loop */

/* close cursor */
EXEC SQL CLOSE C_ROSTER;

/* end error trapping */
/*EXEC SQL WHENEVER SQLERROR CONTINUE;*/
EXEC SQL COMMIT WORK RELEASE;
return;
}
```

ANOTHER EMPLOYEE ROSTER

To use a cursor, the program first must declare it. This is done with a SQL statement that DECLAREs the cursor as standing FOR a SQL query:

EXEC SQL DECLARE C__ROSTER CURSOR FOR
    SELECT LAST, FIRST, INIT, DEPT__NO
    FROM ROSTER;

After a cursor has been declared, it must be opened. You do that with a fairly straightforward command such as:

EXEC SQL OPEN C__ROSTER;

The third step is to FETCH the data from the SQL table and insert it into user variables:

EXEC SQL FETCH C__ROSTER INTO
    :last, :first, :init, :dept__no;

The name of the cursor now represents its associated query. The data are retrieved one row at a time. This command lies within a C loop that has no definite end. At each pass, the cursor will move through the table and retrieve another row. The effect is the same as that produced by the dBASE command DO WHILE .NOT. EOF(). The loop continues until the cursor reaches the end of the file.

Precompile this program, compile, link, and run it and you

should see a familiar-looking display from the UnderFed employee roster.

THERE'S MORE

There's much more than this to writing a professional-level C program. For those who are skilled in that art, ORACLE also offers many advanced programming interfaces. It would take another complete book to explain all the possibilities ORACLE and the C language have to offer in combination. The purpose here is to acquaint you with the basics. As you learn, the ORACLE manual can take you as far as you'd like to go.

You should be able to see, however, that a SQL database need not suffer from lack of a programming interface. C and other languages will give SQL everything the dBASE language gives that system—and much more. For those who are not programmers, there are easier ways ahead.

REVIEW QUESTIONS

1. Name the three steps in compiling a C program to work with an ORACLE database. Which step is not used to compile a normal C program?
2. The precompiler, compiler, and linker all expect certain program name extensions. What are they?
3. What are the two types of SQL commands you can include in a C program?
4. Declarations go in the prologue. What other types of SQL commands should be there?
5. What's the difference between the proper way to use host variables in a SQL command and the same variables in a C statement?
6. What's a VARCHAR?
7. What is an indicator variable?
8. A WHENEVER command has three possible responses. What are they, and what do they do?

ANSWERS

1. The steps, in order, are precompiling, compiling, and linking. The precompiling step is the addition.

2. .PC on a file intended for the precompiler, .C for the compiler, and .OBJ for the linker.
3. Declarations and SQL statements.
4. INCLUDE SQLCA and CONNECT.
5. When used in a SQL command, precede the host variable names with colons. Do not do this in a C statement.
6. A special type of variable character type used in SQL declarations.
7. A variable whose value reflects the absence or presence of errors in an associated host variable.
8. STOP halts the program, CONTINUE ignores the error, and GOTO initiates a programmed response.

18

Put on a Happy Interface

INTRODUCING THE INTERFACES

USING SQL*FORMS

THE SQL SPREADSHEET

"The time has come," Madison said, "to reveal a deep, dark secret. You see, you don't have to sit down at your computer every day and type things like 'SELECT diddlywhump FROM thingamabopper.' You don't have to become an expert programmer, either. You see, we have something called a user interface. Two of them, in fact. They can do all the while and whereas stuff for you. There's a form-drawing utility to make data entry easier for data entry people. For reports and analysis and all that other good stuff, there's a way to pump your SQL data into and out of the ever-popular spreadsheet. Take a look and see what I mean."

INTRODUCING THE INTERFACES

At the risk of repeating the obvious, SQL is not a complete programming language in itself. It is more like having a couple of dozen dBASE commands at your disposal. They are very versatile commands, but SQL lacks all the rest of the dBASE language.

In some SQL products, that's all you get. These are so-called database engines. They are designed to be used by application developers who will use SQL as the basis for their own programs. They will write the necessary code to create a useful product based on SQL.

Other SQL products provide SQL with their own enhancements. The enhancements turn SQL into a finished product you can install and use without further involuntary programming effort. ORACLE is in this class. So are several competing database products.

The extended commands of SQL*Plus are one type of enhancement. The C language connection is another. ORACLE, though, like most of its competitors, also offers a highly finished user interface, complete with designer screens and ease-of-use features that separate day-to-day operators from the need to write programs or even SQL queries. These front-end features vary greatly from product to product. Naturally, it's the ORACLE interfaces that will be discussed here.

IN GOOD FORM

ORACLE has a pair of these. One, called SQL*Forms, gives you the means to create user-congenial, on-screen forms for queries and data entry. You must be familiar with SQL commands to create these screens. The people who use the finished product, though, need not even know that something like SQL exists.

1-2-SQL

The second interface is SQL*Calc, which lets you use SQL in much the same way you would use your favorite spreadsheet. Along with the usual calculations you can make with a spreadsheet, SQL*Calc will execute SQL commands and exchange data with the ORACLE database.

The spreadsheet interface looks much like 1-2-3. In fact, this interface's latest incarnation *is* 1-2-3. A new ORACLE for 1-2-3 that links the popular spreadsheet with an ORACLE database recently reached the market. It works very much as does SQL*Calc, which is the product you'll see discussed here. If you understand one, you should find it easy to switch to the other.

USING SQL*FORMS

ORACLE's form-building tool comes with three manuals of its own. It's a sophisticated screen-building program that can not only put data on the screen but can also establish defaults, validate entries, and even trigger SQL commands and C programs.

This program's many features can't be covered in a chapter any more than C can. Accordingly, the purpose here will be more to illustrate than to instruct. This chapter will be a short demonstration of what SQL can do when it's operated through a front-end program such as SQL*Forms.

FRONT END ALIGNMENT

Like the rest of the ORACLE system, SQL*Forms is protected by a password system. Accordingly, its opening screen looks like Figure 18-1.

FIGURE 18-1   The Opening Screen of SQL*Forms

```
SQL*Forms (Design): Version 2.0.18.12DX - Development on Fri Feb  5 12:32:34 1

Copyright (c) 1986, Oracle Corporation, California, USA.  All rights reserved.


             Username
             Password




        Enter your ORACLE user name and password then
        press End (Accept) to continue.

        Press F8 at any time to show function keys.



Form:          Block:          Page:     SELECT:     Char Mode: Replace
```

After you have successfully passed this barrier, a small window in a large screen will present you with the options in Figure 18-2. You'll be expected to enter a name for the form. Because this one will record transactions, why not call it TRANSACT?

Below the name are several actions you can take with this form. Because TRANSACT doesn't exist yet, the only meaningful thing you can do right now is to CREATE it. Later you will be able to select and modify existing forms, save your work, generate code, and do some general file maintenance.

FIGURE 18-2   The First of Many Options

```
                    CHOOSE FORM
          Name
          TRANSACT
          Actions:
            CREATE      MODIFY      LIST
            RUN         DEFINE      LOAD
            FILE        GENERATE
```

Successive punches of the <Tab> key will position the cursor (we're back to talking about the on-screen version now) in front of the successive options. <Return> will do the same thing. The arrow keys also will move you around within—and, for that matter, without—the window. Once you've reached the item of your choice, the <Home> key will select it. In fact, in this program <Home> is called SELECT. This form of menu navigation is not one of ORACLE's finest accomplishments, but you'll get used to it. Soon you'll be dashing around these windows with all the style and grace of a teenager on a first date.

OPENING ANOTHER WINDOW

As often happens in this system, your selection opens another window. This is the CHOOSE BLOCK window that overlaps the CHOOSE FORM menu (Figure 18-3).

Again, you must provide a name, but this time a name has already been provided for you. A *block* is a section of a form. It corresponds to a database table. The form you want to use now (because I told you so) is SALES.

The easiest way to turn an existing table into a form (you also can do it the other way around) is to select the DEFAULT option. This will present you with a third window that enables you to display a list of the columns in the chosen table. By now, the screen should resemble the spread shown in Figure 18-4.

FIGURE 18-3   Choosing a Block

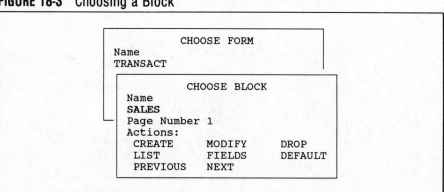

FIGURE 18-4   A Display of Columns for Your Selection

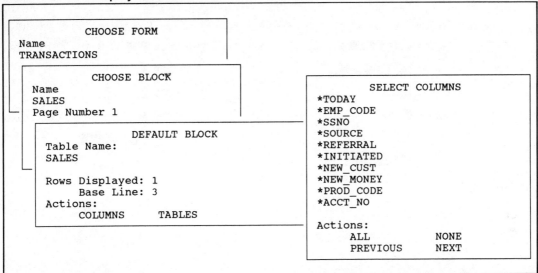

ADVANCE TO THE REAR

If there are any columns you do not want to display on the form, use <Home> to select them. That's not the case this time, so it's time to start backing out window by window. Just as <Home> took you forward, <End>, or ACCEPT, will take you backward. You'll move back to the CHOOSE BLOCK window. Tell ORA-CLE you want to modify the form, and you'll see a screen like that shown in Figure 18-5.

DRAG RACING

The default headings and column titles are simple text entries. You can alter or delete them as you would in any text editor. The data fields, which actually appear as reverse-video blocks, can also be moved. Move the cursor to the one you want to move, hit <F5>, and the field will disappear. Move to the new location, hit <F4>, and it will reappear. You can mark text blocks, using <Home> at each end, and move them in the same way, but often it's just as easy to erase and rewrite the text. A status line at the bottom tells you a few things about what you're up to.

FIGURE 18-5 The Beginnings of a Screen Layout

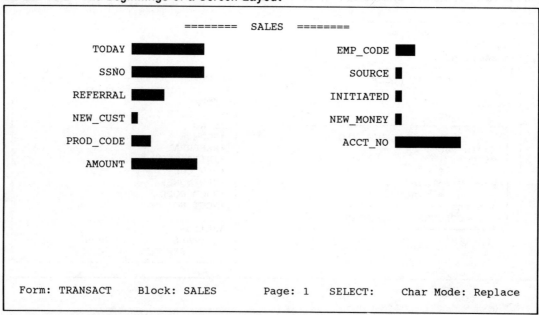

After a bit of fooling around, the display looks like Figure 18-6, which in turn looks something like the original dBASE screen (see Figure 14-1).

ADDING CUSTOMERS

When an employee records a sale, the record must include some data from SALES and some from the CUSTOMER table. After

FIGURE 18-6 A Rearranged Data Entry Screen

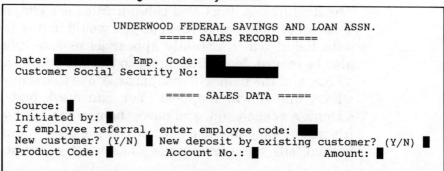

going through the same routine described for SALES, the customer information is added, as shown in Figure 18-7.

VALIDATION AND DEFINITION

The strength of this program is its ability to validate, compute, and format every data item on the screen. It can even use a TRIGGER function to calculate or verify a data entry, using either a SQL query or a C program.

Figure 18-8 shows how to set the current date as the default for the date entry.

The <F2> key, called DEFINE in this program, starts the process. It presents a DEFINE FIELD window with which, among other things, you can establish the data type and the display format. You can also call for a validation block that lets you establish a default value, a validation formula, or both. Here, the $$DATE$$ in the default blank feeds the current date into the variable.

FIGURE 18-7   Customer Data Items Added

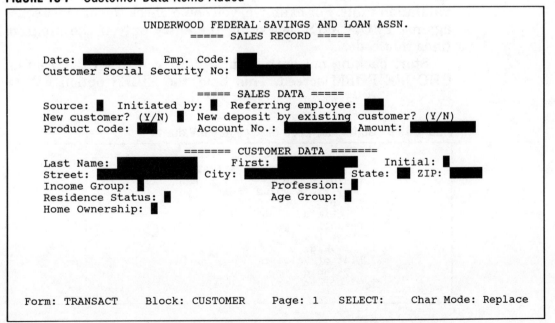

FIGURE 18-8 Setting a Default Value

```
              DEFINE FIELD           Seq # 1
        Name TODAY
                   SPECIFY VALIDATION
        Field Length 9              Query Length 9
        Copy Field Value from:
            Block
            Field
        Default    $$DATE$$
        Range Low
            High
        List of Values:
            Table
            Column
        Help:
        Enter value for : TODAY
```

A VALIDATION EXAMPLE

Figure 18-9 shows another validation window, this one for the
SOURCE field. This is one of the coded entries; the codes range
from 1 to 6. Other possibilities include taking the value from
some other table, or checking an entry against the contents of the
validation table. For example, you could check the product codes
against PRODUCTS, accepting the entry only if the program
finds that code.

Start backing out with <End> until you reach the original
CHOOSE FORM screen. This time, the FILES option will be

FIGURE 18-9 Setting a Range of Acceptable Values

```
                 SPECIFY VALIDATION
        Field Length 1             Query Length 1
        Copy Field Value from:
            Block
            Field
        Default
        Range Low 1
            High 6
        List of Values:
            Table
            Column
```

useful, letting you save your work. Once the saving is finished, generating the form is a separate operation. It appears on the CHOOSE FORM menu, but you'll quickly be instructed to leave the program and issue your own generation command. Shortly, you'll find the same is true of RUN.

RUNNING THE PROGRAM

When you do run this form, you'll see the old familiar screen again, looking like Figure 18-10. This time it's ready for some data entry. The date's already there, thanks to the default established for that field. A couple of other entries have been thrown in, bringing us down to the SOURCE entry. There, just for the heck of it, is an 8.

At the bottom of the screen is a message:

Must be in range 1 to 6

At least this program has the courtesy not to suggest that you've broken the law when you type an incorrect number. The program read the deliberately out-of-range entry and recognized that it exceeded the boundaries of the validation instructions. Change the entry to something within the acceptable range, and you can proceed.

FIGURE 18-10   A Deliberate Mistake

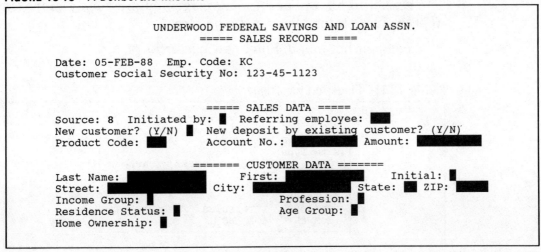

```
                UNDERWOOD FEDERAL SAVINGS AND LOAN ASSN.
                       ===== SALES RECORD =====

        Date: 05-FEB-88  Emp. Code: KC
        Customer Social Security No: 123-45-1123


                          ===== SALES DATA =====
        Source: 8  Initiated by: █  Referring employee: █
        New customer? (Y/N) █   New deposit by existing customer? (Y/N)
        Product Code: █         Account No.: █         Amount: █

                        ======= CUSTOMER DATA =======
        Last Name: █              First: █             Initial: █
        Street: █          City: █            State: █  ZIP: █
        Income Group: █            Profession: █
        Residence Status: █        Age Group: █
        Home Ownership: █
```

TRIGGER

Another kind of validation makes use of the ability to include SQL queries in a form. Such a query is called a *trigger*. For example, one of the leading questions an employee has when a customer wants to open a new account is whether this customer is already on the rolls. What better way to do that than with a query of the customer table?

The program should search the list of existing customers for the Social Security number that uniquely identifies every person. If not found, the program should alert the operator with instructions to complete a new-customer record. Unofficially, of course, this will also alert the employee that there will be no extra points for signing up this customer.

To create a trigger, press < F2 > to define the SSNO field. Select the TRIGGER option from the DEFINE FIELD window (Figure 18-11).

The next window to open will give you an opportunity to write a SQL formula to be executed after the operator has completed this entry. There are also options to trigger a query at other phases of the operation. You can also enter a message to be displayed if the query fails (Figure 18-12). The colon in this query designates the field on the SALES form rather than on the table of the same name.

Figure 18-13 shows what happens when you run this form and enter a Social Security number that obviously is not on file. The screen lights up, and the message you previously prepared appears in a status block at the bottom:

Customer not found. Enter new customer record.

FIGURE 18-11   Finger on the Trigger

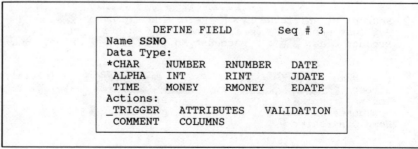

FIGURE 18-12   A SQL Query Triggers Action

```
Seq # 1                TRIGGER STEP          Label
SELECT * FROM CUSTOMER WHERE :SALES.SSNO = CUSTOMER.SSNO




Message if trigger step fails:
Customer not found. Enter new customer record.
Actions:
    CREATE         COPY          DROP          ATTRIBUTES         COMMENT
    FORWARD        BACKWARD      PREV STEP     NEXT STEP
```

A LEADING EXAMPLE

This has just been a quick demonstration of what a good front-end program can do with a SQL database. The main point is that a typical business user will not sit there typing SQL queries. Instead, there will be a data entry screen like the one designed here or like the similar screens developed for so many dBASE applications.

SQL is the database engine around which working applications can be built. Someone else must provide the automatic transmission and power steering.

THE SQL SPREADSHEET

Figure 18-14 should look familiar. Then again, perhaps not. Certainly no spreadsheet user can mistake the layout, although the status and menu lines are at the bottom of the screen instead of at the top as they are in Brand X. Anyone who's followed this book to this point should recognize the contents, even in their

FIGURE 18-13   Ready, Aim, Misfire

```
                UNDERWOOD FEDERAL SAVINGS AND LOAN ASSN.
                      ===== SALES RECORD =====

        Date: 06-FEB-88  Emp. Code: HT
        Customer Social Security No: 000-00-0000
```

FIGURE 18-14 One Familiar Display; Another Familiar Setting

```
         A          B          C          D          E          F          G          H
   1  EMP_CODE  LAST       FIRST      INIT       DEPT_NO    POSITION   SS_NO      DATE_HIR
   2  AD        DAVIDSON   ADDIE      H                1    MANAGER    123-45-6   09-SEP-7
   3  DM        MADISON    DENNIS     W                1    ASST MGR   234-56-7   07-JUL-8
   4  MP        PRESTO     MISTY      D                1    RECEPTIO   456-78-9   19-JUN-7
   5  HT        TUBA       HUBERT     G                2    NEW ACCT   567-89-0   17-MAY-8
   6  SM        MAHONEY    SUZANNE    S                3    TELLER     789-01-2   18-JAN-7
   7  CB        BUCHINSK   CHARLES    B                4    SECURITY   890-12-3   18-DEC-8
   8  VP        PALMER     VERA       M                3    TELLER     901-23-4   23-SEP-8
   9  KC        COLLINS    KATHLEEN   D                2    NEW ACCT   987-65-4   15-OCT-8
  10  RZ        ZIMMERMA   ROBERT     D                2    SUPERVIS   876-54-3   14-OCT-8
  11  PR        ROWE-HAT   PHYLLIS    F                2    NEW ACCT   765-43-2   07-NOV-8
  12
  13
  14
  15
  16
  17
  18
  19
  20
  21
  0% USED,  A1(SQL,A,A)=SELECT * into &a1.k11 FROM ROSTER
  Press HELP (F1) any time.  (Begin SQL with $, formula with +, command with /.)
```

slightly truncated form. What should not be familiar is this particular setting.

SELECT COMMANDS IN A SPREADSHEET

What's happened is that along with the usual text, number, and formula entries, this spreadsheet accepts SQL commands. The specific command is the traditional:

SELECT * FROM ROSTER

For use in the spreadsheet, it is necessary to precede this command with a dollar sign, as the prompt at the bottom of the screen suggests. Just above that line is the command, as embellished and executed by SQL*Calc. It retrieves the rows and columns of the SQL ROSTER table and inserts them into the rows and columns of the spreadsheet.

A HINT OF THE FUTURE

You may be seeing a bit of the future here. All the peope who use spreadsheets can now have the full array of SQL databases and operations at their command. You can query, add to, and even create a SQL table through SQL*Calc. At the same time, the ORACLE folks have found a way to make the popular 1-2-3 perform much as SQL*Calc does.

When you query a SQL table, the program will first spread the table's column headings, or at least those you've selected, across the top of the table. Then, it will tell you how many rows are available for import and ask for your okay to go ahead.

Figure 18-15 is another look at the same display. It's been tidied up a bit with column widths adjusted to display their contents more legibly and the SALARY column set in a MONEY format.

The usual set of options is spread across the bottom of the screen—along with one unusual choice. The ORACLE selection calls up a submenu from which you can execute the most common SQL commands.

SPREADSHEET REPORTING

You can combine the power to retrieve this SQL table with the spreadsheet's power to do calculations on the figures you get

FIGURE 18-15   A Modified Table Display and an Added Option

```
           C        D    E       F            G          H          I
    1 FIRST        INIT DEPT_NO POSITION     SS_NO      DATE_HIRED SALARY
    2 ADDIE        H       1    MANAGER      123-45-6789 09-SEP-79  24000.00
    3 DENNIS       W       1    ASST MGR     234-56-7890 07-JUL-81  21000.00
    4 MISTY        D       1    RECEPTION    456-78-9012 19-JUN-78  43000.00
    5 HUBERT       G       2    NEW ACCT     567-89-0123 17-MAY-87  11500.00
    6 SUZANNE      S       3    TELLER       789-01-2345 18-JAN-79  12400.00
    7 CHARLES      B       4    SECURITY     890-12-3456 18-DEC-86  15000.00
    8 VERA         M       3    TELLER       901-23-4567 23-SEP-85  13450.00
    9 KATHLEEN     D       2    NEW ACCT     987-65-4321 15-OCT-85  13300.00
   10 ROBERT       D       2    SUPERVISOR   876-54-3210 14-OCT-85  13400.00
   11 PHYLLIS      F       2    NEW ACCT     765-43-2109 07-NOV-87  11250.00
   12
   13
   14
   15
   16
   17
   18
   19
   20
   21
0% USED,  C1(Text)=FIRST
Worksheet   Range   Copy   Layout   File   Print   Oracle   Quit
Control ORACLE-worksheet interactions, or show related database information
```

back. For example, you can create a spreadsheet version of the monthly salary report from Chapter 16.

First, you must create a spreadsheet column to accept the new values. The /WORKSHEET INSERT command will do that. Tell the program you want to create a new Column J. Type in the heading MONTHLY, and the worksheet should look like Figure 18-16.

Now, in the first cell of the new column, enter a spreadsheet formula to divide the annual salary by 12. It takes the form:

+I2/12

You're almost ready to copy this formula into the remaining cells of the new column. The default setting in SQL*Calc is an *absolute reference*. Unlike the default in 1-2-3, a copied formula continues to refer to the cells mentioned in the original. Copy the formula now, and you'll have an entire column of I2/12.

You need to establish a relative reference in which the cells to which the formula refers move along with the location of the formula itself. The formula in Row 3 should read I3/12, in row four I4/12 and so on.

A NO-DEFAULT POLICY

There's a trick you can use to accomplish this. Simply enter the cell references in lowercase instead of uppercase letters. The formula in Cell J2 should really read:

+i2/12

FIGURE 18-16   Adding Space for a New Column

	F	G	H	I	J	K	L
1	POSITION	SS_NO	DATE_HIRED	SALARY	MONTHLY	EXTENSION	BRANCH_N
2	MANAGER	123-45-6789	09-SEP-79	24000.00		101	69
3	ASST MGR	234-56-7890	07-JUL-81	21000.00		102	69
4	RECEPTION	456-78-9012	19-JUN-78	43000.00		100	69
5	NEW ACCT	567-89-0123	17-MAY-87	11500.00		109	69
6	TELLER	789-01-2345	18-JAN-79	12400.00		107	69
7	SECURITY	890-12-3456	18-DEC-86	15000.00		108	69
8	TELLER	901-23-4567	23-SEP-85	13450.00		106	69
9	NEW ACCT	987-65-4321	15-OCT-85	13300.00		105	69
10	SUPERVISOR	876-54-3210	14-OCT-85	13400.00		104	69
11	NEW ACCT	765-43-2109	07-NOV-87	11250.00		103	69

When you copy this version to the remaining cells, each will do its calculations in its own row, as you intended. The results should look like Figure 18-17.

EXPANDED REPORTING

You can use the same technique to expand the cross-selling report that also was created in Chapter 16. This report presented the numbers of sales for each employee, then the number of cross-sales to existing customers. Then, it compared the dollar amounts of these sales. The spreadsheet makes it easy to add another dimension to this report: the cross-sale figures as percentages of the employees' totals.

Go to column A2 of an empty spreadsheet. Enter the SQL command to produce the cross-selling report, but without any of the formatting information that was in the earlier version:

```
$SELECT ROSTER.LAST, SOLD.NO, XSOLD.NO,
    SOLD.AMT, XSOLD.AMT FROM SOLD, XSOLD,
    ROSTER WHERE SOLD.EMP_CODE =
    XSOLD.EMP_CODE AND SOLD.EMP_CODE =
    ROSTER.EMP_CODE ORDER BY ROSTER.LAST
```

The results are shown in Figure 18-18.

EXPANSION PLAN

Create a new Column D and another new column G. In Cell D2 enter the formula:

+c2/b2

FIGURE 18-17   A New Column of Calculated Values

```
        F              G            H          I          J          K          L
 1  POSITION       SS_NO        DATE_HIRED  SALARY     MONTHLY    EXTENSION  BRANCH_N
 2  MANAGER        123-45-6789  09-SEP-79   24000.00   2000.00    101              69
 3  ASST MGR       234-56-7890  07-JUL-81   21000.00   1750.00    102              69
 4  RECEPTION      456-78-9012  19-JUN-78   43000.00   3583.33    100              69
 5  NEW ACCT       567-89-0123  17-MAY-87   11500.00    958.33    109              69
 6  TELLER         789-01-2345  18-JAN-79   12400.00   1033.33    107              69
 7  SECURITY       890-12-3456  18-DEC-86   15000.00   1250.00    108              69
 8  TELLER         901-23-4567  23-SEP-85   13450.00   1120.83    106              69
 9  NEW ACCT       987-65-4321  15-OCT-85   13300.00   1108.33    105              69
10  SUPERVISOR     876-54-3210  14-OCT-85   13400.00   1116.67    104              69
11  NEW ACCT       765-43-2109  07-NOV-87   11250.00    937.50    103              69
```

FIGURE 18-18 The Cross-Selling Report Again

	A	B	C	D	E
1					
2	COLLINS	12	4	24987.45	13414
3	ROWE-HAT	9	5	234124	183799
4	TUBA	12	2	275004	898
5	ZIMMERMA	9	3	931366	882726

Remember to use lowercase letters for the column references. Now, you can copy that formula to the rest of Column D and all of Column G. Use that /LAYOUT menu option to format the two percentage columns to two decimal places, and adjust the column widths as necessary. Then, add your own column headings in Row 1, which was left blank for this purpose.

The results of all this are in Figure 18-19. The employees' performance is reflected in percentages as well as in raw figures. It shouldn't be too hard to use the spreadsheet's calculating ability to analyze these figures further. For example, you could add a column listing the employees' goals for the rating period and another expressing their actual performance as a percentage of the goal.

Go ahead and try it. As of this moment, you're on your own.

FIGURE 18-19 The Final Sales Report

	A	B	C	D	E	F	G	H
1	NAME	SOLD	XSOLD	PCT	AMOUNT	XSOLD	PCT	
2	COLLINS	12	4	0.33	24987.45	13414.00	0.54	
3	ROWE-HATTON	9	5	0.56	234124.00	183799.00	0.79	
4	TUBA	12	2	0.17	275004.00	898.00	0.00	
5	ZIMMERMAN	9	3	0.33	931366.00	882726.00	0.95	

REVIEW QUESTIONS

1. In the PC version of ORACLE, which key do you use to SELECT an option from a SQL*Forms menu?
2. SQL*Forms uses the term BLOCK to refer to a specific data entry area on the screen. What is the counterpart to a block within a SQL database?
3. What is the function of the ACCEPT key in SQL*Forms?
4. What is a trigger, and what purposes does it usually serve?
5. What symbol precedes a SQL command in SQL*Calc?
6. How might you make productive use of both a forms-drawing front end and a spreadsheet connection in the same system?

ANSWERS

1. <Home>. The SQL*Calc manual is designed for users of several different types of systems, each with its own key layout. The identity of the SELECT key varies from system to system.
2. A block is the counterpart to a table.
3. ACCEPT, the <End> key on PCs and compatibles, temporarily saves the results of a window operation and returns you to the previous window.
4. A trigger is a SQL command or C program called from within the form. Its most common uses are to validate data entries and to retrieve related data from other tables.
5. A dollar sign.
6. There's no wrong answer to this question. A good combination, though, would be to use the forms utility for data entry and the spreadsheet link to analyze the data.

INDEX

A

Absolute reference, 406
ACCEPT, 309-311, 319, 375, 378, 397, 408, 409
Access control, 202-213, 224, 227, 244-246, 287, 293
ADD, 57
ADD_MONTHS, 160, 163
Administrator, 202, 227, 230, 233, 245-252
ALIAS
    column, 67, 68, 136, 188, 189, 343
    table, 78, 83, 88
ALL, 93-96
Alphanumeric column, 133
ALTER TABLE, 51, 57, 58, 60, 215, 216, 267, 293, 294, 296
Ampersand, 307, 311, 318, 319, 379
AND, 101
ANY, 93-96
Apostrophe, 139, 147, 239
APPEND, 33, 34, 50, 52, 58, 136, 214, 222, 223, 260, 311
Argument, 151
Association, 282, 285, 292
Asterisk
    as error flag, 32, 33
    as wild card, 7, 64, 75, 236
Attribute, 15, 280, 281
AUDIT_TRAIL, 247, 248
Auditing, 227, 246-249, 287, 288
AVG, 124, 127-130, 175, 195, 334

B

Backup, 23, 42, 202, 249, 250
BETWEEN, 71, 72, 80, 81
Binding, 185
Block
    Storage unit, 239, 240, 251
    SQL*Forms, 396, 397, 399, 402, 408, 409
BREAK, 310, 329-334
Breaks
    Ranges, 82
    Reports, 342-344, 358, 359, 378, 379

BTITLE, 326, 327, 337
Buffer, 32, 34, 112, 136, 304-306, 310, 318, 319, 321, 337

C

C statements
    %s, 378
    \n, 378
    float, 383
    printf, 378
    scanf, 378
    structure, 369
    typedef, 369
    while, 378
Capital letters, 116, 153, 366
Catalog, dBASE, 227, 228
CHANGE, 32, 101, 307
Char
    constants, 144
    data type, 18, 48, 132, 139, 140
    display, 132
    functions, 140
    and null values, 171
Characteristic, 280, 282, 285, 292
CLEAR, 119, 133, 310
CLUSTER, 232, 264-269, 270, 290
    dictionary table, 269
    column, 265-268
Cobol, 21, 361, 364
Codd, E. F., 14
Colon, 368, 402
Colons, 373, 379, 385, 391
COLUMN (SQL*Plus command)
    Headings, 13, 150, 154, 238
    NOPRINT, 236
    Numeric columns, 112-115, 117
    Reports, 323, 324, 329, 337, 340, 343, 350, 351, 357
    Width, 132, 133, 150, 154, 238
    WORD_WRAPPED, 241, 244, 252
Columns
    computed, 65, 116, 194, 195
    defined, 15
    heading, 116, 117, 136, 151, 324, 347, 350, 351, 357
    label, 116

411

Here's how to receive your free catalog and save money on your next book order from Scott, Foresman and Company

Simply mail in the response card below to receive your free copy of our latest catalog featuring computer and business books. After you've looked through the catalog and you're ready to place your order, attach the coupon below to receive $1.00 off the catalog price of Scott, Foresman and Company Professional Books Group computer and business books.

✂--

☐ YES, please send me my *free* catalog of your latest computer and business books! I am especially interested in

☐ IBM   ☐ Programming
☐ MACINTOSH   ☐ Business Applications
☐ AMIGA   ☐ Networking/Telecommunications
☐ COMMODORE   ☐ Other _____

Name (please print) _____

Company _____

Address _____

City _____ State _____ Zip _____

Mail response card to: Scott, Foresman and Company
                           Professional Books Group
                           1900 East Lake Avenue
                           Glenview, IL 60025

✂--

PUBLISHER'S COUPON   NO EXPIRATION DATE

SAVE $1.00

Limit one per order. Good only on Scott, Foresman and Company Professional Books Group publications. Consumer pays any sales tax. Coupon may not be assigned, transferred, or reproduced. Coupon will be redeemed by Scott, Foresman and Company Professional Books Group, 1900 East Lake Avenue, Glenview, IL 60025.

Customer's Signature _____